Microsoft®
Private Cloud
Computing

Microsoft®
Private Cloud
Computing

Aidan Finn

Hans Vredevoort

Patrick Lownds

Damian Flynn

WILEY

John Wiley & Sons, Inc.

Acquisitions Editors: Agatha Kim and Mariann Barsolo
Development Editor: Richard Mateosian
Technical Editor: Kristian Nese
Production Editor: Eric Charbonneau
Copy Editor: Kathy Grider-Carlyle
Editorial Manager: Pete Gaughan
Production Manager: Tim Tate
Vice President and Executive Group Publisher: Richard Swadley
Vice President and Publisher: Neil Edde
Book Designers: Maureen Forys and Judy Fung
Proofreader: Candace English
Indexer: Jack Lewis
Project Coordinator, Cover: Katherine Crocker
Cover Designer: Ryan Sneed
Cover Image: © loops7 / iStockPhoto

Dear Reader,

Thank you for choosing *Microsoft Private Cloud Computing*. This book is part of a family of premium-quality Sybex books, all of which are written by outstanding authors who combine practical experience with a gift for teaching.

Sybex was founded in 1976. More than 30 years later, we're still committed to producing consistently exceptional books. With each of our titles, we're working hard to set a new standard for the industry. From the paper we print on to the authors we work with, our goal is to bring you the best books available.

I hope you see all that reflected in these pages. I'd be very interested to hear your comments and get your feedback on how we're doing. Feel free to let me know what you think about this or any other Sybex book by sending me an email at nedde@wiley.com. If you think you've found a technical error in this book, please visit http://sybex.custhelp.com. Customer feedback is critical to our efforts at Sybex.

Best regards,

Neil Edde
Vice President and Publisher
Sybex, an Imprint of Wiley

To my family and friends, who make this possible
—Aidan Finn

I owe big gratitude to my family: my wife Marijcke and our three sons. They have certainly missed me while I've been working on the book. However, they were very supportive and asked me about the progress of my book. I dedicate this book to them.
—Hans Vredevoort

I would like to dedicate this book to my family and friends, but most of all to my wife Lisa, and our precious children.
—Patrick Lownds

To my parents, who started me on this journey, and to all the amazing people in my life
—Damian Flynn

Acknowledgments

A project like this is possible only with the help of family, friends, and colleagues. I'd like to thank them; in particular, the editors at Wiley and Sybex, my coauthors Patrick, Hans, and Damian, and our fellow MVP, Kristian Nese, who was the technical reviewer of this book.

—*Aidan Finn*

When Aidan Finn told me he was planning a new book on the subject of the Microsoft private cloud with several other MVPs, it took me only 10 seconds to quickly consider and say YES! Of course, I had no idea what it would mean in terms of time and effort, but this was just something I had to do—no matter what happened.

Working with Aidan Finn, Patrick Lownds, and Damian Flynn, three highly respected MVPs in the world of Hyper-V and Microsoft System Center, turned out to be a fantastic experience. I am very proud of delivering this Microsoft private-cloud computing book together with them, acknowledging their deep technical knowledge and real-world experience. In fact, a book with such diverse topics could probably not have been written by only one author. Each and every one donated a significant piece of the puzzle on how to effectively build a Microsoft Private Cloud. Nevertheless, we had to make concessions on what to cover and what to ignore. If we would've had the time and space, the number of pages could have easily doubled.

A special thank-you goes to the editors of Wiley and Sybex for their expert advice. Likewise, big thanks go to Kristian Nese, a very enthusiastic and knowledgeable MVP in the System Center and Private Cloud arena. He kindly accepted our request to review the hundreds of pages we submitted.

I really couldn't have written this book without the generous and supportive people of XS4ALL, a leading ISP in the Netherlands, and in particular Joey Hofstede and Alexander Rijnbeek. We were given access to their research network, HP blade servers, HP storage, and HP Virtual Connect, including plenty of processor, memory, network, and storage resources for us to build a fantastic Microsoft Private Cloud.

There are several other people I'd like to thank for their help and advice: Udo Walberer from NetApp; Greg Cusanza, Program Manager in the VMM product team; Jonathan Cusson for his Microsoft Virtualization Visio template. Finally Maarten Goet, managing consultant and MVP of INOVATIV, who donated time for research and writing.

—*Hans Vredevoort*

Writing a book takes a lot of dedication and support. It would not be possible without help from family, friends, and colleagues. I would like to thank my wife, Lisa, for helping to keep all the other stuff together, and my children for being patient. A special thanks to the editors at Wiley and Sybex for making the dream a reality; my coauthors Aidan, Damian and Hans; plus our technical reviewer, Kristian. Finally, I would like to also thank Carmen Summers for giving me the opportunity to work with the product during the TAP and for answering those bizarre questions.

—*Patrick Lownds*

Writing a book can be a long and difficult process; there are many people who help along the way—too many to list individually. I offer my sincere appreciation to you all.

I would like to thank my brilliant and beautiful wife, Breege, for teaching me that great things are born from tiny sparks of inspiration; my coauthors Hans, Patrick, and Aidan, who convinced me that we could write a book; Kristian for his insight; and the editors at Wiley and Sybex.

In addition, a very special thanks to my colleagues at Lionbridge Technologies, especially Oyvind, Steve, and the "Corp IT" Team; and also the System Centre product group in Microsoft, especially Carmen, Kenon, Stephen, Hector, Suveen, Santosh, Travis, and Nigel.

—*Damian Flynn*

About the Authors

Aidan Finn is a Hyper-V Most Valuable Professional based in Ireland, where he works in the IT industry, working with technologies such as Hyper-V and System Center. Known for his blogging, he also has written/contributed to books on Hyper-V, Windows Server, and Windows 7 deployment.

Hans Vredevoort is a MVP in Virtual Machine. He joined System Center and Hyper-V Private Cloud specialist INOVATIV in Amsterdam, the Netherlands. He started specializing in Microsoft Virtualization well before Hyper-V was born, and started blogging and presenting for Hyper-V.nu, which has become a very successful blog and user group focusing on the building blocks for the Microsoft Private Cloud: Hyper-V and System Center. Much of his datacenter experience comes from working for a Dutch system integrator, specializing in Microsoft and HP infrastructures.

Hans was the technical editor of *Mastering Hyper-V Deployment* in the Wiley/Sybex Mastering series, by Aidan Finn and Patrick Lownds.

Currently Hans is involved in a multitude of private-cloud projects and proof of concepts. Active participation in several technical adopter programs (TAPs) on Virtual Machine Manager and Windows Server 2012 has given Hans Vredevoort great advantage and made him an excellent sparring partner in talking about datacenter and private-cloud architecture.

Patrick Lownds is a Virtual Machine Most Valuable Professional based in London, and has worked in the IT industry since 1988. Patrick works with a number of differing technologies, including Hyper-V and System Center. Patrick also contributed to the book titled *Mastering Hyper-V Deployment*, which was also published by Wiley and Sybex, plus he blogs and tweets in his spare time.

Damian Flynn, MVP – System Center Cloud & Data Centre, works as a technical architect of corporate IT infrastructure for Lionbridge Technologies (a localization, logo-certification, search, and content-services company and Microsoft Gold Certified Partner). Damian works closely with the business stakeholders, IT team, and partners, while also incubating new projects. Damian is a member of the Microsoft Windows Sever Futures Council, while actively participating in multiple Microsoft TAP programs, and has been working on infrastructure technologies since 1994, gaining deep knowledge and experience in networking, storage, Linux and Windows servers, virtualization, System Center, etc. He blogs on www.damianflynn.com, tweets from time to time on @damian_flynn, and contributes code on www.codeplex.com.

Contents at a Glance

Contents

Introduction

Private cloud computing is a very hot topic, but there remains a lot of mystery around the subject. What is a private cloud? What are the technical and business reasons to deploy one? How do I design one that focuses on service delivery? Does Microsoft have such an offering?

This book exactly answers those questions, and provides step-by-step instructions on how to build a Microsoft private cloud that can serve as an IT-service-delivery virtualization infrastructure based on Microsoft System Center Virtual Machine Manager 2012. You'll be walked through the entire process: understanding cloud computing, understanding the Microsoft concept of a private cloud, architecting and deploying a private cloud fabric, deploying services, building and managing a private cloud, as well as integrating it with Microsoft's public cloud to create a cross-premises or hybrid cloud.

Who Should Read This Book

This book is intended for people who want to learn how to deploy an infrastructure that focuses on the delivery of IT services, based on a private cloud solution built on Microsoft System Center Virtual Machine Manager 2012. Such people probably fall into three basic groups:

♦ Consultants will want to understand how to sell and deploy solutions based on this technology. This book will educate them about how to deploy services to their clients.

♦ Engineers and IT architects who design the Microsoft private cloud and build corporate infrastructure solutions will learn how to build an optimized platform for the delivery of solutions in a centralized and well-managed environment.

♦ IT Administrators who manage IT infrastructures. These are the people who are responsible for the day-to-day delivery of IT services to their businesses. Understanding how to deploy and/or manage a private cloud will improve how they can perform their duties, and enable them to focus their time on more-interesting work.

Together, we are four MVPs who have different experiences and expertise, with one common goal: we want to share what we have learned over the months about Microsoft's new virtualized infrastructure management, service deployments, and private-cloud solution.

We recognize System Center Virtual Machine Manager 2012 as a considerable leap forward in how you can manage your virtualisation fabric, and in the ability to deploy and maintain complex IT solutions across a variety of virtualization platforms. Not only that, together with the other System Center 2012 products, Virtual Machine Manager 2012 offers a comprehensive private cloud solution.

Once you have read this book, you should be ready when your boss or your customers ask if you know anything about the private cloud. Not only will you be able to answer in the affirmative, but you'll be in a position to successfully advise, design, and deploy the solution.

What You Will Learn

You will learn how to do the following:

◆ Describe the different types of cloud computing, including the private cloud

◆ Understand the Microsoft private cloud

◆ Deploy System Center 2012 Virtual Machine Manager and the fabric which serves as the foundation for your private cloud

◆ Build the components of IT service delivery

◆ Set up private clouds and integrate them with Microsoft's public cloud to create a cross-premises cloud using System Center 2012 App Controller

◆ Implement the System Center Cloud Services Process Pack

What You Need

You should have an understanding of Windows Server 2008 R2 (see *Mastering Microsoft Windows Server 2008 R2*, Sybex 2010) and Windows Server 2008 R2 Hyper-V (see *Mastering Hyper-V Deployment*, Sybex 2010).

To re-create the demonstrations contained within this book you will need the following:

◆ Microsoft Windows Server 2008 R2

◆ Microsoft System Center 2012 Virtual Machine Manager

◆ Microsoft SQL Server 2008 R2

◆ Microsoft System Center App Controller 2012

◆ VMware vSphere 4.1

◆ Citrix XenServer 6.0

◆ A number of servers with baseboard management controllers

◆ A network load balancer (virtual or physical) with support for integrating with Microsoft System Center Virtual Machine Manager 2012

◆ A storage-area network (virtual or physical) with support for the Storage Management Initiative – Specification (SMI-S)

What Is Covered in This Book

Microsoft Private Cloud Computing was written to teach you how to deploy Microsoft's solution even if you are new to cloud computing. Each chapter will progress you from theory to advanced private cloud computing; this book will start with explaining the basics, step you through creating and utilizing the fabric of a private cloud, generating and maintaining services, and creating private and cross-premises clouds based on Microsoft System Center Virtual Machine Manager 2012:

Chapter 1: Understanding Cloud Computing There is a lot of misunderstanding about what cloud computing really is. This chapter will explain why cloud computing came to be, teach you about what makes a cloud, and cover the different kinds of cloud, including the private cloud.

Chapter 2: The Microsoft Private Cloud Here you will learn about the reasoning behind Microsoft's design and what makes this complete solution different from the alternatives.

Chapter 3: Introducing the VMM 2012 Architecture This is where you're introduced to Microsoft System Center Virtual Machine Manager 2012. You will learn about the components of VMM 2012.

Chapter 4: Setting Up and Deploying VMM 2012 Explains the requirements for all the different components of VMM 2012. This chapter also shows you to to install the VMM 2012 components. It also deals with the upgrade from VMM 2008 R2, and the security model.

Chapter 5: Understanding the VMM Library The library is a repository of reusable resources that can be used to deploy virtual machines, applications, and services. In this chapter, you will learn how to manage the VMM library.

Chapter 6: Understanding Network and Storage in VMM 2012 Here you'll learn how to build storage fabrics based on SMI-S, network fabrics based on logical networks and address pools, VLANs, and network load balancer virtual IP (VIP) templates.

Chapter 7: Deploying Hosts and Clusters in VMM 2012 VMM 2012 has the ability to deploy Hyper-V hosts on bare-metal hardware, and build new Hyper-V clusters from them. Here you will learn how to deploy this virtualization infrastructure, as well as how to enable advanced virtualization features such as dynamic optimization and power optimization.

Chapter 8: Understanding Service Modeling A service is where a number of individual IT components are working together to provide valuable functionality to the business. This chapter covers service modeling, how to build Server App-V packages for virtualizing server applications, and how to build service templates using the contents of the VMM Library and the storage and network fabrics, deploy the templates as running services, and maintain those services.

Chapter 9: Creating a Private Cloud Leveraging the knowledge gained in the preceding sections of the book, we can now combine all the resources we have created for our consumption. In this chapter we introduce the administrative tasks of creating a VMM private cloud; we define user roles and demonstrate the delegatation of access to these clouds.

Chapter 10: Working in the Cloud With our cloud created and access provisioned, we assume an end-user persona, and experience the three in box interfaces offered for working on our new clouds, as we demonstrate by deploying virtual machines.

Chapter 11: App Controller and the Public Cloud Building on the previous chapter, we introduce the Microsoft public cloud, and how App Controler provides a single interface to span both the public and private clouds.

Chapter 12: Cloud Services Process Pack In the final chapter of the book we introduce the extensible nature of VMM and System Center by implementing the Cloud Services Process Pack, which builds a top of Service Manager, Orchestrator, and Operations Manager.

How to Contact the Authors

We welcome feedback from you about this book or about books you'd like to see from us in the future. You can reach Aidan Finn by writing to `aidanfinn@hotmail.com`, learn more about his work by visiting `www.aidanfinn.com`, or follow him on Twitter at `@joe_elway`.

If you want to contact Hans Vredevoort, send an email to hans@hyper-v.nu or you can follow him on Twitter at @hvredevoort. Hans frequently blogs at www.hyper-v.nu

You can reach Patrick Lownds by writing to `patrick_lownds@hotmail.com` or learn more about his work by following him on Twitter at `@patricklownds`.

Damian Flynn can be reached on email at `msprivatecloud@damianflynn.com`, you can follow him on Twitter at `@damian_flynn`, and read his technology blog at `www.damianflynn.com`.

Sybex strives to keep you supplied with the latest tools and information you need for your work. Please check their website at `www.sybex.com/go/microsoftprivatecloud`, where we'll post additional content and updates that supplement this book if the need arises.

Part 1

Introduction to Cloud Computing

- ◆ **Chapter 1: Understanding Cloud Computing**
- ◆ **Chapter 2: The Microsoft Private Cloud**

Chapter 1

Understanding Cloud Computing

A massive change is sweeping the world of information technology (IT). Consumers are choosing computing devices of different forms, and they are taking their newfound knowledge and power to the work place. They want IT to deliver services differently, and the IT community has responded with a new service-delivery mechanism called *cloud computing*. Marketers have rushed to use this term, often in confusing ways. This chapter aims to dispel that confusion. It explains the following:

◆ The business challenges that led to cloud computing

◆ What cloud computing is

◆ The main cloud-computing service models

◆ The main cloud-computing deployment models

The Challenges of Traditional Computing

Why do businesses utilize information technology? That's a pretty important question because the answer eventually explains why businesses have started to adopt cloud computing.

Some businesses accuse IT pros of having complex infrastructures so they can have playgrounds. Others say it seems that the goal is merely to sell more servers, storage, networking, and maybe even some expensive software. A rack full of equipment may have pretty lights, but that's not why a business needs IT.

In reality, businesses invest considerable sums of money into all this equipment, software, and consulting for a multitude of reasons: to help manage decision making and strategy; to optimize day-to-day operations; to generate profit; and to gain a genuine competitive advantage. In other words, IT is used to deliver services to the business. IT is all about the applications.

WHAT IS A SERVICE?

Most Windows administrators consider a *service* to be a process or set of processes that provide some functionality to the operating system. That's a technology-related definition, and it's not what businesses generally consider to be a service. Customers view an IT department as a *service provider*. Services—for example, email, Customer Relationship Management (CRM) applications, and Enterprise Resource Planning (ERP) applications—are made of components such as firewalls, switches, servers, storage devices, and Windows services. Those pretty lights are unimportant; what is important is that the CRM application is online and responsive. This emphasis on the delivery of service can be a bit of a mind shift if you've spent years being concerned about the components of services. However, if you can cost-effectively keep those services up and running, you will probably have a happy customer.

Business Challenges

At times, working in IT can seem like a fight. *In the blue corner, we have IT infrastructure administrators, engineers, and consultants. In the red corner, hailing from parts unknown, we have the reigning champions, the software developers and application administrators, who are supported ringside by the business.*

That's how things sometimes seem to work. There are two diametrically opposing forces: the IT pro and the software administrator/developer. Very often their relationship is strained and communication between them is practically nonexistent.

Before we look at the technological challenges the IT pro faces, let's look at the relationship from the perspective of the customer: the business.

Delays, Delays, and More Delays   Delays are the biggest complaint. There is a pressing need to respond to some challenge or opportunity within a limited time frame, and IT is busy doing something less important. The solution is delivered too late, and the project isn't as successful as it should have been.

Unfulfilled Requests   A simple request is made to the IT department, and something completely unexpected is delivered. Why does it seem that the IT department can never keep it simple?

Cost Overruns   A project is launched to look for a simple solution with a small budget. When the IT department becomes involved, it seems to turn into an excuse to get the biggest servers or the latest software. Why is it that they cannot stay on budget?

Unusable Systems   Software just doesn't work as expected because the IT department has put unwarranted lockdowns on the system. They seem to enjoy making the network an impossible place to work.

Unfortunately, businesses are increasingly considering the IT infrastructure to be a roadblock. They view IT as an obstacle to business growth, flexibility, and agility. When faced with an obstacle, a river will always find an alternative route—and that is exactly what businesses are looking for now.

Technology Challenges

There are two sides to every story, and the same day-to-day experiences just mentioned can be viewed from the IT pro's point of view.

Constant Time Pressure   The demands for new infrastructure never cease. Even with the rapid-deployment technologies of virtualization, there are only so many people in the IT department and not enough hours in the day to do everything that is requested by the business. The IT department has become a deployment bottleneck, but it is only because so much is being demanded of the department.

No Clear Requirements   Technology is complex. When a developer asks for a SQL Server virtual machine to be deployed, you need to know the required specifications. There is no such thing as "the usual" or "whatever you think is best." The person designing the application should know its requirements. Eventually, you just have to meet the deadlines and managerial mandates by deploying *something*.

IT Complexities   A hundred-dollar 1TB USB 2.0 external drive is not a suitable storage device for a file share in a data center or computer room. Some developers don't understand that a highly available service requires more than one machine with Windows Enterprise, failover clustering, and shared storage.

Security and Compliance   No one seems to understand the amount of work that must be done to secure systems. Storing a SQL Server administrator username and password in a configuration file in an unprotected file share (even if it is read-only) is not acceptable under any circumstance. Policies are enforced equally to protect the assets of the business, customers, partners, and shareholders. Likewise, systems must be locked down appropriately to comply with regulations such as the Health Insurance Portability and Accountability Act (HIPAA), Basel II, the Sarbanes-Oxley Act, and the European Union Data Protection Directive.

The IT pro and the business user have two very different views of the world, and they will forever be at odds. Or will they? Things are changing, and we might have a trendy phone to thank for it.

How Cloud Computing Is Changing IT Service Delivery

A massive wave of change has swept over the entire IT world in the past few years. The first ripples of the newest tide started in the consumer pool as new devices became available. First there were smartphones and then along came tablet devices. Domestic users flocked to these easy-to-use, attractive, and functional devices that had great battery life. In many ways, these devices are more attractive than the gray, locked-down, devices that IT administrators drop on their desks in the office.

Then these new devices began to appear in the office. At first, executives, who can rarely be refused, demanded these fashionable tools, even though the IT infrastructure was incapable of managing or supporting them. Then users, who are under ever-increasing pressure to achieve results and exceed targets, wanted them. Meanwhile, the IT infrastructure became increasingly locked down and inflexible. Eventually, users dipped into their own wallets or the budgets of their departments to purchase equipment more suited to their needs. They weren't going to wait months for a laptop to be encrypted by headquarters; they had projects to start. They weren't going to use some work-supplied device with a three-hour battery life; they needed to work while on an eight-hour trans-Atlantic flight. Business needs had to be met despite the restrictions the IT department imposed on them. This is what led to the *consumerization* of IT.

The dam has burst, and there is no getting that water back. Business users have figured out that they can find apps for their devices and online business solutions from sources independent of their IT departments. Most new business applications have a web interface, and business users can independently source a business application from outside sources and place it with a hosting company. Users get exactly what they need when they need it.

Facing huge growth, time pressures, and the drive to keep costs low, traditional hosting morphed into a new approach to IT service delivery. *Cloud computing* is the newest delivery model for IT-based business solutions.

What Makes a Cloud?

Cloud computing can mean many things. There are different types and delivery models of cloud computing; due to the confusion caused by marketing and sales people, many people don't understand what cloud computing really is.

Cloud computing is more than just server virtualization. In fact, server virtualization is not even a necessary component of a cloud. It is, however, a mission-critical component that makes some forms of cloud computing feasible.

Possibly one of the best-defined and most referred-to descriptions of cloud computing was published by the National Institute of Standards and Technology (NIST). This brief document (`http://csrc.nist.gov/publications/nistpubs/800-145/SP800-145.pdf`) clearly explains what a cloud is. A *cloud* is a collection of shared (or multitenant) computing resources that are easily accessed and consumed at will. A cloud has the characteristics described in the following paragraphs:

Self-Service Provisioning   Using a simple interface, customers (or business users) can subscribe to cloud services and deploy needed resources. The obvious benefit to this self-service ability is that they can quickly provision their own resources without waiting for the already-busy IT department to do it, so that the business can respond to opportunities and challenges in a timely manner.

This does not eliminate the need for an IT department. The role of the IT administrator has changed from one of deploying services to one of deploying the server, network, and storage fabrics that comprise the cloud; and managing the systems and policies that ensure that the services IT provides are available, secure, and compliant with regulatory or corporate standards.

Broad Network Access   The consumerization of IT means that users are using a never-seen-before diverse variety of devices and technologies to access business services. A cloud must provide access to these devices in a secure and reliable manner across different networks. One of the best ways to make applications available to users on a wide variety of devices is to harness the power of the Web and technologies such as HTML5.

If non–IT pros deploy their own services, then network deployment and configuration must be automated. (Ask typical end users if they know how to configure IP subnets and firewall rules and see how that conversation goes!) Each tenant of the cloud must be secured from the other tenants. They need high levels of fault tolerance for web services, and they want this without interaction from administrators.

Shared Resources   Most people have electricity so they can turn on a light, watch TV, or cook dinner. They do not have a power station in their back yard. This analogy can be applied to businesses. Does every department in a university need to have a computer room and server administrators? Does every small business need to have servers for email and file sharing? These accidental IT organizations can use shared resources to provide these services, and they can provide them with higher levels of expertise at lower costs.

Rapid Elasticity   Businesses planning traditional server deployments must plan for peak levels of consumption. An online retail business must deploy as many machines as it thinks it needs for the months of November and December to deal with the increased workloads of the busiest time of the year. But for the other 10 months, most of that server capacity is underutilized, consuming electricity and space. A cloud resolves this issue by dynamically adding more capacity to a service.

From a technology perspective, this means that there are centralized dense server farms that must be architected and managed. There is a higher ratio of servers to administrators. Automation of management systems and quality control become critical.

Measured Service   A cloud provider measures the cost of resources used by each tenant in the cloud. Some service providers use this data to invoice their customers. For example, an online CRM service provider charges users to make a profit. A cloud in a corporation might cross-charge departments or divisions to recoup the costs of operating and servicing the cloud.

Not all organization structures support cross-charging users or customers. However, the service measurements can be used to display the value that the IT department is bringing to the business.

Now that you can identify what is or is not a cloud, you need to recognize the different types of clouds.

Understanding the Cloud-Computing Service Models

There are three widely accepted types of cloud service models. Each serves a different purpose. A business may choose to use just one, two, or even all three of the cloud types simultaneously as the need arises.

SOFTWARE AS A SERVICE (SAAS)

This model was around long before anyone started talking about cloud computing. SaaS is an online application that you can use instead of one that you install on a server or a PC. One of the oldest examples is webmail. People have been using Hotmail, Yahoo! Mail, and others since the 1990s. Many users of these services do not install an email client; instead they browse to the website of the service provider, log in, and correspond with their friends, family, and colleagues.

Since then the variety of personal and business applications has exploded. Rather than deploying an Exchange Server and a SharePoint farm in a small business or a branch office (which requires servers and time), you can subscribe to Microsoft Office 365 and deploy mailboxes and SharePoint sites in a matter of hours, and users can access those services from anywhere on the planet if they have Internet access.

Other examples include Salesforce CRM, Microsoft Dynamics CRM, Microsoft Windows Intune, and Google Apps.

The strength of SaaS is that any user can subscribe to a service as quickly as they can pay with their credit card. In addition to this, the company doesn't have to deploy or manage an application infrastructure. The experience is not that different from purchasing an app for a smartphone: you find something that meets your needs, you pay for it, and you start using it—with maybe some local configuration on the PC to maximize service. The disadvantage is that these systems are not always flexible and may not integrate well with other business applications your organization requires. SaaS is a generalized service that aims to meet the needs of the majority of the market. The rest of the market must find something that they can customize for their own needs.

PLATFORM AS A SERVICE (PAAS)

Ask any software developer what their biggest complaint about deploying their solutions is, and there's a pretty good chance they'll start talking about server administrators who take too long to deploy servers and never provide exactly what the developers need.

PaaS aims to resolve these issues. It is a service-provider-managed environment that allows software developers to host and execute their software without the complications of specifying, deploying, or configuring servers. An example of a PaaS is Microsoft Windows Azure. Developers can create their applications in Visual Studio and load them directly into Microsoft's PaaS, which spans many data centers across the globe. There they can use compute power, an available and scalable SQL service, application fabrics, and vast amounts of storage space.

A widely used example is Facebook. Many people tend their virtual farms or search for clues to solve murders from their offices using software that executes on Facebook. The developers of those games take advantage of the platform that this expansive social network gives them, and they can rapidly reach a large audience without having to invest huge amounts of time and money to build their own server farms across the world.

The strength of this solution is that you can deploy a new application on a scalable platform to reach a huge audience in a matter of minutes. The hosting company, such as Microsoft, is responsible for managing the PaaS infrastructure. This leaves the developers free to focus on their application without the distractions of servers, networks, and so forth. The weakness is that you cannot customize the underlying infrastructure. For example, if you require new web server functionality or third-party SQL Server add-ons, this might not be the best cloud service model to use.

INFRASTRUCTURE AS A SERVICE (IaaS)

Because it is based on a technology most IT pros already know, IaaS is a model of cloud computing that is familiar to them. IaaS allows consumers to deploy virtual machines with preconfigured operating systems through a self-service portal. Networking and storage are easily and rapidly configured without the need to interact with a network administrator.

Virtualization, such as Microsoft Hyper-V, is the underlying technology that makes IaaS possible. An IaaS cloud is much more than just server virtualization. Network configuration must be automated, services must be elastic and measured, and the cloud should have multitenant capabilities. This requires layers of management and automation on top of traditional virtualization.

The resulting solution allows consumers of the service to rapidly deploy preconfigured collections of virtual machines with no fuss. Software developers or department administrators can customize the virtual machines to suit the needs of the applications that will be installed in them. The working environment is familiar and can easily integrate with almost all technologies in an organization. The disadvantage for some is that there are virtual machines to deploy and operating systems to create and maintain. Subsequent chapters explain how Microsoft Virtual Machine Manager 2012 helps IaaS administrators deal with these concerns.

EVERYTHING AS A SERVICE

The "as a Service" brand has been adopted by many online service providers. There is Storage as a Service, Servers as a Service, Backup as a Service, and the list goes on and on. Most of these are variations of the IaaS or SaaS cloud service models. The names are designed to differentiate their products within a crowded space and, unfortunately, can cause confusion.

Understanding the Cloud-Computing Deployment Models

At this point, you know the traits of a cloud and the different cloud service models. Each of these cloud service models can exist in different locations and have different types of owners, which dictate the deployment model of the cloud.

PRIVATE CLOUD

A *private cloud* is entirely dedicated to the needs of a single organization. It can be on or off premises. An on-premises private cloud resides in the owner's computer room or data center and is managed by the organization's own IT staff. With the on-premises approach, a company has complete control of the data center, the infrastructure, and the networks. An off-premises private cloud takes advantage of the existing facilities and expertise of an outsourcing company, such as a colocation hosting facility. The off-premises approach is attractive to those organizations that don't want to or cannot afford to build their own computer room or data center.

The advantage of a private cloud is that an organization can design it and change it over time to be exactly what they need. They can control the quality of service provided. With the right systems in place, regulatory compliance, security, and IT governance can be maintained. The disadvantage of this deployment model is that it can require a significant investment of expertise, money, and time to engineer the solution that is right for the business.

NOTE   The private clouds discussed in this book are created using Virtual Machine Manager 2012, AppController, and machine-virtualization technologies such as Hyper-V, vSphere, and XenServer.

Private clouds change the role of the IT administrators. Without a private cloud, they are involved in many aspects of application deployment, including virtual machines or physical servers, network configurations, network load balancers, storage, installation of applications such as SQL Server, and so on. With a private cloud, their role becomes one of managing the centralized shared resources and managing the service level of the infrastructure. IT admins create and manage the pools of reusable components and systems that empower and enable businesses to deploy their own services. This means that they provide smarter, higher levels of service that are more valued by businesses.

PUBLIC CLOUD

A *public cloud* is a multitenant cloud that is owned by a company that typically sells the services it provides to the general public. Public clouds are readily available in different types. There are huge geo-located presences such as Windows Azure, Microsoft Office 365, and Amazon Elastic Compute Cloud. You can also find smaller service providers that offer custom services to suit the unique needs of their clients.

The big advantage of public cloud computing is that it is always ready to use without delays. A new business application can be deployed in minutes. The business does not need to invest in internal IT infrastructure to get the solution up and running. Doesn't this sound like it might be the way forward? Doesn't it sound as if outsourcing is finally going to happen and make IT pros redundant? Not so fast, my friend!

There are a few issues that can affect the choice of an informed decision maker. Where is the public cloud located? What nationality is the company that owns that cloud? The answers to these questions can affect compliance with national or industrial regulations. What sort of support relationship do you have with your telecom provider? Do you think a public cloud service provider will be that much different? Maybe the public cloud service provider has a fine support staff—or maybe they prefer to keep you 5,000 miles away on the other end of an email conversation. How much can you customize the service on the public cloud and how well does it integrate with your internal services? Maybe your job as an IT engineer or administrator is safe after all.

CROSS-PREMISES CLOUD

Things are not always black or white. The strengths of the private cloud complement the weaknesses of the public cloud, and vice versa. Where one is weak, the other is strong. Most organizations can pick and choose the best offerings of both cloud deployment models.

The *cross-premises cloud,* also known as a hybrid cloud, uses a private cloud and a public cloud at the same time, with services spanning both deployments.

Recall the online retail company that needs to rapidly expand and reduce their online presence for seasonal demands. This company can use a private cloud to store sensitive customer information. The private cloud data can be integrated with a public cloud such as Windows Azure. Azure provides huge data centers; application administrators can quickly expand their capacity during the peak retail season and reduce it when demand subsides. The company gets the best of both worlds: control of security and compliance from the private cloud, cost-effective elasticity and scalability from the public cloud, and a single service spanning both.

This book describes how to create such a cross-premises cloud using Virtual Machine Manager 2012 and AppController.

COMMUNITY CLOUD

A *community cloud* is one that is shared by many organizations. This open cloud can use many technologies, and it is usually utilized by organizations conducting collaborative scientific research. It offers participants features of both the public and the private cloud. Together, they can control the security and compliance of the cloud while taking a shared risk. They also get access to a larger compute resource that spans their cumulative infrastructures.

Because of their open nature, community clouds are extremely complex. A community cloud is a shared risk. Security and compliance are only as strong as the weakest member, and there will be competition for compute availability. Even in a private cloud, company politics are significant. One can only imagine the role that politics will play in a community cloud that is owned and operated by several state agencies.

Summary

Businesses need a new way to deploy IT services. Traditional computing has become expensive and an obstacle to the agility that is required to be competitive.

Cloud computing enables a business to deploy or subscribe to services as it needs them. A cloud features self-service, broad network access, centralized shared resources, and measurement of service usage.

There are different cloud service models. Infrastructure as a Service (IaaS) enables users to deploy customizable preconfigured business-ready virtual machines. Platform as a Service (PaaS) enables developers to rapidly deploy applications without worrying about servers or operating systems. Software as a Service (SaaS) allows customers to instantly subscribe to online applications.

Each cloud service model can be deployed in a number of ways. A private cloud is dedicated to the needs of a single organization. A public cloud is owned and operated by a service provider and enables its customers to subscribe to its services. A cross-premises (hybrid) cloud is a mixture of public and private clouds that offers the best of both. A community cloud is one that is shared and operated by a number of organizations with common goals.

Business computing has been evolving. The mainframe came and went. It was replaced by client/server computing, which has changed over the past decade with various forms of virtualization. The consumerization of IT has changed the way users access their information and applications, and now the forecast for IT service delivery is cloudy for the foreseeable future.

Chapter 2

The Microsoft Private Cloud

Chapter 1, "Understanding Cloud Computing," explained the traits of a cloud, a private cloud, and Infrastructure as a Service (IaaS). This chapter introduces the Microsoft vision of a private cloud and describes each component of the greater solution.

Most of this book focuses on the roles of System Center Virtual Machine Manager 2012 and System Center App Controller 2012 in the delivery of a private cloud. As you progress through the chapters, we'll examine these products in greater depth.

Consultants and customers alike need to know the benefits of the Microsoft private-cloud strategy for their businesses.

This chapter explains the following:

◆   The Microsoft strategy for the private cloud

◆   How the Microsoft strategy benefits the customer and the business

◆   The functions of System Center in the Microsoft private cloud

The Microsoft Private-Cloud Strategy

Chapter 1 questioned the role and necessity of IT in business today. IT exists to provide a service to a business. That service enables business applications to drive business operations, enable partnerships, create profits, and so on. If you ask a roomful of CEOs which virtualization product is at the bottom layers of their IT infrastructure, only a few (and they probably work for Microsoft, VMware, or Citrix) will know or even care. What they care about is the delivery, flexibility, agility, and quality of the service.

Virtualization is an important piece of the puzzle. Virtualization is an ingredient of the Microsoft private cloud. Businesses care about services, not virtualization—but what exactly are services? *Services* (the things that a business really cares about) are line-of-business applications created and managed by developers and application administrators.

Let's take a trip down memory lane to find out how Microsoft has evolved its private-cloud strategy for delivering an IT service to a business.

The Development of the Microsoft Private Cloud

Microsoft recognized the importance of services to business in the early to mid-2000s and has been evolving an infrastructure-management and -enabling solution that delivers the services business demands. At one point, Microsoft called their solution Dynamic Systems Initiative

(DSI). Featuring Systems Management Server (SMS) 2003 and Microsoft Operations Manager (MOM) 2005, DSI offered IT-infrastructure automation. By utilizing DSI, IT professionals could be more effective in response to demands for change by their businesses.

Microsoft developed these products further and branded them as System Center. System Center Configuration Manager (ConfigMgr or SCCM) 2007 (and later R2 and R3) replaced SMS 2003. System Center Operations Manager (OpsMgr or SCOM) 2007 (and later R2) replaced MOM 2005. Then System Center Data Protection Manager (DPM) 2007 (and later 2010) appeared on the scene. System Center Virtual Machine Manager (VMM) 2007, 2008, and 2008 R2 provided a virtualization-management solution. They were joined by Service Manager 2010, while Microsoft acquired a product called Opalis. Although these products span many years, they are sometimes referred to as System Center 2007.

While DSI aimed to provide just automation to the system administrator across Microsoft products, System Center 2007 expanded into providing automation and *service management* across Microsoft and non-Microsoft products in a strategy known as the Dynamic Data Center. Microsoft recognized the importance of compliance, of service-level agreements (SLAs) to the customer (external or internal), and of security. In other words, Microsoft, instead of focusing entirely on the virtualization layer, recognized that the service, and everything that comprises it, is important.

System Center 2012 and the Microsoft Private Cloud

Microsoft System Center has grown from a loose collection of automation tools into a tightly integrated service-management solution. In 2010, Microsoft released System Center Virtual Machine Manager Self Service Portal 2.0 (or SCVMMSSP 2.0 for short), which provides a private cloud layer that can abstract the virtualization infrastructure managed by System Center Virtual Machine Manager 2012. SCVMMSSP 2.0 was a nice first try, and it was not widely adopted. Not long after the release of SCVMMSSP 2.0, Microsoft announced that more was to come from the System Center product groups in 2012. This announcement is part of the reason SCVMMSSP 2.0 hasn't been widely accepted.

System Center 2012 features a new generation of products that build on the automation of DSI and the service management of the Dynamic Data Center, and drive Microsoft into the private cloud. A private cloud enables a business to be more responsive to threats and opportunities by enabling the business to deploy and change services without intervention by the IT department. The role of IT is to provide the shared resources, with automatically provisioned fault-tolerant networking. Services that are deployed should be measured and capable of elasticity to respond to spikes in demand. These are all the traits of a private cloud (see Chapter 1).

Server-based applications are nothing without the client devices to access them, the network to connect to them, and the processes that regulate the business. System Center is a complete solution, encompassing the entire service and infrastructure stack and enabling the IT department to deliver this service.

Talk of cloud computing usually strikes fear into the hearts of traditional server and desktop administrators. But the Microsoft private-cloud strategy doesn't make administrators redundant. It changes their role. They shift from a service-deployment role to an engineering function. Instead of deploying virtual machines or software, they engineer the systems that enable the business to deploy what they need, when they need it, in a manner that is compliant (with process standards and regulations), automated, secure, scalable, controlled, measurable, and dependable. The administrators manage the shared resources of the private cloud. They have more time for engineering. This is exactly what they want to do (because playing with this stuff is fun for computer geeks), and this is exactly what the business wants from IT (because they can deploy what they want for themselves).

IS THE PRIVATE CLOUD FOR EVERYONE?

This question causes debate and will continue to do so for some time. There are two basic arguments:

◆ The features of the private cloud can benefit any business, no matter its size. Even server administrators who are responsible for service deployment can take advantage of the automation systems of the Microsoft private cloud.

◆ A true private cloud separates the role of the server/virtualization administrator from that of the service-deployment administrator. If both functions are indeed performed by a single person or team of people, then adding all of the complexity of a true private cloud makes no sense.

What is not arguable is that every administrator, even one with just a few servers and PCs to manage, can benefit from systems that improve the quality and speed of service they provide. Microsoft's strategy has something for everyone in this line of work. The foundation of the Microsoft private cloud, Virtual Machine Manager 2012, is of huge benefit to anyone managing a farm of virtualization servers, as the rest of this book explains.

Beneficiaries of the Microsoft Private Cloud

Can it really be possible that the Microsoft approach is a win-win-win strategy? Of course, skeptics will say that only Microsoft will win. They'll continue to struggle with service quality and speed while clinging to their failed strategy. Those who are open-minded enough to listen to reason, to consider an alternative, and to give the Microsoft private cloud an honest opportunity to prove itself will soon see how much it offers to all involved.

The Customer Business   Fortunately, the people paying the bills will benefit from the Microsoft private cloud! They care about accessing critical line-of-business applications, collaborating with partners, and reaching out to customers. They care about flexible and agile services that enable the business to react to threats and opportunities before it is too late. A private cloud provides all this.

The Microsoft private cloud not only pays attention to the application layer of the service, but it also manages the complete application stack, including clients (PC, virtual desktop, remote desktop, or mobile device), compliance and security, and the network that connects users to the service.

Importantly, the Microsoft private cloud does this by providing licensing for System Center 2012 without charging customers a prohibitive tax, something that cannot be said for alternative solutions. Strangely enough for Microsoft licensing, System Center 2012 licensing is pretty simple to understand. You typically license each virtualization host for the System Center suite—and that's it! Consult your large account reseller (LAR), distributor, or value added reseller (VAR) to learn more about how you can license the Microsoft private cloud based on System Center 2012 for your business.

The Customer Systems Administrators or Engineers   Neither IT techies nor their company management want the IT department to be putting out fires or doing boring and repetitive work. System Center 2012 allows the IT department to take control of the entire IT infrastructure, from the network all the way through to the application layer, and manage the security, delivery, and compliance of the entire stack. This leverages automation for the processes that are repetitive, enables management by exception for scaled-out infrastructures, and empowers users to help themselves in a controlled and measured manner. It might sound too good to be true, but System Center users know how it can enable administrators to improve the way they work.

Any system that enables the balance to shift from reactive to proactive, from firefighting to interesting engineering, and from heated discussions with the boss and users to a service where the business acknowledges the value that you can provide deserves serious consideration.

The System Integrator or Consultant   There was a time when service providers had reasonable profit margins when reselling hardware or software to their customers. With increased competition and tougher economies, those days are a distant memory. Profits are made by providing expertise to customers in the form of consulting.

Some prefer a curious approach. They drain their customers' budgets by reselling a software solution that deals only with the challenges of virtualization infrastructure. Software sales earn the company a lower margin. Customers have less budget remaining for consulting, and the service providers have less potential for those profit-earning service hours/days.

The Microsoft private-cloud solution takes a different approach. It leverages virtualization solutions that may already exist at the client site, thereby protecting existing investment. However, the focus is on the service-delivery side of the private cloud. With economical and simple licensing, the service provider can shift from a low-margin software-sale-first approach to a high-margin services-sale-first approach.

SYSTEM CENTER 2012 LICENSING

Before System Center 2012, licensing Microsoft's systems-management products could be confusing. There were many options and variations, depending on the product, the complexity of your applications, the size of your environment, and the type of Microsoft licensing programs with which you were involved.

Microsoft listened to the feedback and simplified the licensing for System Center 2012. You don't have to buy different agent types or management licenses, and you don't have to buy different management-server products. It's a simple system.

If you want to manage physical servers or lightly virtualized hosts, purchase the Standard-edition Server Management License (SML). This includes licensing for a physical server and up to two operating-system environments (OSEs)—that is, virtual machines—with all the features of all System Center 2012 products. Note that if your host has four virtual machines, you can buy two Standard SMLs for that host to license all four of the OSEs.

If you want to manage or build a highly virtualized environment, such as a private cloud, with System Center 2012, purchase the Datacenter-edition SML. Not only can you manage the licensed host, but you also get licensing to manage an unlimited number of virtual machines on that licensed host with all of System Center 2012.

You license physical servers (such as virtualization hosts) on a per-physical-processor basis. Each SML includes licensing for two physical processors. For example, if you want to license a host that has four processors, you need two SMLs.

Microsoft released a data sheet with more details on SMLs at

```
http://download.microsoft.com/download/1/1/1/11128EC7-2BE7-480C-9D46-
4ECECA9E481A/System%20Center%202012%20Licensing%20Datasheet.pdf
```

and an FAQ can be found at

```
http://download.microsoft.com/download/8/7/0/870B5D9B-ACF1-4192-BD0A-
543AF551B7AE/System%20Center%202012%20Licensing%20FAQ.pdf.
```

Contact your VAR, distributor, or LAR if you have questions about System Center licensing.

That's enough of the high-level strategy discussion. It is time to learn a little more about the components of System Center 2012 to prepare you for the rest of the book.

System Center 2012 in the Microsoft Private Cloud

We have spent a lot of time talking about clouds and the Microsoft strategy. It is time to learn a bit more about what makes up a Microsoft private cloud.

Virtualization

Virtualization (such as vSphere, XenServer, or Hyper-V) enables server consolidation and rapid deployment of virtual machines. Virtualization is the start of the journey to the private cloud, not the destination.

Actually, virtualization is a critical piece of the private cloud. Without it, you cannot realistically provide rapid, flexible, self-service delivery of services or a collection of consolidated shared resources.

By abstracting services and machines from hardware, virtualization makes it possible for an IT department to build a library of reusable resources that can be made available to the business. Self-service, quality control, automation, and flexibility are leveraged by System Center 2012 to build the Microsoft private cloud.

System Center 2012 Roles

System Center 2012 offers several products that enable the private cloud. Each of them plays a vital role in Microsoft's solution.

SYSTEM CENTER 2012 CONFIGURATION MANAGER (SCCM OR CONFIGMGR)

SCCM 2012 is a lifecycle-management solution that provides tools to help administrators look after the IT infrastructure, from client to server. The 2012 release provides a solution to empower users to deploy software to their own PCs.

With ConfigMgr 2012 in place, administrators can centrally manage PCs, servers, virtual machines, and mobile devices such as Windows Phone, Android, and iPhone/iPad. Administrators can do the following:

◆ Perform zero-touch deployment of operating-system images to computers

◆ Deploy software and service packs according to policy

◆ Distribute security updates for Microsoft, partner, and custom products

◆ Audit hardware and software, storing knowledge of the infrastructure in a central database

◆ Determine configuration compliance and use policy to autocorrect noncompliant configurations

◆ Centrally manage Forefront Endpoint Protection 2012, Microsoft's antivirus product for desktop and server operating systems

The consumerization of IT has created a demand for self-service provisioning of services (cloud computing) and apps. With a new user-centric approach, ConfigMgr 2012 enables administrators to package software, making it available to users from a portal. Company-wide licensed or free software can be installed automatically and immediately when requested by a user; other software can require an approval workflow to be completed before the software can be installed on the user's PC.

ConfigMgr offers automated discovery of services deployed in the private cloud and complete control over licensing, configuration, standardization, and security. Without this functionality, the business would be subject to all sorts of threats, including licensing non-compliance, security issues, and nonstandardization. This solution makes end users happier too, because they can drive change when they need to and react to the daily challenges of doing their jobs.

SYSTEM CENTER 2012 OPERATIONS MANAGER (SCOM OR OPSMGR)

What good is delivering a service if you cannot ensure the quality of that service? SCOM is an enterprise monitoring solution for the complete IT service.

The Network The link between a service and the consumer of that service is a critical IT resource. OpsMgr 2012 adds network-fabric discovery and monitoring to its arsenal, enabling complete service-delivery monitoring.

Hardware Building on server and storage partnerships with Microsoft, OpsMgr can use the manufacturer's own knowledge and expertise to monitor the hardware that provides virtualization and storage fabrics.

Virtualization Virtualization is an enabling layer of the private cloud, so it should be monitored. A black box that can negatively impact the performance of business services is not acceptable.

Operating System   This enables administrators to determine the health and performance of the operating system that is hosting business services, including Windows, Linux, and UNIX.

Applications   Expertise is provided by Microsoft and partners for the applications (such as IIS and SQL Server) that you install in your virtual-machine operating systems.

Many line-of-business applications are custom-developed and have no prepackaged monitoring expertise. There are ways to provide external monitoring, but issues sometimes fall between the cracks of the opposing forces of IT administrator and application developer. OpsMgr 2012 adds built-in monitoring for .NET and for Java 2 Platform, Enterprise Edition (J2EE) applications, offering visibility into the health and performance of those applications, even if the developers have not bothered with logging and monitoring.

Client Perspective   It is great when traditional monitoring of IT components reports that everything is healthy, but it is infuriating when the console is all green while users are complaining about an outage or performance issue. For example, a web application may appear to be running and performing OK, but if there's a bug in the web application that causes a failure, IT finds out only when users complain.

OpsMgr 2012 can monitor services from a client's perspective. This can vary from basic availability and responsiveness to replaying recorded transactions to ensure that the expected results occur. This enables IT to start reacting to issues as soon as the service degrades, even if everything appears to be OK from the server perspective.

Service-Level Agreement   A service comprises many infrastructure and application components. This relationship can be modeled, and the level of performance and availability to the business can be measured. The business can then use this to evaluate the success of service delivery by IT infrastructure and application developers/administrators, making OpsMgr 2012 an infrastructure (private cloud and Microsoft's public cloud, Windows Azure) *and* business solution.

With OpsMgr 2012, a business can monitor everything that makes up the private cloud and the services that are hosted by it. This shift from focusing just on the virtualization layer can greatly improve the performance and availability of business-critical services.

System Center 2012 Virtual Machine Manager (VMM)

VMM 2012 is the system that ties together the infrastructure components and the reusable resources that make the private cloud, and it deploys the services that are required by the business:

Fabric Management   A *fabric* is a collection of infrastructure resources that are components of the private cloud. VMM 2012 is able not only to manage, but also to deploy Hyper-V hosts and clusters to bare-metal machines. Remember that the business doesn't care which kind of virtualization is used. If you have XenServer or vSphere, VMM 2012 protects your investment by letting you include those products in your virtualization fabric. This means that services can be deployed across any of the big three virtualization platforms. Network (IP configuration and load balancers) and storage (for VM and data placement) fabrics can be provisioned for virtual machines so that they are automatically configured.

Resource Management VMM has been capable of reacting to errors detected by OpsMgr using a feature called performance and resource optimization (PRO). PRO is not a dynamic feature; it waits for a warning or a fault. This feature continues in System Center 2012, but it is joined by much more.

Dynamic optimization enables VMM to dynamically load-balance virtual machines and their workloads across the virtualization infrastructure. A new power-management feature enables VMM to consolidate virtualized workloads down to fewer virtualization host servers during times of low utilization. Idle hosts can be powered down, further reducing the electricity bills of the IT infrastructure.

One of the best features of VMM is the *library*. This is a reusable collection of resources such as virtual-machine templates, virtual-machine profiles, ISO files, and scripts. The 2012 version adds more resources, such as Server App-V packages for SQL Server and IIS (which enable services to be packaged and easily deployed to virtual machines as virtualized programs that run in a server operating system), SQL database packages, application packages, and website packages. The contents of this library are the ingredients of a service.

PowerShell lives on and expands as a scripting and enhanced command-line solution in VMM. With PowerShell, administrators can automate operations and build more complex tasks than can be performed in the administration console.

A hotly requested feature for VMM arrives in the 2012 version. The VMM service can be clustered, making it highly available. This is critical if VMM is to be the beating heart of the private cloud, deploying and managing the infrastructure, as well as deploying services for the business.

Cloud Management Private clouds can be built from the virtualization hosts that are managed by VMM. Permission to deploy services can be delegated to end users, and this can be quota- and policy-controlled by VMM administrators.

Service Management The service template is a new feature that joins all of the pieces together and enables end users to deploy a complete IT-based service.

Administrators can define one or more templates that describe common application architectures. This can include networks, network load balancers, virtual machines (numbers and elasticity per role in the service), virtual-machine templates, Server App-V packages, and so on. End users can select one of these service templates and deploy it. After a few minutes, anything from a single virtual machine to a complex n-tier application can be deployed on their behalf—with IP configurations completed, network load balancers operating, and services such as IIS and SQL Server up and running.

Maintaining security is a big concern for businesses because of the self-service nature of the private cloud. Administrators can automate the deployment of security updates to the virtualization fabric (Hyper-V hosts) and to the components of the services.

Quite a bit of growth has occurred since the days of VMM 2008 R2. Most of this book focuses on how you can use these pillars to deploy and manage a private cloud. VMM 2012 won't be discussed much here, because the remainder of the book focuses on it and how it enables the Microsoft private cloud.

SYSTEM CENTER 2012 APP CONTROLLER

App Controller is a new product that provides a single, seamless self-service interface for deploying and managing services across VMM-managed private clouds and the Microsoft Azure public cloud. It simplifies service deployment and enables the owner to pick and choose the right cloud for each service. You will learn more about this cross-premises or hybrid cloud solution in Chapter 11, "App Controller and the Public Cloud."

SYSTEM CENTER 2012 DATA PROTECTION MANAGER (DPM)

One of the most important functions of the IT department is to protect the services and data of the business in case of disaster. DPM is Microsoft's backup and recovery solution. With it you can back up data from Hyper-V–based services in a few ways:

In-VM Backup   A DPM agent can be installed in each VM to back up the entire virtual machine or just the data. An in-VM backup is an inefficient way to back up an entire virtual machine, but it is an effective way to back up just the important business data, such as file shares and databases.

Storage-Level VM Backup   A DPM agent is installed on every Hyper-V host server to enable the backup of entire running virtual machines, as if they were just a collection of a few files with some metadata. This makes restoration of a lost or corrupted virtual machine quick and easy. This type of backup allows you to mount virtual machines and restore data from them, but it is not intended for restoring databases and other such applications that require consistency between files.

A Combined Approach   By combining frequent in-VM backups with infrequent storage-level VM backups, you can back up business data on a regular basis (for example, every hour), and you can back up virtual machines less regularly (for example, once a week, once a month, when computer account passwords change, or when security updates are applied). This approach optimizes data transfer over the network, greatly reduces the time it takes to restore a lost virtual machine, and offers the granularity of an in-VM backup.

DPM 2012 offers direct-to-disk backup of data on a block-level basis. This means that only the changes to files are backed up, unlike the traditional and inefficient full/incremental approach. Backup data can be streamed to tape, and it can be replicated to another DPM server's disk for off-site storage.

New features of DPM 2012 include

- Centralized management of many DPM servers from a central console

- Role-based management

- Certificate-based protection for machines that are not members of the Active Directory forest

- The ability to store many protection groups (policies) on a single tape

- Item-level recovery from SharePoint farms

- Improved and faster backup of Hyper-V virtual machines

SYSTEM CENTER 2012 ORCHESTRATOR

Formerly known as Opalis, Orchestrator 2012 is known as a *runbook automation solution*. Orchestrator is intended to automate repetitive tasks by comprising many steps, which span one or more systems.

Every organization's IT department has many examples of such tasks. There will be a folder of processes, where some operation requires a skilled IT operator to spend the business's valuable time executing a sequence of steps, clicking and typing exactly what is documented. There is almost no variation in the implementation of the process.

Orchestrator makes it possible for organizations to automate repetitive processes that span many systems. The business wins because it gets predictable, timely results. IT operators can use the saved time to benefit the business. And let's face it: no one enjoys doing this kind of donkey work; they'd rather be doing something more interesting.

With System Center 2012 Orchestrator, you can automate processes across heterogeneous systems from Microsoft, HP, IBM, EMC, BMC, CA, and even VMware, using provided integration packs. Third-party integration packs can be purchased, and more can be developed in-house as required.

If you've worked with Opalis in the past, you will be happy to learn that the reliance on Java has been dropped. Orchestrator 2012 also features a much tighter integration with the rest of System Center 2012 to facilitate cross-platform automation in the Microsoft private cloud.

SYSTEM CENTER 2012 SERVICE MANAGER (SCSM)

The name of this product is pretty descriptive; SCSM is all about delivery of service to the business. SCSM accomplishes this in three ways:

Self-Service   A customizable service catalog presents a set of services that span both the infrastructure and application layers. End users, departmental IT staff, application administrators, developers, and so on can request operations to be completed on their behalf. Leveraging automation, such as the runbook or process automation provided by Orchestrator 2012 or the System Center Cloud Services Process Pack, SCSM 2012 enables those noncentral IT staff to request the system to do work on their behalf. The automation systems perform the work, and other systems monitor it for exceptions. The role of central IT shifts from doing that repetitive work to engineering the automation systems and monitoring them for performance and reliability.

Process Compliance and Automation   SCSM 2012 can reach into the databases of ConfigMgr 2012 and OpsMgr 2012 to learn about the infrastructure and services that IT provides to the business. SCSM 2012 can then be used to achieve business goals, such as IT-risk, governance, and compliance solutions.

Management   SCSM 2012 can be referred to as a help-desk solution, but that does it a disservice. It is also capable of being an automated management solution by building in workflows for problem management, SLA management, and service management (helpdesk). With all this talk of private clouds, computers, and automation, it's easy to forget that humans are part of the equation and they require assistance from time to time.

System Center 2012 is a complete solution spanning all components of the private cloud, from creating the cloud to monitoring service delivery. The central piece in the creation of a private cloud is System Center Virtual Machine Manager 2012. Part 2 of this book, "Fabric and Service Management," will teach you how to build the infrastructure of your first Microsoft private cloud.

Summary

In this chapter you learned that the Microsoft private-cloud strategy is to emulate the goal of the private cloud. It uses the System Center 2012 suite of integrated products to focus on service delivery and management, which are directly relevant to the business, bringing you beyond virtualization.

Each of the System Center products plays a role in building the private cloud, deploying services, monitoring the fabrics and services, protecting the business, providing automation and self-service, and integrating with the Microsoft public cloud, Azure. System Center Virtual Machine Manager 2012 and System Center App Controller play central roles in the creation, management, and service deployment of a Microsoft private cloud.

Part 2

Fabric and Service Management

Chapter 3

Introducing the VMM 2012 Architecture

Virtual Machine Manager 2012 has become the main tool for building the Microsoft private cloud and is now an important member of the System Center 2012 family of management products. This chapter describes the following:

- ◆ How VMM evolved from a patched-together collection of managers to today's sophisticated tool

- ◆ The capabilities of VMM that make it a complete solution for managing private clouds

- ◆ The architecture and main components of a VMM private cloud

Exploring the New Capabilities of VMM 2012

The traditional data center has a large variety of servers, clusters, hypervisors, network devices, storage devices, and other equipment. Most physical servers host dozens of virtual machines. Those virtual machines in turn host a variety of operating systems and applications. Most of them run some version of Windows and Linux. Another trend that can be observed in more and more enterprises is the combined use of several hypervisors. Hyper-V and XenServer have joined VMware, and the most appropriate hypervisor is chosen for a particular workload or scenario. Notably, Hyper-V R2 has made a lot of progress in the past two years, and the advent of Hyper-V in Windows Server 8 promises a breakthrough of Microsoft virtualization for both server and client. Multi-hypervisor is here to stay!

Your IT environment can be large, medium, or small; regardless of size, the chances are high that you work in the kind of heterogeneous environment described in the previous paragraph. You may already use or may be contemplating using several Microsoft System Center 2012 management applications. Most likely you will upgrade from their previous versions. Even if you haven't decided to upgrade, you should take a look at the different members of the System Center family: Operations Manager is a capable monitoring and reporting solutions for heterogeneous environments with Windows, Linux, and VMware. You might have considered using Data Protection Manager to protect your Windows applications and Hyper-V virtual machines. Perhaps you have already set up Configuration Manager for deploying and updating your clients and servers. You may even have thought of applying Service Manager in combination with Orchestrator to control the flow of your IT and data-center processes. Creating some sort of synergy across the different parts of your data center would really help your IT team.

Now that you have started to figure out how to transform your traditional data center into a private cloud, you need to take a closer look at Virtual Machine Manager (VMM). If Hyper-V is already a hypervisor of choice in your environment, you have probably implemented VMM 2008 R2 to deal with a collection of virtual machines. This product was nothing more than an extension of Hyper-V Manager and Failover Cluster Manager, although for some tasks you had to resort to the native Hyper-V and clustering tools. VMM 2008 R2 was not always aware of changes performed in the other tools, which could cause unexpected behavior. Not so with VMM 2012! Considerable effort was put into making VMM the primary tool for managing Hyper-V, VMware, and XenServer—and into avoiding the use of other managers. VMM 2012 is positioned to be the primary aid in building the foundation for a Microsoft private cloud that is not confined to Microsoft virtualization. It is surrounded and integrated with the other System Center 2012 modules to offer you superior control of the ever-expanding, diverse ecosystem of IT Infrastructure and, most important, the applications or services that help your organization operate successfully.

In summary, this piece of management software is aimed at the virtualized data center. It helps to configure and manage not only virtualization hosts and virtual machines but also the relevant networking and storage resources. Resource pooling is one of the essential characteristics of the cloud. VMM enables you to combine many of your server, storage, and network devices and organize them into capacity pools. This is a big step in the right direction, because traditionally these resource silos were managed separately and required dedicated IT staff. With its very good deployment capabilities, VMM makes it easy for you to create and deploy virtual machines and applications (or *services*, as they are now called). This product release and the other members of the System Center 2012 suite will help you build and operate the private cloud.

New Functionality

In this section, we'll briefly look at the tremendous amount of new functionality introduced with VMM 2012.

VMM Deployment

◆   You can install VMM in a Windows failover cluster. As of this release, it is possible to build a highly available VMM management server, allowing quick VMM failover while you perform hardware or software maintenance on one of the cluster nodes.

VMM Security Configuration

◆   Taking Operations Manager as its example, VMM allows you to create Run As accounts. It simplifies and speeds up the process of providing credentials while accessing or configuring a certain device or other cloud object. You don't have to remember all the passwords, and you control who is able to use those Run As accounts.

◆   You can create a Delegated Administrator and Self-Service User role to provide finer control in VMM. You don't want to assign full control to your fabric and clouds to all members of your IT department. You can delegate control to certain people and specify which parts of the fabric they can access.

◆ You can create a Read-Only Administrator user role and several other existing roles, such as the Delegated Administrator and Self-Service User roles. If you want to keep control over the private cloud but want certain users or customers to have a read-only view of their cloud objects, you can give them permission to view their own host groups, virtual machines, clouds, and library servers.

VMM Fabric Configuration

◆ You can discover physical servers without an operating system on the network and add the bare-metal servers to VMM management by installing a version of Windows Server that includes the Hyper-V role. This gives you the power to rapidly deploy a large number of physical servers and automatically configure them according to organizational standards.

◆ With minimal effort, you can create an operational Hyper-V cluster by joining multiple standalone Hyper-V servers. The wizard quickly collects all relevant data and configures the cluster automatically. You can also validate the cluster after you make changes, add or remove nodes, or uncluster the corresponding Hyper-V servers.

◆ You can manage Citrix XenServer hosts. This makes VMM the first private-cloud management solution that supports the three leading hypervisors. Because its architecture is similar to that of Hyper-V, XenServer is a logical extension of the hypervisors that could be managed in the previous version of VMM.

◆ You can create and configure networking resources consisting of logical networks, IP-address pools, MAC-address pools, load balancers, and VIP templates, which can be used to deploy virtualization hosts and virtual machines on any of the supported hypervisor platforms. With networking integration, administrators and delegated administrators can configure and assign networking resources without the full-time involvement of a specialized network administrator.

◆ You can create and configure storage resources with one or more storage classifications and pools, storage providers and storage arrays. By utilizing deep storage integration, administrators can assign storage to Hyper-V virtualization hosts without the full-time involvement of a specialized storage administrator. Of course, storage expertise and assistance are required during the configuration phase of VMM and the integration of all supported storage arrays. Once an agreed portion of enterprise storage has been made available to the storage pool by the storage administrator, the administrator can independently assign storage capacity to one or more private clouds. In the current release, this functionality is available only to Hyper-V hosts and clusters.

◆ You can scan Hyper-V and fabric-management servers to make sure they comply with a defined update baseline. You can verify the compliance status of these servers and use a configured Windows Server Update Services (WSUS) server to perform update remediation. Compliance management applies to Hyper-V servers and clusters, VMM management servers, VMM library servers, Windows software update servers and WDS/PXE servers.

◆ You can automatically schedule resource balancing of virtual machines across host clusters that support live migration technologies (*dynamic optimization*).

◆ You can automate the power management of virtualization hosts that have been idle for some time. Idle hosts can be automatically switched off after a graceful live migration of the virtual machines. When required, these hosts will be automatically switched on based on workload requirements (*power optimization*).

VMM Cloud Configuration

◆ In VMM, one or more private clouds can be created for an organization or department to organize a selected number of virtualization hosts in combination with a pool of storage, a variety of networking resources, and VMM library resources. If you are a hosting provider, you probably have a cloud for each customer. Virtual machines and services can be deployed to those private clouds.

◆ Server application virtualization (Server App-V) is integrated into VMM, adding the ability to create sequenced applications for deployment by VMM.

◆ The concept of a capability profile is introduced in VMM to define or to limit the resources that can be used by a virtual machine in a private cloud. There are default capability profiles for Hyper-V, VMware, and XenServer, but you can also create your own.

◆ Application profiles with configuration details about Server App-V, Microsoft Web Deploy, and SQL Server data-tier applications (DACs) can be created in VMM to deploy scripts, applications, and services in the private cloud.

◆ You can create a SQL Server profile with special instructions for a SQL instance when used with a SQL Server DAC as part of a virtual machine or service.

◆ You can deploy virtual machines to private clouds by means of virtual-machine and service templates.

◆ The Service Template Designer is introduced in VMM to create service templates, which can be used to deploy services to a cloud.

◆ You can scale out a service by adding additional virtual machines to a service that has already been deployed.

◆ You can update an existing service template using version management. If combined with multiple update domains and load-balanced virtual machines, it is possible to update an already deployed service without downtime for users.

◆ You can transfer service templates and virtual-machine templates by means of export and import.

◆ You can mark file-based/physical library resources as equivalent objects in different and often distant VMM libraries so that any identical file object (.vhd file, .iso file, or custom object) can be used from any VMM library when a virtual machine is deployed from a template. This enables you to use a single template across multiple sites.

Changed Functionality

Support for the following software is deprecated in the current version of VMM:

◆ Microsoft Virtual Machine Manager 2005 R2

◆ VMware ESX 3.0 and ESXi 3.0

◆ Microsoft SQL Server Express (VMM 2012 requires a fully featured version of Microsoft SQL Server)

The previous version of VMM already had limited self-service, but users had to log into a web portal that had limited functionality. Self-service users can now benefit from the VMM console and are not limited to using the web portal.

Resources for VMM 2012

For more information about VMM 2012, you can refer to the following URLs:

System Center Downloads

http://technet.microsoft.com/en-us/systemcenter/cc137824

Documentation

◆ System Center 2012 Technical Library:

http://technet.microsoft.com/en-us/library/hh546785.aspx

◆ TechNet Library:

http://technet.microsoft.com/nl-nl/library/gg610610(en-us).aspx

◆ Microsoft Download Center:

www.microsoft.com/download/en/details.aspx?id=6346

Websites

◆ Microsoft Server and Cloud Platform:

www.microsoft.com/en-us/server-cloud/system-center/virtual-machine-manager.aspx

◆ VMM 2012 Survival Guide:

http://social.technet.microsoft.com/wiki/contents/articles/vmm-2012-survival-guide.aspx

◆ Virtual Machine Manager blog:

http://blogs.technet.com/b/scvmm/

◆ Storage and Load Balancer Provider downloads:

http://social.technet.microsoft.com/wiki/contents/articles/scvmm-2012-storage-and-load-balancer-provider-downloads.aspx

◆ VMM 2012 Error Codes:

http://social.technet.microsoft.com/wiki/contents/articles/4906.aspx

Community (MVP) blogs

http://kristiannese.blogspot.com

http://aidanfinn.com

http://damianflynn.com

http://hyper-v.nu

http://mountainss.wordpress.com

http://workinghardinit.wordpress.com/author/workinghardinit/

http://hyper-v-server.de

Understanding the VMM Architecture

Designing and building a private cloud can be an interesting adventure, if not virgin territory. "Think before you build" is good advice, but it's difficult to plan something in a field that is mostly unknown to you. That's why you bought this book. Because there is little guidance in the land of private clouds, the following chapters will take you by the hand and guide you through that uncharted territory. This chapter doesn't yet focus on installing hardware or software components; it is intended to help you before you start your journey.

Prior chapters explain what a private cloud can mean to your company, its employees, and its customers. Your team has agreed to build that promising private cloud for your organization and you need to prepare for that daunting project. Although many components of the private cloud may be familiar to you, welding them all together requires new insights. Take some time to prepare. Read as much as you can about the cloud concept. Talk with your colleagues and your peers in the social media. Check the relevant blogs and forums on the Internet. Begin to define what you expect to achieve with the private cloud. Don't forget to involve corporate management; you need to know what they expect from IT.

So far you are doing quite well. What you are learning from this book should help you build an environment in which to learn, to test and verify your assumptions, and get hands-on experience building the foundation for your private cloud. Take ample time to think and to prepare for the journey.

Use your imagination and try to sketch the general picture. You can always adapt and modify your ideas before you finally begin to build your first production private cloud. Even after you build the infrastructure components of the private cloud, flexibility is your friend. After all, isn't that what you expected when you started to think of building a cloud in the first place? Cloud computing is still in its infancy. This is the time to experiment, learn from your mistakes, and adjust as necessary.

Your first step in designing a private cloud is to understand the major building blocks. A private cloud is built around familiar physical building blocks such as servers and clusters, networks, and storage. The generic word used for them is *fabric*. In the storage world, the word *fabric* is used to describe a collection of interconnected storage devices (SAN switches, storage arrays, tape robots, and so forth). In the context of the cloud, the term *fabric* includes servers, clusters, and networks, as well as storage.

So *fabric* is the pretty little word that encompasses the vast physical foundation of the private cloud. However, when you start thinking about architecting that fabric, it is a good idea to take a satellite view of your surroundings. Imagine booking a trip on one of the first commercial space flights. While in orbit, you get a fairly good opportunity to look at the world you thought you knew well, but now as you look down, you behold its abstraction, the impressive overall view from your shuttle window. While picturing the fabric as the foundation of the private cloud, you do not need to zoom in on the details just yet. Let's put in the bigger blocks first: servers and clusters, networks, and storage.

If you're not sure whether a private cloud would be appropriate or if you fear your company might be too small, think about the scale and complexity of your IT operations. Even if you have a limited number of physical servers and virtual machines, building a private cloud could mean making a new start with new principles to fight the often time-consuming manual labor needed to deploy servers and virtual machines and attach networks, VLANs, and all the different storage options. Instead of looking at the individual pieces, it is time to look at them as a fully functional and interconnected fabric. The biggest gains come from changing your attitude toward standardization, automation, elasticity, and self-service. Together the results will be rewarding, whether your private cloud is small, medium, or large.

If your cloud will serve a small number of customers, it will have one cluster with a few hosts, network, and storage devices. If your company has bigger aspirations, you may have hundreds of hosts, several networks, multiple locations with hundreds of VLANs, multiple load balancers, and numerous storage arrays. When you picked up this book, you were already convinced of the advantages that a private cloud offers you, your company, and the consumers of your cloud. You already want to build one. All you have to do is find out if your theory can land on earth and become a common practice.

Take your binoculars and zoom in one level. Ignore objects such as domain controllers, DNS servers, and DHCP servers. The relevant servers are virtualization hosts of several different flavors, clusters combining multiple virtualization hosts, and a variety of management or auxiliary servers. Think of hosts that manage deployment, hosts for managing and monitoring both virtual and physical machines, and hosts that take care of update management—and don't forget the prospect of a rapidly growing number of virtual machines.

The next major component of the fabric is the network. Again, this assumes that all the physical switches, routers, and load balancers that make the LAN and WAN are in place. The network either has no VLANs or the network administrator has already logically divided the network into multiple virtual LANs, each representing a location or a specific purpose. Wouldn't it be nice if you could abstract those networks by using meaningful names and you could find a way to manage the pools of static IP addresses?

The third important building block is storage. Without an abundance of storage, a cloud has little substance. *Storage* is the collection of storage arrays, pools of disks, and the individual disks (often called LUNs by SAN admins) assigned to servers. Like the networking component, storage is often in the hands of a specialized admin. More often than not, that dependency on specialists will prolong the deployment of new services. Wouldn't it be great if the consumer or an application administrator could easily recognize the different storage silos? Wouldn't it make your job easier if you could assign the appropriate quality and quantity of storage to a virtual machine, service, or entire cloud with little effort?

If self-service is one of the most important and useful characteristics of a private cloud, then self-service users shouldn't have to understand the technical building blocks in the cloud landscape. These artifacts should be completely abstracted.

Components of VMM

Depending on the size and scale of a private cloud, VMM can be deployed on one or several servers. If your environment is limited to a few Hyper-V hosts, all the components can be installed on one server. If you expect to host dozens or even hundreds of hosts with different hypervisors and possibly thousands of virtual machines, you need to take a more careful look at where to place the different components of VMM. A primary reason for this is to increase scalability, flexibility, serviceability, and availability.

Chapter 4 looks at the requirements for a number of different configurations. It gives a general overview of the different VMM components and how they can be distributed across multiple servers and locations.

Figure 3.1 gives an architectural view of VMM 2012 and shows some of the components described in the preceding paragraphs.

FIGURE 3.1
The VMM architecture

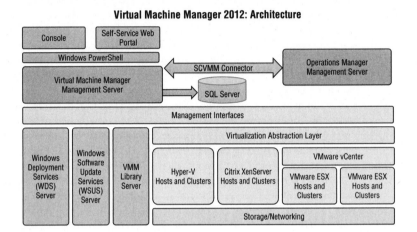

Virtual Machine Manager 2012: Architecture

VMM MANAGEMENT SERVER

The central component of VMM is the VMM management server, which runs as a Windows service on each VMM server. This component is the first one to be installed and is responsible for communicating with the SQL Server database and for storing and retrieving the configuration, including all objects that are created and managed by VMM. This core service also stores performance information about the different fabric resources.

The VMM management server has a broker function and is responsible for the following tasks:

◆ Communicating with the database server for storing and providing information when a VMM client asks for information via the VMM console or a PowerShell cmdlet.

◆ Communicating with hosts via VMM agents and executing commands

◆ Communicating with VMM library servers via a VMM agent and executing commands

◆ Communicating with XenServer servers and executing commands

◆ Communicating with VMware vCenter servers and expediting commands

◆ Starting and stopping jobs

◆ Monitoring jobs

◆ Reporting progress, success, and failure

◆ Communicating with System Center components

The VMM management server is also supported in a virtual machine but should ideally be isolated from the servers it manages. A good location for a VMM server could be a Hyper-V cluster dedicated to System Center 2012 management.

A default installation of the VMM management server is performed on a single machine. This may make sense in a testing and development environment. The setup can be done quickly and easily. If you are setting up VMM for a private cloud of some size, your admins, users, or customers depend on it, so consider making VMM highly available.

If you are going to operate an enterprise-level private cloud, consider the consequences if your VMM-related servers are unavailable for a day, two days, a week, or possibly even longer. After you spend a good amount of time deploying and configuring VMM, the database will be filled with all relevant objects and resources. Several other cloud admins, application admins, or even external customers will depend on VMM. At that point, VMM will become a very important piece of software and will be the spider in the web of your private cloud. If you decide to cluster VMM, do you think making VMM highly available will suffice? You will need to cluster the database as well as the virtual-machine libraries.

Because all three functions (VMM management, VMM database, and VMM library) can't be in the same physical or guest cluster, it would perhaps be better to take another approach. Apart from VMM, you will probably also implement other members of the System Center 2012 family. Most management applications have the same high-availability requirements. In such cases, a good approach is to take two or more physical servers, provision some shared storage, build a Hyper-V cluster, and deploy the System Center products as Hyper-V highly available virtual machines. With all three important VMM components, you can also create three separate guest clusters: a two-node SQL Server guest cluster, a two-node VMM management server cluster, and a two-node file cluster for the VMM libraries. Of course, if you have already clustered the database and file servers, you can concentrate on building a highly available VMM management server. Chapter 4, "Setting Up and Deploying VMM 2012," describes how to do this.

VMM DATABASE

The VMM database is a Microsoft SQL Server database, which is installed on the VMM server itself, on a dedicated SQL Server machine, or on a SQL Server cluster. As of VMM 2012, a full version of SQL Server is required (see Chapter 4 for the exact requirements) and must be available before the other components can be installed. In a larger private cloud, a separately clustered SQL Server is highly recommended. It protects against problems with either the physical server or the SQL Server services and configuration. Monthly maintenance can be performed more easily, because vital services can be failed over between the nodes in the SQL cluster.

Size and scalability determine where to place the VMM database. As you will see in Chapter 4 in the section on VMM requirements, it is feasible to place the VMM database in a virtual machine (cluster) too.

VMM CONSOLE

The VMM console offers the primary graphical user interface for all private cloud administrators, delegated admins, read-only admins, and self-service users. However, what you can see and manage in the VMM console depends on your role. Some admins need to have full access to all fabric resources, such as servers, network, and storage. If you are in a consuming role, you only need to see your own clouds and have access to the computing, network, and storage resources for which you have permission. As a consumer, you want to quickly and efficiently deploy new virtual machines and services, deploy applications, and deploy the images that contain them. For such self-service users, the underlying infrastructure is invisible and fully abstracted as explained in Chapter 6, "Integrating Networking and Storage into VMM 2012," and Chapter 7, "Deploying Hosts and Clusters in VMM 2012."

The VMM 2012 interface differs considerably from earlier versions. The first remarkable difference is the ribbon, the flexible and context-sensitive tool used to access most detailed functions. As you can see on the bottom left of Figure 3.2, there are more Wunderbars, now called *workspaces*, and they have changed. Administration is now called Settings. It allows you to view or configure a variety of different settings. The Library and Jobs bar is still there, but Hosts has been placed under the new Fabric workspace, which hosts not only Servers but also Networking and Storage. Finally, the Virtual Machines category is now combined with Services in VMs and Services.

FIGURE 3.2

The VMM 2012 user interface

Navigation pane   Ribbon

Workspace   Detail pane   View pane

The VMM console is automatically installed with VMM Management Server, and a VMM console icon is placed on the desktop. The VMM console can be installed separately on a management computer and allow you to connect to VMM remotely. When you install the VMM console, you also get the VMM command shell, PowerShell. While the console is built on top of PowerShell, the console does not provide access to all the functionality available through a PowerShell cmdlet.

VMM COMMAND SHELL

The VMM command shell is the true engine of VMM. Like the console, the command shell is installed with each VMM management server. By default, two PowerShell modules are imported to the VMM server: `virtualmachinemanager` and `BitsTransfer`. You can check which commands are available in the module by issuing the following command:

```
Get-Command -Module -virtualmachinemanager
```

The `BitsTranfer` commands are used by VMM to start, stop, and suspend background intelligent transfer service (BITS) jobs. These jobs transport large quantities of data between systems, cleverly employing bandwidth only as it becomes available. VMM has a lot of bit transfers to do, so this module is loaded by default.

VMM LIBRARY

The VMM library (Figure 3.3) provides an easy way to configure a repository of the resources that help create a virtualization host, a virtual machine, an application, or service. Examples are `.iso` image files, virtual hard-disk files (`.vhd, .vmdk`), VM templates, PowerShell scripts (`.ps1`), Answer Files (`.inf, .xml`), SQL Server scripts (`.sql`), MSDeploy packages (`.zip`), Server App-V packages (`.osd`), virtual floppy (`.vfd, .flp`) files, driver files (`.inf`), Custom Resources (`.cr`), and complete clones of virtual machines. Chapter 5, "Understanding the VMM Library," is dedicated to the VMM library.

FIGURE 3.3
Overview of the VMM Library

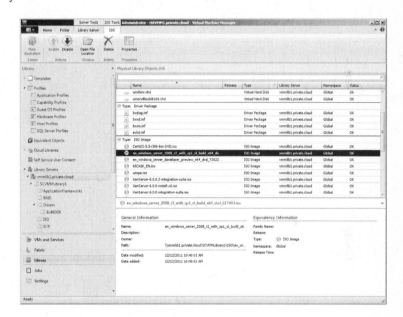

VMM SELF-SERVICE PORTAL

With VMM 2012 you can optionally install a web-based VMM Self-Service Portal. This component allows you to create a controlled environment where self-service users can create and manage their own virtual machines via a web interface. You can enable an application administrator to author, deploy, manage, and decommission applications in the private cloud. It is a good idea to configure this portal on a separate machine that hosts Internet Information Services (IIS).

VMM 2012 Topology

If you combine all the components and add the virtualization host and auxiliary servers WSUS and WDS, the topology of Virtual Machine Manager 2012 resembles the landscape of Figure 3.4.

FIGURE 3.4
Overview of the
VMM 2012 topology

VMM Console
Administrator
Delegated Administrator
Read-Only Administrator
Self-Service User

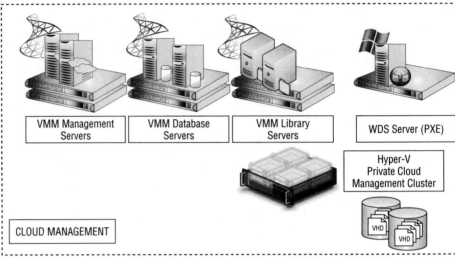

VMM Management
Servers

VMM Database
Servers

VMM Library
Servers

WDS Server (PXE)

Hyper-V
Private Cloud
Management Cluster

VHD

VHD

CLOUD MANAGEMENT

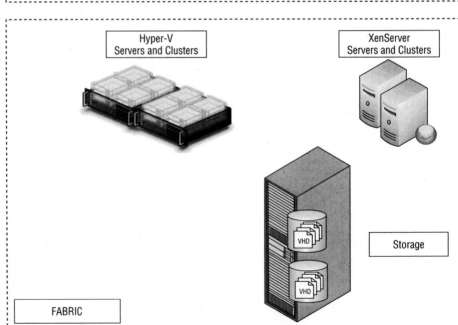

Hyper-V
Servers and Clusters

XenServer
Servers and Clusters

VHD

VHD

Storage

FABRIC

Web Console
Self-Service User

WSUS Server

System Center 2012
Servers

VMware vCenter
Servers

Self-Service Portal
Servers

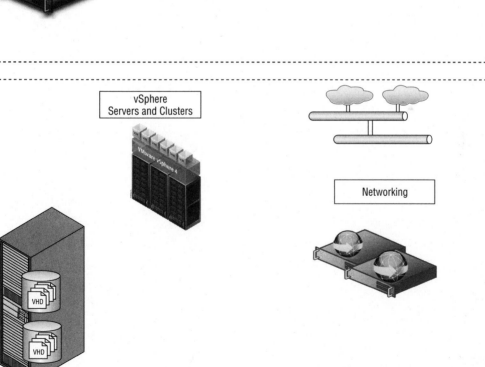

vSphere
Servers and Clusters

Networking

Ports and Protocols

When you set up the VMM management server, you can assign a number of ports for protocols that are used to communicate with a variety of devices as well as for executing file transfers between the different VMM components. As a security best practice, these default ports may be changed. VMM must be uninstalled (with retention of the database) and reinstalled to change any of these ports. Figure 3.5 shows the default ports that are configured when VMM and the VMM console are installed.

FIGURE 3.5
Default ports for VMM and the VMM console

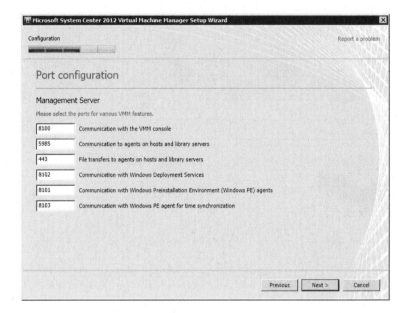

The default settings for the ports are listed in Table 3.1. Figure 3.6 represents these ports pictorially.

TABLE 3.1: The VMM Default Ports

CONNECTION TYPE	PROTOCOL	DEFAULT PORT
SFTP file transfer from VMware ESX 3.x hosts	SFTP	22
VMM management server to P2V source agent (control channel)	DCOM	135
VMM management server to load balancer	HTTP/HTTPS	80/443
VMM management server to WSUS server (data channel)	HTTP/HTTPS	80/8530
VMM management server to WSUS server (data channel)	HTTP/HTTPS	443/8531 (SSL)
BITS port for VMM transfers (data channel)	BITS	443
VMM library server to hosts file transfer (data channel)	BITS	443 (Max: 32768)
VMM host to hosts file transfer (data channel)	BITS	443 (Max: 32768)

TABLE 3.1: The VMM Default Ports *(CONTINUED)*

CONNECTION TYPE	PROTOCOL	DEFAULT PORT
VMM self-service portal to VMM self-service portal web server	HTTPS	443
VMware Web Services communication	HTTPS	443
SFTP file transfer from VMM management server to VMware ESX Server 3i	HTTPS	443
OOB connection SMASH over WS-Man	HTTPS	443
VMM to VM data channel	HTTPS (BITS)	443
VMM to Windows host data channel	HTTPS (BITS)	443 (Max: 32768)
OOB connection IPMI	IPMI	623
VMM management server to remote SQL Server database	TDS	1433
Console connections (RDP) to VMs via Hyper-V hosts (VMConnect)	RDP	2179
VMM management server to Citrix XenServer host (customization data channel)	iSCSI	3260
Remote desktop to virtual machines	RDP	3389
VMM management server to VMM agent on Windows Server–based host (data channel)	WS-Management	5985
VMM management server to in-guest agent VMM to Virtual Machine (control channel SSL)	WS-Management	5985
VMM management server to VMM agent on Windows Server–based host (control channel SSL)	WS-Management	5986
VMM management server to XenServer host (control channel)	HTTPS	5989
VMM console to VMM management server	WCF	8100
VMM self-service portal web server to VMM management server	WCF	8100
VMM console to VMM management server (HTTPS)	WCF	8101
Windows PE agent to VMM management server (control channel)	WCF	8101
VMM console to VMM management server (NET.TCP)	WCF	8102
WDS Provider to VMM management server	WCF	8102
VMM console to VMM management server (HTTP)	WCF	8103
Windows PE agent to VMM management server (Time Sync)	WCF	8103
VMM management server to Storage Management Service	WMI	Local call
VMM management server to cluster PowerShell interface	PowerShell	n/a
Storage management server to SMI-S provider	CIM-XML	Provider specific port
VMM management server to P2V source agent data channel	BITS	User-defined

FIGURE 3.6
Overview of VMM
2012 ports and
protocols

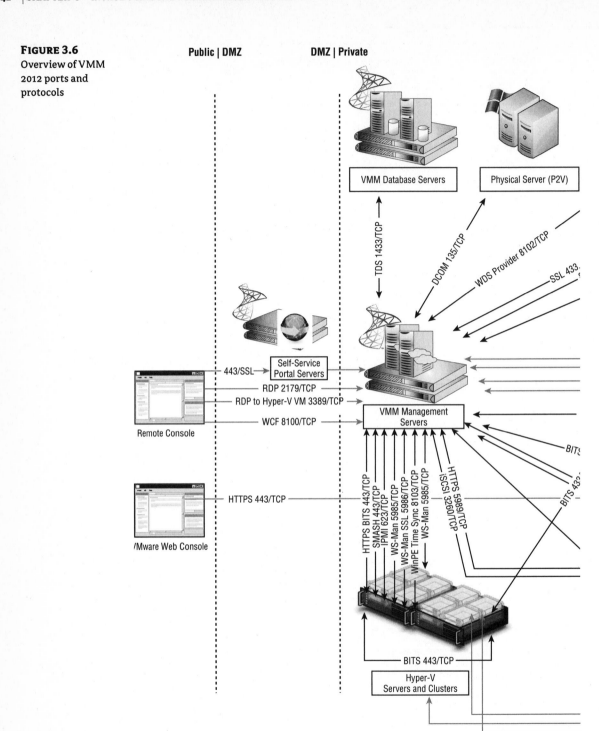

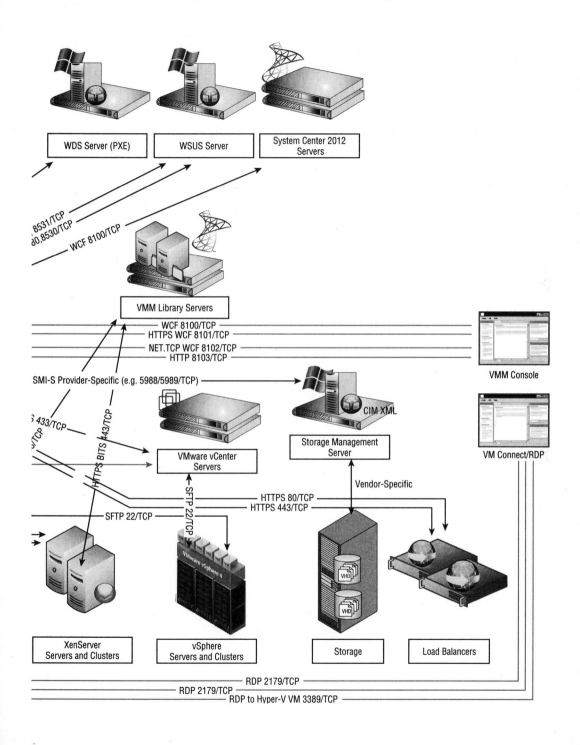

WDS Server (PXE)

WSUS Server

System Center 2012
Servers

8531/TCP
80,8530/TCP

WCF 8100/TCP

VMM Library Servers

WCF 8100/TCP
HTTPS WCF 8101/TCP
NET.TCP WCF 8102/TCP
HTTP 8103/TCP

VMM Console

SMI-S Provider-Specific (e.g. 5988/5989/TCP)

CIM XML

S 433/TCP
/TCP

HTTPS BITS 443/TCP

VMware vCenter
Servers

Storage Management
Server

VM Connect/RDP

Vendor-Specific

SFTP 22/TCP

HTTPS 80/TCP
HTTPS 443/TCP

SFTP 22/TCP

SFTP 22/TCP

VHD

VHD

XenServer
Servers and Clusters

vSphere
Servers and Clusters

Storage

Load Balancers

RDP 2179/TCP
RDP 2179/TCP
RDP to Hyper-V VM 3389/TCP

Summary

VMM arose from Microsoft's attempts to control its virtualization and cluster failover facilities. VMM 2008 R2 provided an incomplete solution, but VMM 2012 finishes that job and adds facilities for building and managing Microsoft private clouds.

A Microsoft private cloud rests on a fabric of servers, clusters, networks, and storage. By abstracting these elements, VMM 2012 enables the key cloud features of resource pools, elasticity, and self-service.

VMM 2012 is built on the VMM management server, which brokers requests between clients and the software underlying the abstracted fabric elements that clients see. It uses a full SQL Server database to keep track of all the pieces. Clients and administrators can communicate with the management server using a GUI, a command shell, or a self-service portal.

A key feature of private clouds is that all underlying fabric resources (virtualization hosts, storage, and network) are abstracted from the consumer of the private cloud.

Setting Up and Deploying VMM 2012

The previous chapter discussed the new Virtual Machine Manager capabilities, the components of this private cloud–management product, and how the components relate to each other. The focus now shifts to preparing for VMM setup and deployment. This chapter shows you how to do the following:

◆ Relate VMM requirements to your business needs

◆ Prepare to install VMM

◆ Install and configure VMM

◆ Use clustering to ensure high availability

Discovering VMM 2012 Installation Requirements

Don't just grab the installation media and execute the setup. First take a little time to study the installation requirements. Installing VMM and its components isn't rocket science, but it is important to review requirements that might influence the following choices:

◆ Should you upgrade your current version or simply reinstall?

◆ Should all the components be on one server or distributed?

◆ Should there be one physical location or several?

◆ Should there be a separate database server or cluster?

◆ Should there be separate library shares, an existing fileserver, or cluster?

◆ Should you use Hyper-V only or a mix of hypervisors?

◆ Should there be highly available VMM?

◆ Where is the best place for the self-service portal?

◆ How does VMM update management fit into your current updating strategy?

Studying the VMM 2012 installation requirements can help you answer these questions before you install the software.

The number of servers you'll need for VMM depends on whether you are using a single server or distributed components with high availability for some components.

As recommended in Chapter 3, "Introducing the VMM 2012 Architecture," one suitable approach is to create a management or infrastructure cluster based on Hyper-V and build your components inside multiple virtual machines. You can start with a two-node cluster of capable physical hosts and build guest clusters for those components that support high availability. This increases cost, but it considerably improves flexibility, scalability, and availability. You will probably add other System Center 2012 modules after VMM, so build a good foundation.

If you are building a private cloud and expect it to grow substantially, you should distribute the VMM components across a number of servers and, ideally, each in its own (virtual) machine. If you base your cluster on Windows Server 2008 R2 Datacenter edition, the number of Windows licenses is not an issue because you are entitled to an unlimited number of licenses.

Many of Microsoft's minimum and recommended requirements are open for debate. Ignore the minimum values and be generous on the recommended ones. If you build your System Center virtual machines on Hyper-V, setting a dynamic maximum memory value, the memory-demand information in Hyper-V Manager will give you good idea about its real-life requirements if you leave it running for a while. Set the minimum memory value to at least 2 GB to avoid a failed memory requirement during setup. It will save you from another reboot.

VMM Management Server

The hardware and software requirements for the VMM management server largely depend on the number of virtualization hosts it manages, the locality of the database, and the location of the VMM library shares. Check the requirements for those as well if you separate these components.

For the best scalable approach, use a dedicated (virtual) machine for the VMM management server and place the VMM library and database in their own (virtual) machine (clusters). Monitor the server's resources with System Center tools such as Operations Manager to determine whether additional resources are required.

The general requirements for the VMM management server include the following:

◆ The VMM management server must be a member of an Active Directory domain.

◆ The name of the VMM management server can have a maximum length of 15 characters.

◆ Startup memory should be 3 GB if the VMM management server runs on a Hyper-V R2 SP1 host with dynamic memory enabled.

◆ Running the VMM management server on a failover cluster requires Windows Server 2008 R2 Enterprise or Datacenter edition.

Table 4.1 lists recommended hardware requirements for the VMM management server. Table 4.2 lists software requirements.

TABLE 4.1: Recommended Hardware Requirements for the VMM Management Server

HARDWARE COMPONENT	UP TO 150 HOSTS	MORE THAN 150 HOSTS
Processor	Dual x64 CPU, 2.8 GHz	Dual x64 CPU, 3.6 GHz
RAM	4 GB	8 GB
Disk	40 GB (without local VMM database)	50 GB (without local VMM database)
	150 GB (with local, full version of Microsoft SQL Server)	150 GB (with local, full version of Microsoft SQL Server)

TABLE 4.2:   Software Requirements for the VMM Management Server

SOFTWARE REQUIREMENT	NOTES
A supported operating system	A full installation of Windows Server 2008 R2 (Standard, Enterprise, or Datacenter) with SP1 or later.
Windows Remote Management (WinRM) 2.0	Setup requires the WinRM service to be started. In R2 the Windows Remote Management (WS-Management) service is set to start automatically (delayed start).
Microsoft .NET 3.5 SP1	The VMM Setup Wizard installs this automatically.
Windows Automated Installation Kit (WAIK) for Windows 7	WAIK is a requirement for the VMM Setup Wizard. It can be found at the Microsoft Download Center: http://www.microsoft.com/en-us/download/details.aspx?id=5753
SQL Server	Check the SQL Server requirements in the VMM database section.
Service Account	If you plan to use a domain account for VMM, make it a member of the Local Administrators Group.

VMM Console

Installing a VMM management server automatically includes installing the VMM console. This section describes the requirements for installing the VMM console on a separate computer.

As noted in the previous section, the VMM management server must be a member of an Active Directory domain. Table 4.3 lists recommended hardware requirements for the VMM console. Table 4.4 lists the software requirements.

TABLE 4.3:   Recommended Hardware Requirements for the VMM Console

HARDWARE COMPONENT	UP TO 150 HOSTS	MORE THAN 150 HOSTS
Processor	Dual x86 or x64 CPU, 1.0 GHz	Dual x86 or x64 CPU, 2.0 GHz
RAM	1 GB	2 GB
Disk	2 GB	4 GB

TABLE 4.4:   Software Requirements for the VMM Console

SOFTWARE REQUIREMENT	NOTES
A supported operating system	A full installation of Windows Server 2008 R2 (Standard, Enterprise, or Datacenter) with SP1 or later. Windows 7 (Professional, Enterprise, or Ultimate) with SP1 (x86 and x64).
Windows PowerShell 2.0	Included in supported operating systems.
Microsoft .NET 3.5 SP1	The VMM Setup Wizard installs this automatically.

VMM Self-Service Portal

The general requirements for the VMM self-service portal include the following:

♦ Installation must be on a separate (virtual) machine.

♦ The self-service portal cannot be installed on a domain controller.

♦ Client computers accessing the self-service portal must use Internet Explorer 8 or later.

The requirements for the VMM self-service portal depend on the number of simultaneous connections to the web server. Monitor the server's resources with System Center tools such as Operations Manager to determine whether additional resources are required. Table 4.5 lists recommended hardware requirements for the VMM self-service portal. Table 4.6 lists software requirements.

TABLE 4.5:   Recommended Hardware Requirements for the VMM Self-Service Portal

HARDWARE COMPONENT	10 CONNECTIONS OR FEWER	MORE THAN 10 CONNECTIONS
Processor	Single x64 CPU, 2.8 GHz	Single x64 CPU, 2.8 GHz
RAM	2 GB	8 GB
Disk	20 GB	40 GB

TABLE 4.6:   Software Requirements for the VMM Self-Service Portal

SOFTWARE REQUIREMENT	NOTES
A supported operating system	A full installation of Windows Server 2008 R2 (Standard, Enterprise, or Datacenter) with SP1 or later.
Web server (IIS)	The Web Server (IIS) role is required, including the following IIS role features: .NET extensibility, ASP.NET, default document, directory browsing, HTTP errors, IIS 6 metabase compatibility, WMI compatibility, ISAPI extensions and filters, request filtering, and static content.
Windows PowerShell 2.0	Included in supported operating systems.
Microsoft .NET 3.5 SP1	The VMM Setup Wizard installs this automatically.

VMM Database

The general requirements for the VMM database portal include the following:

♦ The VMM database server must be a member of an Active Directory domain. If that domain differs from the one containing the VMM server, a two-way trust relationship must exist between the two domains.

♦ The name of the server cannot exceed 15 characters.

◆ The SQL instance needs to be case-insensitive with collation type `SQL_Latin1_General_CP1_ CI_AS`. Types other than `Latin1` are supported as long as the collation type is `CP1_CI_AS`.

◆ The required server roles for the VMM admin account on the VMM database are dbcreator, process admin, and security admin.

◆ Database role membership should be db_owner.

USING A REMOTE EMPTY DATABASE FOR VMM INSTALLATION

In some environments, permissions on SQL Server databases make installing VMM difficult. In June 2010, Kerim Hanif, a Microsoft program manager, published a blog entry about how to get around that problem by specifying a remote empty database:

`http://blogs.technet.com/b/scvmm/archive/2010/06/21/using-a-remote-empty-database-for-vmm-installation.aspx`

The hardware requirements for the VMM database server depend on the total number of hosts you manage (see Table 4.7). Monitor the server's resources with System Center tools such as Operations Manager to determine whether additional resources are required.

TABLE 4.7: Recommended Hardware Requirements for the VMM Database Server

HARDWARE COMPONENT	UP TO 150 HOSTS	MORE THAN 150 HOSTS
Processor	Dual x64 CPU, 2.8 GHz or faster	Dual x64 CPU, 2.8 GHz or faster
RAM	4 GB	8 GB
Disk	150 GB	200 GB

Consult Table 4.8 for the software requirements for the VMM database server.

TABLE 4.8: Software Requirements for the VMM Database Server

SOFTWARE REQUIREMENT	NOTES
A supported operating system	A full installation of Windows Server 2008 R2 (Standard, Enterprise, or Datacenter) with SP1 or later. If SQL Server is clustered, only Enterprise and Datacenter are supported.
SQL Server versions	◆ SQL Server 2008 R2 Datacenter (32-bit and 64-bit) with SP1 or later ◆ SQL Server 2008 R2 Enterprise (32-bit and 64-bit) with SP1 or later ◆ SQL Server 2008 R2 Standard (32-bit and 64-bit) with SP1 or later ◆ SQL Server 2008 Enterprise (32-bit and 64-bit) with SP2 or later ◆ SQL Server 2008 Standard (32-bit and 64-bit) with SP2 or later

VMM Library Server

The VMM library server (Figure 4.1) is essentially a store for the physical files that serve as the building blocks for Hyper-V hosts, virtual machines, and services. The templates and metadata are actually stored in the VMM database. Examples include the following:

◆ VM and service templates

◆ Service deployment configurations

◆ Virtual hard disks

◆ ISO images

◆ Scripts

◆ Several types of profiles

◆ Stored virtual machines and services

◆ Update baselines and catalogs

FIGURE 4.1
Examples of VMM
library contents

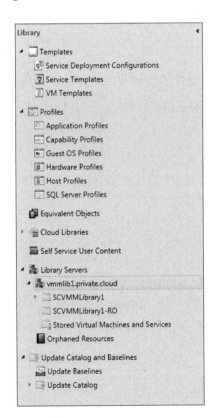

The general requirements for the VMM library server include the following:

◆ The VMM library server must be a member of an Active Directory domain. If that domain differs from the one containing the VMM server, a two-way trust relationship must exist between the two domains.

◆ The name of the server cannot exceed 15 characters.

◆ VMM includes support for highly available library shares on a failover cluster.

◆ VMM requires an SMB/CIFS-based file server. It does not support case-sensitive file servers such as Windows Services for UNIX or NFS.

SYNCHRONIZING VMM LIBRARIES

VMM does not include a synchronization feature for copying data between libraries. VMM also does not support DFS namespace (DFSN) and DFS replica (DFS-R). If you want to use another tool to synchronize library data, you have to move not only the physical files but also the metadata for objects stored in the VMM database.

The hardware requirements for the VMM library server largely depend on the size of the files in the library. Table 4.9 lists the recommended hardware requirements. Table 4.10 lists the software requirements.

TABLE 4.9: Recommended Hardware Requirements for the VMM Library Server

HARDWARE COMPONENT	RECOMMENDED HARDWARE REQUIREMENT
Processor	Dual x86 or x64 CPU, 3.2 GHz or faster
RAM	2 GB
Disk	Depends on the number and size of library files

TABLE 4.10: Software Requirements

SOFTWARE REQUIREMENT	NOTES
A supported operating system	A core or full installation of Windows Server 2008 R2 (Standard, Enterprise, or Datacenter) with SP1 or later (x64). If the VMM library is clustered, only Enterprise or Datacenter SKU is supported.
	A core or full installation of Windows Server 2008 with SP2 (x86 or x64). If the VMM library is clustered, only Enterprise or Datacenter SKU is supported.
	Windows Server 2008 R2 with SP1 or later is the preferred operating system.
Windows remote management (WinRM) 1.1 or 2.0	WinRM 1.1 is included in Windows Server 2008 and the WS-Management service is set to start automatically (delayed start).
	WinRM 2.0 is included in Windows Server 2008 R2, and the WS-Management service is set to start automatically (delayed start).

Virtual-Machine Hosts

VMM 2012 is the first private cloud–management system that supports the three major hypervisors:

◆ Microsoft Hyper-V

◆ VMware ESX

◆ Citrix XenServer

With this release, Microsoft no longer supports Virtual Server 2005 R2, so you must migrate Virtual Server VMs to Hyper-V before you install VMM.

VMM 2012 supports both individual hosts and clusters on all three hypervisor platforms. Both Hyper-V and XenServer can be managed directly by a VMM agent. Because there is no published API for managing VMware ESX hosts and clusters directly, VMM requires that VMware vCenter Server be added to the VMM fabric as an intermediate management server.

Table 4.11 lists the versions of Microsoft Hyper-V hosts and clusters that VMM supports. Tables 4.12 and 4.13 list the corresponding information for VMware and Citrix hypervisors.

TABLE 4.11: Supported Microsoft Hyper-V Versions

OPERATING SYSTEM	EDITION	SERVICE PACK	SYSTEM ARCHITECTURE
Windows Server 2008 R2 (Full or Core)	Enterprise or Datacenter	SP1 or later	X64
Hyper-V Server 2008 R2	Not Applicable	SP1 or later	X64
Windows Server 2008 (Full or Core)	Enterprise or Datacenter	SP2	X64

TABLE 4.12: Supported VMware ESX Versions

REQUIREMENT	NOTES
VMware vCenter Server 4.1	Check VMware product documentation for exact requirements.
Virtual machine host and cluster versions	Hosts that are managed by a vCenter Server that is managed by VMM: ◆ ESXi 4.1 ◆ ESX 4.1 ◆ ESXi 3.5 ◆ ESX 3.5

TABLE 4.13: Citrix XenServer Versions

REQUIREMENT	NOTES
Citrix XenServer 6.0 or later	Check Citrix product documentation for exact requirements.

Citrix XenServer - Microsoft System Center Integration Pack 6.0.0.2 or later	Check the MyCitrix website for additional information about this Integration Pack:
	 `www.citrix.com/english/mycitrix/`
	 `http://support.citrix.com/article/CTX131571`

Hyper-V Host Deployment to a Bare-Metal Computer

A *bare-metal computer* is a server that has never been used or has to be newly provisioned with an operating system. In VMM you can connect to one or more physical servers via a baseboard management controller (BMC) — which is essentially a computer within a computer — initialize, partition, and format its disks, copy a VHD with a sysprepped installation of Windows Server 2008 R2 Enterprise or Datacenter, and finally add the Hyper-V role. This is a fully automated, standardized procedure. It allows rapid deployment of new Hyper-V hosts. You can also overwrite existing server configurations and bring them under VMM management.

Table 4.14 lists the requirements for bare-metal deployment.

TABLE 4.14: Hardware and Software Requirements for Bare-Metal Deployment

REQUIREMENT	NOTES
WDS/PXE server	Windows Server 2008 R2 SP1 with Windows Deployment Services (WDS) role installed, which serves as a PXE server. The bare-metal server boots from this PXE server via WinPE and gets installed and configured via an automated process in VMM 2012.
One or more physical servers with a baseboard management controller (BMC)	Requires support for one of the following out-of-band management protocols: ◆ Intelligent platform management interface (IPMI) versions 1.5 or 2.0 ◆ Data center management interface (DCMI) version 1.0 ◆ System management architecture for server hardware (SMASH) version 1.0 over WS-Management (WS-Man).
Windows Server 2008 R2 operating-system image	Because bare-metal deployment in VMM uses a boot-from-VHD method for deploying an operating system, currently only Windows Server 2008 R2 is supported. In this case, Windows is allowed to boot from a virtual hard disk, which is provisioned by VMM from the VMM library.

UPDATE YOUR BMC FIRMWARE

For BMC devices supporting the SMASH protocol, an update of the BMC firmware may be required. See the vendor support site for your server hardware.

Update Management

VMM integrates with Windows Server Update Services (WSUS) for managing updates of the servers in the VMM fabric. Servers supported for update management include the following:

◆ Virtual machine hosts

◆ Library servers

◆ VMM management servers

◆ WDS/PXE servers

◆ WSUS server

The following tasks are available:

◆ Configure one or more update baselines

◆ Scan servers for compliance with attached baselines

◆ Remediate servers and clusters to make them compliant again with the baselines

The general requirements for update management are as follows:

◆ In small environments, the WSUS server can be combined with the VMM management server.

◆ In larger private clouds with higher-volume updates, a dedicated WSUS server is recommended. In this case, the WSUS management console must be installed on the VMM management servers.

◆ If WSUS is installed on a server other than the VMM server, Microsoft Report Viewer 2010 must be installed on the WSUS server. This report viewer has a dependency on .NET 3.5 SP1 or .NET 4.0.

◆ VMM is also supported to work with System Center Update Publisher configured for full content updates. Metadata-only updates cannot be added to an update baseline in VMM 2012.

Table 4.15 lists the software requirements for update management.

TABLE 4.15: Software Requirements for Update Management

REQUIREMENT	NOTES
Windows Server Update Services (WSUS) 3.0 SP2 (64-bit)	◆ Location: Microsoft Download Center www.microsoft.com/download/en/details.aspx?id=5216 ◆ It can be either the root server with a connection to Microsoft Update or a downstream WSUS server. ◆ VMM does not support a WSUS replica server. ◆ The WSUS server can be either dedicated or an existing WSUS server. ◆ VMM supports a WSUS server that is managed by Configuration Manager 2012. This requires additional configuration.

VMM Monitoring and Reporting

If you combine VMM 2012 with Operations Manager 2007 R2 or Operations Manager 2012, you get additional information about the health and performance of your private cloud and the virtual machines and hosts that reside there. VMM and SCOM enable this by using performance and resource optimization (PRO).

VMM AND SCOM INTEGRATION

Install the correct version of Operations Manager Console on the VMM management server. It must correspond with the Operations Manager version with which you are integrating.

The integration of VMM 2012 and Operations Manager 2007 R2 or 2012 offers you improved reporting functionality (what-if queries) in SCOM if the SQL Server analysis servers are installed on the Operations Manager reporting server. The minimum version of Analysis Services must be SQL Server 2008 with SP2.

Figure 4.2 shows a diagram view of a VMM 2012 service that is monitored in Operations Manager 2012.

FIGURE 4.2

SCOM 2012 diagram view of a VMM 2012 service

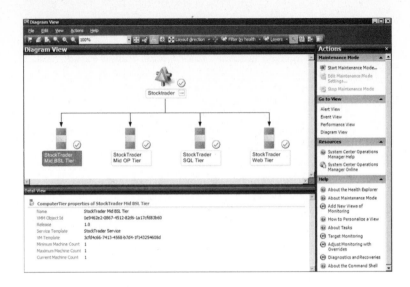

Setting Up and Discovering VMM

So far this chapter has covered the requirements for VMM and its components. The next part of the chapter focuses on installing and discovering VMM. You are now ready to install VMM based on the topology you have chosen. The following pages deal with standalone and highly available VMM servers, as well as upgrading from VMM 2008 R2 SP1. So get out your VMM 2012 media and start the action!

Preparations for Installing VMM

To make installing VMM a smooth experience, prepare as follows:

◆ Check your design for networking details, naming standards, network ports, installation locations, required software, and software versions.

◆ Prepare your physical/virtual machines and clusters before installing VMM.

◆ Join the machines to your Active Directory domain.

◆ Create a dedicated domain account for VMM 2012 and add that account to the local Administrators group on the VMM management server.

◆ Install the Windows Automated Installation Kit (WAIK) for Windows 7.

◆ Install Microsoft .NET Framework 3.5 SP1 (VMM can autoinstall this feature for you if you skip this step).

◆ Install a supported version of SQL Server or ensure that you have access to an existing SQL Server installation.

◆ Prepare file locations and shares for the VMM Libraries.

If you have planned to install a highly available VMM server, you must also do the following:

◆ Configure an Active Directory domain for distributed key management (DKM).

◆ Prepare Hyper-V clusters for the VMM management, database, and library servers.

CREATING A DOMAIN ACCOUNT FOR VMM

Although you may be tempted to use the local system account with VMM, there is a number of reasons why a domain account is the best choice. This account must be a member of the local Administrators group on the VMM management server. A domain account for VMM is required for the following situations:

◆ If you use a highly available VMM management server.

◆ If you plan to use shared ISO images with Hyper-V virtual machines you need to perform additional configuration as described on this webpage:

`http://technet.microsoft.com/en-us/library/ee340124.aspx`

◆ When your VMM hosts reside in an Active Directory with a disjointed namespace. This is the case when the fully qualified domain name of a Windows server in AD does not equal the FQDN in DNS. You must also add the SPNs of the DNS host FQDN to Active Directory Domain Service if you want to add a Hyper-V host or cluster. For more information, go to the following website:

`http://technet.microsoft.com/en-us/library/gg610641.aspx`

TIP   As a best practice, do not share the domain account used for VMM 2012 with any other server or service. Removing a Hyper-V host from VMM also removes the domain account from the local Administrators group of that host.

CONFIGURING DISTRIBUTED KEY MANAGEMENT

The VMM database contains sensitive data about many of your private cloud building blocks. Examples are license keys or admin accounts and their passwords. This is not the kind of information you want unauthorized people to access. For this reason, VMM employs encryption to protect the sensitive data and allow you to store this sensitive information external to the VMM servers.

In fact, VMM uses Active Directory as a redundant and well-protected store for the VMM encryption keys. Of course, you are dependent on your Active Directory admin colleagues, so they must have procedures in place to protect and recover Active Directory in case disaster strikes. Your organization will have a much bigger problem if they don't.

If you install a standalone VMM server, realize that the configuration of distributed key management (DKM) is optional, but nevertheless a recommended practice. However, if you plan a clustered installation of VMM, then you simply have no choice. DKM is a requirement for highly available VMM.

If you are also an Active Directory admin, you can use your credentials to create a container with a descriptive name like VMMDKM somewhere in your AD tree. It doesn't really matter where you place this container as long as you find a logical place for it. If you place the container in the root of your tree, its corresponding LDAP, for example, will be CN=VMMDKM, DN=PRIVATE, DN=CLOUD.

By default the AD groups domain admins, enterprise admins, and AD user SYSTEM have full permissions to this object and its descendant objects. Authenticated users have only read and list permissions. Members of the Administrators group have read, write, and create control, but by default cannot delete child objects.

To create this container, follow these steps:

1. Log into one of your domain controllers with domain admin privileges and start `adsiedit.msc` from an administrative command prompt.

2. In the ADSI Edit console, right-click ADSI-Edit and connect to your Active Directory domain services.

3. Right-click the desired container or organizational unit and select the object container; select New ➤ Object (Figure 4.3). Type the name of your DKM, such as **VMMDKM**, and then click Next and Finish.

4. Find the LDAP string. Right-click the new container and select Properties. Then find the attribute distinguishedName under the Attribute Editor tab (Figure 4.4).

FIGURE 4.3
Creating a
container for DKM

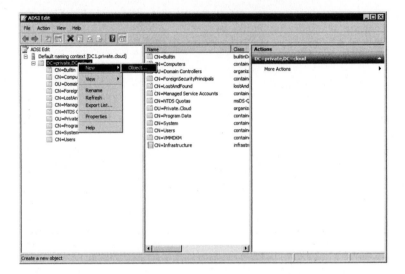

FIGURE 4.4
Using the Attribute
Editor

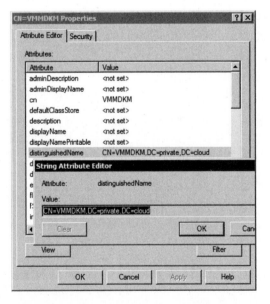

5. From the Security tab, select Domain Admins and click the Advanced button. Choose This Object And All Descendant Objects and set Full Control.

6. Check the Apply These Permissions check box and click OK.

You have now finished preparing to use distributed key management for either a standalone or a highly available VMM installation.

> **TIP** If you want to view the LDAP in Active Directory and Computers, make sure you have selected Advanced Features in the View menu. If you then view the properties of the DKM folder you created earlier, you can find the LDAP under the Attribute Editor tab (it will have a distinguished name similar to adsiedit).

Installing the VMM Server

If high availability is not at the top of your list and you haven't planned to install VMM on a separate management or infrastructure cluster with live migration capabilities, then this installation procedure is meant for you.

On the VMM setup screen, you have access to several tools that might be of interest before you start the actual installation: they include release notes, an installation guide, and a VMM configuration analyzer. From this location, you can also perform a local agent installation, which is discussed later in the book.

1. Log in with appropriate credentials and verify that all programs are closed and there are no pending restarts on this machine.

2. Find the VMM installation location, right-click `setup.exe` and start it with administrative privileges.

3. Ensure that the "Get the latest updates to Virtual Machine Manager from Microsoft Update" check box is checked.

4. Click Install.

5. On the Select Features To Install page, select VMM Management Server. The VMM console is automatically installed for every VMM management server and is, therefore, auto-selected. Leave the VMM self-service portal for installation later on a separate server.

> **NOTE** If you are installing on a Windows failover cluster, VMM Setup takes appropriate action automatically. See the next section on installing a highly available VMM Server.

6. On the Product Registration page, enter your registration information. You need not immediately provide a product key during setup. You can provide a product key after setup by using the VMM console. If you leave the Product Key field empty, VMM will be installed as an evaluation edition. Click Next.

7. Accept the license agreement and click Next.

8. Choose one of the two options regarding the Microsoft Customer Experience Improvement Program (CEIP). If you think you can benefit from it, answer Yes, I Am Willing To Participate and click Next.

9. Consult your design and enter the correct path for the VMM installation location. You probably don't want to install VMM on the default Windows drive. Click Next to continue.

10. VMM setup will then check to see if you have fulfilled all other prerequisites. Some of them you can simply correct and then click the Check Prerequisites Again button. If you have insufficient memory or if there is a pending restart on your computer, you have to correct this first, restart the computer, and restart the VMM setup. If all is well, click Next.

11. On the Database Configuration screen (Figure 4.5), provide information about the database server. If you already have access to the database with your current credentials, you need only enter the server and instance name. VMM automatically inserts VirtualManagerDB as the new database. If your SQL server listens to a different port or requires alternative credentials, specify them on this page. If the database was created outside VMM or already exists from an earlier attempt, you can decide on an alternative name or first back up and remove that database from the database server. Click Next.

FIGURE 4.5
Configuring the database

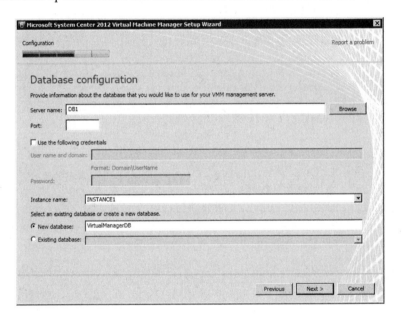

12. At the Configure Service Account And Distributed Key Management page, you can choose between a local system account and a domain account. Provide the domain and the username of an existing domain account. If you are in doubt, reread the paragraph about creating a domain account earlier in this chapter. You get this option only if you are installing the standalone version of VMM. You can change from a local system account to a domain account, but to do so you must uninstall VMM, preserve the database, and then reinstall.

13. On the same page, you can also specify where to store the encryption keys. If in doubt, go back to the paragraph on configuring DKM earlier in this chapter. If you might put VMM on a cluster later, select the Store My Keys In Active Directory radio button, paste the LDAP value, and click Next.

14. On the Port Configuration screen, accept the default TCP ports or choose your own. Be careful when you change these ports. Document the ports you have chosen and also

provide the correct ports when connecting to this VMM server from a remote VMM console or when you connect with other servers and components in the VMM fabric.

15. On the Library Configuration screen, create a new library share with a name and location of your choice or use an existing library share. The default location, `C:\ProgramData\Virtual Machine Manager Library Files`, is probably not the best location, because a library can grow quite quickly and the local drive is typically not large. Create a directory on an available drive with plenty of disk space. Note that on a highly available VMM installation you are expected to configure a VMM library location after installing VMM.

16. The Installation Summary screen lets you review all the settings. Go back if you want to correct a setting, and click Install when you are satisfied with all your selections.

17. If all went well, this brings you to the final page, showing that the setup of the selected VMM components is complete. Leave the "Open the VMM console when this wizard closes" check box enabled, and click Close to enjoy the rich new VMM 2012 user interface, which will open the gate to your private cloud.

18. The VMM console offers `localhost:8100` as its default connection to the VMM server. You can change this to the name and custom port dependent on your chosen configuration. If you expect to be logging in with different sets of credentials, you can leave the check box Automatically Connect With These Settings set to off and click Connect.

Making the VMM Server Highly Available

With the advent of private clouds as the primary IT landscape for your organization, VMM is likely to become so important that you cannot afford to see it offline for very long — if at all. Unexpected downtime affects not only administrators. The private cloud model extends to many of your delegated admins, the different groups of application owners and self-service users, as well as your customers who might be losing money if they cannot manage their part of the cloud.

Your private cloud design should aim at avoiding downtime for this important component of VMM, but other components should certainly not be neglected and should be made highly available as well. Let's start with a small environment managing only a few virtualization hosts. For this configuration, you might have chosen to install a physical machine with VMM, including all components on a single piece of hardware. This means you have combined the management server with the VMM database, the VMM library, and maybe even the Windows Update server. Of course, server hardware is often very high-quality these days, but if that server's hardware fails and you cannot start the operating system or VMM, how long can you afford to be without VMM's functionality when someone asks you to build a new VM, add some capacity, or deploy a service? Even in small environments, this will not be a professional solution. Even if you can restore a backup in just a few hours, you might still lose important changes.

There are several ways you can build a better foundation for VMM. A safe method is to put the important components in different virtual machines to become not only more scalable, but also much more flexible in transferring those virtual machines between different physical hosts. Even if you don't have any form of clustering yet, the virtual machines are much easier to protect than physical machines. Backing up and restoring a few virtual machines will make your life much easier, as you have probably become accustomed to in recent years.

The second approach is to build separate clusters for SQL Server, the highly available library share servers, and the VMM management service. Keep in mind that you cannot combine the

VMM management service and VMM library directly on top of a Windows failover cluster, because you cannot deploy a VMM library agent on the same server as the VMM management server. Combining the VMM library component with the VMM database component is an option. You can place the active database server instance on one node and the highly available file server on another. In case of a hardware failure on one node, both components can live together for a while. The disadvantage is that you have to build at least two clusters of physical Windows 2008 R2 servers just to avoid a hardware failure.

The third option is closer to what you would expect from a private cloud: high availability, scalability, flexibility, and manageability. In this configuration, you take two or more capable physical servers, install Windows Server 2008 R2 (Enterprise or Datacenter) with the latest service pack and important hotfixes, enable the Hyper-V R2 role, enable the failover-cluster feature, add shared storage, and build a multi-node Hyper-V R2 cluster. As in the first approach, all VMM components are either installed in one virtual machine or, preferably, across multiple virtual machines. Apart from tolerance for a physical node failure, you get the additional benefits of live migration, dynamic memory, dynamic storage, and so forth. Of course, if a physical server fails, the guests on that node in the cluster will go down as well but are quickly restarted on one of the other cluster nodes. This Hyper-V cluster is called a *management cluster*, dedicated to one or more System Center components. Other terms you might come across are *infrastructure cluster* or *private cloud management cluster*. The important thing is that you decouple management from the clouds and services you need to manage. Each is fully independent of the other. If your VMM 2012 server is on one of the production clusters, it can suffer if any of the production clusters fail. Of course, there is only a small chance that this will happen, but if it does you are much better off if your VMM 2012 management server, its database, library, and other related management servers are still up and running.

TIP Even though you have installed SP1 for Windows Server 2008 R2, you should be aware of hotfixes that make your Hyper-V cluster more robust. You can find a list of required and optional hotfixes at the following location:

http://social.technet.microsoft.com/wiki/contents/articles/1349.hyper-v-update-list-for-windows-server-2008-r2.aspx

For a list of cluster hotfixes for Windows Server 2008, paste this URL into your browser:

http://social.technet.microsoft.com/wiki/contents/articles/2008
.list-of-cluster-hotfixes-for-windows-server-2008-r2.aspx

The last and most complete option is to combine the functionality of a Hyper-V host cluster with one or more guest clusters for the most central VMM components, such as the VMM database, the VMM management server, and the VMM library. Web servers hosting the self-service portal can be load-balanced across multiple servers, and any other server that supports some sort of high availability can be added to this concept. This option offers the best of both worlds. It not only protects against hardware failures; it also enables you to patch one virtual cluster node after failing over the virtual SQL server, the virtual VMM service, or the virtual VMM library server and shares.

NOTE Because Hyper-V virtual machines in Windows Server 2008 R2 only support iSCSI for shared storage, you need an iSCSI storage solution to build a guest cluster. If you don't have access to iSCSI storage, you can leave the SQL server on a physical cluster and install VMM Management Server in a guest cluster. This is allowed because the SCVMM Service is configured as a generic service cluster resource and does not require shared storage. You still need to find a highly available solution for the VMM library file shares. Microsoft recommends that you do not use file shares on data drives because they can affect SQL Server's behavior and performance. If you want to create a file-share resource, use a different, unique network name and IP address for the resource.

Hyper-V in Windows Server 2012 also supports virtual fibre channel host bus adapters in Hyper-V guests. This will make it easier to build guest clusters when you have access to only fibre channel shared storage.

This does not entail much extra expense. The Hyper-V hosts are already installed with Enterprise or Datacenter editions of Windows. This means you are entitled to four guest OS licenses in the former and an unlimited number of guest OS licenses in the latter. Therefore, building a guest cluster will not add more cost. The Datacenter editions are licensed per processor socket and allow unrestricted virtual-machine migrations between hosts. Using one edition or the other is largely dependent on the number of virtual machines that can live on any of the hosts in the cluster. When you double the number of guests for clustering purposes, the Enterprise edition might quickly prove more expensive than the Datacenter edition.

BEST PRACTICE: SEPARATING MANAGEMENT FROM PRODUCTION

A combination of a Hyper-V host cluster with one or more guest clusters or load-balanced guests is the configuration of choice for medium to large private clouds. Separating the private cloud–management cluster from the private cloud production clusters provides better performance and flexibility. This design is more secure and more highly available. This concept is also easy to extend to other members of the System Center 2012 family.

Now you know why a highly available VMM management server is important. The following instructions show you how to install VMM on a cluster (whether physical or virtual).

CREATING A FAILOVER CLUSTER

If you have never built a cluster, rest assured that the days are long gone when building a cluster involved a touch of magic or a lot of luck. Since Windows 2008, failover clustering has really become a no-brainer because it involves only a few easy steps.

Before you start building guest clusters, you should already have a Hyper-V cluster ready to use. Aidan Finn's *Mastering Hyper-V Deployment* (Sybex, 2011) is a good source of information about deploying Hyper-V hosts and clusters.

Follow these steps to create a generic, guest failover cluster:

1. Prepare at least two servers with Windows Server 2008 R2 SP1 or later and enable the Failover Clustering feature.

2. Configure two network adapters and rename the connection names to **Backend** and **Cluster**. The Backend NICs should be in your server's IP subnet. The Cluster adapter can be in an isolated network, which only connects the cluster nodes. This network is used for cluster communication. Check to see if you can reach the individual nodes from the network and that each node can use the cluster network. Check both the IP address and DNS name.

3. Ask your SAN administrator to provide one small disk (1 GB) to the two servers you use for the cluster. This can be a disk presented via an iSCSI network. Only iSCSI is currently supported. The disk is a *witness* disk. Both cluster nodes should be able to see this disk. If you are using multiple paths, make sure MPIO or your vendor's device-specific module (DSM) is installed and configured.

CLUSTER QUORUM

In a server cluster, a quorum is a small database that keeps track of the servers in the cluster, lets them know which of them is active, and helps them communicate if the direct channels between them fail. This book is not about building clusters, but it is good to know that there are several quorum methods for protecting the shared disk resources in the cluster. Without a quorum, multiple servers might inadvertently write to the same disk, causing corruption. There are several quorum methods—node majority, disk witness, and file-share witness—depending on the number of nodes in the cluster. As a best practice for a two-node cluster, a quorum or witness disk must be provided. With an uneven number of nodes, a majority node quorum is advised. With an even number of nodes spread across two sites, a file-share witness on a third location is advised. Each node, witness disk, or witness share counts as one vote. As long as there is a majority of votes, the cluster remains operational. It is possible to change the quorum type without affecting the cluster. If there is no majority of quorum votes, the cluster service is stopped on all cluster nodes because the protection of shared disks can no longer be guaranteed. A more detailed description of cluster quorums can be found here:

```
http://blogs.msdn.com/b/clustering/archive/2011/05/27/10169261.aspx
```

4. Open Disk Manager (`diskmgmt.msc`), and choose Rescan Disks from the Action menu. Bring the newly presented 1 GB disk online, initialize it, create a partition, and format it. Name the disk **Witness** and assign it a drive letter (W:, for example).

5. Start Failover Cluster Manager (`FailoverClusters.SnapInHelper.msc`), right-click it, and select Create A Cluster (Figure 4.6).

FIGURE 4.6
Creating a cluster

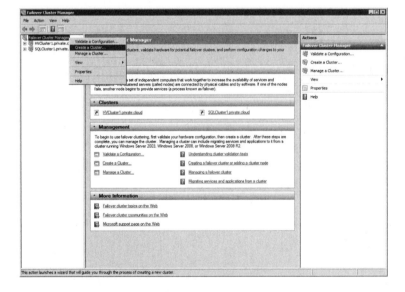

6. Read and accept the Before You Begin screen and click Next.

7. Enter the cluster node names and click Next.

8. Enter the cluster name, check the IP subnet, and complete the IP address. Click Next.

9. Confirm the cluster settings and click Next.

10. Check the cluster report, act on missed requirements, and click Finish.

This generic cluster configuration is now ready for a highly available VMM installation.

CHECKING THE REQUIREMENTS

As a requirement for installing a highly available VMM, double-check that the following are true:

◆ A SQL Server installation on a single physical or virtual machine (see the requirements for a VMM database component in this chapter) or a clustered SQL installation is available in the same domain (or in a fully trusted domain) as the VMM management server.

◆ Microsoft Failover Clustering is installed, configured, and tested.

As a test, a cluster resource such as an extra shared (cluster) disk can be failed over between nodes.

◆ Active Directory is configured for distributed key management. (See the section on configuring DKM.)

◆ Optionally, one or more highly available file shares are available in the same domain (or in a fully trusted domain) as the VMM management server.

◆ You have already created a domain user for VMM 2012 with appropriate permissions. This account should be a member of the local Administrators group on each cluster node (Figure 4.7).

◆ All other basic requirements for the VMM management server are complete.

FIGURE 4.7
VMM 2012
domain user

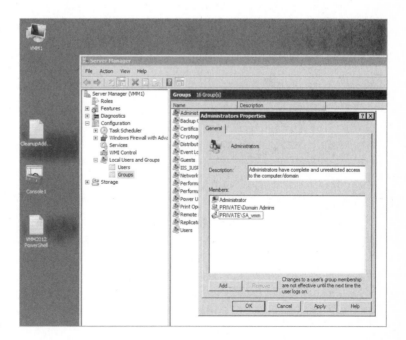

SETTING UP A HIGHLY AVAILABLE VIRTUAL MACHINE MANAGER

On the VMM 2012 setup screen, you have access to several tools that might be of interest before you start the actual install; they include release notes, an installation guide, and a VMM configuration analyzer. From this location, you can also perform a local agent installation, which is discussed later in the book.

Perform the following procedure to install a highly available VMM management server:

1. Log in with the appropriate credentials and verify that all programs are closed and there are no pending restarts on this machine.

2. Find the VMM installation location, right-click `setup.exe`, and start it with administrative privileges.

3. Ensure that the "Get the latest updates to Virtual Machine Manager from Microsoft Update" check box is checked and you have Internet access.

    This ensures that you use the latest version of the installation software. Setup also checks for updates after installation.

4. When you are ready, click Install.

    Setup checks for Microsoft .NET Framework 3.5 SP1 and installs it automatically if necessary.

5. As soon as you select VMM Management Server on the Select Features To Install page, setup detects that you are installing on a cluster. The VMM console is automatically installed for every VMM management server and is, therefore, autoselected. Leave the VMM self-service portal for installation later on a separate server.

    If you expand the installation options with the up arrow, Setup shows you additional information about the component. From here, there is a link to view all installation requirements.

6. Click Next when you are ready.

7. On the Product Registration Information screen, provide a product key if you have one, and click Next.

    If you leave the Product Key field empty, VMM is installed as an evaluation edition. You can provide a product key after setup is complete by using the VMM console.

8. Accept the license agreement and click Next.

9. To participate in Microsoft's Customer Experience Improvement Program (CEIP), select Yes. Otherwise, select No. Click Next.

10. Consult your design and put in the correct path for the VMM installation location. You probably don't want to install VMM on the default Windows drive. Click Next to continue.

11. If Setup displays warnings about missing prerequisites, resolve them and click Next.

    In some cases, you can correct the problem and click Check Prerequisites Again. If you have insufficient memory or a pending restart, you must restart the computer and restart the installation.

12. On the Database Configuration screen, provide information about the database server. If you can access the database with your current credentials, you only have to enter the

server and instance name. VMM automatically inserts VirtualManagerDB as the new database. If your SQL server listens to a different port or requires alternative credentials, specify them on this page. If the database was created outside VMM or already exists from an earlier attempt, use a different name, or first back up and remove that database from the database server. If you encounter problems connecting to your remote SQL server, make sure you have enabled TCP/IP for remote connection on your SQL Server instance and the required ports are enabled in the Windows Server firewall to allow connection.

13. At the Cluster Configuration screen, provide the name of the highly available VMM server (for example, **HAVMM1**). Also specify which networks and IP addresses to use in the cluster. Specify at least one IP address in the Backend network and click Next.

14. On the Configure Service Account And Distributed Key Management page, you cannot choose the local System account. In a highly available VMM management server, a domain account is required, so provide the domain and the username. In the Distributed Key Management section, you have no choice but to accept to store the encryption keys in Active Directory. Provide the LDAP value for its location and click Next.

15. On the Port Configuration screen, you can either choose to accept the default TCP ports or choose your own. Be careful changing these ports. Do not only document the ports you have chosen, but also provide the correct ports when connecting to this VMM server from a remote VMM console or when you connect with other servers and components in the VMM fabric. Click Next.

16. On the Library Configuration screen, you can just continue because in a highly available VMM server setup you have to configure library locations after the installation of VMM 2012 has finished. Click Next.

17. The Installation Summary screen gives you an opportunity to review all settings. Go back if you want to correct a setting and click Install when you are satisfied with all your selections.

18. If all steps went well, this will bring you to the final page showing that the setup of the selected VMM components is complete. Leave "Open the VMM console when this wizard closes" checked, and click Close to enjoy the rich new VMM 2012 user interface, which will open the gate to your private cloud.

19. The VMM console offers `localhost:8100` as its default connection to the VMM server. You can change this to the name and custom port appropriate to your configuration (for example, `havmm1:8100`). If you expect to be logging in with different sets of credentials, leave "Automatically connect with these settings" unchecked, and click Connect.

Upgrading from VMM 2008 R2 SP1

If you have servers running the previous version of VMM, you can save some of your existing data by doing the extra work of upgrading rather than doing a fresh installation. Most existing data falls into one of the following categories:

◆ Data about your virtualization hosts that will be rediscovered after they are added to a clean VMM 2012 installation.

◆ Data that cannot migrate and must be re-created in the new installation

The value of database contents that are not in one of these categories determines whether upgrading is worth the extra work. Although the majority of VMM library files can migrate, objects such as VM templates may need to be re-created based on the VHDs in your current library. The following restrictions apply to upgrading data:

◆ Back up data before upgrading. A failed upgrade cannot undo the changes it makes.

◆ System Center Operations Manager 2007 connections as well as performance and resource optimization (PRO) configurations, are lost.

◆ Job history is lost.

◆ TCP ports cannot be changed during upgrade.

◆ Some encrypted data, like passwords stored in templates and profiles, must be reentered manually.

Distributed Key Management (DKM) is a new feature in VMM 2012, and choosing either a local system account or a domain account is important for preserving encrypted data. Table 4.16 provides details about preserving encrypted data during upgrades.

TABLE 4.16:   Preserving Encrypted Data During Upgrades

Account Used When Upgrading	VMM 2008 R2 SP1 Service Account	VMM for Service Account	Not Using DKM	Using DKM
Any valid administrative account	Local System	Local System	Encrypted data is preserved.	Encrypted data is preserved.
Any valid administrative account	Local System	Domain account	Encrypted data is not preserved.	Encrypted data is preserved.
Any valid administrative account	Domain account	Local System	Not supported.	Not supported.
Same domain account as the VMM 2008 R2 SP1 service account	Domain account	Domain account	Encrypted data is preserved.	Encrypted data is preserved.
Different domain account from the VMM 2008 R2 SP1 service account	Domain account	Domain account	Encrypted data is not preserved.	Encrypted data is not preserved.

UPGRADE REQUIREMENTS

On many occasions a clean install is the best approach. Before you decide, consider these upgrade requirements:

◆ VMM 2008 R2 servers must have SP1 installed.

Upgrading older versions such as VMM 2007, VMM 2008 and VMM 2008 R2 (without SP1) is not supported.

◆ VMM 2008 R2 SP1 must be installed on Windows Server 2008 R2.

If your server runs the older 64-bit version of Windows Server 2008, you must upgrade the operating system before starting an in-place upgrade of VMM.

◆ A full version of SQL Server 2008 R2 or SQL Server 2008.

If your previous VMM version runs on an Express version of SQL, you must first upgrade the database/database server.

◆ SQL Server 2008 R2 Command Line Utilities installed on your VMM server.

While not a strict requirement, this generates a warning during the prerequisites check. Install the SQL Server 2008 R2 feature pack to solve this.

◆ Old versions of the Windows Automated Installation Kit (WAIK) must be uninstalled before you install WAIK for Windows 7.

◆ NET 3.5.1.

The VMM 2012 prerequisite check automatically enables the .NET Framework, which is part of Windows Server 2008 R2.

◆ Windows Remote Management (WinRM) 2.0 must be enabled.

WinRM 2.0 is part of Windows Server 2008 R2.

◆ Upgrade of Virtual Server 2005 R2 SP1 to Hyper-V.

◆ Upgrade of older versions of VMware ESX and VMware vCenter Server.

◆ Upgrade of VMM library servers running on Windows Server 2003.

After you upgrade VMM, remove and upgrade the old library servers to Windows Server 2008 SP2 or higher.

MOVING THE VMM DATABASE

If you are running an unsupported version of SQL Server, you must move the database to another server. Another possible reason for moving the database is to upgrade to a highly available VMM server.

These are the steps to move the database:

1. Use the VMM backup tool in VMM 2008 R2 SP1 or use the tools in SQL Server to make a backup of the existing VMM database.

2. Install a server with a supported version of SQL Server and copy the database to this server.

3. Use the SQL Server tools to restore the database. If you run System Center Data Protection Manager, you can restore the VMM database directly to the new database server. DPM takes care of the conversion process.

PREPARING THE UPGRADE

Before you start the upgrade complete the following steps:

1. Verify that all jobs on your current VMM server have been completed.

2. Close all connections to the VMM server (VMM consoles, VMM command shells, VMM self-service portal).

3. Check that there are no pending restarts and close all other programs on the VMM Server.

4. Log on with a valid administrative account.

5. If you have not done this already, make a full backup of the VMM database.

PERFORMING THE UPGRADE

Take these steps to perform the upgrade:

1. Start the VMM 2012 Setup Wizard on the VMM 2008 R2 SP1 server and click Install.

2. Confirm that you want to upgrade to VMM 2012.

3. On the Features To Be Upgraded page, click Next.

4. Provide the requested product-registration information and click Next.

5. Enter your product key, or leave it empty if you want to install the evaluation version, and click Next.

6. Accept the license agreement and click Next.

7. Select the desired Customer Experience Improvement Program (CEIP) option and click Next.

8. Enter a new path for installing VMM 2012. Click Next.

9. Correct any issues found during the prerequisite check.

10. Provide the database-connection information and click Next. If the connection fails with your current credentials, you can change them and retry.

11. On the Configure Service Account And Distributed Management screen, provide the account to be used by the VMM service. Be careful to check Table 4.16 again if in doubt.

12. Under the Distributed Key Management section, provide the LDAP information for DKM. Click Next.

13. Accept the port-configuration details (they cannot be changed during upgrade) and click Next.

14. If the VMM self-service portal was installed on the VMM server, click Next on this page.

15. If the upgrade compatibility report finds any issues, click Cancel and fix the issues. Otherwise, click Next to continue the upgrade.

16. Review the Installation Summary screen. Go back by clicking Previous, or click Install to start the upgrade.

17. If the resulting message states "Setup Completed Successfully," click Close to finish the upgrade.

By default the VMM console opens. You can immediately start to discover VMM 2012.

Installing a Management Console

Installing the VMM management server automatically installs the VMM console. By contrast with earlier versions, if you install the VMM management server on a separate computer, you no longer need to install a VMM console on every Operations Manager server. For Operations Manager 2012 to integrate with VMM 2012, you are not required to install a VMM 2012 console, which really simplifies the integration experience.

Use the following steps to install the VMM console:

1. Log in with the appropriate credentials and verify that all programs are closed and there are no pending restarts on this machine.

2. Find the VMM installation location, right-click `setup.exe` and start it with administrative privileges.

3. On the setup screen, click Install.

If Microsoft .NET Framework 3.5 SP1 is not installed you get a warning. VMM Setup will take care of that if you click OK.

4. Select VMM Console and click Next.

5. Answer appropriately on the license agreement and CEIP screens. Click Next.

6. Answer appropriately on the Microsoft screen and click Next.

7. Accept or change the default installation location, which is `C:\Program Files\ Microsoft System Center 2012\Virtual Machine Manager` and click Next.

8. If all prerequisites are met, you can continue with Next or else make appropriate changes, click on Check Prerequisites Again, and click Next if Setup can continue.

9. On the Configuration screen only one TCP port can be set. You can leave the default of port 8100 for communication with the VMM management server or change to the port definition in your design. Click Next.

10. Review the Installation Summary screen and continue by clicking on Install.

11. If the installation completes successfully, click Close and log into the VMM console. Don't forget to type the correct name of the VMM server or cluster and its correct port name.

Installing a Self-Service Portal

Before you install the self-service portal, it is important to check the hardware and software requirements. Verify that the Web Server (IIS) role is enabled with all its required features. You may want to install the self-service portal on its own dedicated server(s).

To install the VMM Self-Service Portal, perform the following steps:

1. Log in with the appropriate credentials and verify all programs are closed and there are no pending restarts on this machine.

2. Find the VMM installation location, right-click `setup.exe,` and start it with administrative privileges.

3. On the VMM 2012 setup screen, click on Install. If Microsoft .NET Framework 3.5 SP1 is not installed, you will get a warning. VMM Setup will take care of that if you click on OK.

4. On the Select Features To Install page, select VMM Self-Service Portal and click Next.

5. Accept the license agreement and click Next.

6. Accept or change the default installation location, which is `C:\Program Files\ Microsoft System Center 2012\Virtual Machine Manager,` and click Next.

7. If all prerequisites are met, you can continue with Next or else make the appropriate changes, click Check Prerequisites Again, and click Next if Setup can continue.

8. On the Configuration screen, fill in the name of the VMM server, the TCP port (which defaults to 8100), and the TCP port for connections to the self-service portal (which defaults to 80).

You normally change the self-service portal port to 443 if you use an SSL connection. If the IP address for the self-service portal is shared with other websites, check Provide Host Header For Portal Access and specify the host header for the portal. Click Next.

9. Review the Installation Summary screen and continue by clicking on Install.

Adding or Removing a PXE Server

A PXE server is used for bare-metal deployment of Hyper-V servers. PXE services can be added by enabling the Windows Deployment Services (WDS) role on a Windows Server 2008 R2 server. The WDS server requires no configuration, but be careful to install WDS with the following information:

◆ After the WDS role has been added, right-click Windows Deployment Services and choose Configure Server.

◆ Choose a path different from the OS partition (for example, `D:\RemoteInstall`).

◆ Select both the deployment server and the transport server options.

◆ You don't have to add any images to the WDS server because VMM uses a VHD file that you will create later and place in the VMM library.

◆ You don't have to configure any of the PXE response settings either because VMM uses its own PXE provider.

◆ Place the PXE server in the same subnet as the physical servers that you want to use for bare-metal deployment of Hyper-V servers.

Take the following steps in the VMM console to add an existing PXE server to VMM:

1. Select the Fabric workspace, expand the Servers folder in the navigation pane, and right-click PXE Servers. Select Add PXE Server (Figure 4.8).

FIGURE 4.8
Adding a PXE server

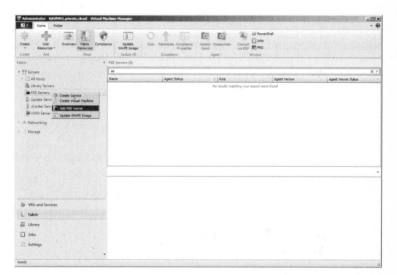

2. Enter the name of the PXE server, select a Run As account with proper domain access, and click OK.

   To check the progress, click the Jobs workspace and select Set Up A New PXE Server Job in the details pane.

Follow these steps to remove a PXE server:

1. Select the Fabric workspace, expand the Servers folder in the Navigation pane, select PXE Servers, right-click the PXE server in the details pane, and select Remove.

2. Select a Run As account with proper domain access and click OK.

You can also add or remove a PXE server via PowerShell, which can be accessed either from the ribbon and the PowerShell icon or via Start ➢ Program Files ➢ Microsoft System Center 2012 ➢ Virtual Machine Manager ➢ Command Shell.

If you start PowerShell from the command prompt, you can see if the VMM module is loaded by issuing the following command:

```
PS C:\get-module
```

```
ModuleType Name                        ExportedCommands
---------- ----                        ----------------
Manifest   BitsTransfer                {Start-BitsTransfer, Remove-BitsTransfer,
                                        Resume-BitsTransfer, Get-BitsT...
Binary     virtualmachinemanager       {Start-SCComplianceScan, Add-SCLibraryShare,
                                        Get-SCLibraryServer, Get-SC...
```

Add a PXE server with the PowerShell cmdlet in Listing 4.1.

LISTING 4.1:   Adding a PXE Server

```
PS C:\> $Credential = Get-SCRunAsAccount "Run_As_Domain_Admin"
PS C:\> Add-SCPXEServer -Computername "WDS1.private.cloud" -Credential $Credential


Name               : WDS1.private.cloud
ManagedComputer    :
ServerConnection   : Microsoft.SystemCenter.VirtualMachineManager.Remoting
                     .ServerConnection
ID                 : dbb330e0-4ea8-476a-988c-27a4cff54877
IsViewOnly         : False
ObjectType         : PxeServer
MarkedForDeletion  : False
IsFullyCached      : True
```

Remove a PXE server with the PowerShell cmdlet in Listing 4.2.

LISTING 4.2:   Removing a PXE Server

```
PS C:\> $Credential = Get-SCRunAsAccount "Run_As_Domain_Admin"
PS C:\> $PXEServer = Get-SCPXEServer -ComputerName "WDS1.private.cloud"
PS C:\> Remove-SCPXEServer -PXEServer $PXEServer -Credential $Credential -Confirm

Confirm
Are you sure you want to perform this action?
Performing operation "Remove-SCPXEServer" on Target "WDS1.private.cloud".
[Y] Yes  [A] Yes to All  [N] No  [L] No to All  [S] Suspend
[?] Help (default is "Y"): y
```

```
Name              : WDS1.private.cloud
ManagedComputer   :
ServerConnection  : Microsoft.SystemCenter.VirtualMachineManager.Remoting
                    .ServerConnection
ID                : 24372cbb-b00e-4e12-8c3e-039e836c2335
IsViewOnly        : False
ObjectType        : PxeServer
MarkedForDeletion : True
IsFullyCached     : True
```

Adding or Removing an Update Server

Take the following steps to add an existing WSUS server to VMM:

1. Select the Fabric workspace, expand the Servers folder in the navigation pane, and right-click Update Server. Select Add Update Server (Figure 4.9).

FIGURE 4.9

Adding an update server

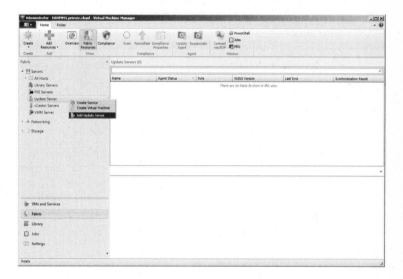

2. Enter the name of the WSUS server, select TCP/IP port 8530, select a Run As account with proper domain access, and click OK.

Take the following steps to remove a WSUS server from VMM:

1. Select the Fabric workspace, expand the Servers folder in the navigation pane, select Update Server, right-click the WSUS server in the details pane, and click Remove.

2. Select a Run As account with the proper domain access and click OK.

TIP   Clicking the View Script button creates a PowerShell cmdlet based on the selections you made in the previous dialog. You can modify and reuse this cmdlet and save it to the VMM library.

You can also add an update server with the PowerShell cmdlet in Listing 4.3.

LISTING 4.3:   Adding an Update Server

```
PS C:\> $Credential = Get-SCRunAsAccount -Name "Run_As_Domain_Admin"
PS C:\> Add-SCUpdateServer -ComputerName "WSUS1" -TCPPort 8530 -Credential ↩
$Credential

Name                              : WSUS1.private.cloud
Port                              : 8530
IsConnectionSecure                : False
ServerType                        : RootUpdateServer
Version                           : 3.2.7600.226
UsesProxy                         : False
ProxyServerName                   :
ProxyServerPort                   : 0
ProxyUserName                     :
UpstreamServerName                : Microsoft Update
UpstreamServerPort                : 80
SynchronizationType               : Manual
SynchronizationFrequencyPerDay    : 0
SynchronizationTimeOfTheDay       : 1/1/0001 1:00:00 AM
SynchronizationStatus             : Idle
LastSynchronizationDetails        : Microsoft.SystemCenter.VirtualMachineManager.
                                    LastSynchronizationDetails
Languages                         : {Hebrew, Portuguese, Japanese, Greek...}
UpdateCategories                  : {Antigen, Bing, BizTalk Server, Developer
                                    Tools, Runtimes, and Redistributables...
                                    }
UpdateClassifications             : {Beveiligingsupdate, Definitie-updates,
                                    Essentiële update, Functiepakket...}
DownloadExpressPackages           : False
DownloadUpdateBinariesWhenApproved : True
StoreUpdateFilesLocally           : True
AutoApproveWsusInfraUpdates       : True
AutoApproveNewRevisions           : True
AutoDeclineExpiredRevisions       : True
ManagedComputer                   : WSUS1.private.cloud
CanChangeConfigurationProperties  : True
ServerConnection                  : Microsoft.SystemCenter.VirtualMachineManager.
                                    Remoting.ServerConnection
ID                                : be9a89a5-fe69-4b7d-9b4f-87f0308ea5a8
IsViewOnly                        : False
ObjectType                        : UpdateServer
MarkedForDeletion                 : False
IsFullyCached                     : True
```

You can remove an update server with the PowerShell cmdlet in Listing 4.4.

LISTING 4.4:   Removing an Update Server

```
PS C:\> $Credential = Get-SCRunAsAccount -Name "Run_As_Domain_Admin"
PS C:\> $UpdateServer = Get-SCUpdateServer -ComputerName "WSUS1.private.cloud"
PS C:\> Remove-SCUpdateServer -UpdateServer $UpdateServer -Credential $Credential
```

```
Name                                  : WSUS1.private.cloud
Port                                  : 8530
IsConnectionSecure                    : False
ServerType                            : RootUpdateServer
Version                               : 3.2.7600.226
UsesProxy                             : False
ProxyServerName                       :
ProxyServerPort                       : 0
ProxyUserName                         :
UpstreamServerName                    : Microsoft Update
UpstreamServerPort                    : 80
SynchronizationType                   : Manual
SynchronizationFrequencyPerDay        : 0
SynchronizationTimeOfTheDay           : 1/1/0001 1:00:00 AM
SynchronizationStatus                 : Idle
LastSynchronizationDetails            : Microsoft.SystemCenter.VirtualMachineManager.
                                        LastSynchronizationDetails
Languages                             : {Hebrew, Portuguese, Japanese, Greek...}
UpdateCategories                      : {Microsoft Research AutoCollage, Microsoft
Security Essentials, Virtual Server, Systems Management Server...}
UpdateClassifications                 : {English Service Pack, Update, Applications,
                                        Definition-updates...}
DownloadExpressPackages               : False
DownloadUpdateBinariesWhenApproved    : True
StoreUpdateFilesLocally               : True
AutoApproveWsusInfraUpdates           : True
AutoApproveNewRevisions               : True
AutoDeclineExpiredRevisions           : True
ManagedComputer                       :
CanChangeConfigurationProperties      : True
ServerConnection                      : Microsoft.SystemCenter.VirtualMachineManager.
                                        Remoting.ServerConnection
ID                                    : 722008b7-a9cb-42af-b008-0f5c4b789d3e
IsViewOnly                            : False
ObjectType                            : UpdateServer
MarkedForDeletion                     : True
IsFullyCached                         : True
```

Creating Host Groups

By default, there is one host group called All Hosts. Whenever you add a virtualization host, it will be placed in this folder. If you have many hosts, you can create additional host folders and organize them in a hierarchical way. VMM allows you to create a deep folder structure, but in most cases a simple hierarchy is better.

There is a number of good reasons for placing virtualization hosts in their own separate host group. As you can see by examining the properties of the All Hosts group, you can configure several aspects of host-group properties.

Placement Rules   Placement rules help VMM identify the best virtualization hosts when it deploys a new virtual machine (VM). Such a rule assigns one or more selections that either allow or block placement of a virtual machine on hosts in the host group. You can assign values to up to ten custom properties (see the final item in this section). You specify one of the four choices shown in Figure 4.10 for each of the custom properties. At the time of deployment, VMM compares the VM's values with the rules and allows or blocks deployment of the VM to a host in the group.

Note the difference between "must" and "should." "Must" is evaluated as binary yes or no, while "should" acts as a more flexible gatekeeper allowing placement of a virtual machine on a host if the conditions conform to the placement rules.

FIGURE 4.10
Creating a placement rule in a host group

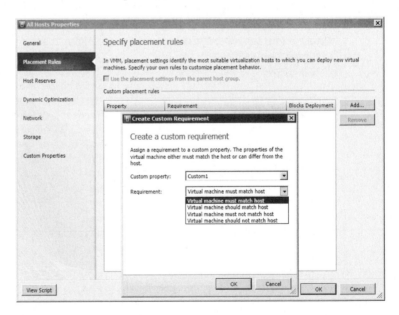

Host Reserves   You can specify that the servers in a host group require certain resources (CPU, memory, disk speed and capacity, network bandwidth) to support the host operating system. Before deploying a VM to a server in the group, VMM ensures that the VM can run without consuming any of the reserved resources. Otherwise, it does not deploy the VM and returns an error.

Dynamic Optimization   If the host group contains clusters, this is the place to configure how aggressively to balance the load among the VMs in the cluster. Chapter 7, "Deploying Hosts and Clusters in VMM 2012," provides more information about dynamic optimization.

Network   In VMM 2012, it is possible to associate a host group with one or more network resources. The topic of networking can also be found in much greater detail in Chapter 6, "Understanding Network and Storage in VMM 2012." Just remember that you can specify network resources on a host-group level. Also note that these are not limitations but associations that self-document the network resources that are available to all hosts in this host group.

◆ Logical networks

◆ Load balancers

◆ IP pools

◆ MAC pools

Storage   If one or more storage arrays are visible to VMM, this screen shows you the storage (both storage groups and logical units) allocated to the host group. Chapter 6 provides more details.

Custom Properties   You can specify a set of custom properties for controlling placement of VMs. Each property is one of the following object types:

◆ Virtual machine

◆ Virtual machine template

◆ Host

◆ Host cluster

◆ Host group

◆ Service template

◆ Service instance

◆ Computer tier

◆ Cloud

You assign each a value to be used in placement rules.

If you have only a few hosts, you might just as well leave them in the All Hosts folder and change the properties in the host group. Be careful not to set the placement rules and host reserves too strictly and make it impossible to place a virtual machine.

When you design your private cloud, also pay proper attention to how to spread your hosts and clusters across the different host groups and specify the placement rules, the host reserves, the network and storage associations, as well as the custom properties that will help you differentiate between the hosts.

There are endless ways of grouping hosts; but by using some of the techniques mentioned in the previous paragraphs, you can probably keep the number of host groups to a minimum. These are a few examples of organizing the host-group hierarchy:

Organize by Location   If you don't have any multisite clusters, this is probably a good approach; but remember that a cluster in VMM is a unit, and the individual nodes cannot be spread across multiple host folders.

Organize by Functionality   If your virtualization hosts are mostly dedicated to a certain type of virtual machines or a particular functionality or department, you can organize the hosts using the name of the functionality or department.

Organize by Hypervisor   If it is relevant to group the hosts by hypervisor, create one host group for each hypervisor in your organization.

Organize by Datacenter   A good way to organize dozens or even hundreds of hosts is to group them by the datacenter in which they reside. Of course, you can make further subgroups per datacenter, but don't overdo it. Limit yourself to two or three levels at most. Remember to keep it simple!

Organize by Development Stage   If your organization uses a Development, Test, Acceptance, Production (DTAP)-type of method, you can create a host group for every step in the development cycle.

Before you reach your final host-group organization, test a few of the previously mentioned types and take a look at the different host-group properties. These are the steps to create a host group:

1. Select the Fabric workspace, right-click All Hosts, and select Create Host Group.

2. Type the name of the host group by replacing the text New Host Group.

There are several ways to modify the host group's name or location. By right-clicking the host, you have several options, like Rename, Move, or Delete. You can also find the properties from this context-sensitive menu.

The default host group, All Hosts, cannot be renamed, moved, or deleted. Child host groups can be created under each level. VMM does not stop you from creating a 20-level host-group tree, but this is far from desirable.

If you have added one or more hosts to a child host group, the host groups above that level cannot be removed. First move the virtualization host to another host group and then delete the folder or the entire tree.

Adding a Hyper-V Host to a Host Group

After you set up your host-group structure, you can add new hosts to those groups or move existing hosts from the All Hosts folder to the newly created child host groups.

These are several ways of adding a host to VMM:

1. Select the Fabric workspace, right-click the host folder, and select Add Hyper-V Hosts And Clusters or a corresponding Citrix or VMware alternative.

2. In the Add Resource Wizard, select the first option if you know your host is in a trusted Active Directory domain. If the Hyper-V role is already enabled, the wizard continues to add that host. If not, it enables the Hyper-V role automatically. Click Next.

3. In the Credentials section, either manually specify the credentials for the host or click Browse For An Existing Run As account. If you have not yet created a Run As account with domain administration privileges, click Create Run As Account. If there is an account available, just click the correct Run As account, then click OK and then Next.

4. If you know the names of the candidate hosts, enter each computer name on a separate line in the Discovery Scope section. You can also specify an IPv4 or IPv6 address for locating the virtualization hosts, and you can choose to skip AD verification by clicking the check box underneath the Computer Names text box. An alternative method of selecting hosts is by specifying an Active Directory query to search for candidate Windows Server computers, which is relevant only for hosts that are or will be Hyper-V hosts. When you are ready, click Next.

5. In the Target Resources section, select the computers you want to add as hosts and click Next.

6. In the Host Settings section, select the target host group and add one or more placement paths as default locations for storing virtual machines on the hosts. If you are readding hosts that already have the right VMM agents installed, check the "Reassociate this host with this VMM environment" check box. When you are ready, click Next.

7. On the Summary page, you can still go back with the Previous button or click Finish if you are happy with your choices.

   You can check progress by selecting the Jobs workspace and viewing the details of the Add Virtual Machine Host job (Figure 4.11). You'll discover a separate job for each host you are adding. In effect, the job adds a virtual-machine host after checking if the host has been deployed before (so it will not have to install an agent). If the host is new, VMM installs a VMM agent and enables the Hyper-V role if necessary. If things go wrong or not all requirements are met, you can find the job details on the Summary tab.

FIGURE 4.11
Checking the job details

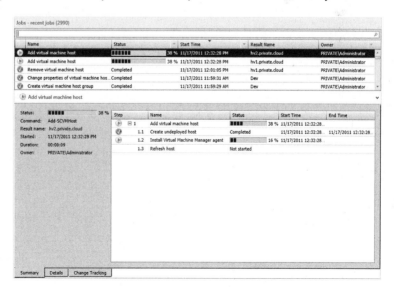

If you need to add Hyper-V hosts that are not in the same Active Directory forest, you can find more information in Chapter 7.

An existing virtual machine host can also be placed in a host group from the Fabric workspace under All Hosts and by selecting Fabric Resources from the ribbon (Figure 4.12). Right-click the name of the host, select Move To Host Group, and select the requested host group.

FIGURE 4.12

Placing a host into a host group

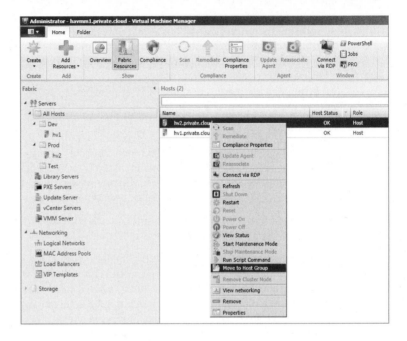

If you would like to see the host-group or host-group path in the Hosts view, right-click the column bar and select Host Group or Host Group Path. This is only one example of adding one of many available columns in the View pane.

ADDING XENSERVER AND VMWARE HOSTS

VMM 2012 was built with full multi-hypervisor management capabilities. It is also possible to add Citrix XenServer and VMware ESX virtual-machine hosts. Although some features for adding hosts—such as bare-metal deployment and update management—are relevant only to Hyper-V hosts, most of the important VM, library, cloud, application, and service functionality is fully applicable to all types of supported VM hosts. Chapter 7 explains adding a Citrix XenServer and VMware vCenter/ESX Server in more detail.

Configuring VMM Settings

The Settings workspace is the place to establish a variety of general settings for the product. The following sections describe the available settings.

GENERAL

The General section contains the following settings:

Customer Experience Improvement Program Settings   During setup you were asked if you wanted to participate in CEIP. In this section, you can enable or disable your participation.

Database Connection   This provides a read-only view of the database settings: database server name, database instance, and database name.

Library Settings   The refresh interval that VMM uses to index the files on library shares is initially set to one hour. You can either switch indexing off or set a refresh interval (in hours).

Remote Control   The VMConnect port is initially set to 2179. You can change it.

Self-Service Settings   You can specify the email address shown to self-service users in the event of a problem.

Network Settings   This provides access to a number of options for logical and virtual networks, as shown in Figure 4.13. By default, a logical network is created and matched based on its first DNS suffix label. If you change the match setting to Network Connection Name and then add a new Hyper-V host, the Add Host Wizard adds all existing network connections (network adapter names) on the host to VMM. These virtual networks are added to Logical Networks in the Fabric workspace. You can also specify a second matching option to be used if the first fails. In that case, the virtual networks (virtual switches) known to the Hyper-V host are added to Logical Networks.

On this screen, you can also choose whether VMM creates a new logical network if the host network adapter is not associated with a logical network.

Guest Agent Settings   You can configure the way VMM communicates with the VMM guest agent. This can be via either FQDN or IP address.

Network Settings and Guest Agent Settings can also be set via PowerShell. The following command disables auto-creation of logical and virtual networks:

```
PS C:\> $vmmServer = Get-SCVMMServer -ComputerName "havmm1.private.cloud"
PS C:\> Set-SCVMMServer -AutomaticLogicalNetworkCreationEnabled $false ↵
-LogicalNetworkMatch "NetworkConnectionName"↵
-AutomaticVirtualNetworkCreationEnabled ↵
$false -BackupLogicalNetworkMatch "VirtualNetworkSwitchName"
```

The following command enables communication via IP address between VMM and VMM agent:

```
PS C:\> Set-SCVMMServer -UseIPForVMGuestCommunication $true
```

FIGURE 4.13

Logical and virtual network options

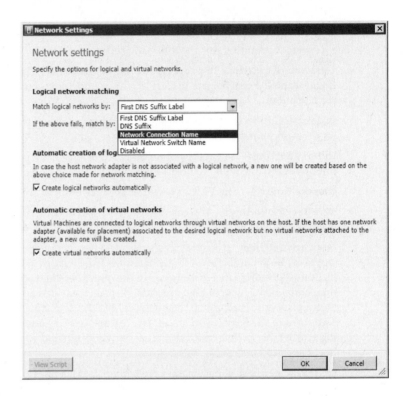

SECURITY

Security and delegation in VMM 2012 are controlled by User Roles and Run As accounts. Compared to the previous versions of VMM, this is one area of great improvement.

User Roles

User roles play an important role in delegating access to the different parts of your private cloud and the different workspaces in VMM 2012.

If you open Security\User Roles under the Settings workspace, there is initially only one user with the Administrator user role. Except for adding a description, you can only add or remove Active Directory user accounts as members of this role.

Members of the Administrator role can perform all administrative actions on all objects that are governed by VMM. There are a few tasks that can only be performed by the Administrator role:

◆ Adding Citrix XenServer hosts and clusters (pools) to VMM management

◆ Adding Windows Server Update Services (WSUS) servers to VMM for update management of the servers in the VMM Fabric

Creating new roles is also a task that can only be done by members of the VMM Administrator role. These user roles can be one of three profile types:

Delegated Administrator   A user with delegated administrator rights can perform all tasks on objects within their assigned scope. They cannot change any VMM settings and cannot add or remove members from the Administrator user role. They cannot add Citrix XenServer servers or WSUS servers.

Read-Only Administrator   Users of this type can view properties, status, and job status of objects within their assigned host groups, clouds, and library servers, but they cannot modify the objects. This user role is suitable for auditors. This role also defines the specific Run As account for the Read-Only administrator to view relevant objects.

Self-Service User   Users with this profile can create, deploy, and manage their own virtual machines and services by using the VMM console or a web portal. A self-service user role specifies which tasks users can perform on their virtual machines and services and can place quotas on computing resources and virtual machines.

Depending on the profile, different options can be set. In the definition of the delegated administrator and read-only administrator, you can not only add Active Directory users as members to the User role, but also select specific library servers and Run As accounts that are authorized for use.

A scope assignment based on the resources in one or more host groups can be defined for all three profiles. The VMM administrator has full access to all resources and cannot be altered under the User Roles section, so there is no Scope section for the Administrator role.

The Self-Service user role can be scoped to one or more specific clouds defined by the VMM administrator. Additionally, specific resources such as VM templates and service templates can be assigned to users of this role. A library path location can be specified for uploading data to be shared with other members of the same role. Unique to this role is a fine-grained list of actions that can be allowed or disallowed, as shown in Figure 4.14.

FIGURE 4.14
Setting permitted actions for self-service users

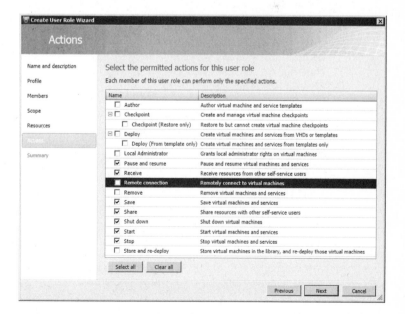

The following PowerShell commands set permitted actions for the Self-Service user role:

```
PS C:\> Set-SCUserRole -JobGroup "c7cfbbbd-248b-472f-b991-7a52ec65b756" -Permission ↩
@("PauseAndResume", "CanReceive", "Save", "CanShare", "Shutdown", "Start", ↩
"Stop") -ShowPROTips $false -UserRoleDataPath "\\vmmlib1.private.cloud\ ↩
SCVMMLibrary1-Test"
PS C:\> $libResource = Get-SCVMTemplate -ID "5c307a0a-5f6f-464a-8e7a- ↩
78c18077dc2f"
PS C:\> Grant-SCResource -Resource $libResource -JobGroup "c7cfbbbd-248b-472f-b991- ↩
7a52ec65b756"

PS C:\> New-SCUserRole -Name "Development Cloud User Role" -UserRoleProfile ↩
"SelfServiceUser" -Description "" -JobGroup "c7cfbbbd-248b-472f-b991- ↩
7a52ec65b756"
```

Run As Accounts

VMM protects Run As account credentials on the operating system level by means of the Windows data protection API (DPAPI). DPAPI uses a Triple-DES algorithm with strong keys. This cryptographic method is safer than password-based data protection.

VMM also uses the distributed key management (DKM) mechanism to store encryption keys in Active Directory, as described in the installation section of this chapter.

Many security-sensitive actions in VMM require credentials. Typing a password for every action in the GUI or in PowerShell is neither secure nor intuitive. As you are probably already accustomed to in System Center Operations Manager, VMM now also allows you to create Run As accounts as safely protected credentials for accessing different types of servers, storage, and network devices.

Run As accounts can be created from the Settings workspace by selecting Run As Account from the Navigation pane. These are the steps for adding a Run As account:

1. Choose Create Run As Account from the ribbon and type the name of the account. Add a description to explain the purpose of this Run As account to your fellow private-cloud admins. The account can be an Active Directory account or just any username/password combination. Be sure to uncheck Validate Domain Credentials if you are adding a Run As account that is not known in AD.

2. Enter the corresponding domain\username plus password and click OK.

TIP   As with any type of object you create in VMM 2012, it is a good idea to define a naming scheme for your Run As accounts. Use a prefix like RA_ or Run_As preceded by a meaningful name or type such as Run_As_Domain_Admin or RunAsStorage. Devote a section in your design to listing the different Run As accounts

3. If you have applied this Run As account with one or more resources, you can return to the Run As Host definition and go to the Consumers section to see which objects use this Run As account.

The Access section of the Run As account properties shows who created the account and which user roles and users are related to this account.

For additional security, it is possible to temporarily disable a Run As account if you want to tightly control when such an account is used.

A Run As account can be deleted by right-clicking it and choose Delete.

Servicing Windows

In the Settings workspace under Servicing Windows, a VMM administrator can define one or more scheduled servicing windows. These schedules allow you to reserve time for scheduling services outside of VMM. You can set start time, duration (in minutes or hours), and a recurrence pattern (daily, weekly, monthly).

Servicing windows can be associated with individual hosts, clusters, virtual machines, or services. During the specified times, you can use other applications to perform maintenance on the specific objects.

Use the following steps to subscribe a host to a servicing window.

1. Select the Fabric workspace, select a host, and right-click to select Properties.

2. In the Servicing Windows section, click Manage and add or remove a servicing window, and click OK.

3. Click OK one more time to finish.

Backup

You can quickly create a backup of the VMM database. Before you do this, make sure you have prepared a shared directory to which the SQL server has access.

1. Create a shared folder and provide access to the domain account used for the SQL server.

2. Select the Settings workspace and click Backup on the ribbon.

3. Provide a location.

To restore a database, VMM offers a command called SCVMMRecover in the C:\Program Files\Microsoft System Center 2012\Virtual Machine Manager\bin directory.
The syntax of SCVMMRecover is

```
SCVMMRecover [-Path <location>] [-Confirm]
```

The command requires the path of the VMM database location and a confirmation. Before you start the database restore, close the VMM console on all computers. A VMM database recovery can be started as follows:

```
C:\Program Files\Microsoft System Center 2012\Virtual Machine Manager\bin>SCVMMR ↵
ecover.exe -path \\vmmlib1\backup\VirtualManagerDB-02122012-191629.bak -confirm
SCVMMRecover 2.0 - Virtual Machine Manager database recovery command-line tool.
Copyright (c) 2008 Microsoft Corporation. All rights reserved.

Virtual Machine Manager database recovery completed.
```

Summary

This chapter covers all aspects of setting up and configuring VMM as the control center for your private cloud. It details the installation requirements for all VMM components.

You should now understand the design considerations behind the installation choices that VMM provides, and you should have made those choices optimally for your situation. You should be able to determine if a highly available setup of VMM and its important components, such as the database and library, are appropriate for your private cloud setup.

You were given several things to consider when you're deciding whether to migrate from the previous version of VMM or start with a fresh install.

You have seen how different auxiliary components, such as an update server and a WDS/PXE server, can be integrated in VMM. You now also know how to deal with host groups, how to add a domain-integrated Hyper-V host to a host group, and how to configure the items under settings.

You are now ready to learn about another central component of your private cloud, the VMM library.

## Chapter 5

Understanding the VMM Library

The VMM library is a catalog that provides access to all the resources you need to support a cloud, whether they are stored on library shares or in the VMM database. The library can also store virtual machines when they are not in use; therefore it is effectively a resource for everything deployed to the private cloud.

This chapter covers all aspects of setting up, configuring, and maintaining the VMM library, including the following:

- Understanding the requirements for building a library

- Deploying library servers and shares

- Associating library servers with particular host groups

- Keeping resources such as VHDs, ISOs, and templates in the library and using them to create and deploy virtual machines

- Installing and configuring fabric patching within the environment

- Scanning for compliance and remediating the server fabric

Introducing the Library Role in VMM

The VMM library acts as a central resource for all that is deployed to the private cloud. Leveraging the library will help you promote a consistent set of standards as you build out your private cloud; it will also encourage the reuse of IT-approved configurations and images.

A default library share is created as part of the VMM installation process. During the installation, the default is to create a library share on the VMM management server. This is located on the system drive in

```
%systemroot%\ProgramData\Virtual Machine Manager Library Files
```

and the default share name is MSVMMLibary. Additional library servers and library shares can be added post-installation, via the VMM Administration console.

Certain considerations need to be made as to the design of your library-server architecture. During a proof of concept or for a small production implementation, leveraging the default library share might be appropriate; however, as you move to a mid-to-large-scale production environment, concerns over scalability and high availability will drive the design of your library-server architecture, as shown in Figure 5.1.

FIGURE 5.1
Sample library-
server architecture

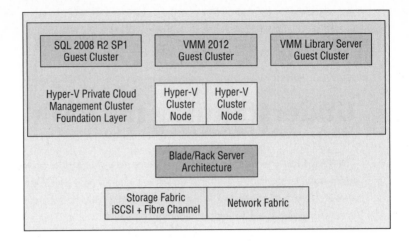

As a best practice, Microsoft recommends that you make the library server highly available by using a file share managed by a Windows failover cluster. This library share might reside on an existing Windows failover cluster that might host other services and applications, or it might reside on a dedicated Windows failover cluster as either a guest cluster running within the private cloud-management fabric or as a dedicated, physical Windows failover cluster outside of the management fabric.

VMM supports adding a file share on a Windows failover cluster using the following operating-system versions and editions:

◆ Windows Server 2008 SP2, Enterprise Edition, x86 or x64

◆ Windows Server 2008 SP2, Datacenter Edition, x86 or x64

◆ Windows Server 2008 R2 SP1, Enterprise Edition

◆ Windows Server 2008 R2 SP1, Datacenter Edition

Library-Server Hardware Requirements

A number of factors influence the hardware requirements for your library servers. However, the library server is a repository; its main tasks are to store and retrieve content. Therefore, storage capacity and Input/Outputs per Second strongly influence your library design, the level of change within the environment, the number of library servers, and their geographical placement all are factors.

There are no hard and fast answers here. Chapter 4, "Setting Up and Deploying VMM 2012," lays out the requirements for a library server.

REAL-WORLD VMM LIBRARY-SERVER SIZING

Sizing any type of server can be a challenge; and while there is no one single answer, we want to give you some insight into the hardware sizing for our production library servers.

We have at present around 45 cloud-based projects, and each cloud project has an average of 10 virtual machines running on the server fabric.

Because each of our library servers runs within a virtual machine, we have allocated two logical processors and a dedicated 1 GbE network adapter. The memory allocation for this virtual machine is 2 GB. The disk capacity is approximately 1 TB.

Hyper-V Guest - Virtual-Machine Library			
Windows Server 2008 R2 SP1 Enterprise Edition x64			
Network Adapter 0 (1 GbE) - vSwitch 1			SCSI Controller 0
IDE Controller 0 Boot Disk (VHD)	IDE Controller 0 DVD Drive	IDE Controller 1 Data Disk (1 TB VHD)	IDE Controller 1 <available>
2 GB RAM			
Logical Processor 1		Logical Processor 2	

The 1 TB of disk space accommodates approximately 240 virtual hard disks (VHDs), which are base operating-system images and approved patches, totaling around 700 GB. Another 290 GB contains approximately 250 CD/DVD images (ISO files), which mainly contain Windows distributions that are locale/Multilingual User Interface-specific.

Adding Library Servers

VMM is not limited to a single library server. In designing the logical architecture for your VMM implementation, you might decide to add additional library servers because your implementation spans more than one data center or because you need to support one or more remote sites. Having all the required files available locally enhances the performance of your virtual environment and reduces network traffic.

Use the following procedure to add a library server to VMM:

1. In the VMM console, select the Library workspace (Figure 5.2).

2. On the Home tab, in the Add group, click Add Library Server. The Enter Credentials screen appears.

FIGURE 5.2
Library servers
and shares

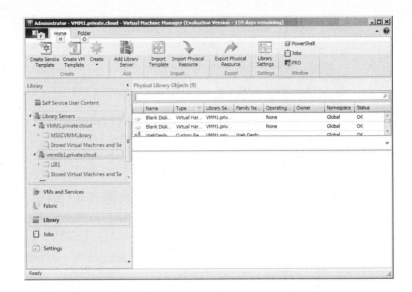

3. Enter the username and password for a domain account that has administrative rights on the server you intend to add as your library server, and click Next.

   You can use a Run As account or you can manually specify a set of credentials in the format `domain\user`. If you need to create a Run As account, you can do so from the Select Run As Account screen.

   The Select Library Servers screen appears.

4. Enter the domain and computer name of the server you want to add, and click Add.

   If you don't know the server name, you can use the Search button to help you find it. By default VMM does not perform Active Directory name verification, but you can require verification by unchecking the check box.

5. When the intended server's fully qualified domain name appears in the Selected Servers box, click Next. The Add Library Shares screen appears.

ADDING A HIGHLY AVAILABLE LIBRARY SERVER

If you plan to implement a highly available library server, select the Client Access Point that is associated with the file server. An informational pop-up message indicates the VMM agent will be installed on all nodes in the cluster.

---

6. Select the check box next to each library share you want to add, and optionally select the check box in the Add Default Resources column. Click Next.

   If you ask for default resources, VMM adds the `ApplicationFrameworks` folder to the library share. Resources in the `ApplicationFrameworks` folder include x86 and x64 versions of the Server App-V agent and sequencer, Windows PowerShell cmdlets for Server App-V, and Microsoft web deployment tools. The folder also includes scripts that add application profiles in a service template or install virtual applications and web applications during service deployment.

The Summary screen appears.

7. Review the settings and click Add Library Servers.

The Jobs window opens, enabling you to follow the progress and ensure that the library server and share are added successfully. You should see them in the Library Servers node of the VMM console (Figure 5.2).

Adding a Library Share

Your VMM library server is composed of one or more file shares, which are either local to the management server or are located over the network, on file shares managed by VMM.

Before a library share can be added to the library server, you must manually create the shared folder on the intended server, in advance of adding the library share to VMM.

Use the following procedure to add an additional library share to VMM:

1. In the VMM console, select the Library workspace.

2. Expand the Library Servers node, and select the library server where you want to add the share.

3. On the Library Server tab, click Add Library Shares. The Add Library Shares screen appears.

4. Select the check box next to the library share you want to add, optionally select the check box in the Add Default Resources column, and click Next. The Summary screen appears.

5. Review your settings and click Add Library Shares.

The Jobs window opens, enabling you to follow the progress and ensure that the share is added successfully. You should see it in the Library Servers node of the VMM console.

Associating Library Servers to a Host Group

Library servers can be added to host groups to further organize them. This is accomplished by modifying the properties of a library server in the VMM console. During placement, VMM uses this association as an input to help determine where to obtain library resources.

Use the following procedure to associate a library server with a host group:

1. In the VMM console, select the Library workspace.

2. In the Library pane, expand the Library Servers node, and select the library server you want to associate with a specific host group.

3. On the Library Server tab, click Properties. The General Properties dialog box opens.

4. In the Host Group drop-down list, click the host group with which you want to associate the library server. Optionally check the Allow Unencrypted Transfers check box. Click OK.

By default, all file transfer operations into and out of the library use SSL encryption (MPPE and RC4). This is enabled by default in VMM and nothing specific needs to be configured to make this work.

If you have already implemented another form of encryption within your environment (for example, IPSec) or have otherwise secured your environment, you can use unencrypted file transfers to improve performance during virtual-machine creation and migration.

ASSOCIATING LIBRARY SERVERS

You can associate a library server with only one host group, as defined in your host-group hierarchy. However, child host groups (host groups below the main host group you select during association) are automatically associated with the library server. It is also possible to associate more than one library server with a single host group.

Adding Resources to the Library

Before the library can function and serve a purpose, you must add content to it. Content resides either in files or in the VMM database. This section shows you how to add content of each type.

Adding File-Based Resources

Adding file-based resources like VHDs, ISOs, and deployment scripts must be done manually, outside of VMM. When you add files to a library share, the files do not appear in the library until after the next library refresh. The default and minimum library refresh interval value is 1 hour.

To make files available immediately, you must manually refresh the library server or share. If you move files within or between library shares, you must manually refresh the destination shares. During a library refresh, VMM indexes the files stored on the library share and then updates the Library workspace with the resource listings.

To add file-based resources to the library, do one of the following:

◆ Without using the VMM console, browse to the library share and then manually copy the files you need.

◆ In the VMM console, in the Library workspace, expand Library Servers, right-click a library share, and click Explore. Again manually copy the files you need.

◆ In the VMM console, on the Home tab, use the Import Physical Resource and Export Physical resource options to move file-based resources between library shares.

Use the following procedure to refresh the library server:

1. In the VMM console, select the Library workspace.

2. In the Library pane, expand the Library Servers node, right-click the library server you want to refresh, and select Refresh.

During a library refresh, VMM indexes the files stored on the library share and then updates the Library workspace and resource listings. Not all files are indexed, and not all indexed files are displayed in the Library workspace. The following file types are the ones added as library resources during library refreshes:

- Virtual hard disks— `.VHD` files (Hyper-V and Citrix XenServer) and `.VMDK` files (VMware)

- ISO image files— `.ISO` files

- PowerShell scripts— `.ps1` files

- SQL Server scripts— `.sql` files

- Web Deploy (MSDeploy) packages— `.ZIP` files

- SQL Server data-tier applications (DACs)— `.dacpac` files

- Server App-V packages— `.osd` files

- Driver files— `.inf` files

- Answer files— `.inf` and `.xml`

- Custom resources folders—those with a `.cr` file extension

- Virtual floppy disks— `.vfd` (Hyper-V) and `.flp` (VMware)

The following configuration-file types are indexed but are not added to the Library workspace as library resources:

- Virtual machine export files— `.EXP` (Hyper-V) `.VMX` (VMware)

- Virtual machine saved-state files— `.VSV` (Hyper-V)

- Virtual machine memory files— `.BIN` (Hyper-V)

- Virtual machine configuration files— `.VMTX` (VMware)

- VHDs, ISOs, and VFDs that are attached to a virtual machine

Adding Templates and Profiles

A *template* is a library resource that consists of a number of other configuration components. Typically, these components are stored in the VMM database (with the exception of the virtual hard disk) and are not represented as physical files in the Library workspace. They include the following:

- Hardware profile

- Guest operating-system profile

- Capability profile

- Application profile (which is part of a service template)

- SQL server profile (which is part of a service template)

- Virtual hard disk

Templates provide a standardized group of hardware, software, and application settings you can consistently reuse to create multiple new virtual machines configured with those settings applied. VMM supports two types of templates:

◆ virtual-machine template

◆ Service template (which is covered in Chapter 8, "Understanding Service Modeling")

CREATING A HARDWARE PROFILE

A *hardware profile* is a library resource that contains the hardware specifications that will be applied to a new virtual machine or to a virtual-machine template. A hardware profile contains specifications for things like the CPU, memory, floppy drive, COM ports, video adapter, DVD drive, and network adapters; it also contains the priority given to the virtual machine when resources are allocated on a virtual-machine host and specifies which capability profile to leverage when validating your hardware profile.

After specifying a hardware profile for a specific virtual machine, you can go back and change the settings that were imported. These changes do not affect the hardware profile, nor is any association maintained with the hardware profile after the virtual machine is created.

Use the following procedure to create a new hardware profile:

1. In the VMM console, select the Library workspace.

2. On the Home tab, in the Create group, click Create and select Hardware Profile. The New Hardware Profile screen appears.

3. Enter a name and description for your hardware profile.

4. Click the Hardware Profile tab (Figure 5.3) and configure your hardware profile as appropriate.

CREATING A GUEST OPERATING-SYSTEM PROFILE

A *guest operating-system profile* is a collection of operating-system settings and values that can be imported into a virtual-machine template to provide a consistent operating-system configuration for virtual machines that are deployed from that template.

A guest operating-system profile contains specifications for things like computer name, administrative password, time zone, which roles and features to install (in the case of deploying Windows Server 2008 or above), and which workgroup or domain to join. You can attach a dedicated answer file to apply additional settings outside of the guest operating-system profile.

Guest operating-system profiles are database objects that do not have physical files associated with them within the library. The profiles are configured in the Library workspace, where they are displayed under the Profiles node.

Use the following procedure to create a new guest operating-system profile:

1. In the VMM console, select the Library workspace.

2. On the Home tab, in the Create group, click Create and select Guest OS Profile. The New Guest OS Profile screen appears.

3. On the General tab, enter a profile name and description.

4. On the Guest OS Profile tab (Figure 5.4), configure your guest OS profile as appropriate.

Figure 5.3

Hardware profile properties

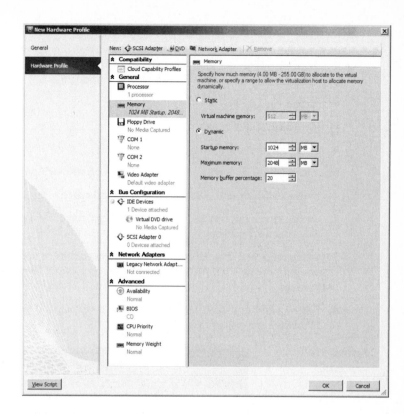

Figure 5.4

Guest OS profile properties

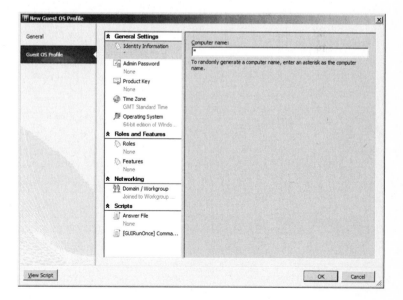

CREATING A VIRTUAL MACHINE TEMPLATE

Virtual-machine templates are used to create new virtual machines, providing a repeatable way of deploying standardized hardware and software settings. A virtual-machine template is a library resource that consists of the following components:

◆ Virtual hard disk

◆ Hardware profile

◆ Guest operating-system profile

Use the following procedure to create a new virtual-machine template:

1. In the VMM console, select the Library workspace.

2. On the Home tab, in the Create group, click Create VM Template. The Select VM Template Source screen appears.

3. Using the Search box, browse to a virtual hard disk or template to be used as the starting point for the new template. Click OK, and click Next. The VM Template Identity screen appears.

4. Enter a name and description for the VM template, and click Next. The Configure Hardware screen appears (Figure 5.5).

FIGURE 5.5
Configuring hardware

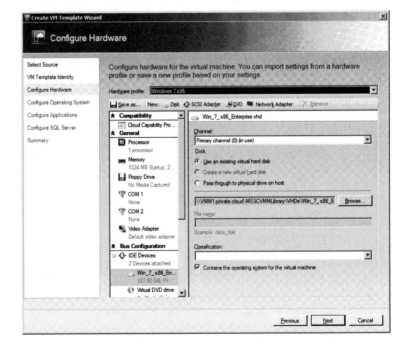

5. Select your predefined hardware profile or configure a new hardware profile and click Next. The Configure Operating System screen appears (Figure 5.6).

FIGURE 5.6

Configuring an operating system

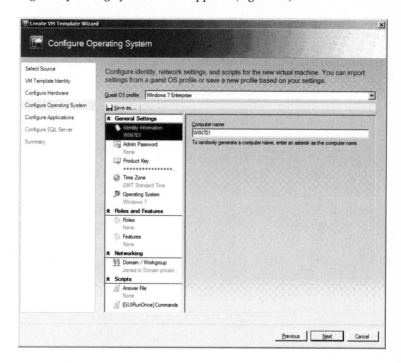

6. Select your predefined guest OS profile or configure a new guest OS profile, and click Next. The Configure Applications screen appears.

7. Click Next.

Note that application configuration is available only for Windows Server guest operating systems. Chapter 8 discusses application profiles in more detail.

The Configure SQL Server screen appears.

8. Click Next.

Note that SQL configuration is available only for Windows Server guest operating systems. Chapter 8 discusses SQL profiles in more detail.

The Summary screen appears.

9. Review your choices and click Create.

CREATING A VIRTUAL MACHINE FROM A TEMPLATE

Creating a virtual machine is one of the main tasks that a VMM administrator will perform, and configuring the multitude of hardware and software settings available can be a fairly repetitive task. The virtual-machine template provides a repeatable way to deploy standardized hardware and software settings.

Use the following procedure to create a virtual machine from a template:

1. In the VMM console, select the VMs And Services workspace (Figure 5.7).

FIGURE 5.7
Creating a VM

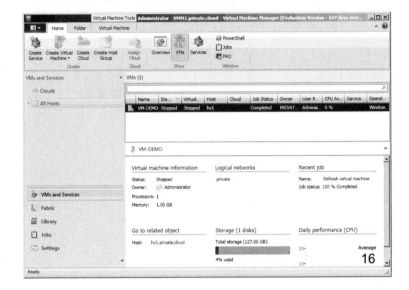

2. On the Home tab, in the Create group, click Create Virtual Machine and select Create Virtual Machine. The Select Virtual Machine Source screen appears.

3. Use the search box to browse to the VM template on which to base the new virtual machine. Click OK, and click Next. The Specify Virtual Machine Identity screen appears.

4. Enter a name and description for the virtual machine. Click Next. The Configure Hardware screen appears.

5. Select a predefined hardware profile or configure a new hardware profile. Click Next. The Configure Operating System screen appears.

6. Select a predefined guest OS profile or configure a new guest OS profile. Click Next.

   The Select Destination screen appears with the To Place The Virtual Machine On A Host option already selected because it is the only option.

7. Click Next. The Select Host screen appears.

8. Select the host best suited for the workload rated by intelligent placement. Click Next. The Configure Settings screen appears.

9. Review the values that will be used to create your new virtual machine. Click Next. The Select Networks screen appears.

10. Select the logical network for your virtual machine to use, the virtual network to bind to, and any VLAN settings to be applied. Click Next. The Add Properties screen appears.

11. Specify the automatic actions for your virtual machine when the virtualization host is either started or stopped. Include or exclude this virtual machine from optimization actions. Click Next. The Summary screen appears.

12. Review the configuration summary and click Create.

STORING VIRTUAL MACHINES IN THE LIBRARY

At some point, you may want to store a previously running virtual machine in the library. By doing so, you can preserve the state of the virtual machine for later use. There are many reasons to preserve a VM. For example, you can use your stored VM to make multiple copies to run several other virtual desktops.

Use the following procedure to store a running virtual machine in the library:

1. In the VMM console, select the VMs And Services workspace, right-click the virtual machine, and select Store In Library. The Select Library Server screen appears.

2. Select the library server you want to use to store the virtual machine, and click Next. The Select Path screen appears.

3. Click Browse, expand the library share, select the directory where you want to submit your virtual machine, and click OK. Then click Next. The Select Library Server screen reappears.

4. Select the library server you want to use to store the virtual machine, and click Next. The Summary screen appears.

5. Review your choices and click Store.

Equivalent Objects

If your VMM library has multiple locations, you'll want users to be able to use resources without regard to location, but you'll want VMM to supply those resources from a local library share if possible. To support this ability, you can define sets of library objects as equivalent. If users request one resource in a set of equivalent objects, VMM can substitute any other resource in that set to satisfy the request.

In previous versions of VMM, the only way to do that was to create different VM templates referring to different library shares. With equivalent objects, you can use a single template and let VMM access the resources from the most convenient location. That is, VMM is location-aware so that you don't have to be.

The resources that you call equivalent must be of the same file type, either virtual hard disk (VHD) or image file (ISO).

NOTE   By default during VMM installation, the custom resources of Server App-V and Web Deployment Framework are automatically added to the library as equivalent objects. If you add multiple library shares and choose to add default resources, when creating a new library share the custom resources are all automatically marked as equivalent.

Use the following procedure to mark file-based resources in the library as equivalent:

1. In the VMM console, select the Library workspace.

2. In the Physical Library Objects pane, click the Type column header to sort the contents of the library by resource type.

3. Select the file-based resources that you want to mark as equivalent.

   Use the Ctrl and Shift keys according to the usual Windows conventions for specifying disjointed selections and ranges.

4. Right-click the selected resources, and click Mark Equivalent. The Equivalent Library Objects screen appears.

5. Specify the Family Name and Release Value, and click OK.

   The objects you marked as equivalent should appear in the Equivalent Objects node of the Library pane in the console (Figure 5.8).

FIGURE 5.8
Equivalent objects

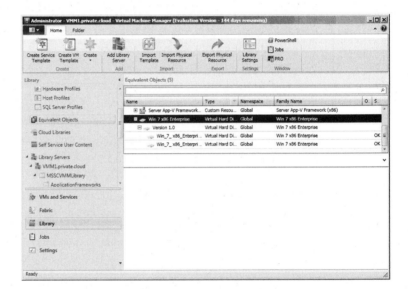

Use the following procedure to modify equivalent file-based resources in the library:

1. In the VMM console, select the Library workspace.

2. In the Library pane, expand the Equivalent Objects node, expand the Family Name and Release Value, right-click the resource object, and select Properties.

3. On the General tab, modify the values as appropriate. To remove an object from a set of equivalent objects, delete the Family Name and Release Value.

Removing Resources from the Library

Library resources can be removed from the Library workspace, and specific library object files that are stored on a library share can be disabled.

When you no longer need a file in the VMM library, Microsoft recommends that you remove the file through the VMM console. If you remove the file from a library share outside the console, any library resources that use that file must be repaired and references to the deleted file must be removed. If you use the Remove option (Library Server tab ➤ Remove Group) to remove the object, VMM lists any dependencies that reference the file; and if you proceed, VMM removes the reference to the deleted file from the library resource that used it.

Disabling Library Resources

Only file-based resources can be disabled in VMM. Use the following procedure to disable a resource in the library:

1. In the VMM console, select the Library workspace.

2. Select the Library Servers node to get an entire view of what file-based resources are available across your entire library infrastructure, or select the library server that hosts the library object you want to disable (Figure 5.9).

FIGURE 5.9

Disabling file-based resources

3. Select the library object in question, and from the Library Object tab in the Action group, click Disable.

   The library object's status changes from OK to OK (Disabled). To re-enable the object, select the library object and from the Action group and click Enable.

Deleting Files from the Library

File-based resources can be deleted from the library server. Use the following procedure to delete a resource from the library:

1. In the VMM console, select the Library workspace.

2. Select the Library Servers node to get an entire view of what file-based resources are available across your entire library infrastructure, or select the library server that hosts the library object you want to delete (Figure 5.9).

3. Select the library object and from the Object tab in the Delete group, click Delete.

   VMM warns you that it will delete the associated file from the library share, not just remove the resource from management.

4. Click Yes to delete the library object.

Removing a Library Share or Server

Use the following procedure to remove a library server or share from management:

1. In the VMM console, select the Library workspace.

2. Expand the Library Servers node and select the library server from which you want to delete the share. On the Folder tab, click Remove.

   VMM informs you that the library share will be removed from management, but that no files will be deleted.

3. Click Yes to remove the library share from management.

Use the following procedure to remove an entire library server from management:

1. In the VMM console, select the Library workspace.

2. Expand the Library Servers node, and select the library server you want to remove.

3. On the Library Server tab, in the Remove group, click Remove.

4. Enter the necessary credentials to connect to the library server.

   Specify an account manually or use an existing Run As account. Either account must have Administrator rights on the library server.

5. Click OK to remove the server from management.

Updating the Catalog and Baselines

With VMM, Microsoft provides the ability not only to build and cluster the virtualization fabric but also to maintain and optimize that fabric, all from a single pane of glass.

VMM requires the x64 version of Windows Server Update Service (WSUS) 3.0 SP2. The WSUS server role can be installed on the VMM management server or on a remote server. Because VMM places an agent on the WSUS server, the supported operating-system version is limited by the VMM Agent prerequisites. The remote server must be running Windows 2008 or higher. No support for Windows 2003 is provided. Chapter 4 describes the requirements for an update server.

Benefits of Managing Fabric Updates with VMM

Managing the server fabric, which includes Hyper-V hosts, Hyper-V clusters, and VMM server roles (i.e., the management server, library servers, Preboot Execution Environment (PXE) servers, and WSUS servers) can be a challenge in terms of compliance and remediation.

VMM supports on-demand compliance scanning and server-fabric remediation. VMM administrators can monitor the update status of the server fabric, scan for compliance, and remediate updates for a selected group of servers. They can also exempt specific servers within the fabric from installing specific updates.

VMM supports orchestrated updates of Hyper-V host clusters. When a VMM administrator performs update-remediation tasks on a host cluster, VMM places one Cluster node at a time into maintenance mode and then installs the selected updates.

If the cluster supports live migration, intelligent placement is used to live-migrate the virtual machines off the Cluster node. If the cluster does not support live migration, as is the case for Windows 2008, then VMM will put the virtual machine into a saved state.

Managing the WSUS Server

After you add a WSUS server under the control of VMM, you should not continue to manage the WSUS server with the WSUS console; this may be one of the reasons you decide to implement a dedicated WSUS server to patch your server fabric.

In VMM, an administrator updates the properties of the update server to configure a proxy server for synchronization and to change the update categories, products, and any supported languages that are to be synchronized by the WSUS server. If you add the update server to VMM in Single Sockets Layer (SSL) mode, you can update the proxy-server credentials for synchronization in the update server's properties. If the update server is not added to VMM in SSL mode, the proxy-server credentials are managed in the WSUS Administration console.

In VMM, administrators and delegated administrators can manage fabric updates. Only administrators can manage the update server and synchronize updates. Delegated administrators can scan and remediate updates on machines that are within the scope of their defined user role. Delegated administrators can use baselines created by administrators and other delegated administrators. However, delegated administrators cannot modify or delete baselines created by others.

Deploying a WSUS Server

To manage updates in VMM, you must either install a dedicated WSUS server or use an existing WSUS server. VMM uses the WSUS Windows Update/Microsoft Update catalog, Windows Update Agent (WUA) integration in Windows Server, and a WSUS server for binary distribution to managed computers.

You can install the WSUS server on the VMM management server. However, Microsoft recommends using a remote WSUS server, especially if the VMM management server is managing a large number of computers. If you install WSUS on a remote server, you must install a WSUS console on the VMM management server and then restart the VMM service.

SHOULD YOU USE A REMOTE WSUS?

If you are managing a large enough environment, you may want to consider implementing a remote WSUS server. A good rule of thumb is to offload the WSUS server away from VMM when the VMM management server is managing more than 150 hosts.

If you plan to use a highly available VMM management server, Microsoft recommends that you use a remote WSUS server. With a highly available VMM management server, you must install a WSUS console on each node of the cluster to enable the VMM service to continue to support fabric updates.

WSUS SERVER PREREQUISITES

Before you install the WSUS server, ensure that the intended server meets all WSUS prerequisites. You must install the Web Server (IIS) role in Windows Server. In addition to the roles or services that are added by default, WSUS requires the following role services:

◆ ASP.NET

◆ Windows authentication

◆ Dynamic content compression

◆ IIS 6 management compatibility

INSTALLING A WSUS SERVER

Use the following procedure to install a dedicated WSUS server to your environment running on Windows 2008 R2 SP1:

1. Launch Server Manager, select the Roles node, and then click Add Roles. The Add Roles Wizard appears.

2. Click Next. The Select Server Roles screen appears.

3. Select Windows Server Update Service, and click Install. The Add Role Services Required For Window Server Update Services screen appears.

4. Note which additional roles are required as a dependency and click Add Required Role Services.

5. Click through the following pages:

   ◆ On the Web Server (IIS) page, click Next.

   ◆ On the Select Role Services page, click Next.

   ◆ On the Windows Server Update Services page, click Next.

6. On the Confirm Installation Selections page, click Install.

7. Click through the following screens:

   ◆ On the Welcome To Windows Server Update Services Wizard page, click Next.

   ◆ On the License Agreement page, click Agree.

   ◆ On the Required Components To Use the Administration UI page, click Next.

   ◆ On the Select Update Source page, accept the default storage location.

   ◆ On the Database Options page, accept the default.

   ◆ On the Website Selection page, accept the default.

   ◆ On the Ready To Install Windows Server Update Services page, click Next.

   ◆ On the Completing The Windows Server Update Services Setup page, click Next.

◆ On the Windows Services Update Configuration Wizard page, click Next.

◆ On the Join The Microsoft Update Improvement Program page, click Next.

The Choose Upstream Server screen appears (Figure 5.10).

FIGURE 5.10
Choosing an
upstream server

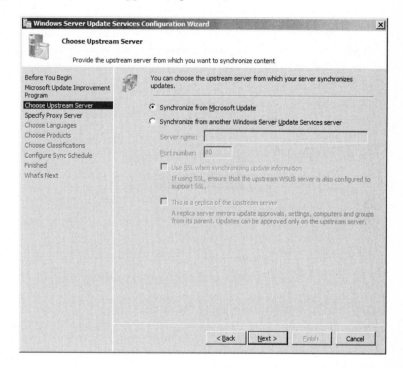

8. Select Synchronize from Microsoft Update, and click Next. The Specify Proxy Server screen appears.

9. Enter the details of your proxy server (if applicable), and click Next. The Choose Languages screen appears.

10. Select the update languages you require, and click Next. The Choose Products screen appears.

11. Select the products for which you want to download updates, and click Next. As a best practice, only synchronize the languages, products, and classifications associated with your server fabric.

   The Choose Classifications screen appears.

12. Select the classifications for which you want to download updates, and click Next. The Set Sync Schedule screen appears (Figure 5.11).

13. Select manual or automatic synchronization. For automatic synchronization, specify the synchronization schedule. Click Next.

14. Click through the remaining screens:

◆ On the Finished Configuration screen, click Next.

◆ On the What's Next screen, click Finish.

◆ On the Installation Results screen, click Close.

15. To verify that WSUS has been installed successfully, use the Windows Start menu and navigate to Administrative Tools ➢ Windows Server Update Services. You should see the Update Services screen (Figure 5.12).

FIGURE 5.11
Setting the sync schedule

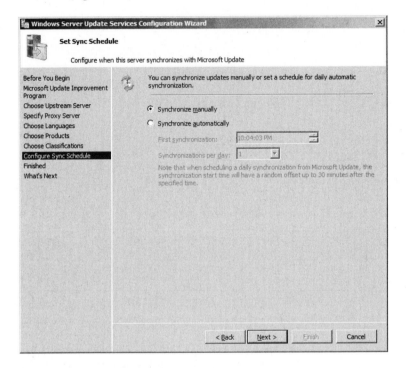

FIGURE 5.12
Windows Server Update Services

16. Click the server name to expand it, and then click Synchronizations to verify that the initial synchronization was successful.

INSTALLING THE WSUS CONSOLE

Use the following procedure to install the WSUS console on your VMM management server. This step is required when the WSUS server is installed on a remote server:

1. Download the x64 version of WSUS 3.0 SP2 (`WSUS30-KB972455-x64.exe`) from the following location:

   `www.microsoft.com/download/en/details.aspx?id=5216`

2. Run the downloaded program. The Windows Server Update Services 3.0 SP2 Wizard appears.

3. Click through the screens:

   ◆ On the Welcome screen, click Next.

   ◆ On the Installation Mode Selection screen, select only the Admin console.

   ◆ On the License Agreement screen, click Accept.

   ◆ On the Required Components screen, click Next.

   ◆ On the Completing screen, click Finish.

4. On the VMM management server, open a command window. From the Start menu, navigate to Accessories ➢ Command Prompt.

5. Enter **net stop scvmmservice** to stop the VMM service.

6. Restart the VMM service by entering **net start scvmmservice.**

   The VMM service starts, and the WSUS console is available.

ADDING THE WSUS SERVER TO VMM

Use the following procedure to add a remote WSUS server to the server fabric and enable update management:

1. In the VMM console, select the Fabric workspace (Figure 5.13).

2. On the Home tab, in the Add group, click Add Resources and then click Update Server. The Add Windows Update Server Services screen appears.

3. In the Computer Name field, enter the fully qualified name of the WSUS server (for example, **wsus1.private.cloud**).

4. In the TCP/IP Port field, specify the port number that the WSUS website uses to listen for connections.

   If you installed WSUS with default values and are using the default website, the TCP/IP port should be 80.

5. Enter the necessary credentials for connecting to the WSUS server.

   Either specify an account manually or use an existing Run As account. Either account must have administrator rights on the WSUS server.

FIGURE 5.13

Updating the server

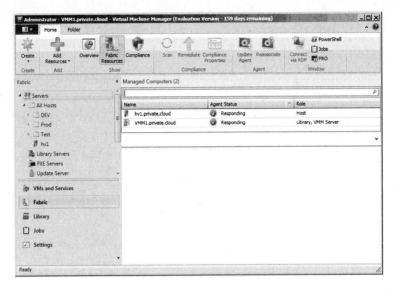

6. Optionally, check the Use Secure Sockets Layer (SSL) check box and click Add.

The WSUS server is added to VMM. It begins to synchronize the updates catalog. Depending on how many update classifications and products you chose when you installed the WSUS server, this operation can take a reasonable amount of time.

Use the following procedure to verify that the remote WSUS server has been added to the server fabric successfully:

1. In the VMM console, select the Fabric workspace.

2. On the Fabric pane, expand the Servers node, and click Update Server. The Results pane shows the recently added WSUS server.

3. In the Library workspace, on the Library pane, expand Update Catalog And Baselines and then click Update Catalog. The Results pane shows the updates downloaded during WSUS synchronization.

Configuring Update Baselines

After you add your WSUS server to VMM, you can prepare to manage updates for the server fabric by configuring update baselines. An *update baseline* contains a set of required updates that is then scoped to an assignment. This assignment can be a host group, a standalone host, a cluster, or a VMM management-server role.

During a compliance scan, servers that are assigned to a baseline are graded for compliance with their assigned baselines. After a server is found to be noncompliant, an administrator can bring the server into compliance through *update remediation*.

Update baselines that are assigned to a host group are applied to all standalone hosts and clusters in that host group, as well as the standalone hosts and clusters in child host groups.

If a host is moved from one host group to another, the baselines for the new host group are applied to that host and the previous baseline will no longer apply, unless that baseline is assigned to both host groups. Explicit baseline assignments to a host stay with that host when it is moved from one host group to another. It is only when the baseline is assigned to a host group that baseline assignments are revoked during the move. You can use either of the following methods to prepare update baselines for remediation:

♦ Use one of the built-in update baselines that VMM provides.

♦ Create your own custom update baseline.

VMM provides two built-in sample update baselines you can use to apply security updates and critical updates to the computers in your VMM environment:

♦ Sample Baseline For Security Updates

♦ Sample Baseline For Critical Updates

Before you can use a baseline, you must assign it to host groups, clusters, or standalone hosts. Use the following procedure to assign servers to the sample security baseline.

1. In the VMM console, select the Library workspace.

2. On the Library pane, expand Update Catalog And Baselines, and then click Update Baselines.

3. On the Baselines pane, right-click Sample Baseline For Security Updates, and select Properties. The Sample Baseline For Security Updates Properties screen appears.

4. On the Updates tab, optionally add or remove update baselines from the baselines that are listed. The Sample Baseline For Security Updates includes all security updates. To ensure that all security updates are applied, do not remove any baselines.

5. On the Assignment Scope tab, select host groups, host clusters, or standalone hosts to add to the baseline. Click OK to save your changes.

Use the following procedure to create a new custom update baseline that you can then assign:

1. In the VMM console, select the Library workspace.

2. On the Library pane, expand Update Catalog And Baselines, and then click Update Baselines.

3. On the Home tab, in the Create group, click Create and then select Baseline.

4. On the General page, enter a name (for example, My Company Critical Updates Baseline) and a description for the update baseline, and click Next.

5. On the Updates page, click Add to include the updates that you want to be in your custom baseline. Enter **security updates** in the Search box to filter the selection, and click Next.

6. On the Assignment Scope page, select the host groups, cluster, or standalone host that you want to apply the baseline to, and click Next.

   You can apply a baseline to servers that are performing any of the VMM roles.

7. On the Summary page, review your settings and click Finish.

   Some updates require that you accept a Microsoft license agreement.

8. To verify that your update baseline was created successfully, on the Library pane expand Update Catalog And Baselines, and click Baselines. The new baseline appears in the Results pane.

Scanning for Update Compliance

Now that you have assigned servers to an update baseline in VMM, you can scan those servers to determine their compliance status against that baseline.

When it scans a server for compliance, WSUS checks the assigned update baselines to determine whether applicable updates are installed. After a compliance scan, each update has a compliance status of Compliant, Non Compliant, Error, or Unknown.

The compliance scan focuses on the updates included in the baseline because you deemed them important for your environment.

The following changes can cause a server's update status to change to Unknown. When one of them occurs, you should perform a scan operation to assess the server's compliance status.

◆ A host is moved from one host group to another host group.

◆ An update is added to or removed from a baseline that is assigned to a server.

◆ A server is added to the scope of a baseline.

Use the following procedure to verify the update-compliance status of your server fabric:

1. In the VMM console, select the Fabric workspace.

2. On the Fabric pane, select the Servers node and click Compliance.

The Results pane displays the compliance status of the servers in the VMM fabric (Figure 5.14). Because you have not yet scanned the server fabric for compliance, the servers that you added to your baseline have a compliance status of Unknown and an operational status of Pending Compliance Scan.

FIGURE 5.14
Viewing the compliance status

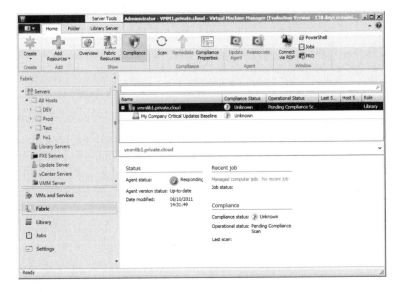

Use the following procedure to scan the server fabric and determine the compliance status against your assigned baseline:

1. In the VMM console, select the Fabric workspace.

2. On the Fabric pane, select the Servers node, click Compliance, and select the server you want to scan.

3. On the Home tab, in the Compliance group, click Scan.

Performing Update Remediation

The task of bringing a server into compliance is known as *update remediation*. In VMM you can choose to remediate all update baselines that are assigned to a server, all noncompliant updates in a single update baseline, or a single update.

Use the following procedure to remediate updates for a nonclustered Hyper-V host that is managed by VMM:

1. In the VMM console, select the Fabric workspace.

2. On the Fabric pane, select the Servers node, click Compliance, and select the server you want to remediate.

3. On the Home tab, in the Compliance group, click Remediate.

The Remediate task is available only when the selected objects are noncompliant. The Update Remediation screen appears (Figure 5.15). If you selected a server to remediate, all updates are initially selected.

FIGURE 5.15
Remediating the update baselines

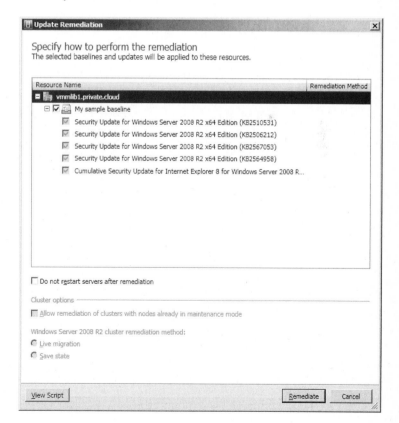

4. Optionally clear specific update baselines, or even individual updates, to determine which updates will be applied.

5. If you prefer to restart the servers manually after remediation, check the "Do not restart the servers after remediation" check box.

6. Click Remediate to start the update remediation process.

There are times when you might not want to apply a specific update even though that update is part of your baseline. When an administrator creates an update exemption for a managed server, that server still remains accountable to an assigned baseline while it is exempted from a particular update in the baseline.

The most common reason for creating an update exemption is that a specific update has placed a managed server in an unhealthy state. The administrator uninstalls the update, which returns the server to a healthy state, and then wants to prevent that update from being reinstalled until the issues around that update have been identified and resolved.

Because the update was uninstalled out of band, the server's update status in VMM remains Compliant until the server is scanned again. The next scan will change the server's status to Non Compliant. To prevent an accidental reinstallation of this update before the issues are resolved, and to provide a valid business justification, the administrator can add an update exemption to the baseline. After the issues are resolved on the server, the administrator can remove the exemption so that the update will be reinstalled during the next update remediation.

Use the following procedure to create an update exemption for a specific server within the server fabric that is managed by VMM:

1. In the VMM console, select the Fabric workspace.

2. On the Fabric pane, select the Servers node, click Compliance, and select the server to which you want to apply an exemption.

3. In the Results pane, expand the appropriate update baseline and click the update you want to exempt.

4. On the Home tab, in the Compliance group, click Compliance Properties. The Compliance Properties screen appears.

5. Select the update or updates to include in the exemption, and click Create. The Create Exemption dialog box appears.

6. In the Notes field, enter information about the exemption, its duration, and the person who authorized it.

7. Click Create.

   The Compliance Properties screen reappears. The status of the update or updates now says Exempt. The update will not be applied to the fabric resource during update remediations until the exemption is removed.

Use the following procedure to remove an update exemption for a specific server within the server fabric that is managed by VMM:

1. In the VMM console, select the Fabric workspace.

2. On the Fabric pane, select the Servers node, click Compliance, and select the server from which you want to remove an exemption.

3. In the Results pane, expand the appropriate update baseline and click the update from which you wish to remove the exemption.

4. On the Home tab, in the Compliance group, click Compliance Properties. The Compliance Properties screen appears.

5. Select the exemption or exemptions to be removed, click Delete, and then click Yes to confirm.

6. Click OK to dismiss the Compliance Properties screen.

7. To perform a compliance scan on a server, in the Results pane click the server to select it. Then, on the Home tab, in the Compliance group, click Scan. The statuses of the update, the update baseline, and the server change to Non Compliant.

8. To return the server to a compliant state, in the Results pane select the update, the update baseline, or the server that is in a Non Compliant state. Then, on the Home tab, in the Compliance group, click Remediate.

Performing On-Demand Update Synchronizations

To get updates, the WSUS server contacts Microsoft Update. WSUS determines whether new updates have been made available by Microsoft since the last synchronization. WSUS downloads the new metadata, and VMM imports the changes into the VMM update catalog.

When the update server is added to VMM, an initial synchronization is performed. VMM does not perform automatic synchronizations after that point. You should perform on-demand synchronizations on a schedule that meets your company's requirements. As a best practice, synchronization should occur at least every 15 to 30 days in accordance with Microsoft security and update release cycles.

Use the following procedure to synchronize updates in VMM with your Microsoft Update:

1. In the VMM console, select the Fabric workspace.

2. On the Fabric pane, expand Servers, click Update Server, and then click Fabric Resources.

3. On the Update Server tab, in the Update Server group, click Synchronize.

Use the following procedure to manage configuration changes with the WSUS server:

1. In the VMM console, select the Fabric workspace.

2. On the Fabric pane, expand Servers, click Update Server, and then click Fabric Resources.

3. On the Update Server tab, in the Update Server group, click Properties.

4. On the Proxy Server tab, if applicable, configure WSUS to use a proxy server when synchronizing updates, or update the port for a proxy server that is already in use.

5. On the Update Classifications tab, select each update classification you want to synchronize.

6. On the Products tab, select each product to include in update synchronizations.

7. On the Languages tab, select each supported language to include in update synchronizations.

8. Click OK to apply any changes you make.

Summary

This chapter covered all aspects of setting up and configuring the VMM library, installing and configuring fabric patching, scanning for compliance, and remediating your server fabric. Now that you understand the factors behind the installation options VMM provides, you should be prepared to make optimal decisions for your own unique situation. In the next chapter you will learn about additional aspects of your private cloud environment: networking and storage.

## Chapter 6

Understanding Network and Storage in VMM 2012

Fabric has no product number. It is an abstract concept, not something you can order. It comprises all the components that together form the physical infrastructure of a cloud. Whether it is your private cloud, a hosted cloud, or Windows Azure (Microsoft's public cloud), the underlying infrastructure must be in place before it can be used to deploy a service consisting of one or more virtual machines and applications. This chapter contains the following topics:

♦ Creating Logical Networks and sites

♦ Creating IP pools and MAC pools

♦ Setting up load balancers and VIP templates

♦ Discovering and configuring storage arrays with Storage Management Initiative–Specification (SMI-S)

♦ Managing storage pools and assigning logical units

♦ End-to-end storage mapping from the VM to the array

In VMM, the fabric is the domain of the VMM administrator, who can create, add, modify, configure, or remove the different fabric components. These are the three major building blocks:

♦ Networking

♦ Storage

♦ Servers

This chapter deals with networking and storage. Chapter 7, "Deploying Hosts and Clusters in VMM 2012," deals with servers. Although the VMM graphical user interface (GUI) presents them in a different order, you should configure networking and storage before you deploy new Hyper-V servers or create a cluster out of standalone Hyper-V servers.

As you can see in Figure 6.1, servers, networking, and storage have further subdivisions.

FIGURE 6.1
The fabric

Preparing Network Integration

VMM helps you organize your networks for the private cloud into easy-to-grasp concepts. Although you should not need to add all your networking equipment to VMM or fully configure your entire network from VMM, doing so is certainly a very good start and network functionality in VMM will be expanded in the future. Networking is so well integrated into VMM that deploying virtualization hosts, virtual machines, and other services (including the applications that run on top of them) is easy.

VMM helps by organizing network subnets and VLANs into Logical Networks, IP address pools, and MAC address pools. Network load balancers and Virtual IP (VIP) templates are used to integrate network components with private clouds and services with flexibility and scalability in mind.

The previous version of VMM had network locations and network tags. These settings were used to place VMs and to determine whether networks on different hosts were the same. You could connect physical network adapters to different virtual networks, but only one address could be set as the location. A moving VM could, therefore, keep or correct connectivity with the proper network. The network tag could specify a specific purpose for a virtual network if it was attached to the same physical network. In practice, these network settings were rarely used.

VMM 2012 has better networking functionality, including features you cannot ignore as an administrator and that are easy to use if you are a self-service user. As we explained in Chapter 3, *abstraction* is the key word. The complexity of the network with its different VLANs, subnets, IP schemas, gateways, and DNS servers is masked from the private cloud consumer. It is up to the private cloud administrator to understand this complexity before setting up the network components of the fabric.

Although networks are usually tied to a specific location, their purpose may still be the same. Let's say you have a network for production and a network facing the Internet. These networks could each have one or more subnets—and it is quite likely that if you have multiple sites, these subnets will not be the same. For this reason, VMM offers the concept of *Logical Networks*. The Logical Networks LAN, DMZ, and WAN have different IP ranges on different locations (unless the network administrator has stretched VLANs). The Self-Service user, however, doesn't know about all these details and is just interested in connecting a VM to the LAN, the DMZ, or the WAN. Being able to use these simple and easy-to-understand logical names makes VMM Logical Networks a strong ally. The next sections describe how you can configure networking in VMM to make networks easy to use for self-service users and how you connect these networks to the different private clouds.

Configuring Network Settings

Before creating Logical Networks and sites, you should take a look at the network settings that determine how networks are automatically created when you add one or more existing virtualization hosts. The network settings can be found in the Settings workspace (bottom-left corner of the VMM Console window).

Under Settings ➢ General ➢ Network Settings, you can specify several options that define the general network settings to autocreate logical and virtual networks, which are enabled by default (Figure 6.2).

FIGURE 6.2
The Logical
Network Matching
options

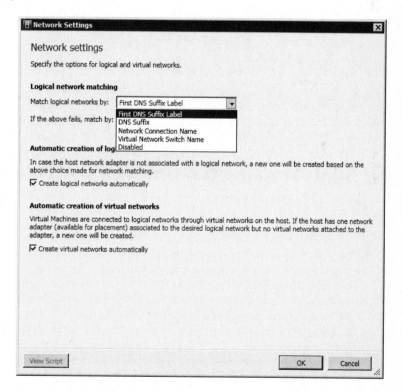

Physical network adapters are matched with Logical Networks only when a host is added to VMM management and only when the host does not have any associated Logical Networks.

When a virtualization host is added to VMM, you can set whether Logical Networks are automatically created when a host network adapter is not associated with a Logical Network.

Similarly, you can either enable or disable the autocreation of virtual networks based on whether or not the host network adapter is connected to a Logical Network.

By default Logical Networks are automatically created under the described circumstances (Figure 6.3).

FIGURE 6.3
Global network settings

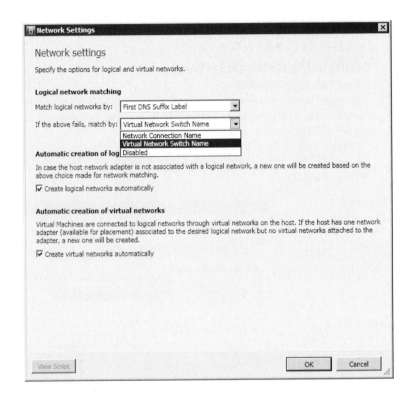

Creating Logical Networks and Network Sites

Logical Networks in VMM are especially helpful when you have a network across multiple locations. You will likely have Internet access on all locations; you could call that network Frontend, but have different definitions per site. In fact, a Logical Network is simply an abstraction of the physical network infrastructure that can be organized by a number of connectivity properties. A Logical Network is a combination of one or more network sites, each comprising an IP range, a subnet, and a VLAN. Once defined, a Logical Network can be easily applied to assign networks to virtualization hosts, single VMs, or a set of VMs that are part of a multitiered service. So, if the web tier requires Internet access, you just have to connect the Frontend network to it. As you will see later, you can also introduce load balancers and assign them to a host group and service in a similar fashion.

It is possible to have an empty Logical Network without any configured sites, but this will not add much functionality other than documenting that network. A Logical Network derives its functionality from its network site definition, which allows associations with VLANs and subnets to host groups. In VMM, IP subnets use a CIDR notation.

WHAT IS CIDR?

The Classless Inter-Domain Routing (CIDR) notation is a compact specification of an IP address and its associated routing prefix. It is an IP address–allocation and route-aggregation methodology used for both IPv4 and IPv6 networking. It is constructed from the IP address and the prefix size, the latter being equivalent to the number of leading 1 bits in the routing prefix mask. The IP address is expressed according to the standards of IPv4 or IPv6. It is followed by a separator character (/) and the size is expressed as a decimal number.

Examples: `192.168.1.0/24`, representing 256 IPv4 addresses (`192.168.1.0` - `192.168.1.255`)

`2001:bc4::/48`, representing the IPv6 addresses from `2001:bc4:0:0:0:0:0:0`

to

`2001:bc4:0:ffff:ffff:ffff:ffff:ffff`

To create a logical network, follow these steps:

1. In the VMM console, open the Fabric workspace.

2. Expand Networking, right-click Logical Networks, and select Create Logical Network. Alternatively, click Create Logical Network on the ribbon in the Fabric workspace.

3. In the Create Logical Network Wizard on the Name page, enter a meaningful name and description (Figure 6.4). Click Next.

FIGURE 6.4
Naming the Logical Network

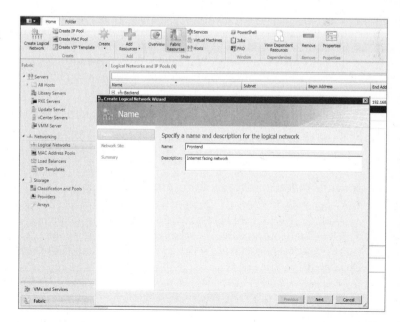

4. You can add one or more network sites by clicking Add on the Network Site page. Click Next.

5. Accept the default Network Site name or, preferably, change it to a more meaningful name, such as **Frontend_Amsterdam** (Figure 6.5). It is possible to associate one or more host groups to this site and insert one or more VLANs and IP subnets. Select the desired host groups, enter the VLAN and IP subnet, or click Insert Row if you want to insert additional VLANs and IP subnets. Click Next when you are finished.

FIGURE 6.5
Associating the VLAN and subnet

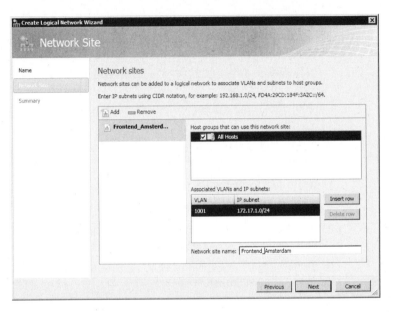

6. Select at least one host group and one VLAN/IP subnet pair. If you enter only the VLAN ID, a DHCP address will be used instead of a static IP address for this network. If you leave the VLAN empty and enter only the IP subnet, the VLAN is automatically changed to 0, which means that VLANs will not be used for this network, assuming your host's network adapter is placed in Access mode.

7. On the Summary page, confirm the settings and click Finish.

If you want to change the properties of the Logical Network, go back to Fabric ➢ Networking ➢ Logical Networks and select the network to be changed.

Manually Removing Dependent Resources

You cannot delete a Logical Network if there are still dependencies on other objects, such as network sites, virtual network adapters, host network adapters, load balancers, or load-balancer templates. You must remove them before you can remove the Logical Network. You can check what dependencies are active by right-clicking the Logical Network and selecting View Dependent Resources.

In Figure 6.6, two Hyper-V servers depend on the Logical Network called Management. The Logical Network can't be removed until these dependencies no longer exist.

FIGURE 6.6
Dependent
resources

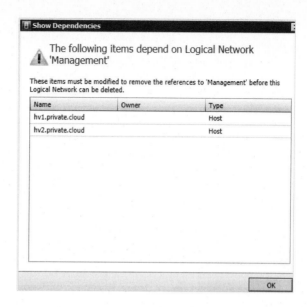

Figure 6.7 shows how a host network adapter is connected to a Logical Network in the properties of the Hyper-V servers. Right-click the identified servers one by one, select Properties ➢ Hardware, and move down to Network Adapters. If you click on the adapter connected to the Logical Network, you can deselect the logical networks associated with this adapter.

FIGURE 6.7
Connecting a host
network adapter

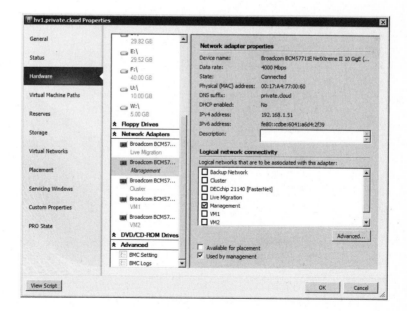

When all the dependencies are removed, you can finally delete the logical networks by right-clicking it, and clicking Remove and Yes to confirm the deletion.

TIP To use Logical Networks with port groups in VMware ESX hosts, use VMware vCenter to configure the port groups. VMM does not automatically create them on ESX hosts. Also, make sure to associate the correct VLANs with the Logical Networks.

Creating IP Address Pools

In VMM you can create static IP address pools, which make it easy to allocate IP addresses to both hosts and VMs. In fact, all supported hypervisors (Hyper-V, VMware ESX, and XenServer) can benefit from this functionality. By assigning one or several subnets to your logical network definition, you can create an IP address pool for each subnet, including all relevant details such as network sites, relevant host groups, Virtual IP (VIP) addresses, reserved addresses, gateways, DNS servers, and WINS servers (at least if you still use the NetBIOS-based-name resolution method). You can create an IP address pool scoped to a host group with only a name and an IP range.

Once you have created a Logical Network and one or more sites, you can add an IP address pool and specify which network site and IP subnet it belongs to.

To create an IP address pool, follow these steps:

1. In the VMM console, open the Fabric workspace and select Networking And Logical Network. If there are existing IP pools, you can expand the logical network and see the naming conventions used for the other IP address pools. In this example, a new IP pool called IP_Pool_London was added.

2. From the ribbon, click Create and select IP pool or right-click the Logical Network and select Create IP Pool.

3. Provide a name according to your networking naming conventions, add a description, and select an existing Logical Network. Click Next.

4. At the Network Site screen (Figure 6.8), you can use an existing network site or create a new one. If you create a new site, you must also provide an IP subnet and a VLAN ID. If you don't use a VLAN, you can leave the ID set to 0. In the bottom part of the Network Site screen, you can also define which host groups can use this network site. Click Next.

5. Follow the steps to create a Logical Network, as described in "Creating Logical Networks and Network Sites" earlier in this chapter.

6. When you have completed all the other subnet details, click Finish. All of your IP pools will appear under the Logical Network, as shown in Figure 6.9.

FIGURE 6.8

Adding a site with an IP subnet and VLAN

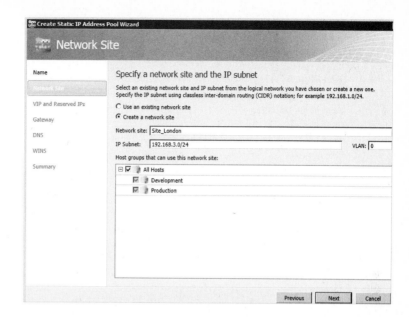

FIGURE 6.9

Logical Network with several IP pools

									Logical Network
IP_Pool_Amsterdam	192.168.1.0/24	192.168.1.1	192.168.1.254	80	71		9		Static IP Pool
IP_Pool_Dublin	192.168.2.0/24	192.168.2.1	192.168.2.254	80	71		9		Static IP Pool
IP_Pool_London	192.168.3.0/24	192.168.3.1	192.168.3.254	254	254		0		Static IP Pool

Viewing Assigned IP Addresses

Currently, the VMM graphical user interface offers no way to see which IP addresses have been assigned to which hosts or VMs. However, you can use PowerShell to view them.

To display a list of assigned IP address for a specific subnet, issue the following code:

```
PS C:\> $IPAddressPool = Get-SCStaticIPAddressPool -IPv4 -Subnet "192.168.1.0/24"
PS C:\> $IPAddressPool

Name                  : IP_Pool_Amsterdam
Description           :
AddressFamily         : InterNetwork
IPAddressRangeStart   : 192.168.1.1
IPAddressRangeEnd     : 192.168.1.254
AvailableDIPAddresses : 71
AvailableAddresses    : 80
```

```
TotalDIPAddresses         : 74
TotalAddresses            : 83
UnassignedAddresses       : 0
UnassignedDIPAddresses    : 0
UnassignedVIPAddresses    : 0
AvailableVIPAddresses     : 9
TotalVIPAddresses         : 9
DNSSearchSuffixes         : {}
DNSSuffix                 : private.cloud
DNSServers                : {192.168.1.21, 192.168.1.22}
DefaultGateways           : {192.168.1.1}
WINSServers               : {}
EnableNetBIOS             : False
IPAddressReservedSet      : 192.168.1.11-192.168.1.180
ReservedAddresses         : 171
VIPAddressSet             : 192.168.1.2-192.168.1.10
Subnet                    : 192.168.1.0/24
IsIPv4                    : True
LogicalNetworkDefinition  : Site_Amsterdam
ServerConnection          : Microsoft.SystemCenter.VirtualMachineManager.Remoting.
                            ServerConnection
ID                        : f8322ffa-636f-464f-b2ff-6af7f943ed6a
IsViewOnly                : False
ObjectType                : StaticIPAddressPool
MarkedForDeletion         : False
IsFullyCached             : True

PS C:\> $IPAddress = Get-SCIPAddress -StaticIPAddressPool $IPAddressPool ↵
-Assigned
PS C:\> $IPAddress


Name                  : 192.168.1.181
Address               : 192.168.1.181
AllocatingAddressPool : IP_Pool_Amsterdam
AssignedToID          : e4008576-4742-4f57-94b5-e6f4d7de3e7c
AssignedToType        : VirtualNetworkAdapter
Type                  : DedicatedIP
State                 : Assigned
Description           : DC3
ServerConnection      : Microsoft.SystemCenter.VirtualMachineManager.Remoting.
                        ServerConnection
ID                    : 392d44d6-2378-4599-9742-6bca85adc715
IsViewOnly            : False
ObjectType            : AllocatedIPAddress
MarkedForDeletion     : False
IsFullyCached         : True
```

All assigned addresses are currently saved in an array and can be individually addressed by their position in the array.

```
PS C:\> $IPAddress[1]

Name                  : 192.168.1.202
Address               : 192.168.1.202
AllocatingAddressPool : IP_Pool_Amsterdam
AssignedToID          : f45a659b-e7d2-42a4-a917-cb369e95f710
AssignedToType        : VirtualMachine
Type                  : DedicatedIP
State                 : Assigned
Description           : HVS-SSQL04
ServerConnection      : Microsoft.SystemCenter.VirtualMachineManager.Remoting.
                        ServerConnection
ID                    : f3c893b3-8c8b-47ae-a042-1c63526395bb
IsViewOnly            : False
ObjectType            : AllocatedIPAddress
MarkedForDeletion     : False
IsFullyCached         : True


PS C:\> $IPAddress[2]

Name                  : 192.168.1.207
Address               : 192.168.1.207
AllocatingAddressPool : IP_Pool_Amsterdam
AssignedToID          : db155230-c74e-4d85-ba00-7a214325d9d8
AssignedToType        : VirtualMachine
Type                  : DedicatedIP
State                 : Assigned
Description           : TEST01
ServerConnection      : Microsoft.SystemCenter.VirtualMachineManager.Remoting.
                        ServerConnection
ID                    : 09baba92-2e4e-4ebc-8ddd-827015e8b8be
IsViewOnly            : False
ObjectType            : AllocatedIPAddress
MarkedForDeletion     : False
IsFullyCached         : True
```

If you want to unassign an entry from the IP pool, use this command:

```
PS C:\> $IPAddress[2] | Revoke-SCIPAddress

Name                  : 192.168.1.207
Address               : 192.168.1.207
AllocatingAddressPool : IP_Pool_Amsterdam
AssignedToID          : db155230-c74e-4d85-ba00-7a214325d9d8
AssignedToType        : VirtualMachine
Type                  : DedicatedIP
State                 : Assigned
Description           : TEST02
```

```
ServerConnection      : Microsoft.SystemCenter.VirtualMachineManager.Remoting.
                        ServerConnection
ID                    : 09baba92-2e4e-4ebc-8ddd-827015e8b8be
IsViewOnly            : False
ObjectType            : AllocatedIPAddress
MarkedForDeletion     : True
IsFullyCached         : True
```

The available number of addresses increases from 71 to 72:

```
PS C:\> $IPAddressPool.AvailableDIPAddresses
72
```

As you can see in Figure 6.10, shortly after the IP address is revoked, a job is run to delete the IP addresses marked for deletion.

FIGURE 6.10
Returning IP addresses to the pool

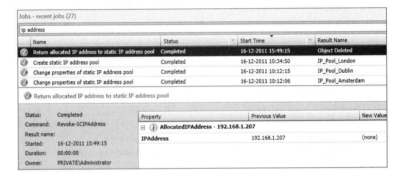

```
PS C:\> $IPAddress = Get-SCIPAddress -StaticIPAddressPool $IPAddressPool ↵
-Assigned
PS C:\> $IPAddress
```

```
Name                  : 192.168.1.181
Address               : 192.168.1.181
AllocatingAddressPool : IP_Pool_Amsterdam
AssignedToID          : e4008576-4742-4f57-94b5-e6f4d7de3e7c
AssignedToType        : VirtualNetworkAdapter
Type                  : DedicatedIP
State                 : Assigned
Description           : DC3
ServerConnection      : Microsoft.SystemCenter.VirtualMachineManager.Remoting.
                        ServerConnection
ID                    : 392d44d6-2378-4599-9742-6bca85adc715
IsViewOnly            : False
ObjectType            : AllocatedIPAddress
MarkedForDeletion     : False
```

```
IsFullyCached        : True

Name                 : 192.168.1.202
Address              : 192.168.1.202
AllocatingAddressPool : IP_Pool_Amsterdam
AssignedToID         : f45a659b-e7d2-42a4-a917-cb369e95f710
AssignedToType       : VirtualMachine
Type                 : DedicatedIP
State                : Assigned
Description          : TEST01
ServerConnection     : Microsoft.SystemCenter.VirtualMachineManager.Remoting.
                       ServerConnection
ID                   : f3c893b3-8c8b-47ae-a042-1c63526395bb
IsViewOnly           : False
ObjectType           : AllocatedIPAddress
MarkedForDeletion    : False
IsFullyCached        : True
```

This PowerShell command lists all statically assigned IP addresses:

```
PS C:\> Get-SCIPAddress | ft address, AllocatingAddressPool, Description, Type, ⏎
State -auto


Address         AllocatingAddressPool    Description       Type         State
-------         ---------------------    -----------       ---          -----
10.0.1.51       IPv4_Pool_Live_Migration hv1.private.cloud DedicatedIP  Assigned
192.168.1.202   IP_Pool_Amsterdam        TEST01            DedicatedIP  Assigned
192.168.2.202   IP_Pool_Dublin           TEST01            DedicatedIP  Assigned
192.168.1.181   IP_Pool_Amsterdam        DC3               DedicatedIP  Assigned
192.168.2.203   IP_Pool_Dublin           TEST02            DedicatedIP  Assigned
10.0.1.52       IPv4_Pool_Live_Migration hv2.private.cloud DedicatedIP  Assigned
192.168.2.182   IP_Pool_Dublin           DC3               DedicatedIP  Assigned
```

Creating a MAC Address Pool

When you install VMM, two default Media Access Control (MAC) address pools use two different ranges. (If you don't need to create custom MAC address pools, you can skip this section.) There is one default pool for both Hyper-V and Citrix XenServer hypervisors and one default pool for VMware ESX hypervisor, as listed in Table 6.1.

TABLE 6.1:   MAC Addresses

MAC ADDRESS POOL NAME	HYPERVISOR	MAC ADDRESS RANGE
Default MAC address pool	Hyper-VCitrix XenServer	00:1D:D8:B7:1C:00 – 00:1D:D8:F4:1F:FF
Default VMware MAC address pool	VMware ESX	00:50:56:00:00:00 – 00:50:56:3F:FF:FF

If you need to create one or more custom MAC address pools, follow these steps:

1. In the VMM console, open the Fabric workspace and select Fabric Resources from the ribbon

2. Expand Networking from the Navigation pane, right-click MAC Address Pools, and select Create MAC Pool (as in Figure 6.11).

3. Enter a name for the MAC address pool, provide a description, and select the relevant host groups. Select Next.

4. Enter the starting MAC address and ending MAC address and click Next.

5. Review the summary and click Finish.

FIGURE 6.11
Creating a MAC pool

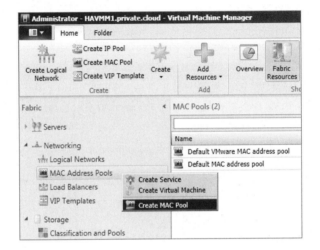

Releasing Inactive IP or MAC Addresses

Under certain conditions, IP or MAC addresses can become inactive. This happens when a host was assigned a static IP address during a bare-metal deployment job and is subsequently removed from VMM management. When removing the host, VMM marks all statically assigned IP and MAC addresses as inactive.

A second example is when a VM goes into a missing state. This can happen if the VM was removed outside VMM. Inactive IP addresses can be removed using the following steps:

1. Using the VMM console, select Logical Networks in the Fabric workspace and expand Networking.

2. Choose Fabric Resources from the ribbon, expand Logical Networks, and select an IP pool.

3. Select Properties ➢ Inactive Addresses.

4. Select one or more addresses, click Release, and then click OK to finish.

Similarly, MAC addresses can be removed with these steps:

1. Select MAC Address Pools in the Fabric workspace and then expand Networking.

2. Choose Fabric Resources from the ribbon, select the MAC Address Pool, and right-click the pool.

3. Select Properties ➤ Inactive Addresses.

4. Select one or more addresses and click Release. Click OK to finish.

Adding and Configuring Load Balancers and VIP Templates

Load balancers are physical or virtual devices that are used to distribute service requests to resources in the private cloud. A *load balancer* is typically used to configure access to applications with fair access, high availability, and scalability in mind. HTTP, HTTPS, and FTP are typical services that are suitable for load balancing because they require dynamic path selection or some sort of failover mechanism if one of the devices happens to fail. Configuration of such load-balancing hardware or its virtualized appliance version is naturally the domain of the network admin.

Configuring and maintaining a private cloud becomes a lot easier when virtualized networks are manageable entities in the VMM fabric. This is true when subnet and VLAN pairs are represented as logical networks in VMM. It is also beneficial when applications and (web) services are automatically referred to a load balancer with an optimal configuration for the specific workload. After all, one of the key differences between a classic data center and a private cloud is that cloud-service management is automated, and therefore repeatable, predictable, and easy to maintain.

Along with the concepts of Logical Networks and IP/MAC pools, VMM introduces two other network abstractions: load balancers and VIP templates. After Logical Networks have been created by the fabric admin, Self-Service users can easily utilize the load-balancing configuration if all they have to do is select the most appropriate template for the applications they are deploying. During deployment and reconfiguration of the service, no administrator intervention is required.

You might be familiar with the tedious and complex process of defining a load-balancer configuration for a specific application and bringing that configuration into production. It takes considerable effort for the server, application, and network admins to get this job done. Much of the work involved needs to be repeated if configurations are changed. It takes precious time and involves risk to take an application out of the load balancer, change the configuration, and put it back again.

DEFINING A LOAD-BALANCER CONFIGURATION

Let's say you are responsible for an application (a web tier, for instance) that could benefit from a load balancer. In many organizations, you'll have to fill out an IP flow diagram, or something like it. You'll need to specify everything that must be behind the load balancers and prepare for possible *persistence mechanisms*. If you need to change or remove one or more servers from the farm, you essentially will need to go back to the drawing table, update the document, and send it to the networking team. You'll have to wait for the machine(s) to be added into the load balancer. Also, during application deployment or application updates, you'll have to make sure the machine is taken out of the load balancer before updating it. You'll need to make sure the machine is ready to go online before you put it back in the pool.

As you saw earlier, you can reserve an IP range for load balancers in an IP address pool that is attached to a Logical Network. A VIP address pool follows the same pattern as an IP address pool. When a VIP is given to a load balancer, it is checked out from the IP pool.

When you are doing load-balancer integration and leveraging VMM to configure the load balancer, VMM not only adds the machine into the right pool during application deployment; it is also smart enough to pull machines out of the pool based on the characteristics a template author has defined, do the upgrade on a particular machine, add it back, and re-enable the pool. So, it is not just the initial configuration of the VIP that VMM takes care of; it also handles the initial setup of the VMs that are placed behind that VIP. VMM also handles the ongoing management and maintenance, ensuring that application users don't experience any downtime.

To get a good overview of the networks you have created so far, go to the Networking workspace and click Overview (Figure 6.12) on the ribbon.

FIGURE 6.12
Overview of networks

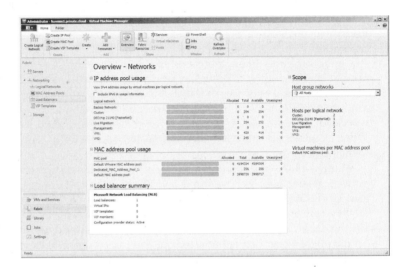

Out of the box VMM comes with one load-balancer configuration provider installed: Microsoft's software-based network load-balancing (NLB) solution, which is an integral part of all current Windows Server editions. Before you add any other load balancers, check to see if a piece of software called a load-balancer provider is available for your specific manufacturer and model. Currently, providers are available for Citrix NetScaler VPX, Brocade ADX, and BigIP F5. Several vendors offer a VM-based version of their load-balancer product, which makes it convenient to integrate into your VMM environment.

TIP Before you add a load balancer, it is important to set up some Logical Networks and IP address pools. If you want to use the load balancer in a service template, the VMs need to have static IP addresses that are automatically assigned from the static IP address pool.

INSTALLING THE LOAD-BALANCER PROVIDER

First, you need to download the latest version of the load-balancer provider offered by the load-balancer vendor. These are the currently known vendors' sites that offer load-balancer providers:

Citrix NetScaler VPX:

`www.citrix.com/English/ps2/products/feature.asp?contentID=2300361&ntref=bottompromo_ns`

Brocade ADX:

`www.brocade.com/partnerships/technology-alliance-partners/partner-details/`
`microsoft/microsoft-systems-center/index.page`

BIG-IP F5:

`https://devcentral.f5.com/weblogs/macvittie/archive/2012/04/20/`
`f5-friday-big-ip-solutions-for-microsoft-private-cloud.aspx`

A load-balancer provider is written in PowerShell, and if no other provider is available for your specific load-balancer hardware, you can always write your own provider.

If you do not have a hardware load balancer at hand, you might want to try Citrix NetScaler (Figure 6.13), which is available as a VM that runs on Hyper-V. It simulates a hardware load balancer and is great for testing purposes. You can download it from My Citrix:

`www.citrix.com/lang/english/publicindex.asp?destURL=/English/myCitrix/index.`
`asp&ntref=Try`

FIGURE 6.13
The Citrix
NetScaler load
balancer

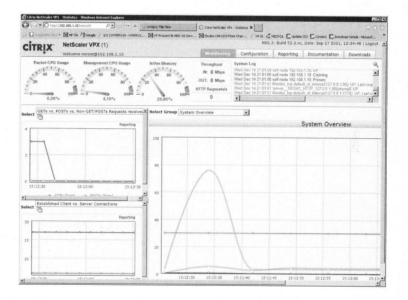

Before you can actually see a load balancer in VMM, you need to install a piece of software called the *load-balancer provider* and then restart the VMM service. Another step you must complete is to add a Run As account specifically for the load balancer.

During setup, you can run a number of tests to validate the existence and connection with the load balancer. After you install the load-balancer provider, the VMM service must be restarted. If you run a highly available (HA) VMM server, you can perform a failover of the VMM management server between the nodes in the cluster.

Installing a Citrix NetScaler Load Balancer Provider

To install a Citrix NetScaler load balancer provider, complete the following steps:

1. From a command prompt, install the downloaded provider: `CitrixNetScalerLoad Balancer.msi`.

2. After the Citrix NetScaler Load Balancer Setup Wizard starts, click Next.

3. If you run an HA VMM server, repeat steps 1 and 2 for the other cluster node.

4. Click Start and run `Services.msc`; right-click System Center Virtual Machine Manager and click Restart. If the VMM console is open, it loses the connection with the VMM server. If you run an HA VMM, the session is automatically reconnected after the first timeout.

To add the provider, follow these steps:

1. Expand Networking in the Fabric pane and select Load Balancers.

2. From the ribbon, click Fabric Resources to see which load balancers are already installed.

3. From the ribbon, click Add Resources to add a new load balancer (Figure 6.14).

FIGURE 6.14
Adding a load-balancer provider

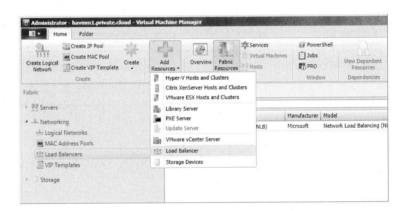

4. Select an existing Run As account or create a new one, and click OK when you are finished. The default credentials are `nsroot` for both the username and password. Press Next.

5. In the host group, specify the host groups for which the load balancers will be available and press Next.

6. On the Manufacturer and Model screen, you can specify Citrix Systems, Inc. for Manufacturer and Citrix NetScaler. Click Next.

7. Specify the load-balancer name or IP address and port number at the Address screen.

8. On the Logical Network Affinity screen, specify the affinity to one or more Logical Networks. The VIP address that is assigned to a load balancer is the front-end address for a service. The dedicated IP addresses that are assigned to the VMs in a service tier are the back-end addresses. Specify the Logical Networks from which VMM should assign the

front-end and back-end IP addresses. Select at least one front-end and back-end Logical Network affinity, as in Figure 6.15. If you don't, the load balancer will not be selected during placement. Click Next.

FIGURE 6.15
Specifying the logical network affinity

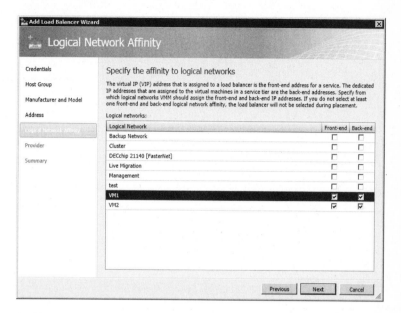

9. Now you are ready to test the Citrix NetScaler load balancer. Simply click Test to see which functions have been implemented and verify the test (Figure 6.16). After checking the results, click Next.

FIGURE 6.16
Testing the load balancer

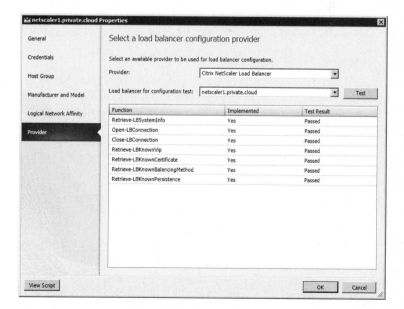

10. When you are ready to confirm the settings on the Summary screen, click Finish. Both the Microsoft and the Citrix network load balancers should appear under Fabric Resources in the Detail pane, as shown in Figure 6.17.

FIGURE 6.17
List of load balancers

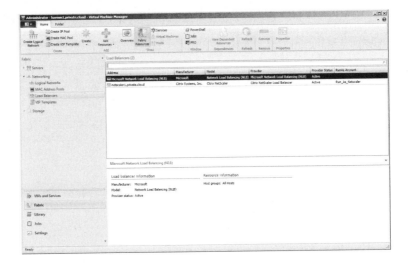

Installing a BIG-IP F5 Load-Balancer Provider

To install a BIG-IP F5 load-balancer provider, complete the following steps:

1. From a command prompt, install the downloaded provider: F5LoadBalancerPowerShellSetup.msi.

2. Use the PowerShell Setup Wizard to install F5 Networks Load Balancer.

If you have access to an F5 hardware load balancer, you can add it using the same procedure used for the NetScaler, including the setup of a Run As account for F5.

DEFINING A VIP TEMPLATE

A VIP template is a collection of load-balancer configuration settings that are optimized for the expected network traffic for a specific application or service offered in a private cloud. In fact, a VIP template represents a combination of the vendor's best practices, the network admin's expertise, and the requirements of application admins for that service.

Because they represent different application requirements, it is quite common to have multiple VIP templates per load balancer. Each VIP template is configured with the following settings:

◆ Template name

◆ Template description

◆ Virtual IP port

◆ Template type

    ◆ Generic if intended for all load balancers

    ◆ Specific if intended for a load balancer specific to a manufacturer and model

◆ Protocol

- ◆ HTTP

- ◆ HTTPS passthrough

- ◆ HTTPS terminate

◆ Persistence type

- ◆ Source IP

- ◆ Destination IP

- ◆ SSL Session ID

- ◆ Cookie

- ◆ Custom

◆ Load balancing methods

- ◆ Least connections

- ◆ Fastest response time

- ◆ Round robin

◆ Health monitors

- ◆ Configurable (You can specify protocol, response, interval, timeout, and retries for a request—for example, Get.)

You can define a generic VIP template before adding any load-balancer providers. A generic VIP template is a load-balancer configuration that applies to all load balancers. Of course, if you want to create a specific VIP template, you need to install the specific load-balancer provider with its specific models and methods.

The following procedure creates a VIP template for applications that need load balancing on port 443 using HTTPS:

1. In the VMM console, select Fabric in the workspace, expand Networking, and right-click VIP Templates in the Navigation pane. Click Create VIP Template.

2. Provide a descriptive template name, description, and VIP port for this template. You might want to include part of the load balancer's name for sorting purposes. The description field can be used to add additional information but is not required. Click Next.

3. On the Type screen, because you are creating a VIP template for a specific load balancer, choose Specific and select the appropriate manufacturer and model. Click Next.

4. On the Protocol screen, specify a protocol for the VIP template. If you select HTTPS, you must specify whether to terminate the HTTPS traffic at the load balancer or to pass it through, still encrypted, to the VM. If you select HTTPS Terminate, you also need to specify the Certificate subject name. Click Next.

5. On the Persistence screen (Figure 6.18), you can select Enable Persistence, which means that the load balancer will always try to direct the same client to the same VM that is behind the load balancer. If you enable persistence, you must choose between several persistence types, depending on the load balancer. Different types come with different options. For example, when you choose Source IP, you must specify a subnet mask to apply. Click Next.

FIGURE 6.18
Specifying
persistence

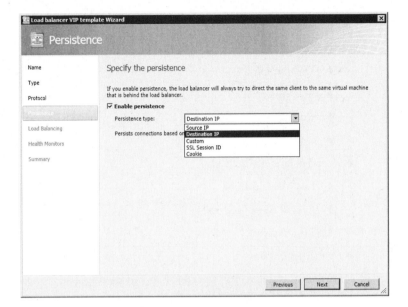

PERSISTENCE

You can set several kinds of persistence for your VIP template. Persistence can be seen as sticky sessions based on conditions supported by your specific load balancer. Not all load balancers support all kinds of persistence. Here are a few types:

Source IP (simple persistence) uses TCP and UDP protocols to direct session requests to the same server based on the source address of a packet.

Destination ID (sticky persistence) uses TCP and UDP protocols to direct session requests to the same server based on the destination IP address of a packet.

SSL Session ID tracks nonterminated SSL sessions using the SSL session ID. Even when IP address changes a persistent session can be kept.

Cookie uses an HTTP cookie stored on the server using the load balancer, which allows the server to reconnect to a website on the same server that was previously visited.

Custom enables you to define persistence on your own terms.

TIP Configuring SSL Termination on your load balancer is useful when you need to configure host header support for your web servers on your back end so you don't need an IP address for every IIS site.

6. On the Load Balancing screen, you can select one of the available load-balancing methods. Click Next.

7. The Health Monitors screen allows you to optionally insert one or more health monitors. Essentially, these are repetitive tests to verify that the load balancer is available. An example is the `Get /.` request, which will execute a `Get` request over HTTPS for the home page of the load balancer and check for a specified header response. Be careful to keep the timeout value below the interval time. Both are measured in seconds. Click Next.

8. The Summary screen allows you to confirm the settings or return to one or more of the previous pages. Click Finish.

Now that you have created a VIP template, you can apply it to one of the service templates in the Service Template Designer (Figure 6.19).

FIGURE 6.19

Using a VIP Template in the Service Template Designer

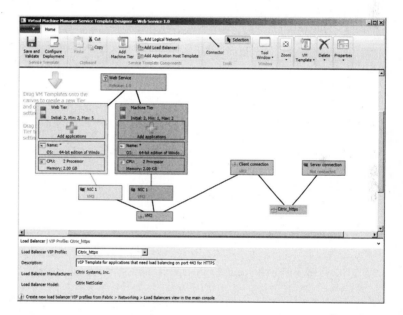

The Self-Service user only has to choose the desired VIP template while deploying a service instance. VMM then uses the correct load-balancer provider and related load-balancer device found within the scope of the host group. It configures the load balancer, creates the VIP, brings up the VMs, attaches them to the proper pool, and enables the VMs used in the service template for load balancing.

Preparing Storage Integration and Automation

Storage is the second of the three major building blocks that make up the private-cloud fabric. In this section, you will learn how to integrate storage arrays from multiple vendors into VMM. After all, when you build a cluster of virtualization hosts, some kind of shared storage will always be part of the solution, whether it is based on iSCSI, fibre channel, or shared SAS. Both hardware- and software-based storage solutions require configuration before your hosts can be clustered.

The biggest storage-related challenge with previous versions of VMM is the lack of visibility beyond the disks and virtual hard disks (VHDs) that Windows and Hyper-V can see. Another challenge is that admins require different tools and consoles to configure storage for their virtualization hosts and clusters.

One way to confront these challenges is to utilize a management standard that looks beyond the products of a single storage vendor. However, if you base your private cloud on VMM 2012, the product should not be built around a proprietary storage stack, nor should it replace the vendor's storage resource–management tools. Given the variety of storage vendors and storage products, Microsoft looked for an industry standard, which they found in SMI-S.

Deep Storage Integration with SMI-S

SMI-S was developed under the auspices of the Storage Networking Industry Association (SNIA) and has been ratified by ANSI. SMI-S defines a method for the interoperable management of a heterogeneous storage-area network (SAN), and describes the information available to a web-based enterprise management (WBEM) client from an SMI-S–compliant common information model (CIM) server and an object-oriented and XML-messaging-based interface to support the specific requirements of managing devices in a SAN.

Although SMI-S v1.0 became an ISO/IEC standard in 2007, many storage vendors continued their own proprietary methods for operating their storage devices. Only a minority of leading storage vendors provided limited support for SMI-S in their devices. This proved to be challenge for Microsoft's intention to apply SMI-S as its standard protocol to communicate with storage devices and fully integrate storage into VMM. Microsoft requests a minimum of the SMI-S provider of version 1.4. On the SNIA web page, you can verify what devices have been tested against this SMI-S version.

At first, SMI-S provided only for identification of the attributes and properties of storage devices. The current version also delivers full discovery and automated configuration of storage devices. For VMM this means you get not only full end-to-end visibility all the way from the VHD to the array controller, but also full configuration of a logical unit (LUN)— provisioning it to a host, partitioning, formatting, and finally using it. Rapid deployment technology for both the physical host and the VM are made possible by this kind of deep storage integration in VMM.

Figure 6.20 depicts the different components in the storage stack that VMM uses based on a combination of WS-Management, WMI, SMI-S, and CIM-XML.

Storage integration in VMM offers the following features:

Discovery   Remote storage is often invisible to non-storage administrators. An important feature, therefore, is being able to discover not only local storage but also shared storage arrays with its storage groups (pools), logical units (LUNs), disks, volumes, and virtual disks.

Resource Mapping   When VMM has discovered all the different storage parts, a VM can be mapped to these specific storage parts. In other words, you can create a full end-to-end map in the VMM console and in PowerShell. Since this overview is dynamic, there is no need to use a spreadsheet to document the storage used by hosts and VMs.

FIGURE 6.20
The VMM storage stack

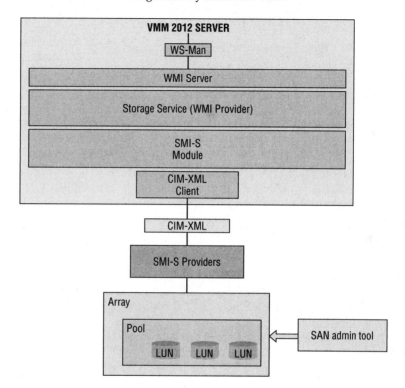

Classification   Your private cloud will have consumers that are unaware of the technical specifications of storage and how they can be used appropriately. Therefore, an easy-to-understand classification model can help the Self-Service user when deploying a VM or a service.

Allocation   Local storage is directly connected to a virtualization host and, therefore, need not be allocated. This is different for shared storage (also referred to as network storage or SAN-based storage). After the VMM service has become aware of this shared storage, it can be allocated to one or more host groups before it can be assigned to a host. Since allocation is a different step from assignment, VMM allows the administrator to allocate storage to a business unit without assigning it to a specific virtualization host or VM.

Assignment   After storage has been allocated to a host group or cloud, private cloud consumers—which can be application owners or administrators—simply look up what storage classifications and capacity is allocated to them and assign it to a Hyper-V host. In traditional IT environments, the process of storage presentation or unmasking is normally done by the storage administrator. In VMM with deep storage integration, assigning storage to a host is fully automated, including the presentation/unmasking part. If the storage is assigned to a Hyper-V cluster, VMM will also create the cluster resources and make them shared across the cluster.

Provisioning   In the previous section, you were dealing with existing storage that was ready to be assigned as new LUNs to a host or cluster. When there is enough capacity available, you might also want to create one or more LUNs and provision them to a host or cluster. There are several ways of provisioning a LUN:

◆ Create new LUN from available storage.

◆ Create a (writeable) snapshot of an existing LUN.

◆ Create a clone of an existing LUN.

Features like snapshotting and cloning often depend on the capabilities of your storage array and are often available as options with additional licenses. Creating a LUN and provisioning it to a host or cluster is basic functionality for all storage arrays.

Decommissioning   When you stop using a host, a VM, or a service, you might want to give back some of the storage to the pool. This process of decommissioning can also be performed by VMM, both via the GUI and via PowerShell.

Storage Classifications

Simplification and abstraction are also relevant to storage. Shared storage arrays are usually considered to be black boxes for everyone but the storage admin. This is why VMM also introduces a simplified model of storage to end users who are creating VMs in a private cloud. In VMM, storage can be classified using a friendly descriptive name.

The storage admin who knows the capabilities of the storage array can create different labels for these different capabilities. They could be as simple as Gold, Silver, and Bronze; but HighIO, MediumIO, and LowIO are descriptive enough (although the latter could easily be too technical for private-cloud consumers). Another example could be HighAvailableStorage and MediumAvailableStorage (LowAvailableStorage would probably be too discouraging to be a serious alternative)—of course, all with the intention to put different price tags to the labels. A self-service user would understand to select Gold, HighIO, and HighAvailableStorage for important enterprise workloads and Bronze, LowIO, and MediumAvailableStorage for testing purposes only.

You can create storage classifications without adding storage arrays to the VMM fabric. Of course, they will not be of much use until a supported array is integrated.

To create Storage Classifications, follow these steps:

1. In the VMM console, click on the Fabric workspace, expand Storage in the Navigation pane, and make sure Fabric Resources is selected in the ribbon.

2. Right-click Classification and Pools and select Create Classification.

3. Enter a name and a description for your storage classification and click Add.

4. Repeat steps 2 and 3 for additional storage classifications.

This is the PowerShell alternative for creating several storage classifications:

```
PS C:\> New-SCStorageClassification -Name "Gold" -Description "Enterprise storage ⏎
(Fibre Channel, 15K, dual-ported, RAID10)" -RunAsynchronously
PS C:\> New-SCStorageClassification -Name "Silver" -Description "Enterprise ⏎
storage (Fibre Channel, 10K, dual-ported, RAID5)" -RunAsynchronously
PS C:\> New-SCStorageClassification -Name "Bronze" -Description "Development ⏎
storage (SATA, 7.2K, dual-ported, RAID5)" -RunAsynchronously
```

When you've finished creating the classifications, you should see something like Figure 6.21. All of the classifications have zero capacity, because no storage arrays have been discovered and integrated into VMM. For the same reason, the number of storage pools is zero.

FIGURE 6.21

Storage classifications

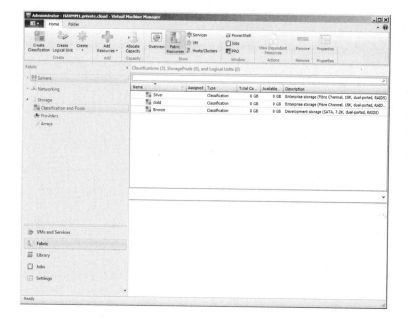

During the discovery of a storage array, you can also create new classifications, as you will see in the next paragraphs.

Discovering Storage Arrays

Your next step is to discover one or more storage arrays. To do that, follow these steps:

1. In the VMM console, go to the Fabric workspace, expand Storage, and select Providers in the Navigation pane while you are in the Fabric Resources view (selectable from the ribbon).

2. Right-click Providers and select Add Storage Devices.

3. On the Specify Discovery Scope screen (Figure 6.22), enter the name of the storage-management server or array controller supporting SMI-S. If you can use SSL as the connection type, you should enter the IP address or FQDN and port 5989. Alternatively, you can use the non-SSL connection in the form of [IP Address | FQDN]:5988. You must also select a suitable Run As account for the storage-management server. It can be created during this step as well. Press Next when you are ready to start the discovery process.

4. After VMM has gathered all the information, it shows you the storage array, its pools (disk groups), manufacturer, model, and capacity on the Gather Information screen. Click Next.

5. On the Select Storage Pools screen (Figure 6.23), select the pools you want to place under VMM management. If you have created storage classifications, you can match the selected

storage pools with your classifications. The assigned classification describes the capabilities of the selected storage pool. Click Create Classification if you want to create a new one. When you are ready, click Next.

FIGURE 6.22
Specifying the discovery scope

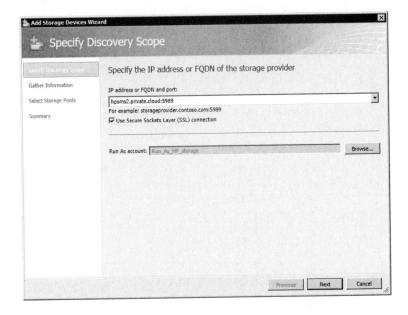

FIGURE 6.23
Assigning classifications to the storage pools

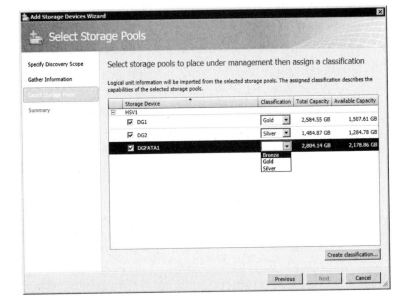

6. On the Summary screen, you can view the storage settings or view the script, which is shown here. Click Finish when you are ready.

```
PS C:\> $array = Get-SCStorageArray -Name "HSV1" | where { $_.ID -eq ↵
"11514140-4997-4893-a243-10ce2ceb3bb5" }
PS C:\> $pools = @()
PS C:\> $pools += Get-SCStoragePool -Name "DG2" | where { $_.ID -eq "81a0bb38- ↵
e0e2-4dc4- 9ce1-93eba03f8ab3" }
PS C:\> $pools += Get-SCStoragePool -Name "DGFATA1" | where { $_.ID -eq ↵
"7915c87c-0c5a- 4871-b6e2-f572cc621bef" }
PS C:\> $pools += Get-SCStoragePool -Name "DG1" | where { $_.ID -eq "0258c221- ↵
e09f-47c3- 9d49-060d48a593f3" }
PS C:\> $classifications = @()
PS C:\> $classifications += Get-SCStorageClassification -Name "Silver"
PS C:\> $classifications += Get-SCStorageClassification -Name "Bronze"
PS C:\> $classifications += Get-SCStorageClassification -Name "Gold"
PS C:\> Set-SCStorageArray -StorageArray $array -AddStoragePoolToManagement ↵
$pools - StorageClassificationAssociation $classifications -RunAsynchronously
```

You can find the array in PowerShell by using the following commands:

```
PS C:\> $arr=Get-SCStorageArray
PS C:\> $arr


ObjectId                            : root/eva:sHPSMS2.PRIVATE.CLOUD:5989;HPEVA_
                                      StorageSystem.CreationClassName=%'HPEVA_Storag
                                      eSystem%',Name=%'50001FE15003E8C0%'
SMDisplayName                       : HSV1
SMName                              : 50001FE15003E8C0
SMNameFormat                        : WWN
ManagementServer                    : HTTPS://HPSMS2.PRIVATE.CLOUD:5989
HardwareIDFlags                     : SupportsPortWWN
MaskingFlags                        : SupportsMasking
ReplicationFlags                    : SupportsMirrorLocal, SupportsSnapshotLocal,
                                      SupportsCloneLocal
ConfigurationFlags                  : SupportsStorageLogicalUnitCreation,
                                      SupportsStorageLogicalUnitDeletion,
                                      SupportsStorageLogicalUnitModification,
                                      SupportsStorageLogicalUnitCapacityExpansion,
                                      SupportsStorageLogicalUnitCapacityReduction
MaskingMaximumMapCount              : 0
MaximumReplicasPerSourceClone       : 1
MaximumReplicasPerSourceMirror      : 0
MaximumReplicasPerSourceSnapshot    : 7
MaskingOneHardwareIDPerView         : False
MaskingPortsPerView                 : AllPortsShareTheSameView
FirmwareVersion                     :
Manufacturer                        : Hewlett-Packard
Model                               : HSV100
```

```
SerialNumber              : P66C5E2AAQV01G, P66C5E2AAQU00U
Tag                       : 50001FE15003E8C0
LogicalUnitCopyMethod     : Snapshot
StorageProvider           : hpsms2.private.cloud:5989
StoragePools              : {DG1, DG2, DGFATA1}
StorageEndpoints          : {50001FE15003E8C0.P66C5E2AAQU00U.hostport1,
                             50001FE15003E8C0.P66C5E2AAQV01G.hostport1,
                             50001FE15003E8C0.P66C5E2AAQU00U.hostport2,
                             50001FE15003E8C0.P66C5E2AAQV01G.hostport2}
StorageInitiators         : {210000E08B826931, 50060B0000C2621C,
                             50060B0000C2621A, 210100E08BB27058...}
StorageiSCSIPortals       : {}
StorageGroups             : {01800710B40805603A2510000080000000005401,
                             03800710B40805603A2510000080000000009401,
                             02800710B40805603A25100000800000000000B001,
                             0C800710B40805603A2510000080000000005601}
TotalCapacity             : 7380428851772
RemainingCapacity         : 5337839042558
InUseCapacity             : 2042589809214
IsCloneCapable            : True
IsSnapshotCapable         : True
IsSanTransferCapable      : True
CreateStorageGroupsPerCluster : False
TotalAllocatedCapacity    : 1327144894464
ObjectType                : StorageArray
Accessibility             : Public
Name                      : HSV1
IsViewOnly                : False
Description               : HSV1
AddedTime                 : 12/28/2011 2:00:10 PM
ModifiedTime              : 12/28/2011 2:16:39 PM
Enabled                   : True
MostRecentTask            :
ServerConnection          : Microsoft.SystemCenter.VirtualMachineManager.
                             Remoting.ServerConnection
ID                        : 11514140-4997-4893-a243-10ce2ceb3bb5
MarkedForDeletion         : False
IsFullyCached             : False
```

As you can see, a lot of information about the storage array is available, including its manufacturer ($arr.Manufacturer), name ($arr.Name), model ($arr.Model), management server ($arr.ManagementServer), supported functions ($arr.ConfigurationFlags), storage pools ($arr.StoragePools), total capacity ($arr.TotalCapacity), and remaining capacity ($arr.RemainingCapacity).

To demonstrate how storage from multiple storage arrays can be used in a standardized way, let's add another storage device.

In Figure 6.24, a list of storage providers specifies the name, management address, status, last refresh time, and credentials used for each device. To view this list, select Fabric, expand Storage, and select Providers while viewing the Fabric Resources.

FIGURE 6.24
List of storage
providers

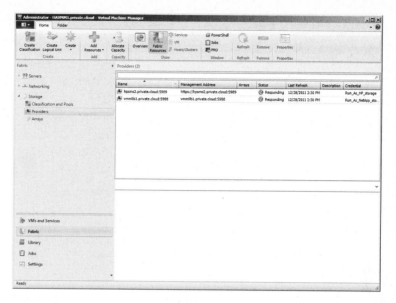

You can view managed storage arrays in the same view by clicking Arrays. The Information pane lists the arrays with their name, total capacity, used capacity, pools, provider name, and status. If you select an array in the list, more information about it (such as the number of LUNs provisioned, assigned and unassigned) appears at the bottom of the screen (Figure 6.25).

FIGURE 6.25
Viewing the array
details

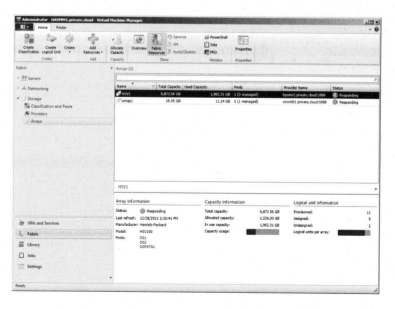

In the ribbon, switch the view from Fabric Resources to Overview to obtain a storage overview with details about used, total, and available storage—including classification use and LUNs per array, as shown in Figure 6.26.

FIGURE 6.26
Overview
of storage use

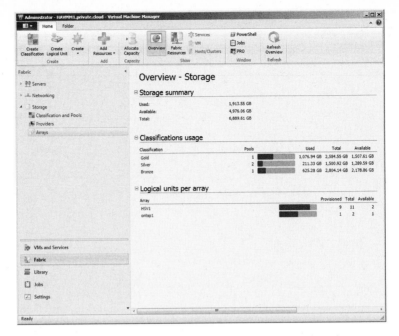

From this overview, you can access shortcuts to classifications and arrays. If you click the Gold classification, for instance, you'll get a detailed view of the storage groups and LUNs classified as Gold (Figure 6.27). To get a better view, you can collapse the Navigation pane by pressing the left-arrow button (←). If you type the name of your pool or LUN, you will see only those logical units.

FIGURE 6.27
Viewing storage
by classification

Creating Logical Units

You can choose to first create one or more LUNs and then allocate storage capacity to a host group or vice versa. You can also leave the creation of LUNs in the hands of the storage admin and allocate only the provisioned storage capacity to host groups. Storage capacity is also assigned to the cloud via the host group.

To create a logical unit, follow these steps:

1. In the VMM console, go to the Fabric workspace, expand Storage, and select Classifications and Pools in the Navigation pane while you are in the Fabric Resources view (selectable from the ribbon).

2. Right-click Classifications and Pools and select Create Logical Unit.

3. On the Create Logical Unit screen, select one of the available storage pools, provide a name, enter an optional description, and designate a size in GB. Press OK when you are ready.

Removing Logical Units

While a logical unit is still unassigned, you can remove the LUN via the following the steps:

1. In the VMM console, go to the Fabric workspace, expand Storage, and select Classifications and Pools in the Navigation pane while you are in the Fabric Resources view (selectable from the ribbon).

2. Expand the pool that contains the logical unit to be removed.

3. Right-click the logical unit and select Remove, as in Figure 6.28. VMM warns you that this action deletes the logical unit and permanently deletes the storage on the logical unit. Press OK when you want to delete the LUN.

FIGURE 6.28
Removing a logical unit

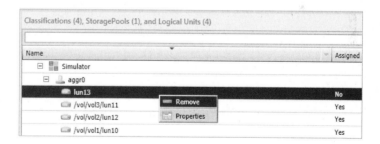

Allocating Storage Pools and Logical Units

After your arrays have been discovered, your storage pools have been classified, and one or more logical units have been created, you are ready to allocate those storage pools and logical units to host groups. Only after these steps can you make disks available to Hyper-V hosts and clusters. To do that, follow these steps:

1. In the VMM console, go to the Fabric workspace, expand Storage, and select Classifications and Pools in the Navigation pane while you are in the Fabric Resources view (selectable from the ribbon).

2. Click Allocate Capacity on the ribbon.

3. On the Allocate Storage Capacity screen, select the intended host group, as shown in Figure 6.29.

FIGURE 6.29

Selecting a host group for storage allocation

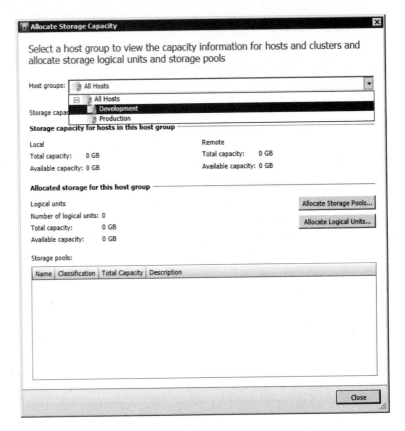

4. Click Allocate Storage Pools. On the Allocate Storage Pools screen (Figure 6.30), select one of the available storage pools and click Add. The storage pool moves from available storage pools to allocated storage pools.

5. If necessary, repeat step 4 to add other storage pools. If you want to remove a storage pool, just select it and click Remove. Click OK when you are finished.

6. On the Allocate Logical Units screen, click Allocate Logical Units to add unassigned LUNs. Click Remove to deallocate LUNs from the host group.

7. Select a logical unit and click Add (Figure 6.31), then click OK when you are finished.

FIGURE 6.30
Allocating the
storage pools

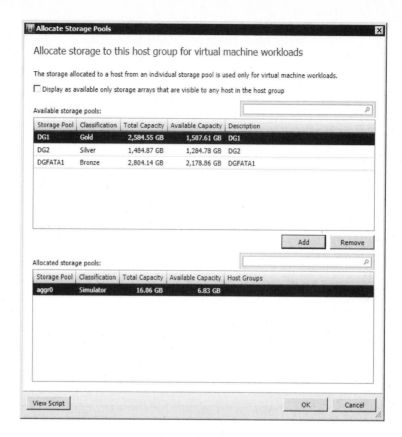

Assigning Storage on a Hyper-V Host

Before you can assign a logical unit to a Hyper-V host, certain prerequisites must be met. Consider the following:

◆ One or more storage arrays should be discovered and classified in VMM.

◆ One or more logical units should be created in VMM, or outside of VMM with the storage vendor's storage-management tool.

◆ One or more storage pools and logical units should be allocated to the host group that contains the Hyper-V host.

◆ Multi-Path IO (MPIO) should be configured on the Hyper-V host and, if available, the vendor-specific device-specific module (DSM) must be installed.

◆ If you are using a Fibre Channel SAN, the Hyper-V host must have connectivity to the array (zoning).

◆ If you are using an iSCSI SAN, there should be a configured iSCSI portal on the Hyper-V host. The iSCSI Initiator service should be started and set to Automatic.

FIGURE 6.31

Adding logical units

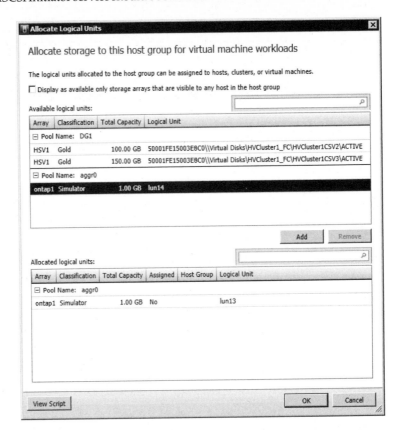

CONFIGURING A SINGLE STORAGE GROUP FOR A HYPER-V CLUSTER

VMM creates one storage group per host and one storage group per cluster node. A storage group can contain one or more of the host's initiator IDs. For iSCSI these are called iSCSI Qualified Name (IQN), and for Fibre Channel these are the World Wide Name (WWN).

For certain storage arrays, only one storage group is preferred for the entire cluster so that all host initiators for all nodes are placed in the same storage group. A single storage group is defined as an object binding multiple related host initiators, target ports, and logical units. In fact, the target ports are used to expose logical units to the host initiators. To configure a single storage group, start a PowerShell screen and enter the following command to find the current state, which should be False by default.

```
PS C:\> $arr = Get-SCStorageArray | where {$_.SMDisplayname -like "ontap1" }
PS C:\> $arr.CreateStorageGroupsPerCluster
False
```

To set the value for `CreateStorageGroupsPerCluster` to True, enter the following PowerShell command:

```
PS C:\> Set-SCStorageArray -StorageArray $arr -CreateStorageGroupsPerCluster $true
```

ADDING AN iSCSI ARRAY TO A HYPER-V HOST

Before you can assign logical disks to a Hyper-V host via iSCSI, you need to configure the iSCSI array in the Storage properties of a Hyper-V host. The Hyper-V host should have its iSCSI portals configured.

1. Go to the Fabric workspace, expand Servers, and expand the host group for the Hyper-V host you are going to configure.

2. Right-click the Hyper-V host, select Properties, and click the Storage tab.

3. If the server can see an iSCSI array, the Add button is enabled (not grayed out).

4. Click Add. On the Create New iSCSI Session screen (Figure 6.32), select the array. You may optionally use advanced settings to select a target portal, target name, and initiator IP.

FIGURE 6.32

Adding an iSCSI array

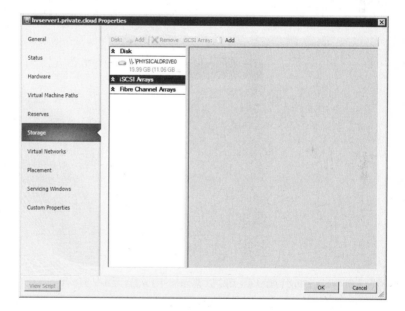

5. Click Create, and then click OK when you are finished

The resulting PowerShell script looks like this:

```
PS C:\> $vmHost = Get-SCVMHost -ComputerName "hvserver1" | where { $_.ID -eq ↪
"b778f655- b014-4a6c-9451-429a3b848f41" }
PS C:\> $iSCSIHba = $vmHost.InternetSCSIHbas | where { $_.ID -eq "9aa491c2-cdcd- ↪
40a3- b590-4c08de6e7817" }
```

```
PS C:\> $array = Get-SCStorageArray -Name "ontap1" | where { $_.ID -eq "8f5a9a4a- ↵
e3a3- 413f-bb14-a3f45e0a9967" }
PS C:\> $targetPortal = $array.StorageiSCSIPortals | where { $_.ID -eq "24871c45- ↵
9def- 4dbe-b6a9-63f453397dd9" -and $_.IPv4Address -eq "172.16.1.10" }
PS C:\> $selectedEndPoint = $targetPortal.StorageEndpoints | where { $_.ID -eq ↵
"434a5ac3- 7337-4a77-b28a-a75153ad1456" -and $_.Name -eq "iqn.1992-08.com.
netapp:sn.99927627,t,0x03E8" }
PS C:\> Set-InternetSCSIHba -InternetSCSIHba $iSCSIHba -TargetPortal ↵
$targetPortal - TargetName $selectedEndPoint -CreateSession -InitiatorIP
"172.16.1.53"
```

When you open the Storage tab on the Hyper-V host's properties again, you will see that an iSCSI session has been created and the configured iSCSI array can be found under iSCSI Arrays, as shown in Figure 6.33.

FIGURE 6.33
Establishing a session with an iSCSI array

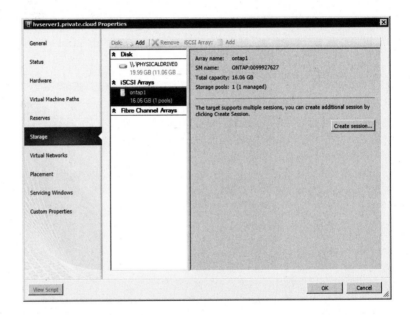

ADDING A DISK FROM AN iSCSI ARRAY TO A HYPER-V HOST

Now that the Hyper-V host can see the iSCSI storage array, you can add one or more disks using the Add button, which is now available.

To add an existing disk, follow these steps:

1. Open the Storage tab of the Hyper-V host properties and click Add (near the word Disk).

2. Select one of the existing logical units. You can also create a new logical unit by clicking Create Logical Unit.

3. Several options are available to partition, format, and label the disk (Figure 6.34). The disk can be mounted with an available drive letter, can be mounted in an empty NTFS folder, or can be left without a drive letter or drive path. This last option is suitable for cluster shared volumes (CSVs).

FIGURE 6.34
Adding a disk

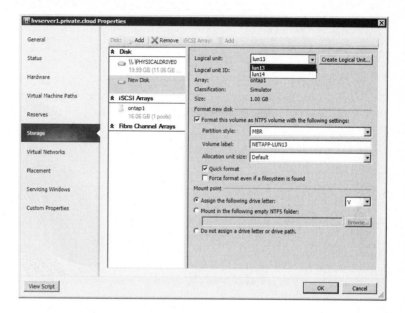

4. View the PowerShell script if you like, and click OK when you are finished.

The resulting PowerShell script looks like this:

```
PS C:\> $vmHost = Get-SCVMHost -ID "b778f655-b014-4a6c-9451-429a3b848f41" ⊃
-ComputerName "hvserver1"

PS C:\> $logicalUnits = @ ()
PS C:\> $logicalUnits += Get-SCStorageLogicalUnit -ID "b0af0c9c-703d-4bcd-9f39- ⊃
d012dcee139b" -Name "lun13"
PS C:\> Register-SCStorageLogicalUnit -StorageLogicalUnit $logicalUnits -VMHost ⊃
$vmHost - JobGroup "17a2e45d-dc96-4fbb-aeea-f5414f748f0a"
PS C:\> $lun = Get-SCStorageLogicalUnit -ID "b0af0c9c-703d-4bcd-9f39- ⊃
d012dcee139b" -Name "lun13"
PS C:\> Mount-SCStorageDisk -MasterBootRecord -QuickFormat -VolumeLabel "NETAPP- ⊃
LUN13" - StorageLogicalUnit $lun -JobGroup "17a2e45d-dc96-4fbb-aeea-f5414f748f0a"
-MountPoint "V:\"

PS C:\> Set-SCVMHost -VMHost $vmHost -JobGroup "17a2e45d-dc96-4fbb-aeea- ⊃
f5414f748f0a" - RunAsynchronously
```

To see if the task completed successfully, click Jobs in the Workspace pane.

You can also go back to the Storage tab in the properties of the Hyper-V host to see if the new logical disk has been added, partitioned, formatted, labeled, and mounted (Figure 6.35).

FIGURE 6.35
Checking for job completion

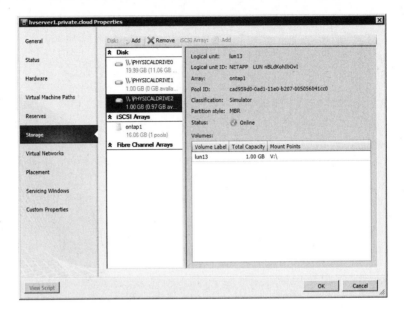

End-to-End Storage Mapping

VMM uses SMI-S as a storage standard to add supported storage arrays and extend your view of storage in VMM, all the way from the VM to the storage array. The best way to see this in action is to use PowerShell to get all the intermediate steps between the VHD of a VM to the logical disk on a storage array.

First, take a look at the properties of the VMM server, assuming you are already connected.

```
# SELECT VMM CLUSTERNAME
PS C:\> $vmmserver = Get-VMMserver "havmm1.private.cloud"

# DISPLAY PROPERTIES OF SELECTED VMM SERVER
PS C:\> $vmmserver
Name                        : havmm1.private.cloud
Port                        : 8100
IsConnected                 : True
ServerInterfaceVersion      : 2.1.0
Profile                     : Administrator
UserRole                    : Administrator
UserRoleId                  : 75700cd5-893e-4f68-ada7-50ef4668acc6
FullyQualifiedDomainName    : havmm1.private.cloud
FQDN                        : havmm1.private.cloud
[shortened]
```

Next, focus on a particular VM called `dc3.private.cloud`. To find everything that is related to storage, run this code:

```
# GET VIRTUAL MACHINE IN PRIVATE CLOUD WHERE NAME OF THE VM IS DC3
PS C:\> $vm = Get-SCVirtualMachine | where {$_.Name -eq "dc3"}) | fl Name, ↵
Location, VirtualMachineState, VirtualDiskDrives, VMHost


Name                 : DC3
Location             : C:\ClusterStorage\Volume1\DC3
VirtualMachineState  : Running
VirtualDiskDrives    : {DC3}
VMHost               : hv1.private.cloud


# MAP FROM VIRTUAL MACHINE TO DISK DRIVE
PS C:\> $vm.VirtualDiskDrives | fl VirtualHardDisk, BusType, Bus, LUN, ObjectType


VirtualHardDisk : W2K8R2SP1_v2_disk_1.vhd
BusType         : IDE
Bus             : 0
LUN             : 0
ObjectType      : VirtualDiskDrive


# MAP FROM VIRTUAL DISK DRIVE TO VIRTUAL HARD DISK
PS C:\> $vm.VirtualDiskDrives[0].VirtualHardDisk | fl Location, HostVolume, VMHost


Location    : C:\ClusterStorage\Volume1\DC3\W2K8R2SP1_v2_disk_1.vhd
HostVolume  : C:\ClusterStorage\Volume1
VMHost      : hv1.private.cloud


# MAP VIRTUAL HARD DISK TO HOST VOLUME
PS C:\> $vm.VirtualDiskDrives[0].VirtualHardDisk.HostVolume | fl MountPoints, ↵
HostDisk, VMHost


MountPoints : {C:\ClusterStorage\Volume1}
HostDisk    : \\.\PHYSICALDRIVE2
VMHost      : hv1.private.cloud


# MAP HOST VOLUME TO HOST DISK
PS C:\> $vm.VirtualDiskDrives[0].VirtualHardDisk.HostVolume.HostDisk | fl ↵
DeviceID, UniqueID, SMLunId, StorageLogicalUnit, VMHost


DeviceID           : \\.\PHYSICALDRIVE2
UniqueID           : 1824538386
SMLunId            : 600508B40010253A00008000026D0000
StorageLogicalUnit : 50001FE15003E8C0\\Virtual Disks\HVCluster1_FC\
HVCluster1CSV1\ACTIVE
```

```
VMHost              : hv1.private.cloud


# MAP HOST DISK TO STORAGE LOGICAL UNIT
PS C:\> $vm.VirtualDiskDrives[0].VirtualHardDisk.HostVolume.HostDisk. ↵
StorageLogicalUnit | fl Name, CopyType, SourceLogicalUnit, StoragePool

Name                : 50001FE15003E8C0\\Virtual Disks\HVCluster1_FC\HVCluster1CSV1\
ACTIVE
CopyType          :
SourceLogicalUnit :
StoragePool       : DG1


# MAP STORAGE LOGICAL UNIT TO STORAGE POOL
PS C:\> $vm.VirtualDiskDrives[0].VirtualHardDisk.HostVolume.HostDisk. ↵
StorageLogicalUnit. StoragePool | fl Name, RemainingManagedSpace,
TotalManagedSpace, StorageArray

Name                  : DG1
RemainingManagedSpace : 1618783911280
TotalManagedSpace     : 2775139431219
StorageArray          : HSV1


# MAP STORAGE POOL TO STORAGE ARRAY
PS C:\> $vm.VirtualDiskDrives[0].VirtualHardDisk.HostVolume.HostDisk. ↵
StorageLogicalUnit. StoragePool.StorageArray | fl Name, TotalCapacity,
RemainingCapacity, IsCloneCapable, IsSnapshotCapable, StorageProvider

Name              : HSV1
TotalCapacity     : 7380428851772
RemainingCapacity : 5337839042558
IsCloneCapable    : True
IsSnapshotCapable : True
StorageProvider   : hpsms2.private.cloud:5989


# MAP STORAGE ARRAY TO STORAGE PROVIDER
PS C:\> $vm.VirtualDiskDrives[0].VirtualHardDisk.HostVolume.HostDisk. ↵
StorageLogicalUnit. StoragePool.StorageArray.StorageProvider | fl Name,
NetworkAddress, TCPPort, StorageArrays

Name           : hpsms2.private.cloud:5989
NetworkAddress : https://hpsms2.private.cloud
TCPPort        : 5989
StorageArrays  : {HSV1}
```

As you can see, integrating storage with SMI-S is very powerful and can give you a wealth of insight, all the way from the VHD in the VM to the array. Finally, virtual storage and physical storage don't have to be treated as distinct entities. End-to-end mapping will help you, as an administrator, troubleshoot issues that are related to the storage stack. The standardized approach of employing SMI-S will help you use identical procedures for storage arrays from different vendors. Provisioning storage to your private clouds with VMM can really help you in your job as a fabric administrator.

Storage Without SMI-S Support

Not all storage has SMI-S support. Does that mean this kind of storage has become useless? No, absolutely not! Local storage does not need SMI-S support because SMI-S is intended for network storage. Local storage is well understood by VMM out of the box.

If you have to deal with storage arrays without SMI-S support, you can still provision LUNs via the management tools offered by your SAN provider. SMI-S does not replace these tools but merely offers a standardized method of talking to a variety of storage arrays from different vendors. The procedure for managing storage with non–SMI-S-supported storage arrays is to create storage pools and LUNs outside VMM, present these LUNs to the servers (in the cluster), and let VMM do the rest. All VMM has to see is one or more raw disks. As soon as you have access to those disks, you can format the volume and convert them into CSVs in the case of Hyper-V clusters.

Of course, if you are looking for a new storage array or if you are replacing your existing storage array, SMI-S support with the minimum version that VMM expects (SMI-S v1.4 or higher) is highly recommended.

Summary

Networking and storage are two of the three important ingredients for building a fabric for your private clouds. If you administer one private cloud, you can dedicate all network and storage fabric components to that single cloud. If you host multiple clouds for different departments, subsidiaries, or external customers, the fabric is shared across multiple clouds. Fabric can be treated as a collection of devices that offer capacity that can grow and shrink as devices are added, removed, or replaced. The important part is that fabric in VMM 2012 is treated as a building block that is fully abstracted from the Self-Service user. The Self-Service user sees only meaningful names that represent physical devices and capacity. The fabric administrator has to take care of all the rest.

Networking and storage themselves can be considered as building blocks for servers or *compute resources*, as they are sometimes called. The next chapter shows how a heterogeneous set of virtualization hosts (Hyper-V, vSphere, and XenServer) can be integrated into a unified management platform for a private cloud that allows independent services (with applications) to run irrespective of the underlying fabric.

## Chapter 7

Deploying Hosts and Clusters in VMM 2012

Chapter 4, "Setting Up and Deploying VMM 2012," introduced Hyper-V hosts. This chapter provides more details about adding and managing Hyper-V hosts, and it explains how to use VMM to create a cluster from Hyper-V servers deployed on bare-metal machines. It shows how to add servers to trusted domains, untrusted domains, and workgroups. It explains how to work with VMware and Citrix virtualization servers in VMM and how to maintain and update Hyper-V clusters.

The chapter includes the following topics:

◆ Deploying Hyper-V clusters on bare-metal

◆ Using dynamic optimization, power optimization, and cluster remediation to keep your Hyper-V clusters healthy, efficient, and up-to-date

◆ Using VMM 2012's improved integration with VMware to deploy and manage ESX/ESXi hosts and clusters

◆ Deploying and managing XenServer hosts and clusters

Adding Existing Hyper-V Servers and Clusters

A new VMM installation has a single, empty host group called All Hosts. Chapter 4 explained how to create host groups and add Hyper-V hosts to them.

You can add an existing Hyper-V server to the VMM-managed fabric using the following methods, all of which install a VMM agent on the server:

◆ Using Windows Server computers in a trusted Active Directory domain

◆ Using Windows computers in an untrusted Active Directory domain

◆ Using Windows Server computers in a perimeter network

The remainder of this section describes these options. A subsequent section describes another option:

◆ Using physical computers provisioned as virtual-machine hosts

This option adds a bare-metal computer with Windows Server 2008 R2 SP1 automatically deployed, including the Hyper-V role. In the Add Resource Wizard, it is the fourth Windows computer location option.

Adding a Hyper-V Server in a Trusted Domain

The large majority of servers that you add to VMM are Hyper-V servers that are members of the same domain as the VMM server or a domain that is trusted by the domain containing the VMM server. Before you can add Hyper-V servers that are located in a trusted domain, the following steps must be taken:

◆ Have one or more servers available that are joined to the same domain, or trusted by the domain that contains the VMM server.

◆ Check the requirements for supported versions of Hyper-V virtual-machine hosts (see Chapter 4).

◆ Check network access to the Hyper-V hosts that are added.

◆ Validate Hyper-V clusters before you add them to VMM (although you can do this from VMM later).

Do not add a Windows server without Hyper-V if the server is not available for a reboot (see the "Adding New Hyper-V Servers" section). To add one or more Hyper-V servers or clusters to the fabric of your VMM environment, follow these steps:

1. In the VMM console, select Fabric, and choose Servers from the Navigation pane. Select Fabric Resources from the ribbon, click Add Resources, and select Hyper-V Hosts and Clusters (Figure 7.1).

FIGURE 7.1
Adding a host or cluster in a trusted domain

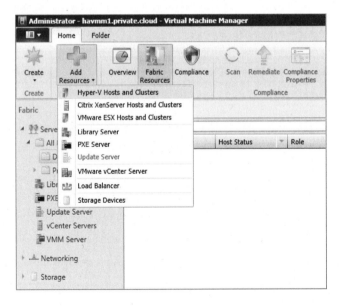

2. In the Add Resource Wizard in the Resource Location tab, choose Windows Server Computers In A Trusted Active Directory Domain. Click Next.

3. On the Credentials tab, enter the appropriate credentials to discover and add a Hyper-V host or cluster or, alternatively, select a Run As account. These credentials will allow you to add the VMM service account to the local Administrators group on the Hyper-V hosts. Click Next.

4. On the Discovery Scope tab, specify one or more Hyper-V servers and clusters. Each server or cluster must be on a separate line. You can identify the hosts by their name, their FQDN, their IPv4 address, or their IPv6 address. By default, the discovery process uses Active Directory (AD), but you can avoid this by checking the Skip AD Verification box. When you have finished your list, click Next.

If you have hundreds of servers, you might not want to specify the hosts for discovery by name; you can specify an Active Directory query to search for the Windows Server computers.

For example, you could search for hosts and clusters that start with the letters *hv* (**hv***) (as shown in Figure 7.2) or that contain the letters *hv* (***hv***).

FIGURE 7.2
Using an AD query
to discover hosts

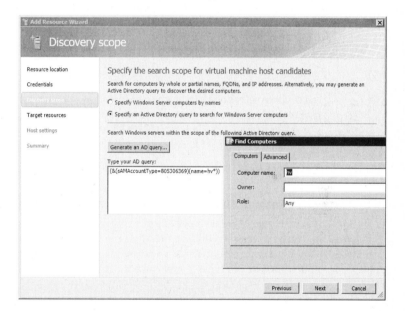

5. The Add Resource Wizard will generate a list of discovered computers; it is up to you to select which computers you want to add as hosts. The wizard will specify the FQDNs of the hosts, the clusters they are in, the OS, and the discovered hypervisor (in this case Hyper-V). As you can see in Figure 7.3, you can discover and add Hyper-V servers in the same step. Click Next.

FIGURE 7.3
Selecting hosts to
be added

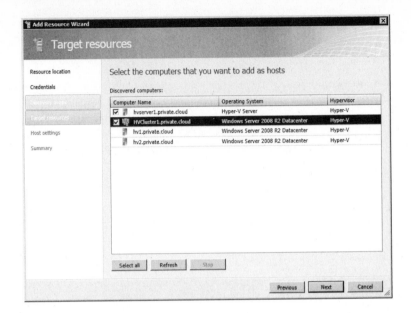

6. On the Host Settings tab, you can specify the host group and VM placement settings. All of these selections can be changed later, so you can ignore most of the other fields. Interestingly, if you want to add a host previously managed by another VMM server, you can select Reassociate This Host With This VMM Environment. This could save some time because the VMM agent might still be installed. When you are done, click Next.

7. When you are satisfied with the results shown on the Summary tab, click Finish.

Adding a Hyper-V Server in an Untrusted Domain

Some of your Hyper-V servers and clusters may be part of an untrusted AD domain. An example of this type of setup would be a hosting provider managing a customer's Hyper-V hosts from their own management domain without trusting the customer's domains.

To set up this type of Hyper-V host, take the following steps to integrate the hosts and clusters:

1. In the VMM console, select Fabric, and choose Servers from the Navigation pane. Right-click the host group to which you want to add the hosts or clusters; or select Fabric Resources from the ribbon, click Add Resources, and select Hyper-V Hosts and Clusters.

2. In the Add Resource Wizard in the Resource Location tab, choose Windows Server Computers In An Untrusted Active Directory Domain. Click Next.

3. On the Credentials tab, specify the appropriate credentials to discover the host in the untrusted AD domain. If the Run As account does not exist yet, you can create one. Select a suitable Run As account, and click Next.

4. Enter the FQDN or IP address of the Hyper-V host in the untrusted domain, and click Add. When you are done adding hosts, click Next.

5. Choose a host group and click Next.

6. Confirm the summary and click Finish. After a minute or so, you will see the Hyper-V in an untrusted AD domain in your Hosts view, as shown in Figure 7.4.

FIGURE 7.4
The Hosts view

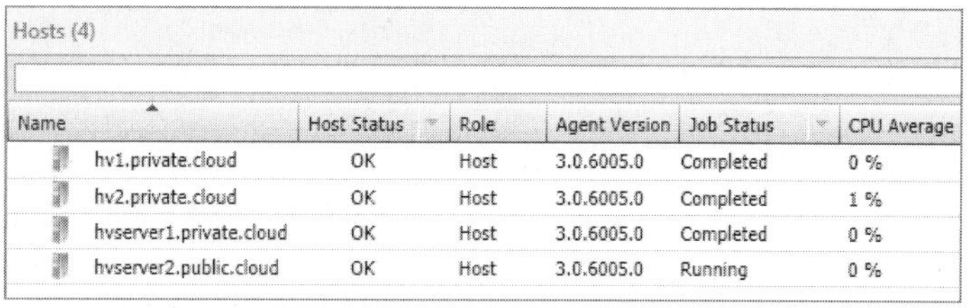

Hosts (4)

Name		Host Status	Role	Agent Version	Job Status	CPU Average
	hv1.private.cloud	OK	Host	3.0.6005.0	Completed	0 %
	hv2.private.cloud	OK	Host	3.0.6005.0	Completed	1 %
	hvserver1.private.cloud	OK	Host	3.0.6005.0	Completed	0 %
	hvserver2.public.cloud	OK	Host	3.0.6005.0	Running	0 %

Adding a Hyper-V Server in a Perimeter Network

You can add a Hyper-V server that is configured to be in a workgroup and is unrelated to any AD domain. Often such Hyper-V hosts are in a perimeter network or DMZ. For this category, an encryption key or a CA-signed certificate is required to authenticate the Hyper-V server from the perimeter network before VMM will accept it.

A non-enterprise scenario for this type of setup is a demo laptop with Windows Server 2008 R2 SP1 plus Hyper-V in a workgroup and several Hyper-V guests, including a domain controller and VMM running on the same laptop. Before you can add the Hyper-V host, you must install the VMM agent locally from VMM media and provide an encryption key. VMM requests this key when you add a Hyper-V Server in a perimeter network. An alternative is to provide a CA-signed certificate.

To add a Hyper-V server in a perimeter network, follow these steps:

1. From the VMM media, run `setup.exe`.

2. Click Local Agent at the bottom of the VMM Install screen under Optional Installations.

3. Click Next on the Welcome screen.

4. Accept the Microsoft Software Notice Terms and click Next.

5. Accept or change the default destination folder of the VMM Agent installation and click Next.

6. Check the box for This Host Is On A Perimeter Network and provide a random file encryption key. By default, it is saved in the root of the VMM Agent installation. You can optionally use a CA certificate for encrypting communications with this host. In this case, you must provide the thumbprint of the certificate (Figure 7.5). Click Next.

7. Choose how VMM contacts this host: either use the local computer name or use its IP address. Click Next.

8. Accept or change the VMM Agent ports used to communicate with the VMM server. By default, VMM Manager uses port 5986 for communications with the virtualization host. VMM uses port 443 to transfer files between VMM and host computers. Click Next to continue.

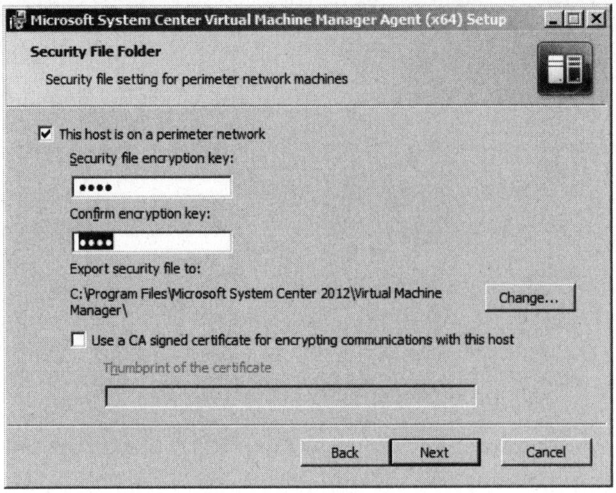

FIGURE 7.5
Specifying the
security file folder

9. If you are ready, click Install to start the installation.

10. Click Finish to complete the local-agent installation.

On the VMM Manager server, you can directly add a Windows server. A reboot of the perimeter host is not necessary. These are the steps:

1. In the VMM console, select Fabric, and choose Servers from the Navigation pane. Either right-click the host group to which you want to add the hosts or clusters or, alternatively, select Fabric Resources from the ribbon and click Add Resources and select Hyper-V Hosts And Clusters.

2. In the Add Resource Wizard in the Resource Location tab, choose Windows Server Computers In A Perimeter Network and click Next.

3. On the Target Resources tab of the Add Resource Wizard, enter the name of the computer, add the encryption key, and provide the path of the security file. You can optionally select the host group to which the perimeter host is added. Click Add.

4. After clicking Add, you can add more Hyper-V perimeter hosts or click Next to continue.

5. Optionally, add one or more virtual-machine paths or use the defaults. Click Next.

6. When you are happy with the results, click Finish.

7. In a short while, your new perimeter Hyper-V hosts will appear in the host groups you selected. You can recognize the hosts easily because they don't have fully qualified domain names. If you had chosen to add perimeter hosts with their IP addresses, you would not have seen the host names.

8. If you right-click a host after it has been refreshed, you can check a large number of properties; just walk down the different tabs. The Status tab should give you an idea about how successful the addition of a host has been (Figure 7.6).

FIGURE 7.6
Checking the host status

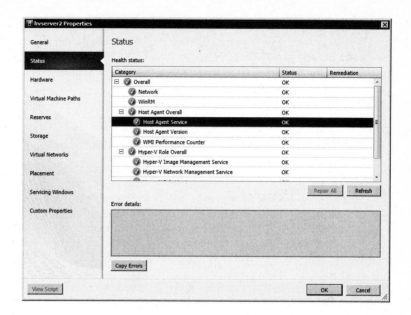

In the Hosts view of one of your host groups, you can add additional fields by right-clicking one of the headers. Check one or more fields and they show up in the current view. The Group By This Column option is at the bottom; this option gives you a great deal of flexibility in the way hosts can be viewed. Figure 7.7 shows an example of the Managed Computers view.

FIGURE 7.7
Group view of managed computers

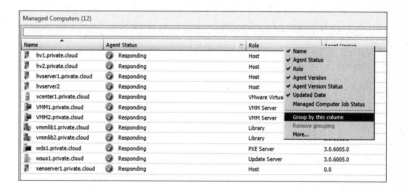

NOTE   For service deployment, a two-way trust is required between the VMM server and the VM guest OS. The domain membership of the Hyper-V host should not impact service and application deployment. That said, a service can be tiered across different hypervisors without any limitations, as long as that two-way trust is maintained.

Adding New Hyper-V Servers

If you want to use a Windows 2008 or 2008 R2 server that doesn't have the Hyper-V role enabled, you can still use all of the previous choices. The Add Resource Wizard enables the Hyper-V role for you; but the server is restarted at least once, so be careful if this server carries production workloads. Of course, according to best practices, a Hyper-V server should be fully dedicated to this role and you should add only servers without other duties.

Adding New Hyper-V Servers with Bare-Metal Deployment

If you have only a few Hyper-V hosts, you don't really need to learn bare-metal deployment. You will probably be able to provision five Hyper-V hosts much faster than you will be able to set up the prerequisites and successfully test a bare-metal deployment with VMM. Nevertheless, if you are just curious about the technology or if your organization expects you to rapidly expand the number of Hyper-V hosts, then bare-metal deployment is for you.

So how does bare-metal deployment work in VMM? First, a number of prerequisites need to be met before you can actually start deploying your first Hyper-V host without ever touching the server. It is always nice to do some work up front and then let the system do all the work for you. You may finally get an opportunity to read your RSS feeds.

Prerequisites

You can find the prerequisites for bare-metal deployment in Chapter 4, but a shortened version of them is given here. Before you can launch a bare-metal deployment, you'll need the following:

◆ A Windows Server 2008 R2 SP1 server with Windows Deployment Services (WDS) serving as a PXE server. There is an alternative route if you cannot implement a PXE server in your environment.

◆ A DHCP server.

◆ Physical hosts that support Hyper-V and include a baseboard management controller (BMC) supporting IPMI, DCMI, or SMASH. In earlier versions, a custom provider route was offered; however, you should use the standard protocols first. Also, be careful to update the firmware to a version that supports one of the required protocols. Examples of supported BMCs include:

   ◆ HP: Integrated Lights Out (iLO)

   ◆ Dell: Dell Remote Access Controller (DRAC)

   ◆ IBM: Remote Supervisor Board (RSB)

◆ A Windows Server 2008 R2 operating-system image.

Bare-Metal Deployment Steps

You'll need to complete quite a few steps for a successful bare-metal deployment. As with most tasks, the process can be broken down into a few basic procedures. Here is an overview of that process.

1. Configure the physical computer:

   ◆ Rack and stack the server(s).

   ◆ Configure the local disk (array, logical disk).

   ◆ Set the BIOS details (virtualization, power, enable PXE).

   ◆ Set the BMC credentials.

   ◆ Disconnect any SAN ports.

   ◆ Update all relevant firmware, especially for the BMC.

2. Optionally, create DNS entries for the new hosts (in case your DNS replication takes a long time).

3. Configure a Windows deployment server (WDS) for Preboot eXecution Environment (PXE) services. Add this server to VMM and have a DHCP server available.

4. Prepare a sysprepped VHD, rename it to reflect its use, and place it in the VMM library. Add other resources such as custom device drivers and unattend scripts to the library.

5. Create one or several host profiles to describe the configurations of the Hyper-V hosts you want to deploy (hostname, VHD file, network, disk, drivers, OS configuration, host settings).

6. Start the Add Resources Wizard to discover physical computers, supply information (host group, host profile), and start the deployment process.

7. As soon as you commit your job, the physical host will turn off and on via the BMC. Then it will boot from the network, look for a PXE server, receive an IP address from a DHCP server, and initiate the bootstrap.

8. Finally, the physical computer will boot into the WinPE (Windows Pre-Execution Environment) that has been prepared by VMM. The WinPE agent will do most of the other work: format and partition the disks, transfer VHD with OS, convert dynamic VHD to fixed VHD, set up booting from native VHD, install matching drivers from the VMM library, deploy OS-customization scripts, enable the Hyper-V role, set up OS-customization scripts, reboot the host; and after the customization is finished, it will install the VMM agent, refresh the host, and enable Hyper-V.

Understanding Physical Machine Management (OOB/BMC)

In VMM you can remotely control a host via out-of-band (OOB) management if that host uses one of the supported BMCs. Think of the concept as a computer within a computer. Even when the host is switched off, you can still independently control the host and perform operations such as power off, power on, and reset.

Microsoft supports several standards-based OOB power-management-configuration-provider options:

◆ Intelligent Platform Management Interface (IPMI) versions 1.5 or 2.0

◆ Data Center Management Interface (DCMI) version 1.0

◆ System Management Architecture for Server Hardware (SMASH) version 1.0 over WS-Management (WS-Man).

TIP   Some BMCs use case-sensitive credentials, so take this into account when you create a Run As account to access your OOB management.

Configuring BMC Settings

After a Hyper-V host has been added to VMM, you'll need to configure its BMC in one of the hardware properties, as described in the following steps:

1. Right-click an existing server and select Properties from the context menu.

2. Select the Hardware tab and scroll to the bottom. Under the Advanced menu, you can manually configure the BMC settings (Figure 7.8). Check the box to enable OOB management for this physical machine, select the OOB power-management configuration provider, provide the BMC address and BMC port, and specify a valid Run As account. Click OK when you are ready.

FIGURE 7.8
Configuring the BMC settings

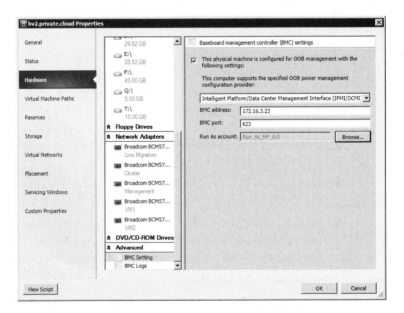

You can now control a server from VMM even if it is in a powered-off state.

Configuring a PXE Server

If you can use a PXE server for bare-metal deployment, your deployment of Hyper-V hosts can be fully automated. Of course, PXE servers are out of the question in some environments. If that is the case, you can bypass a PXE server by preparing a specially configured ISO file from which your bare-metal servers can boot. You can do this manually from USB or a virtual DVD using your BMC, or you can burn that ISO file to create a bootable DVD if you have no other options. On a positive note, the entire bare-metal deployment workflow can still be triggered from VMM with all the other steps and reporting except the PXE-boot part of the workflow.

The next steps explain how to prepare a PXE server based on Windows Deployment Services in Windows Server 2008 R2 SP1. First, place the bare-metal computers you want to convert to Hyper-V servers in the same subnet as your WDS/PXE and DHCP server. You need to do this because PXE boot messages are nonroutable. Note that no customizations are necessary in WDS. You don't have to set any parameters within WDS, and you don't have to add any images or drivers. All you have to think about is where to place the WDS server, because it makes a difference whether you combine the PXE with a DHCP server or keep them separate. As a general best practice, you should keep the two separate if you want to avoid having to perform a custom configuration of your DHCP-server options.

COMBINING WDS AND DHCP ON THE SAME SERVER

If a DHCP server is running on the same computer as the Windows Deployment Server host, check the "Do not listen on port 67" and "Configure DHCP option 60" boxes in your DHCP configuration to indicate that this server is also a PXE server.

Here is how a WDS/PXE server is configured:

1. On the server you have designated for Windows Deployment Services, right, start `servermanager.msc.`

2. Under Server Manager, right-click Add Roles, click Next, and then select Windows Deployment Services. Click Next.

3. At the WDS tab, leave both the Deployment Server and Transport Server role services selected and click Next.

4. On the Confirmation screen, verify that both roles have been selected and click Install. The server may need to be restarted after the installation completes.

5. The Results screen shows you whether the installation of WDS is successful. Click Close.

6. When you expand Windows Deployment Services in Server Manager, a yellow triangle appears in front of the server name. You can configure WDS by right-clicking the server and selecting Configure Server.

7. The next screen explains that the WDS server needs to be member of an Active Directory domain. There should be an active DHCP server on the network, as well as an active DNS server. Also an NTFS partition should be available for image storage. As a best practice, you can make a separate partition available to WDS; but because VMM handles the image, there is no real need for this. Click Next.

8. Select the path for the remote installation folder (`D:\RemoteInstall`) and click Next.

9. On the PXE Server Initial Settings screen, leave the default option on. Do not respond to any client computers. Click Next.

10. The last screen asks you to add images to the server, but you don't need to do this because the image is stored in the VMM library. When you are ready, click Finish.

11. Windows Deployment Services is now ready for action.

Creating Host Profiles

As mentioned in the overview of the bare-metal deployment steps, you need to do a number of things before the actual deployment. Your server's BIOS should be configured for Hyper-V (the usual hardware-virtualization settings), and you might want to do some configuration (enable/disable power management/C-state processor power modes) based on your own preferences.

NOTE In our practice, we often need to switch off advanced power management and disable C-states to avoid crashing hosts and slowing down live migration. We effectively kill the feature that marketing calls *core parking*. If you can afford to thoroughly test your new servers before they go into production, you can experiment with having power-management settings enabled and make your own decision on this topic.

In addition to racking and stacking your servers and setting BIOS, this is a good time to configure your BMCs:

♦ Configure your boot disks or "Boot from SAN" configuration.

♦ Set an IP for a network that can connect to the PXE server and configure the BMC credentials.

♦ Make a record of your servers, including the IP addresses, the MAC addresses of the network adapters, the BMC information, unique server identifiers, and so forth.

Now you are ready to leave your servers in the dark and close the data-center door behind you. You can return to your desk and open your VMM console to remotely control the bare-metal deployment from your management computer. If you have forgotten any of the previous steps, the BMC will save you another trip to the data center. So yes, BMCs are worth investing in, even if you and the servers are in the same building.

The first task in VMM is to create one or more host profiles. A *host profile* is like a template that describes how to configure the bare-metal host. Take the following steps to prepare a host profile:

1. Select the Fabric workspace and choose Home from the ribbon.

2. Expand Profiles in the Navigation pane, or choose Create and then Host Profile from the ribbon.

3. Enter a name and description for the Hyper-V host profile.

4. Because VMM supports deploying only versions of Windows Server that boot from a virtual hard disk (VHD), such as Windows Server 2008 R2, you need to select a VHD file from the library. This VHD must contain a sysprepped image of Windows Server 2008 R2. Browse to the VHD file, and click Next (Figure 7.9).

   If you use a dynamic VHD, this file is automatically converted to a fixed-type VHD during deployment. To speed up testing, you can check the "Do not convert the VHD to fixed type during deployment" check box.

5. On the Hardware Configuration screen, in the Management NIC section, you can obtain an IP address through the DHCP service or allocate a static IP from a logical network, as defined in VMM Networks.

FIGURE 7.9
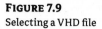

Selecting a VHD file

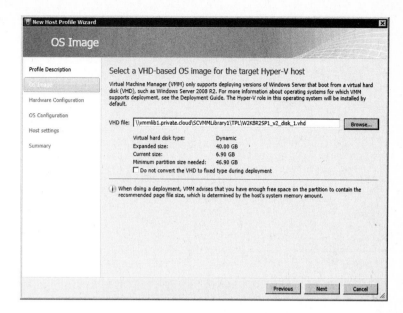

6. In the Disk and Partitions section, you can leave the defaults at one disk with one partition or use the Add Disk and Add Partition buttons to create additional ones.

   Unless your disk is bigger than 2 TB, you can leave the portioning scheme at Master Boot Record (MBR). In this section, you can navigate between disks and partitions. The default primary partition is named OS, uses all remaining free disk space, uses the NTFS file system, and is designated as the boot partition.

7. On the Driver Option section (Figure 7.10) you can leave the default on, automatically applying drivers that match the Plug and Play (PnP) IDs that are discovered on the computer during Windows installation. Or you can specify custom drivers based on a driver tag. This is covered in a later section. Click Next.

8. On the OS Configuration screen, you can specify all relevant settings for configuring the operating system, including joining a domain; specifying the local administrator password, identity information, product key, and time zone; as well as answering files and [GUIRunOnce]commands. Oddly enough, you can't select a Run As account for the local Administrator account. Click Next.

9. On the Host Settings screen, you can provide one or more virtual-machine placement paths. These paths can be configured in VMM later, so just click Next.

10. Finally, you can confirm all settings and click Finish.

FIGURE 7.10
Configuring driver
options

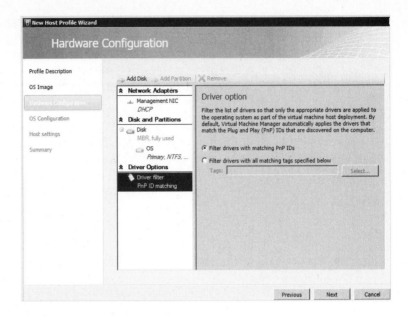

Detailed Bare-Metal Deployment Steps

To better understand the exact steps of a bare-metal deployment, study the process flow. The numbers in the following steps refer to Figure 7.11.

FIGURE 7.11
Explaining the pro-
cess flow of Bare-
metal Deployment

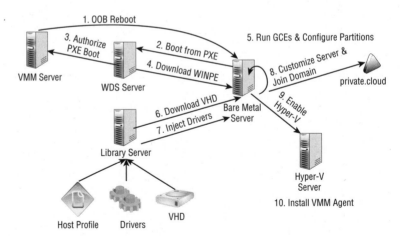

1. The VMM server issues an OOB reboot to the bare-metal server.

2. The bare-metal server boots from the WDS (PXE) server using `boot.wim`.

3. The VMM server receives a request to authorize the PXE boot.

4. The bare-metal server downloads WinPE from the VMM library.

5. WinPE is able to run custom commands and configure partitions on the bare-metal server as defined in a host profile prepared by the administrator. All custom commands connected to a host profile must be prepared in advance (see the "Running Post Deployment Scripts" section for more information).

6. The bare-metal server downloads the VHD from the VMM library.

7. VMM copies the custom drivers to WinPE at runtime and injects these drivers into the VHD automatically, based on the settings in the host profile (using PnP ID matching or tags). These custom drivers are placed and tagged in the VMM library (see the "Adding Drivers" section for more information).

8. The operating system (OS) is customized by the unattend.xml file, and the bare-metal server is joined to the domain as part of the sysprep customization phase when the machine is booted into the VHD for the first time. The domain information is contained in the unattend.xml file that VMM generates. This unattend.xml file contains settings from the host profile and is merged with the custom unattend.xml that the user can add to the host profile.

9. The VMM agent that is running in Windows PE enables the Hyper-V role on the VHD before it is booted for the first time. This is done to save a reboot step later. Although the VMM host agent will also try to enable Hyper-V when it is installed, this step is ignored because it was enabled earlier. This is why you see "Enabling Hyper-V role" twice in the job log.

10. When these steps are complete, the VMM agent is installed.

If you click on the Jobs pane and select the related VMM job, you will be able to see which steps ran successfully and which failed.

NOTE Be careful not to modify the boot.wim file manually. The boot.wim on the WDS server is customized by the VMM server and should not be modified by any method other than using the Update Windows PE action from the VMM UI or the publish-scwindowspe cmdlet.

Discovering and Deploying Hosts

If you have made all the preparations described in the previous paragraphs, you are ready to test your bare-metal deployment. Do not make any special configurations yet. Just see if you can successfully discover the hosts, boot from the PXE server into WinPE, and deploy the VHD with all its configuration steps. If that succeeds, you are ready to make some additional configurations to perfect your bare-metal deployment.

Before you begin the bare-metal deployment, connect to your BMC screen so you can see what happens. If the PXE boot does not kick in automatically, press F12 to manually force the server to boot from the network. In some blade-server enclosure configurations, it is possible to configure a one-time boot for PXE, which will force the server to boot from the network at the next reboot.

Let's kick off a bare-metal deployment by following these steps:

1. In the VMM console, select the Fabric workspace and choose Fabric Resources from the ribbon.

2. Right-click Servers in the Navigation pane and choose Add Hyper-V Hosts and Clusters, or choose Add Resources and then Host Profile from the ribbon.

3. On the Resource Location screen, select Physical Computers To Be Provisioned As Virtual Machine Hosts and click Next.

4. On the Credentials and Protocol screen, specify a valid Run As account to discover computers that use BMC technology, select the correct OOB management protocol, and select a port, as shown in Figure 7.12. Click Next.

FIGURE 7.12
Providing credentials and the OOB protocol

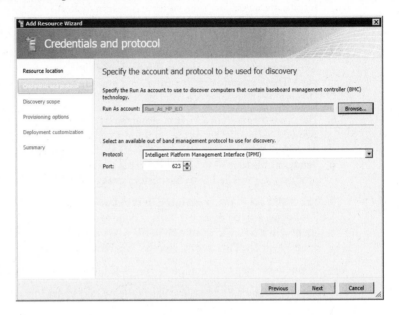

5. On the Discovery Scope tab, specify one IP address, an entire IP subnet, or an IP range, as shown in Figure 7.13. Click Next.

FIGURE 7.13
Discovering bare-metal servers

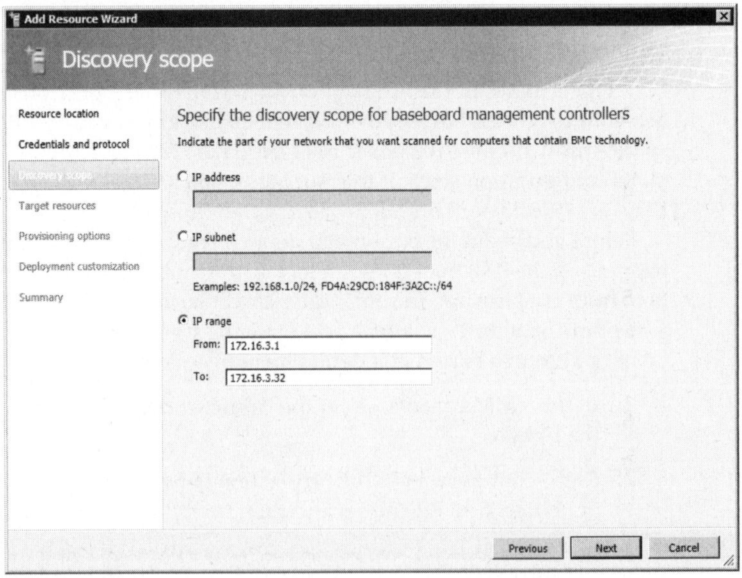

6. On the Target Resources tab, verify the correct IP address and SMBIOS ID before you select one or more servers. Check the correct servers and click Next.

7. On the Provisioning Options tab, select the correct host group, choose the appropriate host profile, and click Next.

   If you had chosen a logical network, the other option would have been available. In that case, you would have to specify the MAC address of the management NIC and its IP configuration on the next page of the wizard.

8. On the Deployment Customization tab, double-check the selected computers, provide names, and click Next.

   If you redeploy a server that already has a computer object in Active Directory, you can check the Skip Active Directory check box for this computer name.

9. When you are satisfied with the summary, click Finish to start the bare-metal deployment.

   Check the job information in the Jobs pane and the BMC screen to see what steps the server goes through.

   As soon as the bare-metal deployment job starts, you can follow its deployment steps. VMM uses BMC to power on the physical machine and initiates the PXE boot. You have exactly 10 minutes before this step times out, and there is no way to get additional information about this step until the server is able to PXE-boot into WinPE.

At this point, the following steps occur without your intervention.

1. When the physical machine has received an IP address it can download the boot.wim from \DCMgr\Boot\windows\Images on the PXE server. If it is successful, it boots into WinPE.

2. WinPE is initialized by the command-line tool wpeinit.exe, and it installs PnP devices, processes unattend.xml settings, and loads network resources.

3. When the network is available, VMM registers the physical machine, configures the disk(s), and starts to transfer the VHD from the VMM library.

4. Now that PXE boot has succeeded and the physical server has successfully started WinPE, progress is shown in the Create A New Host job, as shown in Figure 7.14. VMM uses Background Intelligent Transfer Service (BITS) to deploy the file.

5. If you did not check "Do not convert the VHD to fixed type during deployment" in the host profile, the job converts the VHD from dynamic to fixed.

   Next is the setup of BCD, which enables booting from VHD (also called native VHD).

6. Custom drivers are injected from the VMM library to the correct location in the VHD.

7. The OS-customization script is executed using the information provided in the host profile.

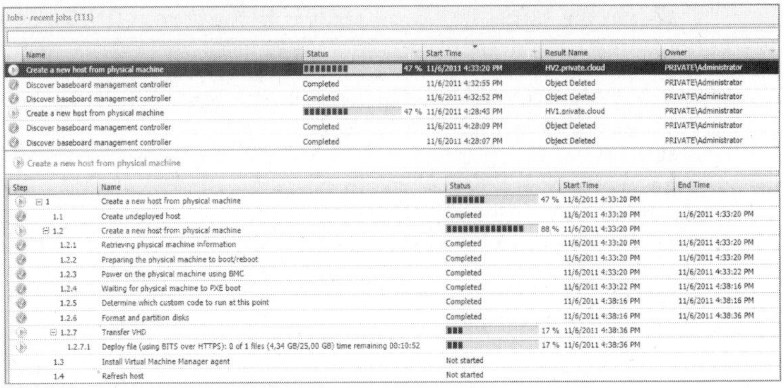

FIGURE 7.14
Progress of the
bare-metal deploy-
ment job

8. After reboot, the matching drivers are installed.

9. Hyper-V is enabled.

10. The OS customization script is run.

11. The server performs a final reboot.

12. The VMM agent is installed.

13. The new host is refreshed in VMM so that all the details become available.

This completes a full cycle of a bare-metal deployment of a Hyper-V server. You can deploy one server at a time; however, if the process works well, it is just as easy to deploy an entire blade enclosure with 16 blades or even more. This is a big time-saver and, most important, you'll end up with identical servers. Uniformly installed servers help you lay a solid foundation for your private cloud.

Adding Drivers

As with any generation of Windows, the operating system includes support for device drivers of the current generation of servers. As soon as a vendor introduces a new server generation with a new class of network or storage devices, you are out of luck and have to do your own plug before you play. Fortunately, VMM offers the opportunity to inject drivers into the VHD from which a Hyper-V host boots. So, if PnP does not recognize any of your server's device drivers, you'll need to do some extra preparation and testing. This is what you have to do:

1. Go to your server vendor's website and download the drivers you need.

2. Extract the driver package to a temporary location.

3. Create a directory called `Drivers` in the root of your VMM library.

4. Create another directory with a short name for your server model. This name is the tag for your custom drivers. The tag is referenced in the host profile that describes the configuration of your server.

5. Copy all extracted drivers to the tag directory.

6. Refresh the library and wait until you can see the `Drivers` directory, including the tag name and the drivers in that directory.

7. To add a custom tag, right-click each driver, select Properties, and click Select.

8. Click New Tag, rename the tag to your tag name, and click Add. Click OK when you are ready (Figure 7.15).

FIGURE 7.15
Adding a custom tag to a driver package

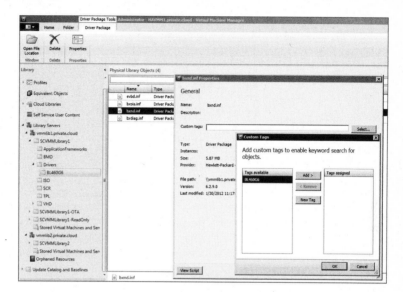

9. If you want to see the custom tags in the library, simply add the Custom Driver Tag column to your view.

10. Find the host's profile, right-click it, and select Properties. Go to the Hardware Configuration tab and click Driver Options. Change from Filter Drivers With Matching PnP IDs to Filter Drivers With Matching Tags, and click Select to choose the tags you prepared earlier. Click OK.

In Figure 7.16, you can see the difference between deploying the same server using custom tags and without custom tags.

You are ready to deploy your bare-metal servers with custom drivers.

TIP Some hardware vendors offer an easy solution to adding custom drivers to the VMM Library. As an example look at HP's whitepaper "Implementing Microsoft Windows Server 2012 Beta on HP ProLiant servers" which is available at
`http://h20000.www2.hp.com/bc/docs/support/SupportManual/c03305495/c03305495.pdf`.

Creating an ISO File

Even if you can't use a WDS/PXE server, you can still fully benefit from using bare-metal deployment for rapidly deploying new Hyper-V hosts. All of the steps remain the same except you don't have to install WDS and add it to the VMM fabric. The requirement for a DHCP server still stands.

FIGURE 7.16

Deploying with custom tags (left) and without custom tags (right)

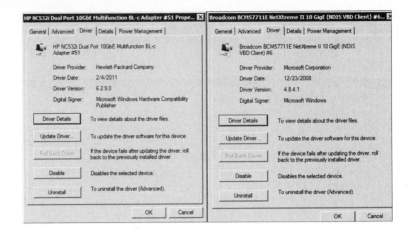

Instead of booting from a PXE server, you can boot from an ISO file that is configured to use the VMM bare-metal deployment script. This ISO file is created by a PowerShell cmdlet. First, start a PowerShell session from within VMM, issue the following cmdlet, and use a valid path in which to create the ISO file. The directory does not have to exist. The command does not give any output if it succeeds, so either check the directory for the existence of the ISO file or check under Jobs.

```
PS C:\> Publish-SCWindowsPE -ISOPath E:\ISO -UseWindowsAIK

PS C:\> dir c:\iso

    Directory: C:\

Mode                LastWriteTime     Length Name
----                -------------     ------ ----
-a---          1/30/2012   1:05 PM  182130688 iso
```

You can burn the ISO file to a disk, place it on a bootable USB drive, or connect to the ISO file through a BMC.

The process then continues as follows:

1. Attach the ISO file or insert a disk/USB drive to physical machine.

2. Run the Add Resource Wizard and choose Physical Computers To Be Provisioned As Virtual Machine Hosts, as you would normally do for bare-metal deployment.

3. When the machine prompts you to "Press enter to boot from DVD," press Enter.

4. The bare-metal deployment continues as usual.

Adding Custom Commands

You can use custom commands in the host profile to prepare certain activities. The next PowerShell code snippet provides an example of a general command executing during the bare-metal process. In this example, a script calls an HP disk utility to delete a RAID configuration and then create a new mirror raid configuration before kicking off the rest of the deployment.

```
#1 Get resource folder location (HPArrayUtility.cr) in the VMM library
PS C:\> $resource = Get-SCCustomResource | where { $_.SharePath -eq "\\ ↩
vmmserver\ ProgramData\Virtual Machine Manager Library Files\HPArrayUtility.cr" }

#2 Get the host profile to be used
PS C:\> $HostProfile = Get-SCVMHostProfile -Name "host gce profile"

#3 Configure Script Command Settings
PS C:\> $scriptSetting = New-SCScriptCommandSetting
PS C:\> Set-SCScriptCommandSetting -ScriptCommandSetting $scriptSetting ↩
-WorkingDirectory "" -PersistStandardOutputPath "" -PersistStandardErrorPath "" ↩
-MatchStandardOutput "" -MatchStandardError ".+" -MatchExitCode "[1-9][0-9]*" ↩
-FailOnMatch -AlwaysReboot $false -MatchRebootExitCode "{1641}|{3010}|{3011}" ↩
-RestartScriptOnExitCodeReboot $false

#5 Run hpacucli.exe with a command to delete the raid configuration
PS C:\> Add-SCScriptCommand -VMHostProfile $HostProfile -Executable "hpacucli. ↩
exe" -ScriptCommandSetting $scriptSetting -CommandParameters "ctrl slot=1 delete ↩
forced" -TimeoutSeconds 120 -LibraryResource $resource

#6 Run hpacucli.exe with a command to create new mirror raid configuration
PS C:\> Add-SCScriptCommand -VMHostProfile $HostProfile -Executable "hpacucli. ↩
exe" -ScriptCommandSetting $scriptSetting -CommandParameters "ctrl slot=1 create ↩
type=ld drives=1:1,1:2 raid=1" -TimeoutSeconds 120 -LibraryResource $resource
```

Running Post-Deployment Scripts

After the new host job finishes, the admin can decide to run one or more post-deployment general command executions (GCEs) — for example, to configure NIC teaming. These GCEs can be initiated from the Run Command action available in the user interface, but they can also be scripted and started by the `invoke-scscript` command PowerShell cmdlet.

Troubleshooting Bare-Metal Deployment

If you can perform a bare-metal deployment without any errors, hats off to you! In practice, you will stumble into one or more gotchas. The following sections provide some hints and guidance for common situations.

PXE BOOT FAILS

When you're configuring a WDS server for PXE, don't configure the same way you would for other purposes. VMM takes full control of the whole process, so all you need to do is a basic WDS role installation. Don't do any configurations or add any images.

A PXE boot can fail for many reasons, including the following:

◆ The PXE server is not in the same subnet as the network adapter that is used to boot from the network.

♦ No DHCP server is available in the subnet used for PXE boot.

♦ PXE and DHCP are on the same server, and no additional DCHP options are set.

♦ The physical server to be provisioned already has a boot partition from another installation.

Make sure you have installed the WDS server according to the detailed requirements described in this chapter.

When the server boots, either press F12 or use your BMC to start it from the network. If everything fails, resort to the procedure explained under "Creating an ISO File."

PXE BOOT SUCCEEDS, BUT WINPE FAILS

You might encounter a situation in which you can boot from PXE and an IP address is provisioned to the server, but the process halts when WinPE kicks in. When the provisioning process halts, you'll probably get a message like "Synchronizing Time with Server." After this, error 803d0010 is displayed, prompting you to check `X:\VMM\vmmAgentPE.exe.etl`. If you are unlucky, this file will be full of blank entries.

A likely reason for the process stall is that WinPE does not have a suitable network driver to continue the installation. Press Shift+F10 to open a command prompt and enter **ipconfig /all** to check for a network configuration.

The Creating ISO method will not help you here because that method also requires a network connection after WinPE boots.

You need to add drivers to the WinPE image that is taken from the Windows Automated Installation Kit location by VMM and deployed to the WDS/PXE server. This involves the following process:

1. Get tags for matching drivers in the VMM library. By default, these are in the following location:

   `c:\Program Files\Windows AIK\Tools\PETools\amd64`

2. Prepare the working directories.

3. Copy the default WIM file to a working directory and use DISM to mount `winpe.wim`.

4. Find the path of each driver that matches the tag and use DISM to insert it into the mounted WinPE image.

5. Commit the changes.

6. Republish the `winpe.wim` to the PXE server(s) managed by VMM.

DISM: DEPLOYMENT IMAGE SERVICING AND MANAGEMENT TOOL

DISM enumerates, installs, uninstalls, configures, and updates features and packages in Windows images. The commands that are available depend on the image being serviced and whether the image is offline or running.

First, check whether the custom drivers can be found in the library with the tags you have given them:

```
PS C:\> $tags = "BL460G6"
get-scdriverpackage | where { $_.tags -match $tags } | select-object class,
inffile,type, tags, provider, version, date | ft -auto

Class        INFFile     Type Tags     Provider                 Version
-----        -------     ---- ----     --------                 -------
system       evbd.inf    INF  {BL460G6} Hewlett-Packard Company 6.2.16.0
net          bxnd.inf    INF  {BL460G6} Hewlett-Packard Company 6.2.9.0
SCSIAdapter  bxois.inf   INF  {BL460G6} Hewlett-Packard Company 6.2.7.0
system       bxdiag.inf  INF  {BL460G6} Hewlett-Packard Company 6.2.3.0
```

You can see some more detail by issuing the following command:

```
PS C:\> $tags = "BL460G6"
PS C:\> get-scdriverpackage | where { $_.tags -match $tags }

[output shows only one driver]

PlugAndPlayIDs   : {B06BDRV\L2ND&PCI_164A14E4&SUBSYS_3101103C, B06BDRV\
                   L2ND&PCI_16AA14E4&SUBSYS_3102103C, B06BDRV\L2ND
                   &PCI_164A14E4&SUBSYS_3106103C,
                   B06BDRV\L2ND&PCI_16AA14E4&SUBSYS_310C103C...}
Tags             : {BL460G6}
TagsString       : BL460G6
Type             : INF
INFFile          : bxnd.inf
Date             : 2/4/2011 12:00:00 AM
Version          : 6.2.9.0
Class            : net
Provider         : Hewlett-Packard Company
Signed           : True
Signer           : Microsoft Windows Hardware Compatibility Publisher
BootCritical     : False
Release          :
State            : Normal
LibraryShareId   : 2dda2b24-bf52-4308-a4df-8c192a097e52
SharePath        : \\vmmlib1.private.cloud\SCVMMLibrary1\Drivers\BL460G6\
bxnd.inf
```

```
Directory           : \\vmmlib1.private.cloud\SCVMMLibrary1\Drivers\BL460G6
Size                : 6153482
IsOrphaned          : False
FamilyName          :
Namespace           : Global
ReleaseTime         :
HostVolumeId        : 9eecdae3-c395-4fd1-a17b-0cd07179eac7
HostVolume          :
Classification      :
HostId              : 64f2e51f-469f-4d6a-9d28-30c06a241fc9
HostType            : LibraryServer
HostName            : vmmlib1.private.cloud
VMHost              :
LibraryServer       : vmmlib1.private.cloud
Cloud               :
LibraryGroup        :
GrantedToList       : {}
UserRoleID          : 00000000-0000-0000-0000-000000000000
UserRole            :
Owner               :
ObjectType          : DriverPackage
Accessibility       : Public
Name                : bxnd.inf
IsViewOnly          : False
Description         :
AddedTime           : 1/25/2012 9:06:33 PM
ModifiedTime        : 1/30/2012 12:23:34 PM
Enabled             : True
MostRecentTask      :
ServerConnection    : Microsoft.SystemCenter.VirtualMachineManager.Remoting
                      .ServerConnection
ID                  : ddf2560a-c718-41c4-bebb-f9eb260f00ff
MarkedForDeletion   : False
IsFullyCached       : True
```

After you have verified the tags of the custom drivers in the library, you are ready to run a script to prepare a `winpe.wim` image with the custom drivers injected.

```
#1 Get tags for matching drivers in the VMM library
# Master WIM = c:\Program Files\Windows AIK\Tools\PETools\amd64\winpe.wim
# Driver tag = winpe
PS C:\> $wim = "c:\Program Files\Windows AIK\Tools\PETools\amd64\winpe.wim "
PS C:\> $tags = "winpe"

#2 Prepare directories
PS C:\> $winpesrcdir = $wim
PS C:\> $workingdir = $workingdir = $env:temp + "\" + [System.Guid]::NewGuid() ↵
.toString()
```

```
PS C:\> $mountdir = $workingdir + "\mount"
PS C:\> $wimfile = $workingdir + "\winpe.wim"
PS C:\> mkdir $workingdir
PS C:\> mkdir $mountdir


#3 Copy default WIM file and mount it using DISM
PS C:\> copy $winpesrcdir $workingdir
PS C:\> dism /Mount-Wim /wimfile:$wimfile /index:1 /MountDir:$mountdir

#4 Find the path of each driver that matches the tag and insert it into mounted
wim using DISM
PS C:\> $drivers = Get-SCDriverPackage | where { $_.tags -match $tags }
foreach ($driver in $drivers)
{
    $path = $driver.sharepath
    dism /image:$mountdir /Add-Driver /driver:$path
}

#5 Commit the changes
PS C:\> Dism /Unmount-Wim /MountDir:$mountdir /Commit

#6 Republish the WIM file to every PXE server managed by VMM
Publish-SCWindowsPE -Path $wimfile

#7 Clean up
PS C:\> del $wimfile
PS C:\> rmdir $mountdir
PS C:\> rmdir $workingdir
```

Step 4 is the part of the script where the drivers are actually injected into the mounted WIM file using DISM:

```
[output shows only one driver]

Deployment Image Servicing and Management tool
Version: 6.1.7600.16385


Image Version: 6.1.7600.16385


Found 1 driver package(s) to install.
Installing 1 of 1 - \\vmmlib1.private.cloud\SCVMMLibrary1\Drivers\DL460G6\
Broadcom10Gb\bxnd.inf: The driver package was
successfully installed.
The operation completed successfully.

Deployment Image Servicing and Management tool
Version: 6.1.7600.16385
```

MACHINE IS NOT DETECTED

If you are using some sort of hardware-virtualization technology, such as HP Virtual Connect, chances are that you not only configured virtual MAC and WWN addresses, but you also virtualized your servers' unique identifiers. If so, you will have a logical serial number and a logical UUID, as shown in Figure 7.17).

FIGURE 7.17
The physical and
logical serial num-
bers and UUIDs

Serial Number	GB8949B8PM
Serial Number (Logical)	VCX0000006
UUID	33383934-3735-4247-3839-34394238504D
UUID (Logical)	41AF9DB5-1AF3-4369-9805-60F8EDE56C51

Because the bare-metal deployment process looks at the physical UUID and not the virtual one, the only way to successfully run the bare-metal deployment job is to use PowerShell. You can start the process in the GUI; but before you kick it off, click the button for viewing the PowerShell command. Save the file, replace the SMBiosGuid with the logical UUID, and copy and paste the cmdlet into a VMM PowerShell command session.

```
PS C:\> $HostGroup = Get-SCVMHostGroup -ID "0e3ba228-a059-46be-aa41-2f5cf0f4b96e" ↵
-Name "All Hosts"
PS C:\> $RunAsAccount = Get-SCRunAsAccount -Name "Run_As_HP_iLO"
PS C:\> $HostProfile = Get-SCVMHostProfile -ID "d3982328-2a4b-48d9-8eaa- ↵
ad5129e8cc5e"
PS C:\> New-SCVMHost -ComputerName "hv1" -VMHostProfile $HostProfile ↵
-VMHostGroup $HostGroup -BMCAddress "172.16.3.22" -SMBiosGuid "41AF9DB5-1AF3- ↵
4369-9805-60F8EDE56C51" -BMCRunAsAccount $RunAsAccount -RunAsynchronously ↵
-BMCProtocol "IPMI" -BMCPort "623" -ManagementAdapterMACAddress "00-17-A4-77-00- ↵
60" -LogicalNetwork "VM1" -Subnet "192.168.1.0/24" -IPAddress "192.168.1.51"
```

SERVER ALREADY EXISTS IN ACTIVE DIRECTORY

A bare-metal deployment will fail if the name of the new server already exists in Active Directory. To side-step the issue, you can skip the AD check. In the GUI, in the Deployment Customization section of the host profile, check the Skip Active Directory check box for the computer name.

If you are using the PowerShell script, just add the following to the cmdlet:

```
-BypassADMachineAccountCheck
```

SERVER ALREADY EXISTS IN VMM

A bare-metal deployment will fail when the name of the server already exists in VMM. In that case, double-check the name and remove it from VMM if appropriate. Removing a server from VMM requires elevated privileges. At any rate, be careful when you have to do this.

Managing Hyper-V Clusters in VMM

If you add a Hyper-V host that is part of a cluster, VMM automatically adds all nodes of that cluster and installs a VMM agent on each. Once the cluster has been inventoried, you can view its properties. Under the General tab, you will not only find the cluster name and host-group location, but also its cluster reserve state. The default is 1, which means that the resources of one cluster node are reserved for high availability. If you start with a one-node cluster and the cluster reserve is 1, the cluster reserve state will not show OK. Of course, for testing purposes, you can change this value to 0. In general, though, you should have one cluster reserve per eight cluster nodes. This means that for a 16-node cluster, you follow best practices by changing this value to 2.

You can obtain more information about the cluster from the tabs of the Properties screen, including the following:

Status   The status displays information such as whether a cluster validation test was run, whether the test was successful or not, and the state of cluster core resources and cluster services.

Available Storage   If the cluster has access to disks that are still in the available storage section, you'll see those disks here. As a best practice, you should have at least one small, shared disk available for testing/validation purposes.

Shared Volumes   A similar view (Figure 7.18) is available for disks that are shared volumes of the cluster. You can also add available disks to the list of Cluster Shared Volumes, remove disks, or convert shared volumes to available storage. Naturally, these tasks are performed only when these disks hold no active virtual machines.

FIGURE 7.18
Viewing shared storage

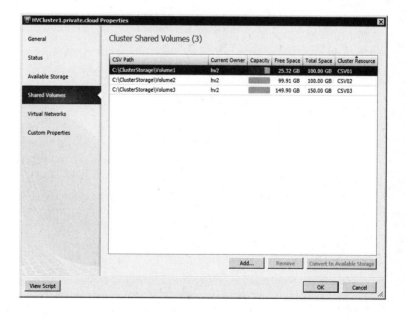

Virtual Networks This tab shows which virtual networks are available to the entire cluster. If you make a spelling error in the name of a virtual network on one of the nodes in the cluster, the virtual network will not show up here.

Custom Properties You can add additional custom properties to the cluster for further identification or custom sorting and grouping.

Once the cluster is managed under VMM, you can perform a number of actions against the cluster:

Create Service You can create a new service on this cluster, based on a service template. A service can be a single- or multitier combination of virtual machines with applications (see Chapter 8).

Create Virtual Machine You can create a new VM based on an existing VM, VM template, or VHD. You can also create a new VM with a blank VHD.

Refresh You can reread all the properties of the cluster and cluster nodes to capture any changes since the last update. The refresh interval is 10 minutes.

Optimize Hosts You can begin a dynamic resource-optimization task for balancing guests across the cluster.

Move to Host Group You can move a cluster to another host group.

Uncluster You can perform what Failover Cluster Manager calls Destroy Cluster. You cannot uncluster if there are still active resources on one of the cluster nodes. If there are, the job will fail with Error 25330 (Figure 7.19).

FIGURE 7.19
A failed Uncluster
Cluster action

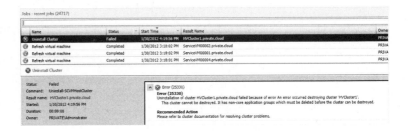

Add Cluster Node Expand the cluster to the current maximum of 16 nodes. The candidate node must have access (a possible owner) to the same shared storage as the other cluster nodes and must be validated before joining the cluster.

This option does not support clusters with *asymmetric storage* (where not all cluster disks are presented to all cluster nodes, which can be useful in multi-site clusters). Asymmetric storage is a feature that was introduced in Windows Server 2008 R2 SP1.

Validate Cluster Revalidate the cluster. The validation status will appear under Status on the cluster's Properties screen.

Remove Remove the cluster from VMM management. The cluster will remain unaltered, but VMM will uninstall its agents from all cluster nodes.

Properties View the cluster's properties, as discussed earlier.

Automated Creation of Hyper-V Clusters

If you've followed along with the discussion, you have added one or more hosts and clusters and brought existing hosts and clusters under VMM management. As soon as you have one or more Hyper-V machines available, you can build clusters from them. Before you create a cluster, you need to prepare all the network and storage connections because VMM validates the potential cluster nodes before they can join the cluster. It is recommended that all cluster nodes be as similar as possible, including but not limited to service packs, Windows updates, and hotfixes.

This is how a cluster can be created from VMM:

1. In the VMM console, select Fabric, and choose Servers from the Navigation pane. Click Create from the ribbon and select Hyper-V Cluster.

2. On the General tab of the Create Cluster Wizard, provide a name for the cluster and select a Run As account or provide a username and password. Click Next.

3. On the Nodes tab, select a host group with available Hyper-V hosts, point at one or more hosts, and click Add to move them to the Hosts To Cluster column. Click Next.

4. On the IP Address tab, either select a static IP pool from which VMM will pick a static IP address, or manually provide a cluster IP address. Click Next.

5. On the Storage tab (Figure 7.20), select any disks you want to cluster. For each, choose the partition style (MBR or GPT), file-system type (NTFS), volume label, whether to quick-format the disk, and whether to add the disk to CSV. Click Next. By default, VMM automatically will select the smallest disk as your quorum disk, depending on the number of cluster nodes. From this Storage view, you can also format the disks and mark them as CSV disks.

FIGURE 7.20
Selecting disks for a cluster

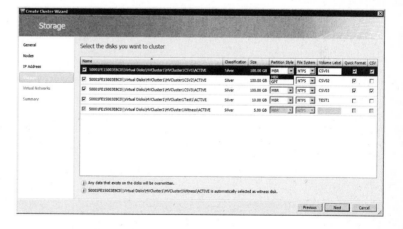

6. On the Virtual Networks screen, select which logical networks to use for creating external virtual networks. Click Next.

7. On the Summary screen, review your settings and click Finish.

You can also add to existing Hyper-V clusters. Take these steps to add a node to an existing cluster:

1. In the VMM console, select Fabric, and choose Servers from the Navigation pane. Right-click the cluster you want to expand and select Add Cluster Node from the context menu.

2. In the Available Hosts column, select the hosts you want to add to this cluster and click Add to move them to the Hosts To Cluster column. Click Add.

3. Select a valid Run As account, or manually add the proper credentials, and click OK.

TROUBLESHOOTING A FAILED ADD CLUSTER NODE JOB

The Add Cluster Node job will fail with Error 25343 if no network adapter matches the cluster virtual network of the nodes in the existing cluster. In that case, prepare the network adapters first, then open the properties of the host, select the hardware tab, and map the network adapters to the proper logical networks, as shown in Figure 7.21.

If the Add Cluster Node job fails with Error 20400, you'll need to take a look at the storage configuration for the node you are adding. You'll find that the disks were not presented to this node, the disks are not online, or VMM is not aware of these disks. Correct the storage configuration and refresh the candidate cluster node.

FIGURE 7.21
Mapping network adapters to logical networks

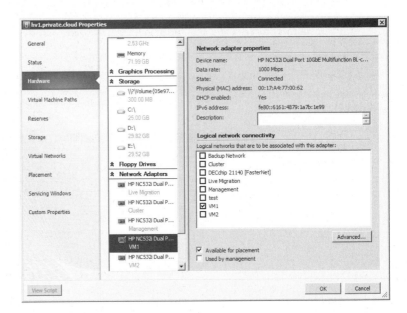

An alternative way to add a node to an existing cluster is to drag the node to the cluster. The Add Node To Cluster Wizard kicks in and you will only have to provide credentials to start the job.

Configuring Dynamic Optimization and Power Optimization

This section deals with dynamic optimization and power optimization — two cluster-optimization techniques that help the cluster to keep load-balanced or can reduce power consumption.

Dynamic optimization refers to the built-in support for load-balancing a cluster. It is no longer dependent on performance and resource optimization (PRO) and integration with Operations Manager, as was the case with VMM 2008 R2. *Power optimization* can help conserve power by shutting down hosts that are not running any workloads. Alternatively, they are turned on again when workload activity increases. Power optimization requires a BMC in the virtualization host.

Both dynamic optimization and power optimization work with Hyper-V, VMware ESX, and XenServer clusters. The respective automated VM migration functionality of the different hypervisors is used to either balance workloads or evacuate a host so that a host can be powered off.

Dynamic optimization and power optimization are configurable on a per-host-group basis. To view dynamic optimization and power optimization in action, you must deploy and run virtual machines on the host cluster.

NOTE   You can configure dynamic optimization and power optimization on any host group. However, the settings have no effect unless the host group contains a host cluster supporting a VM migration technology.

DYNAMIC OPTIMIZATION IN VMM

Dynamic optimization in VMM adds functionality to the host reserve settings from VMM 2008 R2. Like its predecessor, VMM receives its host reserve settings as it is added to the host group.

A host reserve is set by default on the All Hosts host group and can be changed for all underlying host groups. It is also possible to create an underlying host group with different host reserve settings. In such cases, you must deselect "Use the host reserves settings from the parent host group" on the Host Reserves tab of the subgroup's Properties screen. For instance, by default 10 percent of the CPU is reserved, meaning that a host is available for placement until 90 percent of the CPU is utilized.

A different host reserve can also be set at the host level to effectively override the settings of the host group. If no override is set, the host receives the settings of the host group when the host is placed under management by VMM. Also, when a host is moved from one host group to another, the host will inherit the host reserve settings of that group, unless you have set specific host reserves on the host itself.

You can check the current host reserve settings for any specific host or host group by issuing the following PowerShell commands:

```
PS C:\> Get-SCVMHost -computername "hvserver1"
```

```
RunAsAccount                    : Run_As_Domain_Admin
OverallStateString              : OK
OverallState                    : OK
CommunicationStateString        : Responding
CommunicationState              : Responding
Name                            : hvserver1.private.cloud
FullyQualifiedDomainName        : hvserver1.private.cloud
```

```
ComputerName                        : hvserver1
DomainName                          : private.cloud
Description                         :
RemoteUserName                      :
OverrideHostGroupReserves           : True
CPUPercentageReserve                : 30
NetworkPercentageReserve            : 0
DiskSpaceReserveMB                  : 10240
MaxDiskIOReservation                : 10000
MemoryReserveMB                     : 256
```

In the previous example, the host reserve has an override for CPUPercentageReserve. To
check for a specific host group, use this command:

```
PS C:\> Get-SCHostReserve -VMHostGroup Production
```

```
CPUReserveOff                       : False
CPUPlacementLevel                   : 40
CPUStartOptimizationLevel           : 30
CPUVMHostReserveLevel               : 15
MemoryReserveOff                    : False
MemoryReserveMode                   : Megabyte
MemoryPlacementLevel                : 1024
MemoryStartOptimizationLevel        : 1024
MemoryVMHostReserveLevel            : 1024
DiskSpaceReserveOff                 : False
DiskSpaceReserveMode                : Percentage
DiskSpacePlacementLevel             : 10
DiskSpaceVMHostReserveLevel         : 10
DiskIOReserveOff                    : False
DiskIOReserveMode                   : IOPS
DiskIOPlacementLevel                : 1000
DiskIOStartOptimizationLevel        : 1000
DiskIOVMHostReserveLevel            : 1000
NetworkIOReserveOff                 : False
NetworkIOReserveMode                : Percentage
NetworkIOPlacementLevel             : 0
NetworkIOStartOptimizationLevel     : 0
NetworkIOVMHostReserveLevel         : 0
Name                                : Production
ReadOnly                            : False
ConnectedHostGroup                  : All Hosts\Production
OwnerHostGroup                      : All Hosts\Production
ServerConnection                    : Microsoft.SystemCenter.VirtualMachineManager.
                                      Remoting.ServerConnection
ID                                  : aab05537-0406-49d5-9670-5f0a938196b7
IsViewOnly                          : False
ObjectType                          : HostReserveSettings
MarkedForDeletion                   : False
IsFullyCached                       : True
```

As you can see from the output, there are several settings for optimization levels. The value for a reserve is also the starting point for dynamic optimization. In other words, if the `MemoryPlacementLevel` is at 1,024 MB (the default), then `MemoryStartOptimizationLevel` is also set at 1,024 MB, unless it is manually set to another value. The `Set-SCHostReserve` command is used to set host reserves such as placement levels and start optimization levels.

Dynamic optimization is also a property of the host group that can be configured to migrate virtual machines within host clusters with a specified frequency and aggressiveness. If no overrides are set, the host group receives the Dynamic Optimization settings from the parent host group.

By default, the dynamic optimization settings are configured with medium aggressiveness and a frequency of 10 minutes. Aggressiveness can be set in five steps from Low to High (with an intermediate step between Low and Medium and between Medium and High); Aggressiveness defines how eagerly VMM looks for optimization opportunities:

◆ **High:** Balances a cluster for small gains, resulting in more VM migrations

◆ **Medium:** The default setting

◆ **Low:** Balances for only substantial gain, resulting in fewer VM migrations

In Figure 7.22, the Dynamic Optimization settings have been changed to a more aggressive setting but with an hourly interval.

FIGURE 7.22
Overriding the default Dynamic Optimization settings

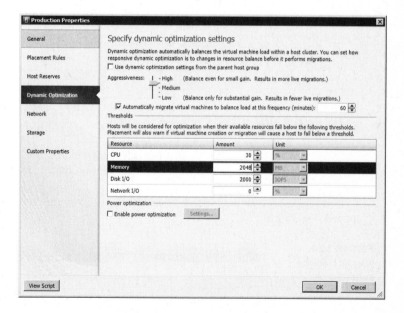

Frequency is set to automatically migrate virtual machines to balance the load every 10 minutes and can be set to a maximum of 2,440 minutes (just over 40 hours). You should test these settings carefully before you automate dynamic optimization. In the current version of Hyper-V, simultaneous migrations are unavailable. Live migrations are queued and wait until the previous migration has finished. If you set the frequency too high, migrations from the previous optimization may not be finished yet.

For dynamic optimization to work, you need clusters with two or more nodes. Any hosts or clusters that do not support migration are ignored. An additional requirement is that VMs must be configured to be highly available and placed on shared storage.

If you want to test dynamic optimization, you can start the process on demand by right-clicking one of your clusters and selecting Optimize Hosts from the context menu.

VMM calculates resource optimizations and proposes a migration for one or more VMs. In the example in Figure 7.23, host hv2 is running all the VMs and VMM proposes to move five VMs to host hv1.

FIGURE 7.23
Calculating optimizations

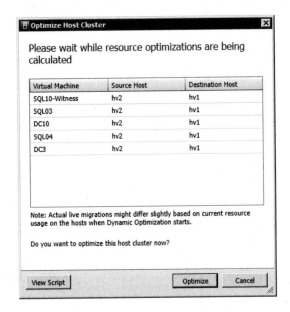

The resulting PowerShell script looks like this:

```
PS C:\> $hostCluster = Get-SCVMHostCluster -Name "HVCluster1.private.cloud"
PS C:\> Start-SCDynamicOptimization -VMHostCluster $hostCluster
```

Under Jobs, you can easily track how VMM optimizes the cluster and which VMs have moved (Figure 7.24).

FIGURE 7.24
You can track the optimization.

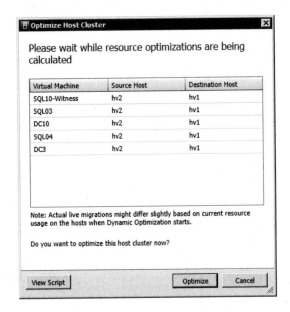

If no resource optimizations are available when you run this command, you will be notified that the host cluster is either within desired resource-usage limits or no further optimization is possible.

POWER OPTIMIZATION IN VMM

Power optimization is functionally part of dynamic optimization. It can only be set if a host group has been configured for dynamic optimization. If you enable power optimization, you effectively allow VMM to power VM hosts off and on based on their actual usage. Before power optimization kicks in, all remaining VMs on that host are migrated to the remaining nodes in the cluster.

By default, power optimization is switched off. If you switch it on, it operates 24 hours a day unless you change the schedule.

There is a difference for power optimization, depending on whether the clusters are created by VMM or outside VMM. For clusters created by VMM, you can set up power optimization for clusters of four or more nodes. For clusters created outside VMM, you need five or more nodes, as shown in Table 7.1.

TABLE 7.1:   Minimum Number of Cluster Nodes for Power Optimization

NODES POWERED OFF	CLUSTER CREATED IN VMM	CLUSTER CREATED OUTSIDE VMM
0	More than 3 nodes	More than 4 nodes
1	4 or 5 nodes	5 or 6 nodes
2	6 or 7 nodes	7 or 8 nodes
3	8 or 9 nodes	9 or 10 nodes

If the number of cluster nodes is sufficient, you can enable power optimization using the following steps:

1. In the VMM console, select Fabric, and choose Servers from the Navigation pane. Right-click the host group you want to enable for power optimization and choose Properties.

2. Click Dynamic Optimization, uncheck "Use dynamic optimization from the parent host group," check "Automatically migrate virtual machines to balance load at this frequency (minutes)," and set it to an acceptable value.

3. Under Power Optimization (bottom of screen), enable power optimization and click Settings.

4. On the Power Optimization Settings screen, click the blue squares to disable or enable power optimization for a particular day and hour as shown in Figure 7.25. If you are a 24x7x365 company and your hosts are constantly utilized, power optimization is probably better switched off.

FIGURE 7.25
Modifying the
power-optimization
schedule

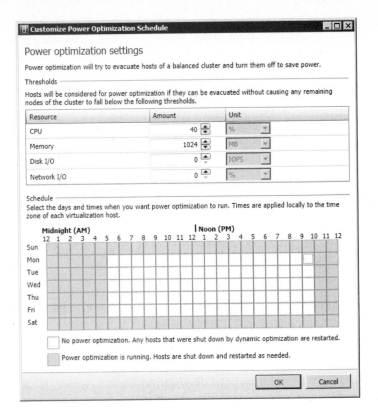

Cluster Remediation

Traditionally, updating clusters has been a laborious task. Windows Server Update Services (WSUS) and System Center Configuration Manager (SCCM or Config Mgr) are still not cluster-aware, so cannot take the risk of automatically updating cluster nodes. If you update a node in a Hyper-V cluster, it reboots without migrating the VMs to another node. Simultaneous reboots of more nodes than the cluster can handle (majority node or other quorum requirements) can take the entire cluster down.

Fortunately, VMM introduces a workflow for updating a Hyper-V cluster based on the assumption that the cluster and the VMs should stay highly available. As when remediating a single Hyper-V host as described in Chapter 5, "Understanding the VMM Library", VMM uses a supported WSUS server as a source for the update catalog and update baselines. To perform the following steps, assume that the update server is already part of the VMM fabric.

These are the steps for setting up cluster remediation:

1. In the VMM console, select Library, and choose Update Catalog and Baselines from the Navigation pane. Right-click Update Baselines and select Synchronize Update Server (Figure 7.26).

2. Click Create on the ribbon and select Baseline.

3. Specify a name and a description and click Next.

4. On the Updates screen, click Add to select all required updates relevant to your Hyper-V cluster. Click Next when you are ready.

FIGURE 7.26
Adding a cluster node

5. On the Assignment Scope screen, select only those clusters that you intend to update with the newly created Hyper-V Cluster baseline (Figure 7.27). Click Next.

FIGURE 7.27
Assigning clusters to a baseline

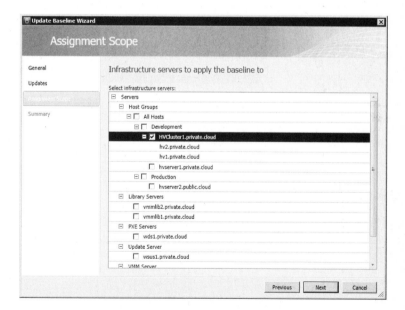

6. Review the summary and click Finish. In the Baselines view, you now see an additional baseline called Hyper-V Cluster with one assigned cluster and one or more updates.

7. Now change to Fabric, expand Servers in the Navigation pane, and click Compliance on the ribbon. Select the Hyper-V cluster you want to remediate. If this is the first time you are updating your cluster from VMM, the compliance status is Unknown and the operational status is Pending Compliance Scan.

8. In the View pane, right-click a cluster and select Scan from the context menu. The operational status changes to Scanning. In the Jobs view you can check progress.

9. When the scan is ready, it reports the compliance status of all cluster nodes. To initiate remediation, right-click the cluster and select Remediate.

10. Before remediation starts, you can make some additional settings. First of all, you should check that the remediation method is Live Migration. You can choose not to restart the servers after remediation and delay this action to a later time. If a cluster node is in Maintenance mode, you need to check the cluster option "Allow remediation of clusters with nodes already in maintenance mode." If there is no need to keep the VMs online during remediation and you want to speed up the entire process, you can also choose to change the cluster-remediation method from Live Migration to Save State (also known as *Quick Migration*). If you are remediating a Windows Server 2008 Hyper-V cluster, this is the only available option.

11. In the Jobs view, the different steps can be monitored.

In the example in Figure 7.28, one of the cluster nodes is placed in Maintenance mode. This effectively evacuates all highly available VMs, installs the updates, reboots the host, and starts a compliance scan. When it is finished, it stops Maintenance mode and moves on to the next cluster node, repeating all the necessary steps until all nodes have been remediated.

FIGURE 7.28
The details of a remediation job

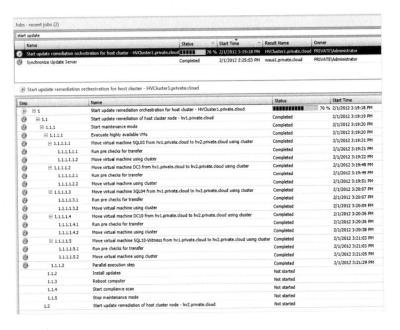

Any non–highly available VMs are put into the Save state.

The cluster-remediation method employed by VMM is fully aware of Hyper-V, its version and migration capabilities, and the state of the cluster nodes. Currently, this remediation process has to be started manually and cannot be scheduled. Of course, you can create a PowerShell script and kick it off at a later time, but you might want to be available while the cluster-remediation process is running.

At the end of the cluster-remediation process, the status should be as shown in Figure 7.29.

FIGURE 7.29
The remediation is complete.

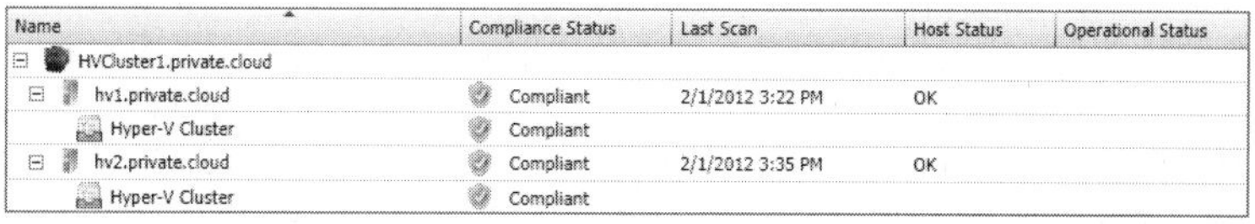

Name			Compliance Status	Last Scan	Host Status	Operational Status
⊟ 🖥 HVCluster1.private.cloud						
⊟ 🖳	hv1.private.cloud		Compliant	2/1/2012 3:22 PM	OK	
	🖳	Hyper-V Cluster	Compliant			
⊟ 🖳	hv2.private.cloud		Compliant	2/1/2012 3:35 PM	OK	
	🖳	Hyper-V Cluster	Compliant			

Adding Existing VMware ESX Hosts

VMM allows you to deploy and manage virtual machines on VMware ESX hosts, as you can with any supported hypervisor. The only difference is that you cannot bare-metal-deploy an ESX host because the chosen native VHD deployment model is not applicable to VMware hosts. Also cluster remediation cannot be applied, because WSUS does not support updating non-Windows hosts. This should not keep you from adding your VMware ESX hosts to VMM, because all the other deployment and management capabilities fully apply to ESX hosts, including creating clouds, creating VMs, and using PowerShell scripting. You can even deploy a multitiered service across multiple hypervisors. Service modeling is described in subsequent chapters.

Because you can't create new VMware ESX hosts, you must first add existing ESX hosts and clusters. Check the requirements in Chapter 4 before you begin, because VMM no longer supports some older versions of ESX and vCenter.

VMM integrates directly with VMware vCenter Server. As soon as vCenter is added to the VMM fabric, you can start adding ESX hosts and clusters.

VMware ESX Integration Improvements

Let's look at some of the differences between managing VMware ESX hosts in VMM 2012 and VMM 2008 R2.

- ◆ As with VMM 2008 R2, VMM 2012 can specify ESX hosts to import or not import an entire vCenter data center.

- ◆ You can add an ESX host to any existing VMM 2012 host group; so in contrast to VMM 2008 R2, you can mix and match Hyper-V and VMware hosts.

- ◆ You can import VMware templates into the VMM library without copying the .vmdk file to the library. Unlike VMM 2008 R2, only the template metadata is registered in the VMM 2012 library, allowing for much faster virtual-machine deployment.

- ◆ If you delete a VMware template from the VMM library, it is not deleted from the VMware data store, as was the case with VMM 2008 R2.

- ◆ Whereas VMM 2008 R2 supported Secure File Transfer Protocol (SFTP) for file transfers, VMM 2012 uses HTTPS for all file transfers between ESX hosts and the VMM library.

Therefore, you no longer need to enable Secure Shell (SSH) to access an ESX host, as was necessary in VMM 2008 R2. Root credentials are needed for file transfers between ESX servers and VMM.

◆ VMM 2012 supports VMware's distributed virtual switch functionality, but you must still configure it from within vCenter. There was no support for distributed virtual switches in VMM 2008 R2

◆ Port groups are still supported, but they must also be configured in vCenter Server. Unlike VMM 2008 R2, the current version of VMM does not automatically create port groups on ESX hosts.

Supported Features

When managing VMware ESX hosts, VMM 2012 supports the following features:

◆ The PowerShell command shell

◆ Placement of VMs and services using host ratings for creation, deployment, and migration of VMware virtual machines

◆ Deployment of VMM services

◆ Private clouds with ESX host resources

◆ Self-service roles and quotas with ESX host resources

◆ Dynamic optimization (but turn off VMware's Dynamic Resource Scheduler)

◆ Power optimization to turn ESX hosts on or off

◆ Live migration (vMotion)

◆ Live storage migration (Storage vMotion)

◆ Migration to and from the VMM library (but VMware thin-provisioned disks become thick when placed in a VMM library)

◆ Network migration between hosts

◆ Maintenance mode

◆ VMM library for storing VMware VMs, .vmdk files, and VMware templates

◆ .vmdk files (older formats created in VMware Server and Workstation have to be converted)

◆ Templates

◆ Standard and distributed vSwitches and port groups

◆ Storage of type VMware Paravirtual

◆ Hot addition and hot removal of virtual hard disks on VMware VMs

◆ Conversion (between VMware VM and Hyper-V VM via V2V process)

◆ Performance and resource optimization (PRO) for monitoring and alerting ESX host via VMM with integration of Operations Manager and PRO

◆ Recognition of VMware fault-tolerant VMs (VMM only shows primary VM on the vCenter server. If it fails VMM recognizes the new primary.)

◆ Dynamic memory

Limitations

Here are some limitations and unsupported features:

◆ VMM does not support VMware VMs with disks on IDE bus. V2V of these machines fails.

◆ Storage must be added to ESX hosts outside of VMM and cannot be provisioned using SMI-S storage automation functionality.

◆ VMM does not automatically create port groups on ESX hosts. Port groups and VLANs must be configured outside of VMM.

◆ VMM does not integrate with VMware vCloud.

◆ You cannot use VMM to deploy vApps.

◆ Update management/cluster remediation is not supported for ESX hosts.

◆ Bare-metal deployment is not supported for ESX hosts.

◆ Dynamic memory is supported only on Hyper-V hosts that are running an OS that supports dynamic memory.

Capabilities

A VM on an ESX host managed by VMM can have the capabilities listed in Table 7.2.

TABLE 7.2:   VMware VM Capabilities

CATEGORY	MINIMUM	MAXIMUM
Processor Range	1	8
Memory Range	4 MB	255 GB
DVD Range	1	4
Hard-Disk Count	0	255
Disk Size Range	0 MB	256 GB
Network Adapters	0	64

Adding a VMware vCenter Server

Before you add a VMware vCenter Server to VMM, check the requirements in Chapter 4. Not all versions are supported.

Secure Sockets Layer (SSL) is used for communication between the VMM management server and the vCenter Server. Either a third-party or a self-signed certificate can be used. Self-signed certificates must be stored in the Trusted People Certificate store.

Before adding the vCenter Server, create a Run As account with the correct Active Directory credentials. This account must have administrative privileges on vCenter Server. A local administrator account on the vCenter Server is also supported.

Adding a vCenter Server does not automatically add VMware ESX hosts. That requires an additional step.

These are the steps to add a VMware vCenter server:

1. In the VMM console, select Fabric, expand Servers from the Navigation pane, and right-click vCenter Server; or click Add Resources from the ribbon and select VMware vCenter Server.

2. Provide the computer name of the vCenter server and specify the correct TCP/IP port (default 443). Also, select your prepared Run As account for connecting to the vCenter server. If you have a certificate, you can leave the "Communicate with VMware ESX host in secure mode" check box checked. Click OK when you are ready.

3. When the VMware certificate appears, click Import.

The PowerShell command to add a VMware vCenter server is

```
PS C:\> $certificate = Get-SCCertificate -ComputerName "vcenter1.private.cloud"
-TCPPort ⤷ 443

PS C:\> $runAsAccount = Get-SCRunAsAccount -Name "Run_As_Domain_Admin"
PS C:\> Add-SCVirtualizationManager -ComputerName "vcenter1.private. ⤷ cloud"
-TCPPort "443" -Credential $runAsAccount -Certificate $certificate
-EnableSecureMode ⤷$true -RunAsynchronously
```

To obtain some extra information about the imported virtualization manager, execute the following code:

```
PS C:\> Get-SCVirtualizationManager -ComputerName vcenter1.private.cloud
```

```
Name                          : vcenter1.private.cloud
SecureMode                    : True
SslTcpPort                    : 443
SslCertificateHash            : 01F5675198A1E88C41228A3F484AC76118D91B0E
NumberOfManagedHosts          : 0
ManagedHosts                  : {}
UnmanagedHosts                : {}
UnmanagedHostClusters         : {}
NumberOfManagedVirtualMachines : 0
Status                        : Responding
```

```
StatusString              : Responding
Version                   : 4.1.0
UserName                  : administrator
Domain                    : private
RunAsAccount              : Run_As_Domain_Admin
ServerConnection          : Microsoft.SystemCenter.VirtualMachineManager.
                            Remoting.ServerConnection
ID                        : 09447c1c-c63e-4d18-97fc-90abf9c9981f
IsViewOnly                : False
ObjectType                : VirtualizationManager
MarkedForDeletion         : False
IsFullyCached             : True
```

Adding a VMware ESX/ESXi Host or Cluster

Now that the VMware vCenter Server has been successfully added to VMM, you can add VMware ESX/ESXi hosts and clusters. Follow these steps:

1. In the VMM console, select Fabric, expand Servers from the Navigation pane, click Add Resources from the ribbon, and select VMware ESX Hosts and Clusters.

2. Select a Run As account with root access to the ESX host you are adding to VMM, and click Next.

3. A list of ESX hosts will appear. Select the hosts you want to add, and click Next.

4. On the Host Settings page, choose a host group for the ESX hosts. Click Next.

5. Review the Summary page and click Finish to confirm.

   If the host status shows OK, then the ESX host has been added successfully. You can also check the status by looking at the job details or by expanding the host group that contains the ESX servers. If the ESX hosts shows OK (Limited), the Run As account does not have root credentials. Another possibility is that you enabled Secure mode without importing the certificate.

To update the ESX-host status, follow these steps:

1. Right-click the ESX host that has an OK (Limited) status and select Properties.

2. Select the Management tab and select a Run As account with root credentials on the ESX host.

3. Click Retrieve to get the certificate and public key for the host. You can view the thumbprint details by clicking View Details.

4. Check the "Accept the certificate for this host" check box and click OK when you are finished.

5. Verify that the host status has changed to OK.

Adding Existing XenServer Hosts

You have seen how to integrate both Microsoft and VMware hypervisors and how to bring these hosts under management in VMM. In VMM 2012, Microsoft introduces a third supported hypervisor, Citrix XenServer. XenServer host management is made possible by a XenServer Integration Pack written by Citrix. Without depending on Citrix XenCenter, this hypervisor perfectly integrates with the VMM Management and Library servers (Figure 7.30).

FIGURE 7.30
Integration of
XenServer in VMM

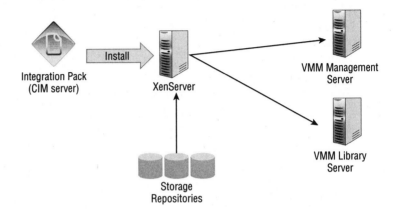

Supported Features

VMM 2012 offers you the following functionality in combination with Citrix XenServer:

♦ Deployment of virtual machines and services using VMM templates

♦ Intelligent placement with host ratings

♦ Paravirtualized VMs (PVs), meaning there is no requirement to use emulated device drivers, freeing up processor time and resources

♦ Highly available VMs (HAVMs)

♦ VM migration (XenMotion) within a resource pool

♦ LAN migration between XenServer and the VMM library

♦ VM conversion using the Physical-to-Virtual (P2V) instead of the Virtual-to-Virtual (V2V) method

♦ Dynamic optimization

♦ Power optimization (requires a BMC in the host for shutdown, power-on, and restart of host)

♦ Maintenance mode (for evacuating a host before maintenance)

♦ XenServer storage with support for all kinds of local and shared XenServer repositories (iSCSI, NFS, HBA, StorageLink). All storage must be added to XenServer outside of VMM.

♦ ISO repositories on NFS or CIFS. The ISO repository must be read-write. Attachment of ISOs is supported only from the VMM library.

♦ XenServer host networking by wrapping a single virtual switch around all of the XenServer switches on a single physical adapter (Figure 7.31)

♦ Windows with highly available VMs

◆ Standard VHDs

◆ Regular start, stop, save state, pause, and shut down VM actions

◆ Enhanced XenServer checkpoints

◆ Guest-console access

FIGURE 7.31
Network integration of XenServer in VMM

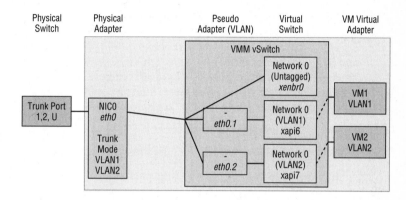

Limitations

You need to be aware of these limitations when integrating XenServer in your private cloud with VMM 2012:

◆ Dynamic memory is not supported.

◆ Virtual floppy drive and COM ports are not available as VM devices.

◆ SMI-S for discovering and configuring storage on XenServer hosts is not supported.

◆ XenServer templates are not supported.

◆ Bare-metal deployment of XenServer hosts is not supported.

Capabilities

Table 7.3 shows supported configurations for VMs on XenServer hosts.

TABLE 7.3:   XenServer VM Capabilities

CATEGORY	MINIMUM	MAXIMUM
Processor Range	1	8
Memory Range	16 MB	32 GB
DVD Range	1	4
Hard-Disk Count	0	7
Disk Size Range	0 MB	2,040 GB
Network Adapters	0	7

Installing Microsoft System Center Integration Pack

Integrating Citrix XenServer into your VMM environment is supported for specific versions of XenServer. The requirements for Citrix XenServer integration can be found in Chapter 4.

Unlike the case with Hyper-V, you cannot create a new XenServer host by means of bare-metal deployment. The XenServer hosts or pools (clusters) must already exist before you can add them to the VMM fabric.

Before you can add a XenServer host or cluster (they are called *pools* in XenServer terminology), you need to prepare XenServer by installing the Microsoft System Center integration pack in Domain 0 (Dom0). Like the first partition or parent partition in Hyper-V, Dom0 is more privileged and has full access to the hardware. When XenServer starts, Dom0 is started automatically after XenServer boots, and you use its console to configure XenServer for VMM integration.

The Microsoft System Center integration pack can be downloaded from MyCitrix. If you don't have an account for MyCitrix, register for one at

```
www.citrix.com/english/mycitrix/
```

Follow these steps to install the integration pack:

1. Mount the ISO of the integration pack.

```
# mkdir -p /mnt/tmp
# # mount <path_to_Integration_Pack_iso/XenServer-6.0.0.2-integration-suite.iso ↵/
mnt/tmp -o loop
```

OR

```
# mount /dev/dvd /mnt/tmp
Mount: block device /dev/dvd is write-protected, mounting read-only
```

2. Start the installation script.

```
# cd /mnt/tmp
# ls
install.sh
ms-scx-1.0.0-32074.i386.rpm
openpegasus-2.10.0-xs1.i386.rpm
xenserver-vnc-control-6.0.0-52391p.noarch.rpm
xs-cim-cmpi-6.0.0.52271p.i386.rpm
XS-PACKAGES
XS-REPOSITORY
# ./install.sh
```

You can check the installed version of the integration pack using a XenServer command:

```
Xe host-param-get uuid=<host-uuid> param-name=software-version
```

After installing the XenServer integration pack, you can verify that the installation was correct by using winrm. On the VMM management server, open a PowerShell console from within VMM (so the virtualmachinemanager module is already loaded).

```
PS C:\> winrm enum http://schemas.citrix.com/wbem/wscim/1/cim-schema/2/Xen_⏎
HostComputerSystem -r:https://<hostname>:5989 -encoding:utf-8 -a:basic ⏎
-u:<XenUser> -p:<Password> -skipCACheck

Xen_HostComputerSystem
    AvailableRequestedStates = 3, 10, 4
    CN = xenserver1.private.cloud
    Caption = XenServer Host
    CommunicationStatus = null
    CreationClassName = Xen_HostComputerSystem
    Dedicated = 2
    Description = Default install of XenServer
    DetailedStatus = null
    ElementName = xenserver1
    EnabledDefault = 2
    EnabledState = 2
    Generation = null
    HealthState = 5
    IdentifyingDescriptions = IPv4Address, ProductBrand, ProductVersion,
    BuildNumber
    InstallDate = null
    InstanceID = null
    Name = 420b6087-a97e-403d-b626-0c3f68dc97a9
    NameFormat = Other
    OperatingStatus = null
    OperationalStatus = 2
    OtherConfig = agent_start_time=1327743281., boot_time=1327743234., iscsi_
    iqn=iqn.2011-12.com.example:5e105dfa
    OtherDedicatedDescriptions = null
    OtherEnabledState = null
    OtherIdentifyingInfo = 192.168.1.71, XenServer, 6.0.0, 50762p
    PowerManagementCapabilities = null
    PrimaryOwnerContact = null
    PrimaryOwnerName = null
    PrimaryStatus = null
    RequestedState = 2
    ResetCapability = null
    Roles = null
    StartTime = 2012-01-28T09:33:54Z
    Status = OK
    StatusDescriptions = null
    TimeOfLastStateChange = 2011-12-11T09:43:27Z
    TimeOffset = 3600
    TransitioningToState = 12
```

Checking the XenServer Hostname

If the XenServer host does not have an FQDN, VMM imports the XenServer based on its IP address. If VMM displays a XenServer host with only its IP address, perform the following steps to correct this:

1. Remove the XenServer host from VMM.

2. Run the following command to check whether the server has a FQDN or not:

```
# Hostname -f
Xenserver1
```

3. From the XenServer console menu, select the Network And Management Interface menu, which shows the hostname along with other information. When the NIC for the management interface is shown, press Enter. Press Enter again to accept the IP-address configuration. Press Tab to go to Hostname and complete the FQDN, as shown in Figure 7.32.

FIGURE 7.32
Changing the host-name of XenServer

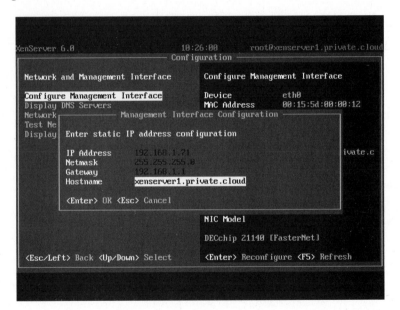

4. Open a XenServer command shell and check the FQDN again with `hostname -f`, which should now show you the full hostname.

```
# Hostname -f
Xenserver1.private.cloud
```

5. Because the certificate is not yet aware of this name change, you have to rename or remove the certificate file (`xapi-sll.pem`).

```
# cd /etc/xensource
# rm xapi-sll.pem
rm: remove regular file 'xapi-sll.pem'? y
```

6. Restart the server.

Adding a XenServer Host or Cluster

Before you add your first XenServer host to VMM, prepare a Run As account with credentials for root access to the XenServer hosts. When you are ready, perform these steps to add a XenServer host or cluster:

1. In the VMM console, select Fabric, expand Servers from the Navigation pane, click Add Resources from the ribbon, and select Citrix XenServer Hosts and Clusters.

2. On the Server Settings screen, enter the FQDN of the XenServer host and accept TCP port 5989 unless you don't want to use the default port. Leave "Use certificates to communicate with this host" turned on, select an appropriate Run As account for the XenServer, and choose a target host group. Click Add and repeat this step for each host or cluster you want to add.

3. Select one of the added hosts and click View Certificate.

4. A thumbprint of the CA Root certificate is shown. Check the name of the host on the certificate and click OK when you are ready.

5. Review the summary and click Finish.

The XenServer host is now added to VMM. Because the integration pack is already installed, this job completes quickly.

The alternative route is to use PowerShell for adding a Citrix XenServer host:

```
PS C:\> $RunAsAccount = Get-SCRunAsAccount -Name "Run_As_XenServer"
PS C:\> $HostGroup = Get-SCVMHostGroup -ID "35fc20ae-fa7c-4395-a55a-0591fe1cf68b" ↵
-Name "Development"
PS C:\> $Certificate = Get-SCCertificate -ComputerName "xenserver1.private.cloud" ↵
-TCPPort 5989
PS C:\> Add-SCVMHost -ComputerName "xenserver1.private.cloud" -TCPPort "5989" ↵
-EnableSecureMode $true -Credential $RunAsAccount -VMHostGroup $HostGroup ↵
-XenServerHost -RunAsynchronously -Certificate $Certificate
```

You are now ready to manage XenServer hosts and clusters as you would any other virtualization host in VMM. Your private cloud has become a truly heterogeneous cloud, and you are ready to deploy virtual machines and services to any of the hypervisors.

Summary

This chapter discussed the deployment of hosts and clusters. Hyper-V hosts that are domain-joined in a nontrusted domain or in a perimeter network need to be treated differently.

The VMM Add Host Wizard makes this task easy. A more ambitious task is the bare-metal deployment method, which transforms servers without an OS into fully operational Hyper-V servers. Building on the previous chapter about integrating storage and networking, you can automate the creation of Hyper-V clusters and configure dynamic optimization and power optimization.

The chapter also showed you how to add a VMware vCenter, including VMware ESX hosts and clusters. The paragraphs on vSphere explain what features are supported, vSphere's capabilities, and its limitations.

Finally, the newly supported Citrix XenServer host was introduced. You learned how to add XenServer hosts without using XenCenter; add a VMware vCenter, including VMware ESX; and you saw the supported features, capabilities, and limitations of this hypervisor platform under the wings of VMM 2012.

## Chapter 8

Understanding Service Modeling

One of the most powerful aspects of VMM 2012 is the ability to combine various library components, to deploy not only a VM, but also a complex n-tier application, across many VMs over different networks. Before you can create and deploy services in VMM, a number of prerequisites need to be met. This chapter introduces service deployment and in an extended example, takes a simple service from deployment through scaling out, exporting and importing a service template, and managing updates. This chapter covers the following main topics:

◆ How service templates enable you to model services and deploy them as easily as VMs

◆ How sequencing captures all necessary steps and resources for distributing and installing an application reliably

◆ The nuts and bolts of preparing, distributing, and updating services and application packages

Introduction to Service Templates

Just as VM templates provide a standardized group of hardware, software, and application settings that you can consistently reuse to create multiple new VMs, a service template provides the information required to create an instance of a service. A service can be as simple as a single tiered application contained within a VM, or it can be a multitier application spanning a number of VMs that are managed as a single entity.

Every service template has a name, which appears in the VMs and Services workspace; has a release value, which indicates the version of the service template; and is constructed from a pattern of one or more tiers, which is a model of your service graphically represented in the VMM Service Template Designer.

Each tier of your service can contain some combination of the following four components:

◆ A VM template (see Chapter 5, "Understanding the VMM Library")

◆ A virtual IP template (see Chapter 6, "Understanding Network and Storage Integration in VMM 2012")

◆ An application profile

◆ A SQL Server profile

APPLICATION PROFILE

An application profile provides the instructions for installing Microsoft Server Application Virtualization (SAV) applications, Microsoft Web Deploy applications, and Microsoft SQL Server data-tier applications (DACs), and for running scripts when deploying a VM as part of a service.

SQL SERVER PROFILE

A SQL Server profile provides instructions for installing an instance of SQL Server when deploying a VM as part of a service.

Preparing the Library for Application Deployment

Before you can commission your service via VMM, you must set up and configure a number of library resources to enable you to deploy your service. These library resources include the following:

- ◆ VM template
    - ◆ Hardware profile
    - ◆ Guest operating-system profile
- ◆ Prebuilt virtual hard disk (VHD)
- ◆ Application profile
- ◆ SQL Server profile
- ◆ Custom resources

You start by deploying a VM template. Then you add or extend additional library resources to allow you to eventually deploy and scale out your service.

Virtual-Machine Templates

A VM template is a library resource that consists of a number of other configuration components:

- ◆ Hardware profile
- ◆ Guest operating-system profile
- ◆ Virtual hard disk
- ◆ Capability profile
- ◆ Application profile
- ◆ SQL Server profile

Creating a Hardware Profile

A hardware profile is a library resource that contains the hardware specifications to be applied to a new VM or to a VM template.

Use the following procedure to create a new hardware profile from within the VMM console. This profile serves as the base hardware profile and is used later in the example deployment.

1. Launch the VMM console, log in with the appropriate credentials, and select the Library workspace. On the Home tab, in the Create group, click Create and select Hardware Profile. The New Hardware Profile screen appears.

2. On the General tab, enter a name and description for the hardware profile.

3. On the Hardware Profile tab (Figure 8.1), configure the hardware profile as appropriate and click OK.

FIGURE 8.1
Configuring the hardware profile

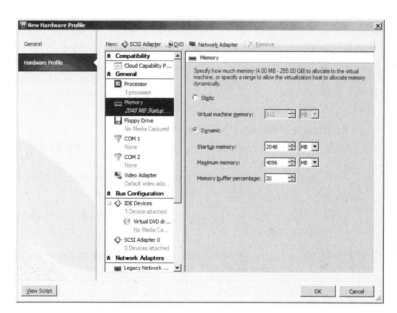

Creating a Guest Operating-System Profile

A guest operating-system profile is a collection of operating-system settings and values that can be imported into a VM template, thereby providing a consistent OS configuration for VMs that are deployed from that template.

Use the following procedure to create a new guest operating-system profile to serve as the base guest operating-system profile and is used later in the example deployment.

1. In the VMM console, select the Library workspace. On the Home tab, in the Create group, click Create, and select Guest OS Profile. The New Guest OS Profile screen appears.

2. On the General tab, enter a name and description for the guest OS profile.

3. On the Guest OS Profile tab (Figure 8.2), configure the guest OS profile as appropriate.

FIGURE 8.2
Configuring the
guest OS profile

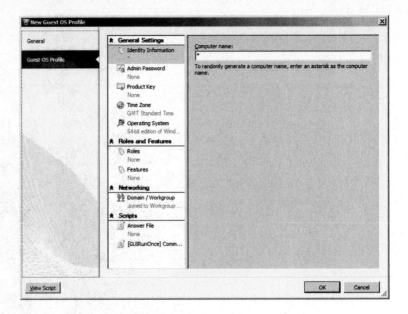

Adding a VHD to the Library

Your library must contain a sysprepped Windows 2008 R2 SP1 VHD. Adding a file-based resource such as a VHD to the library must be done manually. To use the files before the next scheduled library refresh, you must manually refresh the library server or share. To add the required VHD, complete one of the following tasks:

◆ Using Windows Explorer, browse to the library share and manually copy the specific files you need.

◆ In the VMM console, in the Library workspace, expand Library Servers, right-click a library share, and click Explore. Manually copy the specific files you need.

◆ In the VMM console, on the Home tab, use the Import Physical Resource and Export Physical resource options to import and export file-based resources between library shares.

To refresh the library server:

1. In the VMM console, select the Library workspace. In the Library pane, expand the Library Servers node, and right-click the library server you want to refresh.

2. Click Refresh.

Creating a VM Template

With all the basic building blocks in place, the next step is to create a VM template.
Use the following steps to create a new VM template:

1. In the VMM console, select the Library workspace. On the Home tab, in the Create group, click Create VM Template. The Select Source screen appears.

2. Click the radio button for using an existing VM template or virtual hard disk. Click Browse and select the VHD described in the previous section. Click Next. The VM Template Identity screen appears.

3. Enter a name and description for the VM template, and click Next. The Configure Hardware screen appears.

4. From the Hardware Profile drop-down list, select the hardware profile created earlier in this chapter, and click Next. The Configure Operating System screen appears.

5. From the Guest OS Profile drop-down list, select the guest OS profile created earlier in this chapter, and click Next.

6. Click through the following screens to finish the process:

   ◆ On the Configure Applications screen, click Next for the default.

   ◆ On the Configure SQL Server screen, click Next for the default.

   ◆ On the Summary screen, click Create to finish.

Creating Application Packages with Server App-V

One of the major enhancements in VMM 2012 is the capability of VMM to manage Microsoft Server Application Virtualization (Server App-V) packages. Server App-V provides the ability to virtualize an application and abstract the application from the underlying server operating system. Applications are packaged by using a sequencer, which then makes the application files easy to copy, without requiring changes to the application itself. There are five steps to creating a Server App-V package:

1. Install the Sequencer.

2. Launch the Sequencer to monitor the reference server.

3. Install the application on the reference server.

4. Finish the installation and stop monitoring.

5. Save the Server App-V package.

Installing the Server App-V Sequencer

To install the Server App-V Sequencer, you must deploy a VM to act as the reference machine. Use the components you now have in the library to deploy a VM to act as your reference machine. There are a couple of important points to remember when installing Server App-V:

   ◆ Install the Server App-V Sequencer on a clean reference machine.

   The reference machine should be free of other third-party software when you install the Server App-V Sequencer. Otherwise, the sequencing of your application might be interrupted or fail.

   ◆ If you are planning to deploy Server App-V packages to multiple operating system versions, choose the lowest OS version as the OS for your reference machine.

For example, if you want to deploy a Server App-V package to both Windows 2008 R2 and Windows 2008 R2 SP1, then choose Windows 2008 R2 as the OS for your reference machine. Table 8.1 shows the minimum OS requirements for Server App-V.

TABLE 8.1:   OS requirements for the Server App-V Sequencer

OPERATING-SYSTEM VERSION	EDITION	SERVICE PACK	SYSTEM ARCHITECTURE
Windows Server 2003		SP2	x86 and x64
Windows Server 2003	R2	SP2	x86 and x64
Windows Server 2008		SP2	x86 and x64
Windows Server 2008	R2		x64 only
Windows Server 2008	R2	SP1	x64 only

The setup binaries for the Server App-V Sequencer are in a file named `seqsetup.exe`, which by default is on your VMM server, under either x86 or x64 system architecture, in the following directory:

```
c:\program files\microsoft system center 2012\virtual machine manager\sav
```

Take these steps to install the Server App-V Sequencer on the reference machine:

1. Copy the Server App-V Sequencer installation file `seqsetup.exe` to the reference machine.

   Use the version of the installation file that matches the architecture of the reference machine (x86 or x64).

2. Double-click `seqsetup.exe`. The Setup Wizard opens.

3. Click through the following screens:

   ◆ On the Welcome screen, click Next.

   ◆ On the License screen click Accept.

   ◆ On the Customer Experience Improvement screen, click Next.

   ◆ On the Destination Folder screen, click Next to accept the default.

   ◆ On the Ready to Install screen, Click Install.

If it does not detect the Microsoft Visual C++ 2005 SP1 Redistributable Packages (x86) and the Microsoft Visual C++ 2008 SP1 Redistributable Packages (x86), the Setup Wizard installs them.

Creating Your First Package

If you have installed the Server App-V Sequencer on a suitable reference machine, you can start to sequence your first application. The example sequences a sample .NET application called Pet Shop 4.0, which is available for download from the following URL:

```
http://msdn.microsoft.com/en-us/library/aa479071.aspx
```

Before sequencing Pet Shop 4.0, you must ensure that the following conditions exist on the reference machine:

◆ The User Account Control (UAC) is off.

◆ The Web Server role is enabled.

◆ The Web Server Management Tools are enabled.

◆ Web Deploy 2.0 is installed.

Web Deploy enables you to package configuration and content from your installed web applications, including databases, and use the packages for storage or redeployment. Web Deploy is available in your library at

```
C:\ProgramData\Virtual Machine Manager Library Files\ApplicationFrameworks
```

You can also download it from

```
www.iis.net/download/WebDeploy
```

Using the Sequencer

Before you launch the Server App-V Sequencer, make sure that the Pet Shop 4.0 installation files are easily accessible to your reference machine. The procedure for sequencing the Pet Shop 4.0 application has four basic parts:

◆ Start the Sequencer and install.

◆ Perform post-installation tasks.

◆ Create the package.

◆ Store the package in the library.

To start the Sequencer and Install Pet Shop 4.0, follow these steps:

1. On the reference machine, start the App-V Sequencer.

You should be able to do this from the Start menu by navigating to All Programs ➤ Microsoft Server Application Virtualization ➤ Microsoft Server Application Virtualization Sequencer.

The Microsoft Server Application Virtualization Sequencer screen appears.

2. Click Create A New Virtual Application Package. The Prepare Computer screen appears.

3. Resolve any highlighted issues and click Refresh. When no issues are highlighted, click Next. The Select Installer screen appears.

4. Click Browse and navigate to `Microsoft .NET Pet Shop 4.0.msi` (the Pet Shop 4.0 application installer). Click Open and click Next. The Package Name screen appears.

5. Enter **Petshop4** in the Package Name field and click Next.

The Installation screen appears and displays a progress bar. When it finishes, the Security Warning pop-up appears.

6. Click through the following screens:

   ◆ On the Security Warning screen, click Run.

   ◆ On the Welcome To The Setup Wizard screen, click Next.

   ◆ On the License Agreement screen, click Accept.

   ◆ On the .NET Pet Shop 4.0 Information screen, click Next.

   ◆ On the Installation Options screen, click Source Code Only and Next.

The Select Installation Folder screen appears (Figure 8.3).

FIGURE 8.3
The installation-folder options

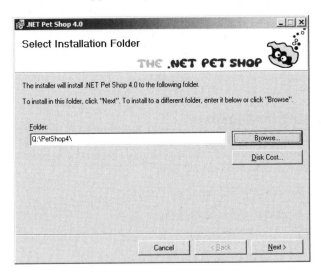

7. Click Browse, change the folder to **Q:\PetShop4** and click Next.

8. Click through the following screens:

   ◆ In Internet Explorer, close the `readme` file.

   ◆ On the Installation Complete screen, click Close.

9. Minimize the Sequencer. The Sequencer continues watching. After you perform the post-installation tasks, maximize it and continue.

To perform the post-installation tasks (such as sequencing Pet Shop 4.0), follow these steps:

1. Open an elevated command prompt (one with administrative rights) and change to **Q:\Petshop4**.

2. Enter `build.bat` and wait for all the actions within the batch file to complete.

When the batch job is done, the message `Press any key to continue…` will appear.

3. From the same command prompt, enter `ecryptWebConfig.bat` and wait for the batch job to finish.

When the batch job is done, the message `Press any key to continue…` will appear.

4. Start the IIS manager.

You should be able to do this from the Start menu by navigating to Administrative Tools ➢ Internet Information Services (IIS) Manager.

5. Expand the Local Host node, right-click the Sites node, and select Add Web Site. The Add Web Site screen appears (Figure 8.4).

FIGURE 8.4

Adding a website

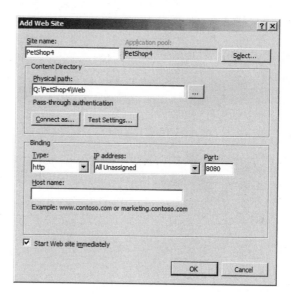

6. Enter **PetShop4** as the site name, `Q:\PetShop4\Web` as the physical path, and **8080** as the assigned port; or use whichever port is appropriate for your environment, and click OK.

7. Using Windows Explorer, copy the Transact-SQL database scripts for Pet Shop 4.0 from `Q:\PetShop4\DatabaseScripts` to a machine that is easily accessible to the reference machine.

You will need these scripts later, when you start to create SQL DACPACs.
To create the package (and continue sequencing Pet Shop 4.0), follow these steps:

1. Maximize the Sequencer, click the I Am Finished Installing check box, and click Next. The Configure Software screen appears.

2. Switch to the VMM management server (or the main library share) and connect to the shared location where the Pet Shop 4.0 database scripts reside.

3. On the main library share, under the `ApplicationFrameworks` folder, create a subfolder called **SQL_TSCRIPTS** and a subfolder within that folder called **PetShop4_SQLDB.CR**.

The `ApplicationFrameworks` folder is created by default during the VMM installation.

4. Copy the Transact-SQL scripts to the `PetShop4_SQLDB.CR` folder.

5. In the VMM console ➤ Library workspace ➤ Library pane, expand the Library Servers node, right-click the library server to which you copied the scripts, and select Refresh.

6 Go back to the Sequencer, and on the Configure Software page, click Next because no first-use tasks need to be managed for Pet Shop 4.0.

The Create Package screen appears.

7. Click Close.

The Deployment Configuration Items screen appears, showing all captured connection strings and application settings (Figure 8.5).

FIGURE 8.5
Configuring
deployment

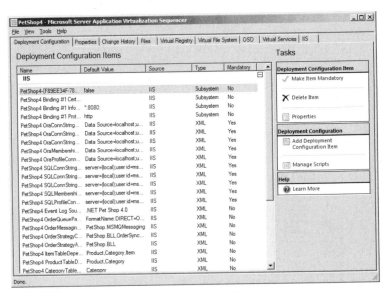

8. From the File menu, click Save and save the Server App-V project to an easily accessible location.

To store the package in the library (and continue sequencing Pet Shop 4.0), follow these steps:

1. Switch to the VMM management server (or the main library share) and connect to the shared location where the Pet Shop 4.0 package resides.

2. On the main library share, under the App-V folder, create a subfolder called **PetShop4** and a subfolder of that folder called **V1**.

If you followed along in Chapter 5, "Understanding the VMM Library," you created the App-V folder. The name V1 stands for version 1.

3. Copy the contents of the sequenced package to the V1 folder.

4. In the VMM console ➢ Library workspace ➢ Library pane, expand the Library Servers node, right-click the library server to which you copied the package, and select Refresh.

The Server App-V package should now appear in the library.

5. Right-click the Server App-V package and select Properties. The PetShop4 Properties screen appears (Figure 8.6)

FIGURE 8.6
PetShop4
properties

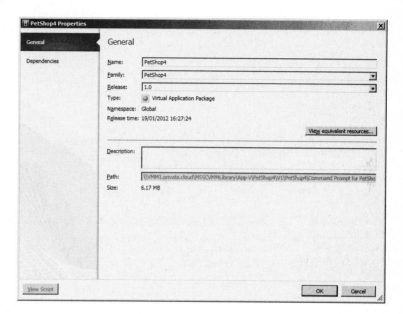

6. On the General tab, in the Family field, enter an application family name (for example, **PetShop4**.) In the Release field, enter a release value (for example, **1.0**), and click OK.

Creating an Application Profile for a Server App-V Application

Application profiles provide the instructions for installing Microsoft Server App-V applications, Microsoft Web Deploy applications, and Microsoft SQL Server DACs, and for running scripts when deploying a VM as part of a service.

To create an application profile for a Microsoft Server App-V application, perform these steps:

1. In the VMM console, select the Library workspace. On the Home tab, in the Create group, click Create, and select Application Profile. The New Application Profile screen appears.

2. On the General tab, enter a name and description for the application profile, and then open the Application Configuration tab (Figure 8.7).

3. Click OS Compatibility and select the OS version and edition on which the application is supported. Click OK. The New Application Profile screen appears (Figure 8.8).

4. Click Add (the green plus sign) and select Virtual Application. Enter a name for the application (for example, **PetShop4 Application**). Click Browse, select the application package that you previously placed in the library, and click OK.

FIGURE 8.7
Setting OS
compatibility

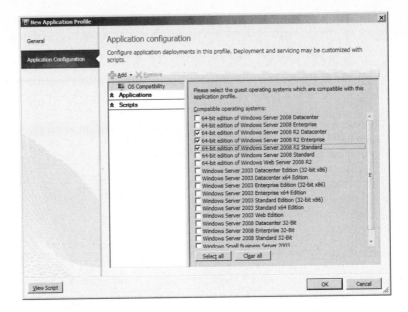

FIGURE 8.8
Configuring the
application

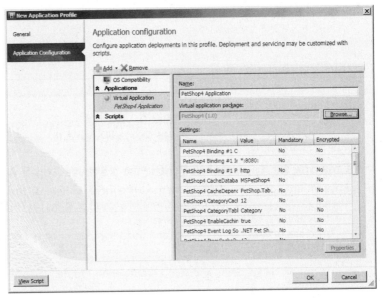

SQL Server Profiles

SQL Server profiles have a key role in rapidly deploying SQL Server within your environment. You decouple the mechanics of installation (called *sysprepping*) from customizing SQL Server for a specific use. The first phase is to perform a standalone SQL Server deployment on a base VM, leaving configuration for a later phase, during which you'll create and use SQL Server profiles.

This approach has the following limitations:

◆ Only Database Engine Services and Reporting Services support standalone deployment.

◆ You can't use standalone deployment in combination with clustering or high-availability scenarios.

◆ You need the installation media when you configure the image.

Performing a Standalone Deployment

You can use the Advanced option within the SQL Server Installation Center to perform a standalone deployment. This installation option is available in all editions of SQL Server 2008 R2.

Although the instructions for performing standalone SQL deployments are not within the scope of this book, there are several articles that do describe how to do it. However, these articles typically do not explain how to use VMM when carrying out the Complete Image phase. The following TechNet article provides good instructions:

```
http://technet.microsoft.com/en-us/library/ee210664.aspx
```

Only the Prerequisites and Prepare Image sections of this article are applicable. The remainder of the configuration uses VMM, as described in subsequent sections of this chapter.

You can also perform the Prepare Image phase from the command line by running the following command:

```
setup.exe /q /ACTION=PrepareImage /FEATURES=SQL,RS
          /InstanceID =<MyInstanceID> /IACCEPTSQLSERVERLICENSETERMS
```

NOTE No matter how you perform a standalone deployment, be sure to make a note of the instance ID, because this value is required when you create the SQL Server profile in VMM.

The instance ID is not the same as the instance name. You can specify both during the Prepare Image phase. The *instance ID* is used only during SQL Server installation and configuration. It is an identifier that enables you to prepare multiple SQL Server instances. The *instance name* is used after installation to connect to a SQL Server instance.

Once you have a standalone deployment of SQL Server, run Windows Sysprep to generalize the operating-system instance and submit the generalized VHD into the library. This is your source VHD for deploying SQL Server.

Use a descriptive name for the VHD file so you can distinguish this VHD from other VHDs in the library. For example, you can rename your VHD to **W2K8R2x64_SQL2K8R2EE.VHD**.

Creating a SQL Server Profile

Now that your standalone deployment of SQL is configured and in the library, use the following procedure to create a SQL Server profile.

1. In the VMM console, select the Library workspace. On the Home tab, in the Create group, click Create, and select SQL Server Profile. The New SQL Server Profile screen appears.

2. On the General tab, enter a name and description for the SQL Server profile. Switch to the SQL Server Configuration tab (Figure 8.9).

3. Click the SQL Server Deployment option. Fill in the name, instance name, instance ID, product key, and installation Run As account. Click Configuration.

FIGURE 8.9
Specifying SQL
Server deployment
options

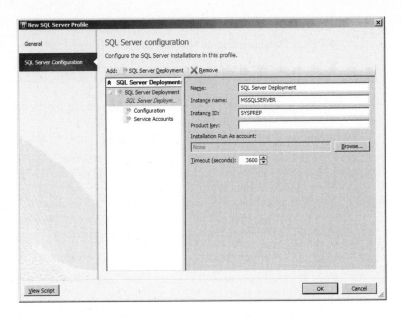

In the Name field specify a name for this SQL Server deployment, and in the Instance Name field, specify the SQL Server instance name: if this value is not set, the default instance name of MSSQLSERVER will be used.

In the Instance ID field (this was the instance ID that you choose during the SQL Server prepare-image step), enter your preconfigured value.

In the Product Key field, specify the product key for the edition of SQL Server you are deploying. If a product key it is not specified and the SQL Server does not have a volume license, then SQL server is installed under Evaluation.

In the Installation Run As Account field, click Browse to select the Run As Account under which you want to run the SQL Server setup.

A Run As account is needed if the Complete Image phase needs to access SQL Server installation media, if the SQL Server installation media is in a network share and a domain account is required to access this share, or when the SQL service accounts need to be domain accounts that will be validated by SQL Server Setup running under this installation account. If this value is not specified, the VMM service account is used by default.

The configuration information appears in the display pane (Figure 8.10).

4. In the Media Source field, specify the path to the installation-media folder containing setup.exe for SQL.

5. In the SQL Server Administrators field, click Add and specify the SQL Server administrator's security group.

FIGURE 8.10
Configuring SQL
Server

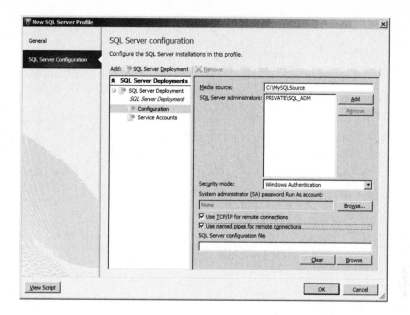

6. In the Security Mode field, specify the SQL Server security mode. If you do not specify a mode, the default value is Windows Authentication.

7. In the System Administrator (SA) Password Run As Account field, specify the password for the SQL Server SA account. The password is required when the security mode is SQL Server Authentication.

8. Set the Use TCP/IP For Remote Connections and Use Named Pipes For Remote Connections check boxes to specify the state of these options for the SQL Server service.

9. In the SQL Server Configuration File field, optionally specify a SQL.ini configuration file that includes the desired configurations not available in VMM. Click Service Accounts.

For further details on how to generate and configure a SQL.ini configuration file, read the following TechNet article:

http://msdn.microsoft.com/en-us/library/dd239405.aspx

The service-accounts information appears in the Display pane (Figure 8.11).

10. Specify the startup accounts for the SQL Server service, SQL Server Agent, and Reporting Services Run As accounts, and click OK.

Now you have all the building blocks in place to deploy a SQL VM via VMM.

FIGURE 8.11
Specifying SQL
service accounts

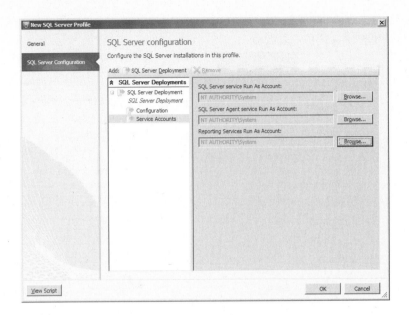

SQL Data-Tier Applications

Since SQL Server 2008 R2, the DAC feature has made it easy for database administrators to package things like databases, tables, users, and logins into a single object for deployment. Its flexibility eases implementation and configuration.

You can use the same DAC for updates or modifications to the underlying platform and for deployment of scale, thereby providing a simplified process for upgrading database servers. A DAC definition contains the following elements:

◆ Definition of all database objects

◆ Definition of all server-level objects

◆ DAC properties that define characteristics of the DAC package

◆ SQL Server selection policies

◆ Files and scripts associated with the DAC package

Only specific objects can be specified in a DAC package as it is being authored or edited. The Extract Data-Tier Application Wizard will not extract a DAC package from an existing database that contains objects that are not supported in a DAC package. The wizard reports the objects it finds that are not supported in a DAC. The following objects are supported in DAC packages:

◆ DATABASE ROLE

◆ FUNCTION: Inline Table-valued

◆ FUNCTION: Multistatement Table-valued

◆ FUNCTION: Scalar

- INDEX: Clustered

- INDEX: Non-clustered

- INDEX: Unique

- LOGIN

- SCHEMA

- STORED PROCEDURE: Transact-SQL

- TABLE: Check Constraint

- TABLE: Collation

- TABLE: Column, including computed columns

- TABLE: Constraint, Default

- TABLE: Constraint, Foreign Key

- TABLE: Constraint, Index

- TABLE: Constraint, Primary Key

- TABLE: Constraint, Unique

- TRIGGER: DML

- TYPE: User-defined Data Type

- TYPE: User-defined Table Type

- USER

- VIEW

Creating a DAC Package

Two methods are available for creating a DAC package that VMM can consume. They are

- Using Visual Studio 2010

- Extracting the DAC package from an existing SQL database

Extracting from an existing SQL database is an easy way to build your first DAC package. You can convert an existing database structure and its related objects to a DAC package. This method doesn't require Visual Studio 2010. It uses SQL Server Management Studio.

To create sample DAC packages, you need an existing SQL server from within your environment or, better still, a dedicated SQL server from your library. You use the SQL server to replay the Transact-SQL files you stored earlier in this chapter, when sequencing the Pet Shop 4.0 application. To create simple DAC packages, follow these steps:

1. Use the `InstallDatabases.cmd` file to execute the T-SQL script.

2. Launch SQL Server Management Studio, connect to the appropriate database server, log in with the appropriate credentials, right-click MSPetShop4, click Tasks, and click Extract Data-Tier Application.

The Management Studio begins to create the DAC (Figure 8.12).

FIGURE 8.12

Extracting a data-tier application

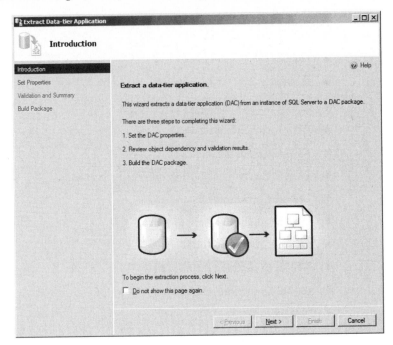

3. Repeat the previous step for the MSPetShop4Orders, MSPetShop4Profile, and MSPetShop4Services databases.

You can edit the DAC packages in Visual Studio 2010 to make modifications or extract the details.

4. Save the DAC packages to an easily accessible location, and hand them off to the application owner or developer.

To store the DAC packages in the library, follow these steps:

1. On the VMM management server (or the main library share), connect to the shared location containing the Pet Shop 4.0 package.

2. On the main library share, create a folder called SQLDAC, create a subfolder called **PetShop4** and a subfolder of that folder called **V1**.

3. Copy the DAC packages to the V1 folder.

4. In the VMM console ➢ Library workspace ➢ Library pane, expand the Library Servers node, right-click the library server you copied the packages to, and select Refresh.

The DAC packages should now appear in the library.

5. Right-click each DAC package in turn and select Properties. On the General tab, in the Family field, enter an application family name (for example, **PetShop4**). In the Release field, enter a release value (for example, **1.0**), and click OK.

Creating an Application Profile for a SQL Data-Tier Application

Creating an application profile for a Microsoft SQL Server data-tier application (DAC) is much the same as creating an application profile for Microsoft Server App-V applications or Microsoft Web Deploy applications.

To create an application profile for a Microsoft SQL Server DAC, follow these steps:

1. In the VMM console, select the Library workspace. On the Home tab, in the Create group, click Create and select Application Profile. The New Application Profile screen appears.

2. On the General tab, enter a name and description for the application profile. In the Compatibility field, select SQL Server Application Host. Then open the Application Configuration tab (Figure 8.13).

3. Click OS Compatibility and select the operating-system version and edition on which the application is supported.

4. Click Add (the green plus sign) and select SQL Server Data-Tier Application. The information within the pane changes (Figure 8.13).

5. In the Name field, enter an application name (for example, `PetShop4 DAC Application`).

6. In the SQL Server Data-Tier Application Package field, click Browse and select the application DAC packages that you previously submitted into the library.

7. Fill in the Authentication Type, Deployment Run As Account, and Uninstall Mode fields, and then click OK.

FIGURE 8.13
Configuring application deployments

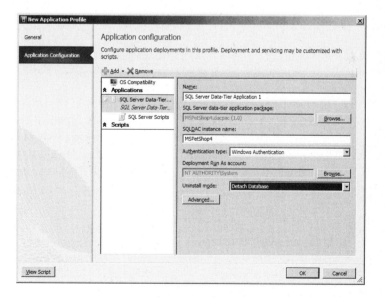

Web Applications

The Microsoft web deployment tool (Web Deploy) is a .NET-based application that provides both a user interface and a command-line shell, which simplifies the management, deployment, and migration of IIS web servers, websites, and web applications.

Use Web Deploy to take a website and its associated resources (for example, COM objects, content, Registry keys, and certificates) and replicate them across a group of web servers; or, more importantly for VMM 2012, create a package and deploy it. Web Deploy integrates with Visual Studio 2010 to simplify the deployment of web-based applications to web servers or web farms.

What Gets Installed

Installing Web Deploy, which is effectively a managed code framework, installs the Web Deploy engine and its public APIs. You can choose the way to install the features (Figure 8.14).

FIGURE 8.14

Web Deploy custom setup

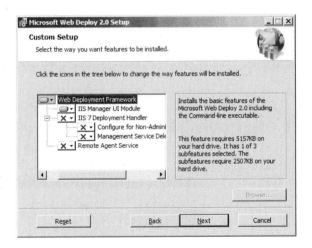

The installed components are as follows:

IIS Manager User Interface Module   Allows the web-server administrator to perform some deployment tasks, mainly packaging or deploying a website or application

IIS 7.0 Deployment Handler   A handler that integrates with IIS Web Management Service, allowing non-administrators or administrators to perform remote operations

Remote Agent Service   An administrator-specific service, based on HTTP and HTTPS, that allows the web-server administrator to connect and perform remote operations

Installing Web Deploy

Installing Web Deploy is a fairly easy and painless task because Microsoft includes the Web Deploy framework in the library. The Web Deploy binaries are at the following location:

```
\ProgramData\Virtual Machine Manager Library Files\ApplicationFrameworks\
```

When you create your VM template, you can add a Pre-Install script to automatically install Web Deploy (Figure 8.15).

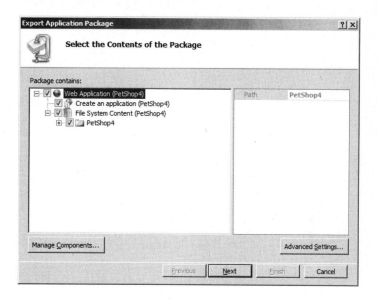

Creating Web Deploy Packages

Two methods are available for creating a Web Deploy package that VMM can consume. They are

◆ Using Visual Studio 2010

◆ Extracting a Web Deploy package from an existing web server

Extracting a Web Deploy package from an existing web server, much like building a DAC package from an existing SQL server, is an easy way to build your first Web Deploy package. To create a simple Web Deploy package, perform these steps:

1. Log onto the reference machine and launch the IIS Manager. Expand the Server node, expand the Sites node, expand Default Web Site, right-click the application, select Deploy, and select Export Application. The Export Application Package screen appears.

By default the Web Deploy package contains the site or application you select (Default Web Site/Pet Shop 4.0) and its content folders.

2. Click Manage Components.

The Manage Components screen appears (Figure 8.16). The first row is the IIS app-provider entry, which is the application. The Provider Name drop-down list contains other potential providers. If you hover over a provider in the drop-down list, you'll see a description and an example path.

FIGURE 8.16
Managing
components of an
application package

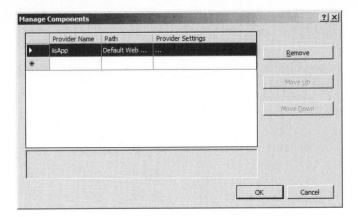

3. Optionally, add other providers from the Provider Name drop-down menu. Click OK.

The Export Application Package screen reappears. If you add providers in step 3, they'll show up in the package-contents tree.

4. Click Next. The Select Parameters screen appears. It shows the parameters for the selected providers.

5. Click Next. The Save Package screen appears.

6. Choose a location and file name for saving your package and click Next.

The wizard completes the packaging process and saves the package to the specified location. The Export Progress And Summary screen appears.

7. Switch to the VMM 2012 management server (or the main library share) and connect to the shared location where the Web Deploy package resides.

8. On the main library share, create a subfolder called **Web_Deploy**, and a subfolder of that folder called **PetShop4_V1**.

9. Copy the contents of the Web Deploy package to the PetShop4_V1 folder.

10. In the VMM console ➢ Library workspace ➢ Library pane, expand the Library Servers node, right-click the library server you copied the package to, and select Refresh.

Basic Sequencing Concepts

Sequencing is the process of discovering and recording the steps and resources necessary to install and set up an application on a system other than the one on which you developed it. The Server App-V Sequencer is the core component for producing Server App-V packages, and it relies on components of the VMM infrastructure to deploy applications.

The Sequencer takes standard, application-installation files and monitors the installation so that it can produce application packages that VMM can understand and consume. The following is a high-level description of the sequencing workflow:

1. Use the standard application installer from the distribution media to install the application while the Sequencer monitors the process.

The Sequencer captures changes to the system as they occur and packages the application to allow VMM to redeploy it.

2. Optimize the package using the Deployment Configuration tab and the associated tabs (Figure 8.5).

The Sequencer generates five or more files: OSD files, an SFT file, an SPRJ file, an XML manifest, an ICO file, and an XML deployment configuration file. VMM needs these files to deploy the application.

3. Install and test the package on a test or development system to ensure that the application installs without errors.

Testing the application does not require VMM directly. You can use the Add-ServerAppVPackage cmdlet to test the package.

4. Deploy the application to the production VMM environment.

Files Created by the Server App-V Sequencer

When it sequences a Windows application, the Server App-V Sequencer produces the following files:

OSD   The open software description (OSD) file provides the information necessary to find the SFT file and set up and launch the application.

SFT   The SFT file contains the core application assets. The Sequencer, without altering the application's installation routine, packages these assets so that VMM can deploy the application.

SPRJ   The Sequencer project (SPRJ) file contains a list of files, directories, and Registry entries that have been excluded. Load this file in the Sequencer to add, change, delete, or upgrade the sequenced application.

Application Manifest   The application manifest XML file contains details such as the version of the OS the application was sequenced on, and the applications, roles, and features that must be on any machine where the package is deployed.

ICO   The ICO file contains the icon associated with the application.

Deployment-Configuration Manifest   The manifest is an XML file containing customized settings that are applied to a specific, virtual application package when the package is run on a target server. The Sequencer detects some deployment configuration settings. You can add others manually.

Configuring the Sequencing Workstation

There are no hard and fast sizing guidelines for determining the hardware configuration of your sequencing workstation, because any sizing guidelines need to incorporate the requirements for the application being sequenced.

The sequencing workstation itself can be a physical server, but using VMs and snapshots (also known as checkpoints in VMM) gives you more flexibility. You can revert to a known working environment when packaging multiple applications.

Sequence the application on a machine that matches the OS and configuration of the target server. You can sometimes sequence on one version of an OS and run the virtualized application on a different version by using the lowest common denominator. However, this scenario is not guaranteed to work for all combinations of applications and operating systems.

Configure the `temp` directories on the sequencing workstation to ensure successful sequencing and improve performance by potentially using a second disk as a location for these files. The Sequencer uses %TMP%, %TEMP%, and its own scratch directory for temporary files.

These locations should contain free disk space equivalent to the estimated installation size. The `scratch` directory is where the Sequencer temporarily stores files generated during the sequencing process. You can easily check the location of the `scratch` directory by launching the Sequencer, clicking Options from the Tools menu, and then modifying the `scratch` directory box in the General tab. By default, the scratch directory location is

```
C:\Program Files (x86)\Server Application Virtualization Sequencer\Scratch
```

Clean Operating System

It is important to sequence an application on your VM with a clean, known, good OS that has no extraneous applications installed. The VM should mirror the server on which the sequenced application will run and contain the lowest common denominator in terms of service packs and hot fixes.

The sequencing workstation should not have anything installed on it that could impact or impede the installation of the application you plan to sequence. This is essential so that the sequenced application package includes all required files. Third-party components or applications may include files that the sequenced application needs. In such cases, the Sequencer won't add those files to the application package.

Server App-V Q: Drive

The Server App-V agent reserves a virtual drive, usually Q:\, on the Windows server. The virtual application executes from this virtual drive. This virtual drive should not be accessed by Windows Explorer and is used only by the Server App-V agent.

The drive is called the Microsoft Application Virtualization Virtual Drive. It is typically the Q:\ drive. However, it automatically moves if necessary at server startup. It is highly recommended to standardize the drive identifier so that you sequence and run the application from the same drive letter identifier. The drive letter identifier is configurable via the following Registry key:

```
\HKEY_Local_Machine\Software\Wow6432Node\Microsoft\SoftGrid\4.5\Client\AppFS
   name equals DriveLetter
   type equals REG_SZ
   data equals Q:.
```

Applications That Work with Server App-V

Server App-V can sequence and deploy most, but not all, applications. It does not support sequencing applications that require device or kernel driver support (for example, antivirus software). It also does not support some large server applications such as Microsoft SQL Server and Microsoft SharePoint.

Server App-V is primarily designed for use with business applications or the business tiers of multitiered applications. There is no list of supported applications for use with Server App-V, but it is optimized to create virtual application packages for applications with the following attributes:

- State persisted to local disk
- Microsoft Windows services
- Internet Information Services (IIS)

- Uses the Registry
- COM+/DCOM
- Text-based configuration files
- WMI providers
- Microsoft SQL Reporting Services
- Local users and groups
- Java

Deploying a Service

In VMM 2012, you use the Service Template Designer to create a service template. The Service Template Designer defines the configuration of the service you are commissioning. The service template includes information about the VMs that make up the service, which applications to install on the VMs, and the network configuration needed for the service.

Service templates can use existing VM templates, or you can define the service without existing VM templates.

Using a service template, you can deploy the service to either a host group or a private cloud. Once the service is deployed, you can easily update the service template and deploy those updates to the already-deployed service. If the demand for your service increases, you can deploy additional VMs to the existing service, by scaling out, in order to provide additional resources for this service. If the demand for your service decreases, you can scale back the additional VMs associated with your existing service.

The following sections show how to create a three-tier application that consists of a web server (front-end tier), application server (middle tier) and database server (back-end tier). Sample files are available for download to help accelerate the process of implementing the example service template at `https://skydrive.live.com/#cid=FD9BAD67005DBCCB&id=FD9BAD670 05DBCCB%21534`

Creating the Web Server–Tier Template

To create a VM template for a web server (front end) tier, follow these steps:

1. In the VMM console, select the Library workspace. On the Home tab, in the Create group, click Create Run As Account. Name the account **SQL_SA**, name the user **SA**, and use **Password1** as the password.

2. In the Library workspace ➤ Home tab ➤ Create group, click Create VM Template. The Select Source screen appears.

3. Click the Use An Existing VM Template Or VHD radio button, and then browse to the base OS VHD, `W2K8R2SP1x64.vhd`. Click OK, and then click Next.

This VHD becomes the starting point for the new template. The VM Identity screen appears.

4. Enter the name **WebServer Template** and a description, and then click Next. The hardware-configuration screen appears (refer back to Figure 8.1).

5. Select the predefined hardware profile from the pull-down list and click Next. The OS-configuration screen appears (refer back to Figure 8.2).

6. Select the predefined guest OS profile from the pull-down menu. Under General Settings ➢ Identity Information, in the Computer Name field, enter **WebSvr##**.

7. Under Roles and Features, click Roles. Select WebServer (IIS) ➢ Management Tools ➢ Application Development ➢ Basic Authentication.

8. Click Features. Select .NET Framework 3.51 ➢ Background Intelligent Transfer Service (BITS) ➢ Messaging Queuing. Click Next. The application-configuration screen appears (Figure 8.8).

9. Click OS Compatibility and select the 64-bit edition of Windows Server 2008 R2 Enterprise as the OS version and edition on which the application is supported. Click Add (the green plus sign) and select Script.

Script information appears in the information pane (Figure 8.17).

FIGURE 8.17
Configuring application scripts

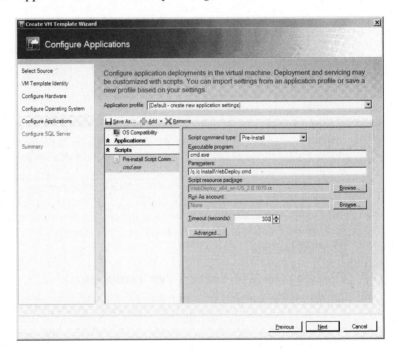

10. Set the fields as follows:

   ◆ In the Script Command Type field, select Pre-Install.

   ◆ In the Executable Program field, enter **cmd.exe**.

   ◆ In the Parameters field, enter **/q /c InstallWebDeploy.cmd**.

   ◆ In the Script Resource Package field, browse to WebDeploy_x64_en-US_2.0.1070.cr.

   ◆ In the Timeout field, enter **300**.

11. Click Add (the green plus sign) and then click Web Application. Name it **Web Application**. Browse to the Pet Shop 4.0 Web Deploy package you created earlier and click OK.

Properties specific to the Web Deploy package will appear in the Settings section (Figure 8.18).

FIGURE 8.18
The settings properties

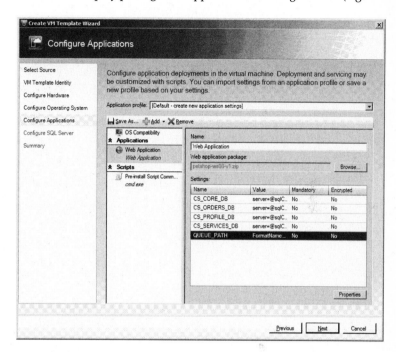

SYNTAX FOR SERVICE SETTINGS

Service settings can contain information such as the computer name, file path, or database connection string, and they can be referenced in a few predefined places within a service template. A service setting is enclosed in a pair of at signs (@); for example, the Computer Name property of Guest OS Profile can be @SQLComputerName@.

Users do not have to define service settings before using them. To further simplify service-template authoring, VMM determines the service settings used in the predefined places and displays their uses.

12. Select each specific property in turn, click Properties, and set the Value fields as follows:

```
CS_CORE_DB   server=@sqlComputerName@;database=MSPetShop4;user id=@
petshopUser@;password=@petshopPassword@; connect timeout=200;min pool
size=4;max pool size=4;
```

CS_ORDERS_DB `server=@sqlComputerName@;database=MSPetShop4Orders;user id=@petshopUser@;password=@petshopPassword@; connect timeout=200;min pool size=4;max pool size=4;`

CS_PROFILE_DB `server=@sqlComputerName@;database=MSPetShop4Profile;user id=@petshopUser@;password=@petshopPassword@; connect timeout=200;min pool size=4;max pool size=4;`

CS_SERVICES_DB `server=@sqlComputerName@;database=MSPetShop4Services; user id=@petshopUser@;password=@petshopPassword@;connect timeout=200;min pool size=4;max pool size=4;`

QUEUE_PATH `FormatName:DIRECT=OS:@lobComputerName@\Private$\PSOrders`

13. Click Add (the green plus sign) and Application Script. Fill in the following fields in the Information pane and click Next:

    ◆ In the Script Command Type field, select Post-Install.

    ◆ In the Executable Program field, enter **cmd.exe**.

    ◆ In the Parameters field, enter **/q /c configure-webtier.cmd**.

    ◆ In the Script Resources Package field, browse to **petshop.wt.cr**.

    ◆ In the Timeout field, enter **300**.

14. On the Configure SQL Server screen, click Next. On the Summary screen, click Create.

Creating the Application Server–Tier Template

To create a VM template for an application server (middle) tier, follow these steps:

1. In the VMM console Library workspace ➢ Home tab ➢ Create group, click Create VM Template. The Select Source screen appears.

2. Click the Use An Existing VM Template Or VHD radio button, and then browse to the base OS VHD, `W2K8R2SP1x64.vhd`. Click OK, and then click Next.

This VHD becomes the starting point for the new template. The VM Identity screen appears.

3. Enter the name **MiddleTier Template** and a description, and then click Next. The Configure Hardware screen appears.

4. Select the predefined hardware profile from the pull-down list and click Next. The Configure Operating System screen appears.

5. Select the predefined guest OS profile from the pull-down menu, under General Settings ➢ Identity Information, in the Computer Name field enter **MidSvr##**.

6. Under Roles And Features, click Roles. Select WebServer (IIS) ➢ Management Tools ➢ Application Development ➢ Basic Authentication.

7. Click Features. Select .NET Framework 3.51 ➢ Background Intelligent Transfer Service (BITS) ➢ Messaging Queuing. Click Next. The Application Configuration screen appears.

8. Click OS Compatibility and select the 64-bit edition of Windows Server 2008 R2 Enterprise as the OS version and edition on which the application is supported. Click Add (the green plus sign) and select Script.

Script information appears in the Information pane.

9. Set the fields as follows:

- In the Script Command Type field, select Pre-Install.

- In the Executable Program field, enter **cmd.exe**.

- In the Parameters field, enter **/q /c InstallSAV.cmd**.

- In the Script Resource Package field, browse to **SAV_x64_en-US_4.7.24.1485.cr**.

- In the Timeout field, enter **300**.

10. Click Add (the green plus sign) and then click Virtual Application. Name it **Web Application**. Browse to the Pet Shop 4.0 virtual application package you created earlier and click OK.

Properties specific to the virtual application package appear in the Settings section.

11. Select the first, fourth, fifth, and sixth specific properties in turn; click Properties, and set the Value fields as follows:

OrderQueuePath `server=@sqlComputerName@;database=MSPetShop4Profile;user id=@petshopUser@;password=@petshopPassword@;min pool size=4;max pool size=4;`

SQLConn1 `server=@sqlComputerName@;user id=@petshopUser@;password=@pet shopPassword@;database=MSPetShop4;min pool size=4;max pool size=4;packet size=3072;`

SQLConn2 `server=@sqlComputerName@;user id=@petshopUser@;password=@petshop Password@;database=MSPetShop4Profile;min pool size=4;max pool size=4;packet size=1024;`

SQLConn3 `server=@sqlComputerName@;user id=@petshopUser@;password=@petsho pPassword@;database=MSPetShop4Orders;min pool size=4;max pool size=4;packet size=1024; timeout=200;min pool size=4;Max pool size=4;`

12. Click Add (the green plus sign) and Application Script. Fill in the following fields in the Information pane and click Next:

- In the Script Command Type field, select Post-Install.

- In the Executable Program field, enter **cmd.exe**.

- In the Parameters field, enter **/q /c configure-midtier.cmd**.

- In the Script Resources Package field, browse to **petshop.mt.cr**.

- In the Timeout field, enter **300**.

13. On the Configure SQL Server screen, click Next. On the Summary screen, click Create.

Creating the Database Server Tier–Template

To create a VM template for a database server (back-end) tier, execute the following steps:

1. In the VMM console ➢ Library workspace ➢ Home tab ➢ Create group, click Create VM Template. The Select Source screen appears.

2. Click the Use An Existing VM Template Or VHD radio button, and then browse to the base OS VHD W2K8R2x64_SQL.vhd. Click OK, and then click Next.

This VHD becomes the starting point for the new template. The VM Identity screen appears.

3. Enter the name **DatabaseTier Template** and a description, and click Next. The Configure Hardware screen appears.

4. Select the predefined hardware profile from the pull-down list and click Next. The Configure Operating System screen appears.

5. Select the predefined guest OS profile from the pull-down menu, under General Settings ➢ Identity Information, in the Computer Name field, enter **SQLSVR##**. Click Next.

The Application Configuration screen appears.

6. Click OS Compatibility and select the 64-bit edition of Windows Server 2008 R2 Enterprise as the OS version and edition on which the application is supported. Click Add (the green plus sign) and select SQL Server Data-Tier Application.

Application information appears in the information pane (Figure 8.19). The subsequent steps create separate application options for the different Pet Shop 4.0 databases.

FIGURE 8.19
Configuring SQL DACPAC

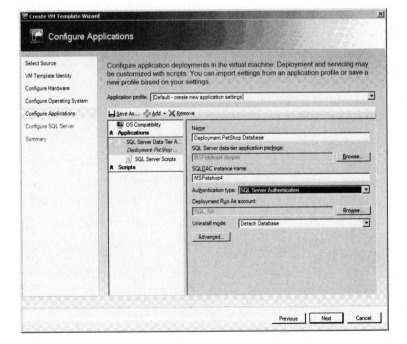

7. Fill in the fields as follows:

   ◆ In the Name field, enter a database name (for example, **Deployment PetShop Database**).

   ◆ In the SQL Server Data-Tier Application Package field, browse to PetShop4.dacpac.

   ◆ In the SQLDAC Instance Name field, don't change anything.

   ◆ In the Authentication Type field, select SQL Server Authentication.

   ◆ In the Deployment Run As Account field, click and browse to the SQL Run As account (SQL_SA) you created earlier.

8. Click Add (the green plus sign) and select SQL Server Data-Tier Application. Repeat step 7, but with database name PetShop Orders Database, and browse to PetShop4Orders .dacpac.

9. Click Add (the green plus sign) and select SQL Server Data-Tier Application. Repeat step 7, but with database name PetShop Services Database, and browse to PetShop4Profiles.dacpac.

10. Click Add (the green plus sign) and select SQL Server Data-Tier Application. Repeat step 7, but with database name PetShop Profiles Database, and browse to PetShop4Services.dacpac.

11. Click Add (the green plus sign) and Script. Fill in the following fields in the Information pane and click Next:

   ◆ In the Script Command Type field, select Post-Install.

   ◆ In the Executable Program field, enter **cmd.exe**.

   ◆ In the Parameters field, enter **/q /c configure-datatier.cmd @sqlAdmin@ @ sqlAdminPassword@**.

   ◆ In the Script Resources Package field, browse to **petshop.sql.cr**.

   ◆ In the Timeout field, enter **300**.

   The Configure SQL Server screen appears (Figure 8.20).

12. Click SQL Server Deployments. Fill in the fields as follows and click Configuration:

   ◆ In the Name field, enter a name for the database server (for example, **PetShop DB Deployment**).

   ◆ In the Instance Name field, enter **MSSQLSERVER**.

   ◆ In the Instance ID field, enter the Instance ID from the standalone installation (for example, **SysPrep**).

   The SQL Server Configuration screen appears (Figure 8.21).

FIGURE 8.20
Configuring SQL
Server instances

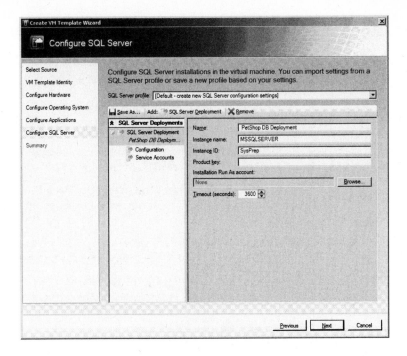

FIGURE 8.21
Configuring SQL
Server

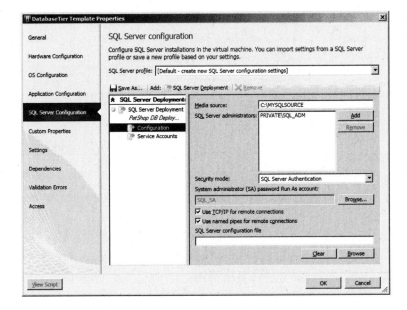

13. Fill in the fields as follows and click Service Accounts:

♦ In the Media Source field, enter **C:\SQLEVAL**.

♦ In the SQL Server Administrators field, click Add to enter your SQL server administrative user or group.

♦ In the Security Mode field, select SQL Server Authentication.

♦ In the System Administrator (SA) Password Run As Account field, browse to the SQL server Run As Account SQL_SA.

♦ Click the Use TCP/IP For Remote Connections check box to enable.

♦ Click the Use Named Pipes For Remote Connections check box to enable.

Account information appears in the Information pane.

14. Fill in the fields as follows, and then click Next and Create:

♦ In the SQL Server Service Run As Account field, browse to NT Authority\System.

♦ In the SQL Server Agent Service Run As Account field, browse to NT Authority\System.

♦ In the Reporting Service Run As Account field, browse to NT Authority\System.

Creating a Service Template

Before you can deploy a service, you must create a service template using the Service Template Designer. In the previous tasks, you created all the necessary VMs to enable you to deploy your first service.

To create a simple three-tier service, perform the following steps:

1. In the VMM console ➢ Library workspace ➢ Home tab ➢ Create group, click Create Service Template. The New Service Template screen appears (Figure 8.22).

FIGURE 8.22
Creating a service template

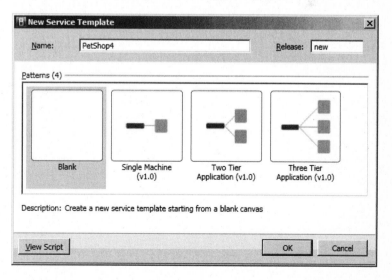

2. Enter **PetShop4** as the name, select the Blank pattern, and click OK. The Service Template Designer canvas appears (Figure 8.23).

FIGURE 8.23
The Service Template Designer canvas

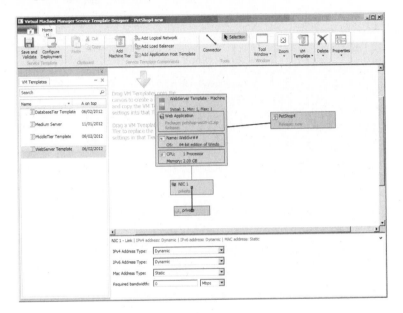

3. From the VM Templates list, drag WebServer Template to the canvas.

4. Click the WebServer template. In the list of scale-out options that appears in the lower-right portion of the screen, check the This Computer Can Be Scaled Out check box and increase Maximum Instance Count to 2.

5. Drag MiddleTier Template and DatabaseTier Template to the canvas so the screen looks like Figure 8.24.

FIGURE 8.24
Designing the service template on the canvas

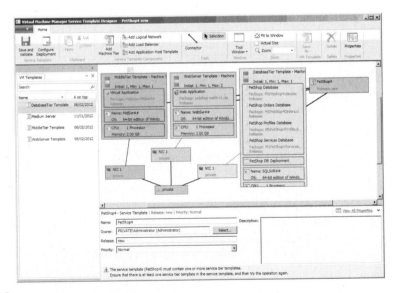

6. On the Home tab, click Save and Validate, wait for the changes to be saved, and then click Configure Deployment. The Select Name And Destination screen appears.

7. Enter `PetShop4 Deployment` as the name and click OK.

VMM determines the best place to put this service and displays the results in a graphical overview (Figure 8.25). The Pet Shop 4.0 Deployment tree under Service Components shows the computer name of each VM in the application.

FIGURE 8.25
Graphical overview of Pet Shop 4.0 deployment

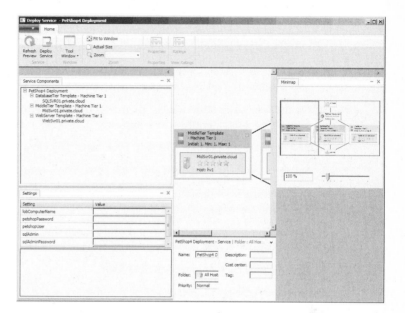

8. Enter the following global settings in the Settings section in the lower-left portion of the screen:

◆ In the lobComputerName field, enter `MidSvr01`.

◆ In the petshopPassword field, enter `pass@word1`.

◆ In the petshopUser field, enter `mspetshop`.

◆ In the sqlAdmin field, enter `sa`.

◆ In the sqlAdminPassword field, enter `Password1`.

◆ In the sqlComputerName field, enter `SQLSVR01`.

9. Click Deploy Service, and then click Deploy.

The service-deployment job starts. You can monitor its progress in the Jobs workspace. When it is complete, the VM and Service workspace should show the status of the created VMs.

Scaling Out a Service

After you deploy a service in VMM, you may need to deploy additional VMs to a tier of the service. You can do this using VMM's scale-out functionality. When you create a tier in the Service Template Designer, you can specify whether that tier can be scaled out and what the minimum and maximum tier size should be. If you try to scale out a tier beyond its maximum size, you'll receive a warning, but VMM won't prevent you from scaling out that tier. Once deployed, both the tier and the service will indicate a status of Needs Attention.

Use the following procedure to scale out a service:

1. In the VMM console, VM And Services workspace, select the host group to which the service is deployed. On the Home tab, in the Show group, click Services. The services appear in the Services pane.

2. Select the service you want to scale out (in this case Pet Shop 4.0 Deployment). On the Services tab, in the Update group, click Scale Out. The Scale Out Tier Wizard opens.

3. On the Select Tier screen, select the tier you want to scale out and click Next. The Specify Virtual Machine Identity screen appears.

4. Enter a name for the new VM, and click Next. The Host screen appears.

5. Select a host for the new VM and click Next. The Configure Settings screen appears.

6. In Operating System Settings, enter the computer name for the new VM and click Next. The Add Properties screen appears.

7. Specify the actions to perform on the VM when the host starts or stops and click Next. The Summary screen appears.

8. Review your choices and click Scale Out.

The scale-out job begins. You can track its progress in the Jobs workspace.

Exporting and Importing Service Templates

In VMM 2012, you can import and export service templates. This enables you to back them up and share them among different VMM environments, such as test, development, and production.

When you export a service template in VMM, tier definitions, hardware settings, guest operating system settings, application-installation settings, and network configurations are saved to an XML file. The export can include sensitive data, such as passwords, product keys, application settings, and global settings that are marked as secure. The sensitive settings can be encrypted to secure the output. During a service-template import, sensitive settings can be included or excluded. If sensitive settings are included, and they were encrypted during the service-template export, the encryption password is required.

You can also choose to export some or all of the physical resources associated with the service template. This can be useful when copying service templates between environments. You can, for example, exclude the virtual hard disks or other elements that are associated with the service template.

When you import a service template into VMM, it validates physical and logical resources that the service template references in the current environment and it allows you to update references to missing resources, such as logical resources, including logical networks and virtual hard disks.

Exporting a Service Template

To export a service template, use the following steps:

1. In the VMM console ➢ Library workspace ➢ Library pane, expand the Templates node. Click Service Templates and in the Templates pane, select the template to export.

2. On the Service Template tab, in the Actions group, click Export. The Export Template Resources screen appears.

3. Optionally, use any of the following steps on that screen.

   A. To export physical resources associated with the service template, under the Physical Resources column, click None. In the Select Resources dialog box, select the physical resources you want to export and click OK.

   B. To overwrite an earlier export file for a selected template, check the Overwrite The Existing Export Files check box.

   C. To include sensitive data such as passwords, product keys, and application and global settings that are marked as secure, check the Export Any Sensitive Template Settings check box. If you select this option, you can configure encryption for the sensitive settings. If you choose not to include sensitive settings, an administrator can provide the settings during template import or by updating the template after it is imported.

   D. To configure encryption for sensitive settings in the template, check the Encrypt Template Settings check box, and enter an encryption password for the XML file.

   E. In the Location box, use the Browse button to select the folder where you want to store the exported service template. The location does not have to be a library share. However, it is recommended that you store exported service templates in the library to ensure access for import.

4. Click OK.

Importing a Service Template

To import a service template, use the following steps:

1. In the VMM console, Library workspace, Library pane, expand the Templates node. On the Home tab, in the Import group, click Import Template. The Import Package Wizard opens.

2. In Package path, browse to the XML file that has the name of the service template you want to import. Optionally, check the Import Sensitive Template Settings check box. Click Next.

If you check the check box, VMM imports sensitive settings such as passwords, product keys, and application and global settings that are marked as secure.

If you choose to import sensitive data and the data is encrypted, you must provide a password.

The Configure References screen appears.

3. Supply the following information and click Next:

   ◆ Enter a name for the service template. If you are restoring a service template, keep the same name.

   ◆ Provide a release value for the service template. If you are restoring a service template, keep the same release value.

   ◆ If the selected name and release match those of an existing service template in the VMM environment, the next step asks whether to overwrite the existing service template.

   ◆ For each logical or physical resource that has a Current Mapping value of None (that is, the resource is missing), click the pencil icon and select a resource that is available in the current VMM environment. The most common missing resources are logical networks and virtual hard disks.

4. If the name and the release value match those of an existing service template in the current VMM environment, click Yes to overwrite or click Cancel to rename the template and retry.

The Summary screen appears.

5. Review your selections and click Import.

Managing and Updating a Service

Managing and updating a service in VMM is the process of modifying an already deployed service. VMM keeps track of which service template is used to deploy a service, so you can make updates to the service template and then use the updated service template to make changes to the deployed service.

VMM supports two different methods for making updates to a deployed service.

◆ Applying updates to existing VMs in place

◆ Deploying a new VM with the updated settings

Applying an update to the existing VMs is less time-consuming; the majority of configuration changes to VMs and application updates can be applied in this way.

To help minimize service interruptions when a tier is being updated in place, you can specify more than one upgrade domain in the tier properties. When the tier is updated, VMM updates the VMs in the tier according to the VMM upgrade domain. VMM upgrades one upgrade domain at a time, shutting down the VMs running within the upgrade domain, updating them, bringing them back online, and then moving to the next upgrade domain in the series. By shutting down only the VMs running within the current upgrade domain, VMM ensures that an upgrade takes place with the least possible impact to your running service.

Conversely, deploying a new VM with updated settings is a more time-consuming process, because you are replacing the existing VMs of the service with new VMs. This approach is best when deploying operating-system updates, such as a service pack for the guest operating system. If applications are installed on your VMs, and those applications have a method for saving and restoring state, you can use a script in the application profile to save the application state before the existing VMs are removed and use a script to restore the application state after the new VMs are deployed.

Creating an Update Template

To copy a service template for the purpose of updating an existing service, follow these steps:

1. In the VMM console ➤ Library workspace ➤ Library pane, expand the Templates node. Click Service Templates, and in the Templates pane, select the service template to copy.

2. On the Service Template tab, in the Create group, click Copy.

The copy appears in the Templates pane. The name is the same, but the release value is Copy of *original service template name*.

3. Right-click the copy and select Properties. The Properties screen appears.

4. On the General page, enter a new release value, and click OK.

Applying Updates to a Deployed Service

Updates are applied in two stages. You prepare the update and then, at a convenient time, you actually apply the update.

To prepare to update a deployed service, perform the following steps:

1. In the VMM console ➤ Library workspace ➤ Library pane, expand the Templates node. Click Service Templates and in the Templates pane, select the service template to update.

2. On the Service tab, in the Update group, click Set Template. The Change Service Template Wizard opens.

3. On the Updated Service Template screen, click Replace The Current Template With An Updated Template For This Service. Browse to the updated template. Click Next. The Settings screen appears.

4. Configure application settings and click Next. The Update Method screen appears.

5. Select whether to make the updates to the existing VMs in place or deploy new VMs with the updated settings. Click Next. The Updates Review screen appears.

6. Review your selections and click Next. The Summary screen appears.

7. Review the settings and click Finish.

To apply a prepared update, do the following:

1. In the VMM console, VMs and Services workspace, select the service to update.

2. On the Service tab, in the Upgrade group, click Apply Template. The Apply Service Template screen appears.

3. Review the updates and click OK.

The Update job begins. When it is done, the VMs and Services workspace should reflect the updated template release value for the service.

Summary

This chapter covered all aspects of setting up, configuring and deploying service templates: preparing the library for application deployment, coming to grips with and understanding the basic concepts of sequencing a line-of-business application with Server App-V, deploying and scaling out a service, and managing and updating a deployed service. You should now understand the considerations behind implementing and commissioning a service that VMM provides, and you should have made your choices optimally for your own unique situation. You are now ready to learn about the next aspect of your private-cloud environment, the private-cloud solution.

Part 3

Private Cloud Solution

## Chapter 9

Creating a Private Cloud

The preceding sections of this book focused on the Virtual Machine Manager (VMM) elements that let you define the fabric of the private cloud. The VMM infrastructure enables you to shield users from the mechanics of deploying resources for their use. Instead, they see an abstraction of the underlying resources that supports the main benefits of private clouds described in Chapter 1, "Understanding Cloud Computing"; those benefits include self-service, access over a network, quick allocation and deallocation of pooled resources, measurement, and optimization.

This final section of the book focuses on using this investment in the fabric. You will form private clouds and provide access to them. You will learn how self-service users consume cloud resources: the interfaces they have access to, and the actions they can execute within the confines of those interfaces. You will be introduced to some management interactions with the public cloud before finally considering the process of formally requesting private clouds for your projects.

This chapter focuses on working with VMM as an administrator. It covers the following topics:

◆ What makes up a private cloud

◆ Access roles

◆ Creating private clouds and managing them through their lifecycle

Identifying Private Cloud Elements

All of the buildup we have carefully focused on until now has been to prepare to ultimately create private clouds. The process of forming these private clouds with VMM is reserved for users who have either Administrator or Delegated Administrator role access. Within the VMM console, clouds can be created using the Create Cloud Wizard or the PowerShell interface. As with all the elements you have defined so far, you will complete this exercise initially using the console and then with PowerShell.

The private-cloud concept embraces many of the elements defined within VMM as the fabric is modeled. Considering the resources and functions that each of these elements offers, administrators can formulate the functionality of the underlying fabric that they expose in the private cloud to address consumer requirements while hiding the physical details from consumers.

In the next few pages, you will review the elements from which you can select to create private clouds.

Host Groups

Addressing a large portion of the physical infrastructure that creates the fabric on which clouds are built, host groups encompass the virtualization hosts and networking services upon which all the virtualization activities of the private cloud are executed. Chapter 5, "Understanding the VMM Library," introduced host groups, hypervisors, and their related capabilities.

Host groups also enable boundaries in VMM to define specific functionality options. They include placement rules, definitions of host reserves for hypervisors; configuration options related to dynamic optimization and power management; and associating both network and storage resources.

As you define a private cloud, you add compute resources from the fabric by assigning the host groups, which will allow you to organize and manage the resources you expose.

Logical Networks

The network resources offered within the private cloud are initially defined within VMM as part of the fabric. Each of the managed hypervisors exposes connections to the native network infrastructure, which may be implemented using physical networks or through virtual LANs. Irrespective of the underlying technologies, these networks are modeled in VMM as logical networks and may be associated with both IP and MAC pools for static-address association, or they may remain dynamic by default. Chapter 6, "Understanding Network and Storage Integration in VMM," explains how these logical networks are defined and associated to the hypervisor host's physical network adapters.

By evaluating the logical networks bound to the hypervisor hosts within the host groups you are associating with the private cloud, VMM determines the logical networks that are available for use within your private cloud.

NOTE Only logical networks that are associated with physical network adapters on hosts in the selected host groups will appear in this list while using the Cloud Wizard.

As you define your private cloud, you must associate at least one logical network so that the hosted services and VMs can communicate.

Load Balancers

As an optional component of the fabric, load balancers may be defined and offered for use within the private cloud. Load balancers are of value only in clouds that deploy services, and these services have one or more application tiers that are identified as scalable. Therefore, these service tiers are stateless by design.

Load balancers are introduced and configured in Chapter 6, while services are presented in Chapter 8, "Understanding Service Modeling."

VIPs

Associated with load balancers, Virtual IP addresses (VIPs) define the virtual service address associated with a service hosted on one or more VMs within the cloud. The VIPs are defined within the fabric of VMM when you configure the load balancer and Logical Networks. VIPs need to be associated with a private cloud only if a load balancer is also associated with it. For more information, see Chapter 6.

Storage

An optional concept in VMM, storage classifications may be applied within the fabric to different classes of storage exposed to clouds. For example, high-speed fiber-channel attached storage could be defined as silver while slower SATA arrays are defined as bronze.

In some environments, all storage is of the same type or all the fabric connections are of the same interface. They may be presented as CSV volumes. In these cases, administrators might determine that no classifications are to be assigned. VMM automatically assigns storage classifications of Local and Remote when using local hard-disk and CSV volumes, respectively.

NOTE   Only storage classifications for storage pools associated with the selected host groups will appear while using the Cloud Wizard. If VMM is not managing storage, then no classifications appear.

Storage configuration and classifications are covered in Chapter 6. The relevant storage classification (if any) is determined when the private cloud is defined by the administrator, depending on the requirements of the customer and the type of load hosted on the VM or as part of the definition of the service.

Cloud Libraries

Libraries are important for the creation and consumption of private cloud services. All of the resources that private clouds offer are related directly to libraries. Chapter 5 explores in depth the topic of libraries and introduces their function and creation; you are strongly encouraged to read it before you create a cloud.

VMM offers the ability to manage resources that have been deposited to a library share, giving private-cloud users an efficient method to provide resources for management and deployment. Table 9.1 summarizes the different uses of cloud libraries.

TABLE 9.1:   Libraries and Shares in the Cloud

LIBRARY	OVERVIEW
Read-only library shares for private clouds	Resources that are to be provided to self-service users for deployment within their cloud. Administrators may store VM images or application-framework resources to the read-only library share for a private cloud so that cloud users can deploy their own VMs or design their own service applications.
Self-Service user-role data paths	Used to offer members of a Self-Service user role a place to upload and share their own resources. This location is the best place for administrators to store resources for a specific Self-Service user role. For example, the development team may share new application packages for services that need to be deployed.
	Permissions on the user data path are controlled through the file system. SCVMM discovers all the files to which the current self-service user has access. Access-control permissions determine whether the users have Read/Write or Read-Only access.
	Only self-service users with the Author or Deploy action can actually use these resources.

TABLE 9.1:   Libraries and Shares in the Cloud *(CONTINUED)*

LIBRARY	OVERVIEW
Self-Service user-role assigned resources	This feature presents VM and service templates available to the self-service users of the cloud.
	If the user role has the Author action, these resources can be utilized as templates for customized resources. Self-service users do not need access to the physical resources that are referenced by templates and assigned profiles.
VM store and recover	This optional share is assigned from a library to a private cloud. It is used to store VMs and services associated to the cloud, but the deployed instance is not required to be actively used. Storing the resources releases valuable capacity from the cloud, which would otherwise be consumed, even if the resource is deployed but powered off.

If you need to assign read-only shares to a private cloud, where administrators can store read-only resources such as .ISO files that will be made available to self-service users, then you must ensure that at least one library share exists that can be assigned as the read-only library share. Self-service users must have the Author permission to access the resources.

TIP   Library shares that are designated as read-only resource locations for a private cloud must be unique; they can't be the same as the library shares used to store VMs or the user-role data path specified for a Self-Service user role.

As you create each new private cloud, you can define a library share for the storage and recovery of VMs or services that you may be hosting as part of your cloud. These resources may not be required to be active at a specific point in time, and they may be stored in this library for safe keeping while releasing the quota capacity they consumed while deployed. This library share is usable only when the administrator has also granted permission for private-cloud users to store or recover items.

Cloud Capacity

Before you create a private cloud, you need to consider its capacity and how it might be measured or constrained. Administrators may need to implement capacity boundaries for different deployments needs. Table 9.2 defines the elements VMM can use as constraints to define the capacity of a cloud.

As an example, memory might be the constraining option for some clouds, limiting the total amount of RAM permitted for all the VMs hosted within a cloud. With dynamic memory, however, some organizations define all their VMs with a maximum RAM limit of, for example, 64 GB. In a scenario such as this, the constraint for RAM is impossible to deploy because VMM defines its boundaries based on the maximum RAM a VM may consume, and not on its dynamically changing actual consumption at a specific point in time.

TABLE 9.2:   Capacity Options

QUOTA TYPE	DESCRIPTION
Virtual CPUs	Sets a limit on processing capacity within the private cloud that is equivalent to the capacity that can be provided by a specified number of CPUs. Applied against running VMs. Setting a CPU quota does not guarantee contiguous capacity (that is, virtual CPUs offered from the same host); it only guarantees total CPU capacity available among hosts in the private cloud.
Memory	Sets a quota on memory (in gigabytes) that is available for VMs that are deployed on the private cloud. Applied against running VMs only. Setting a memory quota does not guarantee contiguous capacity. For example, the private-cloud memory quota may be defined as 4 GB, but the underlying fabric hosts might have only 2 GB of available memory on one host and 2 GB of memory on another.
Storage	Sets a quota on storage capacity (in gigabytes) that is available to VMs deployed on the private cloud. For dynamic virtual hard disks, quota calculations are based on maximum size.
Custom quota (points)	Sets a quota on VMs that are deployed on the private cloud based on total quota points that are assigned to the VMs through their VM templates. Quota points are an arbitrary value that can be assigned to a VM template based on the anticipated size of the VMs. Custom quotas are provided for backward compatibility with Self-Service user roles that were created in VMM 2008 R2.
Virtual Machines	Limits the total number of VMs that can be deployed on the private cloud.

Similarly, storage quotas are calculated only for VMs deployed to the cloud, while VMs within a library of a private cloud are not considered. The virtual hard disk of the machine can also be defined as either static or dynamic, with limits based on the maximum capacity and not the currently expanded size.

Simpler quotas can be implemented by restricting the number of virtual CPUs, or even the total number of VMs on a cloud. However, with careful consideration and understanding of the limits within the capacity-management functions of VMM, these elements can be combined to impose customized boundaries for your private clouds.

Capability Profiles

Because VMM supports multiple hypervisors, capability profiles are available to help define the upper and lower limits for VM capabilities when deployed to these different virtualization technologies. Capability profiles are used to target the hardware profile on a VM. VMM comes with built-in profiles, representing the minimum and maximum limits of the different hypervisors that VMM supports. You can also define your own profiles.

Capability profiles assigned to a private cloud enforce a validation check on the VMs and services being deployed, ensuring that the deployment does not progress if the capability profile is not matched. For example, the virtual hard disk type of the VM can be restricted to ensure that only fixed VHDs can be deployed to the cloud.

Assigning capability profiles to private clouds is a good practice. VM templates also have capability profiles. For these VMs to be successfully deployed on your clouds, the capability profiles of the cloud and template must match.

Additional information about capability profiles appears in Chapter 4, "Setting Up and Deploying VMM 2012."

NOTE   In the Library workspace, you can also create custom capability profiles to limit the resources that are used by VMs created in the private cloud. To view the settings associated with a built-in capability profile or to create a custom capability profile, open the Library workspace, expand Profiles, and then click Capability Profiles. You can view the properties of a capability profile; or on the Home tab, in the Create group, click Create and then click Capability Profile to create a new one.

The Create Cloud Wizard

With all the elements in place, you can now get to the fun part of the process and start creating clouds. VMM simplifies the process by providing a wizard to guide you as you assign each element from the fabric to your new cloud.

In the remainder of this section, you will create two clouds. Table 9.3 shows possible uses for them.

TABLE 9.3:   Sample Clouds

TYPE OF CLOUD	USE
Development	This cloud is used by the engineering team (using the Development Cloud user role) to validate their code as they prepare to create software releases and potential service packages.
Production	Applications hosted in this cloud are published live, for end users.

Prior to creating the cloud, VMM administrators (or delegated administrators) review the submitted requirements for the new cloud, which may include details related to availability, security, and resiliency, and then prepare a plan assigning resources from the fabric to the requested cloud. Table 9.4 shows the resources that might be assigned to the clouds described in Table 9.3.

TABLE 9.4:   Cloud Resources for Grabber, Inc.

RESOURCE	DEVELOPMENT CLOUD	PRODUCTION CLOUD
Host groups	All Hosts\Development	All Hosts\Production
Logical networks	VM1	VM1 and VM2
Load balancers	netscaler1.private.cloud	netscaler1.private.cloud
VIP profiles	Citrix HTTPS	Citrix HTTPS
Storage classifications	Bronze	Gold
Read-only library shares	SCVMMLibrary1-ReadOnly	SCVMMLibrary1-ReadOnly
Storage VMs	\\VMMLIB1\SCVMMLibrary1\StoredVMs\Dev	\\VMMLIB1\SCVMMLibrary1\StoredVMs\Prod
Capability profiles	Hyper-V	Hyper-V

The wizard will guide you through a series of steps to assign the desired fabric resources and present them to users abstractly in the cloud. User roles are used to control access to the cloud.

Using the Create Cloud Wizard

Now that the fabric is defined and you understand the private cloud, you can use the VMM console to create the private cloud with the VMM Create Cloud Wizard. The following procedure creates the Development cloud described in Table 9.4.

NOTE   In the Create Cloud Wizard, if you do not have a fabric resource configured, you can click Next to move to the next page. You can add or remove private cloud resources or modify other settings after you complete the wizard. To do this, right-click the private cloud and then click Properties.

1. Log in to the VMM console as a user with administrator or delegated administrator privileges. If you log in as a delegated administrator, you can use only those resources within your delegated scope.

2. In the VMs and Services view, in the Create section of the ribbon, click the Create Cloud icon. The Create Cloud Wizard appears.

3. Enter a name and description for the cloud and click Next. (For this exercise, the cloud was named Development Cloud.) The Resources screen appears, as shown in Figure 9.1.

FIGURE 9.1
The Resources
screen

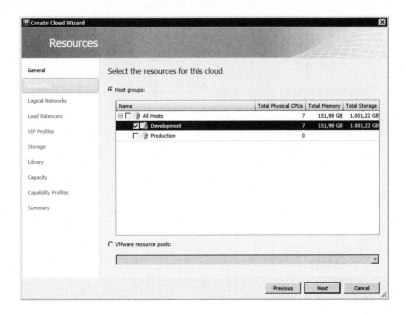

4. Select the host group containing the resources for the cloud and click Next. (For this example, the host group is Development.) The Logical Networks screen appears.

5. Choose the logical networks to use for the cloud and click Next. (For this example, the logical network is VM1.) The Load Balancers screen appears.

6. Choose the load balancers to use for the cloud and click Next. (For this example, the load balancer is `netscaler1.private.cloud`.) The VIP Profiles screen appears.

7. Choose the VIP profiles for the cloud.

The wizard dynamically populates the list based on the load balancer. (For this example, the VIP profile is `Citrix_https`.) The Storage screen appears.

8. Choose the storage classification and click Next.

The wizard presents the available options. This list is empty when the cluster uses local or CSV storage, or when you are a delegated administrator to whom none of the classifications is available. (For this example, Bronze was selected.) The Library screen appears (Figure 9.2).

9. Specify the stored VM path and the read-only library shares and then click Next. (The settings for this example are shown in Figure 9.2.) The Capacity screen appears.

10. Set the capacity for the cloud and click Next.

FIGURE 9.2
The Library screen

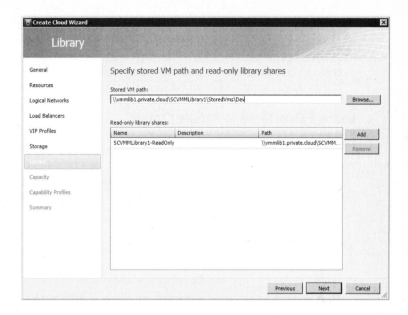

These settings determine how elastic the cloud is. The wizard shows the available resources in several categories, and it lets you assign a capacity up to that amount. (For this example, Use Maximum was checked for each category.) The Capability Profiles screen appears (Figure 9.3).

FIGURE 9.3
The Capability
Profiles screen

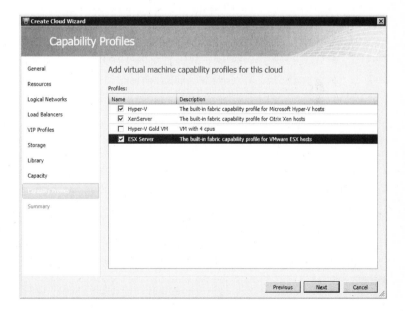

11. Specify the VM capability profiles for the cloud and click Next. The Summary screen appears. (For this example, the built-in profiles for Hyper-V, Xen, and ESX were selected. A custom profile was left unchecked because it did not apply to the Development cloud.)

12. Review your choices and click Finish.

VMM creates the cloud. You can monitor the Create Cloud job in the Jobs window. When the job is complete, you can go to the Library workspace and expand Cloud Libraries to verify the choices you made in step 9. You should see a library that matches the cloud name. If you expand it, you should see the read-only shares and a Stored Virtual Machines and Services node.

Using PowerShell to Create Clouds

The previous section used the Create Cloud Wizard to create the Development cloud described in Table 9.3 and Table 9.4. In this section, you will use PowerShell to create the Production cloud.

To create a cloud using PowerShell, you set PowerShell variables that correspond to the selections you made in the wizard. Then you execute the `New-SCCloud` and `Set-SCCloud` commands.

Begin by generating a new empty variable to hold the list of host groups.

```
$hostGroups = @{}
```

Using the `Get-SCVMHostGroup` command, locate the desired host group and append it to the new variable.

```
$hostGroups += Get-SCVMHostGroup -Name "Production"
```

Next, form the new cloud, assigning it a name, a short description, and the host group. The `$cloud` variable receives a reference to the new cloud. You will use the reference when you add resources.

```
$cloud = New-SCCloud -Name "Production Cloud" -Description "Live Production
Services; Please be careful" -VMHostGroup $hostGroups
```

That was easy, right? The next steps focus on generating a list of resources to attach to the new cloud. The next code block compiles references to the following resources into the `$resources` variable, using the indicated commands:

- Logical networks (`Get-SCLogicalNetwork`)
- Load balancers (`Get-SCLoadBalancer`)
- VIP profiles (`Get-SCVIPProfile`)
- Storage classifications (`Get-SCStorageClassifications`)

```
$resources = @()

$resources += Get-SCLogicalNetwork | Where {$_.Name -like "VM1"}
$resources += Get-SCLogicalNetwork | Where {$_.Name -like "VM2"}

$resources += Get-SCLoadBalancer | where {$_.Name -like "netscaler1.private.
cloud"}

$resources += Get-SCLoadBalancerVIPTemplate -Name "Citrix_https"

$resources += Get-SCStorageClassification -Name "Gold"
```

The next code block sets variables to contain references to the appropriate read-only library shares and the desired capability profiles.

```
$readonlyLibraryShares = @()
$readonlyLibraryShares += Get-SCLibraryShare | Where {$_.Name -like
"SCVMMLibrary1-ReadOnly"}

$CapabilityProfiles = @()
$CapabilityProfiles += Get-SCCapabilityProfile -Name "Hyper-V"
$CapabilityProfiles += Get-SCCapabilityProfile -Name "XenServer"
$CapabilityProfiles += Get-SCCapabilityProfile -Name "ESX Server"
```

With all the references in place, you can add the indicated resources to the new cloud. A reference to this cloud is saved in a variable called `$cloud`, which can be used to tell VMM to which cloud the resources should be added. The `Set-SCCloud` command accepts as arguments the variables that were just created.

```
Set-SCCloud -Cloud $cloud -AddCloudResource $resources -AddReadOnlyLibraryShare
$readonlylibraryshare -AddCapabilityProfile $CapabilityProfiles
-ReadWriteLibraryPath "\\vmmlib1.private.cloud\SCVMMLibrary1\StoredVms\Prod"
```

The cloud now exists and has resources. The following code block uses the `Set-SCCloudCapacity` command to clear all the quota limits.

```
$CloudCapacity = Get-SCCloudCapacity -Cloud $Cloud
Set-SCCloudCapacity -CloudCapacity $CloudCapacity -UseCustomQuotaCountMaximum
$true -UseMemoryMBMaximum $true -UseCPUCountMaximum $true -UseStorageGBMaximum
$true -UseVMCountMaximum $true
```

This section and the previous one demonstrate how easy it is to create private clouds. VMM enables you to pull elements of the fabric together to form a cloud and hide the details from the users. They manipulate abstractions of the actual underlying resources, and VMM handles the details.

After you put a cloud into service, you may need to add or remove elements of the fabric to address changing user requirements. For example, you may need to add additional RAM (called *expanding the cloud*) or remove other elements, such as processors (called *contracting the cloud*). Such expansion and contraction illustrate the elasticity of clouds.

With a little imagination, you should be able to make these changes pretty painlessly using either PowerShell or the VMM interface. Later in this chapter, you'll see exactly how.

Understanding User Roles

Now that you've created the private cloud, you need to grant users access to it. Like other products in the Microsoft System Center suite, VMM implements a role-based access control (RBAC) solution to help you delegate and manage access to features and functions.

ROLE BASED ACCESS CONTROL (RBAC)

Is a method of regulating access to resources based on what users do rather than on who they are. *Roles* are defined according to job competency, authority, and responsibility within the enterprise. For example, developer and QA manager might be roles in an organization. Administrators define roles, which ideally change rarely. Individual users can belong to one or more roles and can move into and out of roles as their circumstances change.

Access is the ability to perform a specific task, such as view, create, or modify objects, or to see or manipulate specific resources.

In contrast to conventional methods of access control, which grant or revoke user access on a rigid, object-by-object basis, RBAC roles can be easily created, changed, or discontinued as the needs of the enterprise evolve, without having to individually update the privileges of every user.

This approach allows you to configure and customize the *scope* (items that can be managed) and *profiles* (which define what actions can be executed on the items managed), resulting in flexible and granular control for consumers of the new cloud services.

VMM implements four profiles that offer a predefined feature and functionality set. The personas of each of these respective profiles are introduced in the next section, and include the Virtual Machine Administrator, Delegated Administrator, Read-Only Administrator, and Self-Service User. Their hierarchy and span can be seen in Figure 9.4, illustrating Self-Service Users as the most restrictive access presented only as Clouds, while the three Administrator profiles have varying levels of administrative access based on the combination of both their assigned role and scope.

FIGURE 9.4
The user-role profile's span

User Roles and Scope

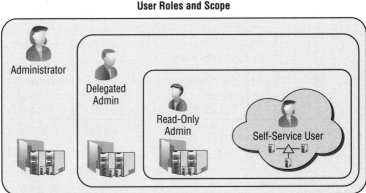

To define a user role there are two steps:

1. Select the VMM profile that defines the function of the role and then define the scope of access with which the role is permitted to interact.

2. Select the Active Directory members who will have this role.

The scope of the role depends on the functionality offered by the selected profile. Members of the role can be either Active Directory users or, as recommended, Active Directory groups. Active Directory users and groups can be members of multiple user roles.

Figure 9.5 illustrates the combination of profiles, scope, and membership that defines the user role.

To illustrate the flexibility exposed via this combination, we consider the boundaries created through each of the elements; initially specifying Membership

◆ Determines which users are part of a particular user role

◆ Assign members as AD Users or preferably AD Groups

◆ Lets you include members in multiple user roles

FIGURE 9.5
Defining user roles

Understanding User Roles

Membership
➕
Profile
➕
Scope
＝
User Role

Membership
- Determines which users are part of a particular user role
- Assign members as AD Users or preferably AD Groups
- Lets you include members in multiple user roles

Profile determines
- Which actions are permitted
- Which user interface is accessible
- How the scope is defined

Scope determines
- Which objects a user may take actions on

Adding Profiles further defines the role by

◆ Determining which actions will be permitted

◆ Determining the accessibility offered or masked to the underlying fabric

◆ Determining how the scope should be defined

And finally this is completed by applying a Scope filter to

◆ Determine which objects the user role may take actions against

As additional user roles are created, the flexibility of the RBAC solution will become more apparent. User roles are hierarchical by design; the use and management of the fabric and its clouds can be delegated multiple times, permitting the environment to scale to fit the organizational requirements. Figure 9.6 illustrates this hierarchy with a sample approach that might be implemented to segregate a fabric and delegate administrative access.

FIGURE 9.6
A sample user-role-delegation hierarchy

Delegating Administration

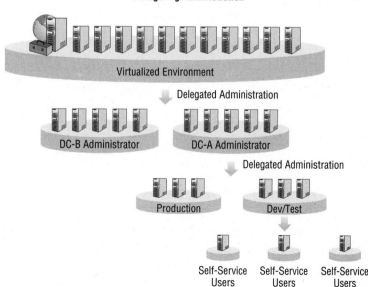

VMM Profiles

In this section, you will learn about the attributes of the different profiles offered within VMM, along with both the functionality and scope they can expose and consume. With this knowledge, you will be able to create user roles to manage and operate your private clouds and their foundational fabric.

ADMINISTRATOR

The Administrator profile is not actually available to use in the roles you create in VMM. This profile is reserved for the Administrator user role that is automatically created when you install VMM. Members of the local Administrators group on the VMM server are automatically granted membership in this role, along with the user account used to install the VMM server.

The properties that define the Administrator profile/role include the following:

◆ There is unrestricted access to all VMM resources.

◆ No additional customization is available or required.

◆ Only administrators can add stand-alone XenServer hosts and clusters (pools).

◆ Only administrators can add a Windows Server Update Services server.

DELEGATED ADMINISTRATORS

The Delegated Administrators profile functions similarly to the Administrators profile except that Delegated Administrators is available for assignment in new roles. More importantly, it permits access scoping, which allows the associated members to divide their resources into groups while still retaining administrative autonomy.

Delegated administrators may further delegate the resources they manage by creating additional delegated administrators who manage part or all of the resources over which the parent delegated administrators have scope; but they cannot delegate access to resources that they themselves have no permission to use.

This functionality can be useful in many different business scenarios. As an example, assume the fabric is distributed across two geographically dispersed data centers, each having its own infrastructure team with responsibility for their local fabric.

The properties of the Delegated Administrators profile include the following:

◆ It can be scoped down to a single host group.

◆ It can be scoped down to a single library share.

◆ Its members are restricted to viewing status and jobs within their scope.

◆ Its members are restricted to viewing resource properties within their scope.

◆ It has administrative privileges to all resources within scope.

READ-ONLY ADMINISTRATORS PROFILE

As with delegated administrators, read-only administrators can have their access scoped. The Read-Only Administrators profile, however, restricts its members to a read-only experience across all access to the resources in their scope. A product of this read-only administrative access is an additional restriction denying these administrative members the ability to create additional user roles.

There are many scenarios where this role may be useful, including training for and monitoring of the cloud fabric. The functions offered by this profile include the following:

- It can be scoped down to a single host group.

- It can be scoped down to a single library share.

- Its members are restricted to viewing status and jobs within their scope.

- Its members are restricted to viewing resource properties within their scope.

- Scoped Run As accounts are restricted to viewing only.

SELF-SERVICE USERS

The Self-Service Users profile provides the primary experience users encounter while working within the cloud. It uses a granular list of action permissions. Users interact in a customized environment for creating, deploying, and managing VMs and services in a private cloud.

In addition, users can use either the VMM console or the VMM command shell to create and manage resources. Self-service users can view status, resource capacity and quota usage, jobs, and Performance and Resource Optimization (PRO) tips (if authorized) for their cloud, VMs, and services.

Working primarily in the cloud, self-service users should neither know nor care about fabric elements, including host groups, hosts, library servers, or any other administrative configuration. As a result, they have no view of the VMM Fabric workspace, because this layer is completely abstracted from their profile. Chapter 10, "Working in the Cloud," introduces the cloud from the consumer's perspective.

Self-service users see cloud libraries, which display physical resources that are available to them through private clouds. The Cloud Libraries node shows each of the private clouds in the scope of the Self-Service user role. Each private-cloud node displays physical resources on read-only library shares that have been configured for the cloud.

NOTE Administrators see both the Library Servers node and the Cloud Libraries node. Delegated Administrators see only the library servers and cloud libraries that are within the scope of their user roles.

The Self-Service User Data node shows physical resources that users have access to on the user data path for their Self-Service user role. Access-control permissions in the file system determine what the users see.

In the Templates and Profiles nodes, self-service users can see only the templates and profiles that they own, that were assigned to their role, or that were shared by other self-service users.

The user data path, which is initially defined when a Self-Service role is created, enables its members to upload and share the physical resources they will use to create service templates and deploy services. Each Self-Service user role has only one user data path for all the private clouds within the scope of that role. The user data path must be in a library share.

Access to the physical resources on a user data path is controlled through the file system. To enable members of a Self-Service user role to use and share their own resources in VMM, grant Read/Write permission on the folder to all role members.

In the Library workspace, Self-Service users can see any resources for which they have permissions on the Library pane, in the Self-Service User Data node. However, only members of a Self-Service user role that has the Author action assigned to it can use the resources to create profiles and templates in VMM.

To enable members of a Self-Service user role to use their own application packages to create service templates and deploy services in VMM, configure a user data path for the Self-Service user role and grant Read/Write permission on the folder.

When a template is to be shared by all the members of a Self-Service user role, the template should have no owner assigned; this will allow members of the Self-Service user role with Author, Deploy, or Deploy (Template Only) actions to use the template. When an owner is assigned to the template, only the owner can use the template.

If authorized, self-service users can share resources with other Self-Service user roles by using the Share and Receive action. This allows users to share profiles (hardware, OS, application, and SQL), templates (VM and service), and services.

When launching the VMM console, self-service users who are members of multiple user roles must select the role under which they wish to work.

TIP Multiple instances of the console can be launched simultaneously when the user wants to interact with more than one user role. If they are members of a Self-Service role, administrators can use this feature to debug issues that users report.

TIP To quickly launch new instances, use the Open New Connection shortcut on the ribbon's Menu button.

The properties of the Self-Service profile include the following:

◆ It can be scoped to a single host group for VM creation.

◆ It can be scoped to a single library share for VM storage.

◆ It can be scoped to logical and physical resources in the library.

◆ Its members are restricted to their own user data paths in the library.

◆ It can be restricted to specific templates for VM creation.

◆ It can be used to manage resource quotas.

◆ It permits access to PRO tips.

◆ It can be scoped to clouds, with per-cloud quota customizations.

User-Role Elements

Along with the various profiles offered for user roles, a number of additional elements are defined as part of the process of creating user roles. This section provides an overview of the different elements and how they can be used to customize the user roles you create to define access to the fabric and clouds.

MEMBERS

Members of a user role are selected from the hosting Active Directory domain. Normally, following best practices, members are assigned to the role as Active Directory groups rather than Active Directory users.

So that all members of a role can share ownership of all the VMs created by other members, you can create a security group in Active Directory and assign that group to the user role.

An alternative method for sharing resources among self-service users is to use the Share and Receive actions (discussed in Table 9.5) which enable resource owners who are self-service users to share individual resources with one or all members of a Self-Service user role.

NOTE   If you are troubleshooting and need to test a user role's access, add yourself as a member of that role.

QUOTA

You can utilize a user role to define a quota at two different scopes.

The first scope is for all members of the user role, and it defines the combined total quota for all the members of the user role in a cloud. The quota cannot exceed the capacity already defined on the private cloud.

The second scope is per member of the user role; you can use it to restrict the amount of cloud resources any single member of the user role can consume, up to the maximum capacity defined for all users of the role accessing the private cloud or the total capacity defined for the private cloud.

NOTE   Quotas apply only to deployed VMs. If a Self-Service user role has permission to store VMs, the quota does not apply to VMs that are stored in the library.

RESOURCES

As users are offered access to a private cloud, additional resources may be needed so they can use the clouds to which they have access. Resources in a read-only library are available only to users who have been assigned the Author action.

Private-cloud users who are assigned the Author action can be assigned template and service resources so they can deploy them to the clouds within their scope.

When sufficient resources are available, administrators can grant access to additional elements within their clouds, including profiles, templates, and additional objects that are not hosted in the library.

ACTIONS

For users to operate within a cloud, actions must be configured to define how that interaction will occur. VMM offers a number of actions for managing both services and VMs.

These actions can control how users can interact with the cloud for deploying both services and VMs. Scoping additionally enables the option to restricting this access, ranging from the full permission of authoring templates, to modifying settings of existing templates, or limited to just deploying preconfigured templates of VMs or Services.

Table 9.5 shows the actions that can be defined for Self-Service user roles.

TABLE 9.5: Action Permissions for Self-Service Users

CLOUD ACTIONS	DESCRIPTION
Author	Grants permission to create and edit templates and profiles, including hardware profiles, operating-system profiles, application profiles, SQL Server profiles, VM templates, and service templates.
Deploy	Grants permission to deploy VMs and services from templates and virtual hard disks that are assigned to their user role. However, they have no rights to author templates and profiles for VMs and/or services.
Deploy (From Template only)	Grants permissions to deploy VMs and services from templates and virtual hard disks that are available to the active users scope. This action however does not permit users to author new templates.
Share	Allows members to grant resources they own to other Self-Service user roles. Shareable resources include hardware profiles, operating-system profiles, application profiles, SQL Server profiles, VM templates, VMs, service templates, and services. A self-service user must be the owner of a resource to share it. The Self-Service user role that receives the shared resource must be assigned the Receive action.
Receive	Allows members to receive resources that are shared by members of other Self-Service user roles.
Remove	Grants members permission to remove their own VMs and services.
Start	Grants members permission to start their own VMs and services.
Stop	Grants members permission to stop their own VMs and services.
Pause and Resume	Grants members permission to pause and resume their own VMs and services.
Shut down	Grants members permission to perform an orderly shutdown of their own VMs and services.
Checkpoint	Grants members permission to create, edit, and delete checkpoints for their own VMs and to restore their VMs to a previous checkpoint. Checkpoints are supported only on VMs and not on services.
Checkpoint (Restore only)	Grants permission to restore their own VMs to a checkpoint but not to create, edit, and delete checkpoints.
Store	Grants permission to store VMs in the VMM library. VMs stored in the library do not count against a user's VM quotas.
Local Administrator	Grants permission to serve as a local administrator on their own VMs. Important: Be sure to select the Local Administrator action on any Self-Service user role that has the Deploy (From Template) action selected. This action enables those users to set the local Administrator password during VM and service deployment. Self-service users who are granted the Deploy action do not need this action to be able to set Local Administrator credentials.
Remote Connection	Grants permission to connect to their VMs from the VMM console and the VMM self-service portal.

RUN AS ACCOUNTS

A *Run As account* is a container used to store user or system credentials. Although most VMM wizards permit end users to supply credentials interactively, in some scenarios users may not have permission to know a specific password or the job being executed may not be interactive.

In these situations, Run As accounts can be associated with the template or profile. Self-service users might later be delegated access to one of these templates for use within their cloud; they will benefit when Run As accounts help VMM join the new VM or service deployment, joining a secure domain utilizing these stored credentials.

Run As accounts can be created by administrators and by self-service users with the Author action.

Managing User Roles with the Create User Role Wizard

User roles are a critical function of the administration of a VMM environment; and to assist in configuring these roles, VMM has yet another of its magical wizards standing by to guide you through the task of both creating and customizing user roles. In this section, you will learn about the process of managing, creating, and removing user roles in VMM using the Create User Role Wizard.

User roles are hierarchical in scope, in that if a new user role is created by delegated administrator A, this role is not visible to delegated administrator B. This hierarchy is not visibly presented in the VMM console. The Parent role (creator) of a user role can be viewed only through the use of PowerShell.

```
$Get-SCUserRole | Select name, parentuserrole
```

In the next few pages, you will configure sample user roles using the VMM Create User Role Wizard.

Managing Administrators

The Administrator role is mandatory in VMM. You cannot remove or duplicate the existing Administrator role. If you are an administrator, you can add users to this role or remove them. Use the following procedure to do so:

1 In the VMM console, open the Settings workspace. In the Settings pane, navigate to Security ⇨ User Roles ⇨ Administrator. On the Home tab of the ribbon, in the Properties group, click Properties. The Create User Role Wizard appears.

2. Click Members. The Members screen appears.

3. To remove a member, click the name in the Members pane and click Remove. To add a member, click Add and select the member from the Select Users, Computers, or Groups dialog box.

You can select an Active Directory user or group. After you click OK, VMM validates your selections before appending them to the members list.

VMM does not apply the changes until you click Next to leave the Members screen.

Creating a Delegated Administrator

To create a new Delegated Administrator user role, the user performing the exercise must already be a member of the Administrator role or an existing Delegated Administrator role.

If the role is being created by a delegated administrator, the delegation scope can only be granted on resources that are within the grantor's scope, including host groups, library servers, and Run As accounts. Use the following procedure to create a Delegated Administrator user role:

1. In the VMM console, open the Settings workspace. In the Settings pane, navigate to Security ⇨ User Roles. On the Home tab of the ribbon, in the Create group, click Create User Role. The Create User Role Wizard appears.

2. Enter a name and description for the new role and click Next. The Profile screen appears.

3. Click the Delegated Administrator radio button, and click Next. The Members screen appears.

4. Add members to the new role, as in the procedure in the previous section, and click Next.

The Scope screen appears (Figure 9.7). The figure shows the choices available to an administrator performing this procedure. A delegated administrator might see fewer choices.

FIGURE 9.7
The Scope screen

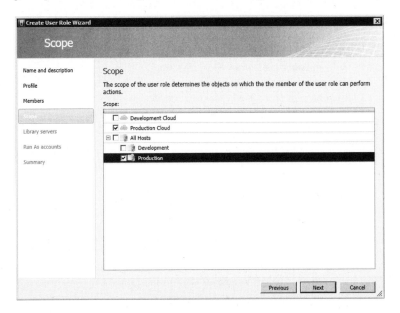

5. Check the boxes by the items you want to place in the scope of the new user role and click Next. The Library Servers screen appears.

6. Use the Add button to look for existing library servers to make available to the new user role. Then click Next. The Run As Accounts screen appears.

7. Use the Add button to look for existing Run As accounts to make available to the new user role. The Summary screen appears.

8. Review your choices and click Finish.

After you create a delegated administrator, you can change members, scope, library servers, and Run As accounts in the Properties dialog box for the user role.

Creating a Read-Only Administrator

The process of creating a user role for a Read-Only Administrator is exactly the same as creating a Delegated Administrator user role, except that you select Read-Only Administrator on the Profile screen. Similarly, the permissions and scope allowed for creating this role are the same as for a Delegated Administrator role.

The process to create user roles using PowerShell is similar to the one you used to create private clouds.

Begin creating your new user role by providing a name, description, and profile, just as you would on the first two pages of the Create User Role Wizard. The variable $userrole receives a reference to the newly created role.

```
$userrole = New-SCUserRole -Name "Production Helpdesk" -UserRoleProfile
"ReadOnlyAdmin" -Description "Helpdesk support"
```

Next, create the variable $resourcesToAdd to hold the list of resources to add to the scope of the new user. Successive lines of code add the host group (Production), cloud (Production Cloud), library server (vmmlib1.private.cloud), and Run As account (Run_As_Domain_Admin).

```
$resourcesToAdd = @()

$resourcesToAdd += Get-SCVMHostGroup -Name "Production"

$resourcesToAdd += Get-SCCloud -Name "Production Cloud"

$resourcesToAdd += Get-SCLibraryServer| where {$_.Name –like "vmmlib1.private.
cloud"}

$resourcesToAdd += Get-SCRunAsAccount -Name "Run_As_Domain_Admin"
```

The next line adds both a new member (PRIVATE\Production Helpdesk Group) and the Resources we just created to the role.

```
Set-SCUserRole -UserRole $userrole -AddMember @("PRIVATE\Production Helpdesk
Group") -AddScope $resourcesToAdd
```

Creating a Self-Service User

Self-service is one of the main purposes — perhaps the most important purpose — of private clouds. A Self-Service role combines the Active Directory user account of a potential cloud user with the Self-Service profile.

The honor of creating Self-Service User roles is reserved for administrators and delegated administrators, who can grant the roles access to resources within the grantor's scope. VMM offers a rich set of features for Self-Service roles, as you saw earlier.

To create a Self-Service User role, follow the same steps as for creating a Delegated Administrator role, except in step 3, click the Self-Service User radio button.

In step 4, you can only select clouds, because self-service users do not see the fabric of the cloud. This should bring you to the Quotas screen (Figure 9.8).

FIGURE 9.8
Assigning quotas to self-service users

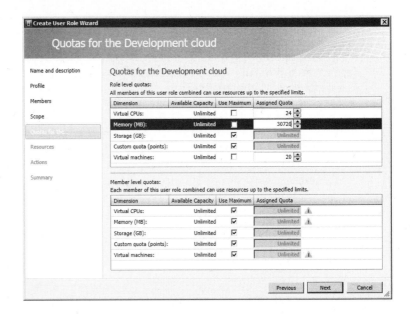

To finish creating a Self-Service user role, follow these steps:

1. Assign quotas and click Next.

The cloud may already have a quota assigned to it. If so, the more restrictive of the two quotas applies. The quota can be defined as a shared quota for all members of the role, or limits per role member. Figure 9.8 shows a shared quota.

2. Specify resources and the user role data path, and click Next.

The Resources screen appears (Figure 9.9). Members of the user role already have access to resources in the associated library, but you can give them access to additional templates or services. The user role data path specifies the library location to which members of this role can upload data.

3. Specify the permitted actions for this user role and click Next.

The Actions screen appears. Refer to Table 9.5 for the actions you can permit members of this role to perform. The Run As Accounts screen appears only if you specify the Author or Deploy actions. If it appears, you can add Run As accounts by clicking the Add button.

4. Review your choices and click Finish.

The Summary screen appears. VMM starts a job to create the new user role. Once the new role exists, you can use the console to change its properties.

FIGURE 9.9
The VMM Create
User Role Wizard's
Resources screen

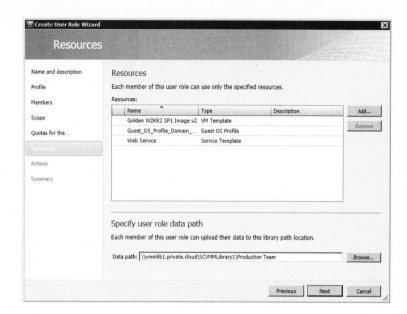

Managing a Private Cloud

The remainder of this chapter describes common tasks that administrators execute while supporting and maintaining private clouds.

Managing Cloud Use

Any user of a private cloud can monitor its resources. To do so in the console, go to the VMs and Services workspace, expand the Clouds node, and select a private cloud. On the Home tab of the ribbon, in the Show group, click Overview. Figure 9.10 shows the kind of information available.

Also, in the Show group, you can select VMs or Services to view information about the VMs and services deployed to the private cloud.

Changing the Cloud's Capacity

In response to customer requests or your own proactive monitoring, you might need to expand a private cloud.

Before increasing a cloud's capacity, check the capacity of the underlying fabric. If the new cloud capacity exceeds the capacity of the fabric, you must first add hosts or other resources to the fabric.

If you have administrative permissions for a cloud, you can modify its capacity by right-clicking the cloud and opening its properties. Then select the tab containing the settings you want to modify.

FIGURE 9.10

Overview of a cloud

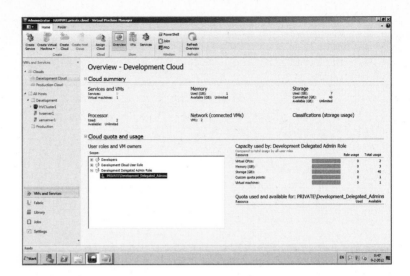

Take the following steps to modify the capacity of the cloud:

1. In the console, open the VMs and Services workspace, locate the cloud, and click it. On the Folder tab of the ribbon, click Properties. The Cloud Properties dialog appears.

2. Highlight the Capacity tab, adjust the capacity, and click OK.

VMM applies the changes.

POWERSHELL SNIPPIT: CHANGING CLOUDS USING POWERSHELL

Modifying a cloud using PowerShell is straightforward. The code below changes the capacity of a cloud called Development Cloud, expanding the VM Count quota to 20.

```
$myCloud = Get-SCCloud -Name "Development Cloud"
Set-SCCloud -Cloud $myCloud -VMCount 20
```

Managing Shared Resources

VMM allows you to configure Self-Service user roles to enable owners of VMs and service templates to share their resources with other members of their own Self-Service user role, with another Self-Service user role, or with an individual member of another Self-Service user role.

The Share action enables a Self-Service user role to share resources; the Receive action enables a Self-Service user role to receive resources that are shared by another Self-Service user role.

SHARING RESOURCES BETWEEN SELF-SERVICE USER ROLES

As a self-service user with permission for the Share action, use the following procedure to share a resource with another Self-Service role that has permission for the Receive action.

NOTE This procedure can also be performed by administrators. The Access tab lists resources that Self-Service user roles can access either through sharing or through assignment. To perform this procedure, delegated administrators must have the resource and the Self-Service user role in the scope of their user role. After an administrator assigns a resource to a Self-Service user role, the resource is added to the Resources tab of the Self-Service user role.

1. In the console, open the Library workspace, navigate to the resource you want to share, and select it. On the Tools tab of the ribbon, in the Properties group, click Properties. The Properties screen appears.

   If you do not have the required permissions, the selection buttons are disabled (grayed out). The Self-Service Owner field shows the current owner (if any) of the resource. The Users list displays the names of self-service users and Self-Service user roles that share the resource.

2. Make the desired selection and click OK to save the updated properties.

   To share the resource with another member of the Self-Service user role, use the Select button to select the user account. To share the resource with other Self-Service user roles, select each Self-Service user role that should receive the resource. Only user roles that have the Receive action assigned to them appear in the list.

   To share the resource with an individual user of a Self-Service user role different from yours, select the user and the user role. Only the selected role member receives access to the shared resource.

Assigning Access to a Private Cloud

A private cloud can be shared between one or more user roles. To assign the private cloud to an existing user role, follow these steps:

1. In the console, open the VMs and Services workspace and expand the Clouds node. Locate and select the private cloud that you want to assign.
2. On the Home tab of the ribbon, in the Cloud group, click Assign Cloud. The Assign Cloud screen appears.
3. Make the desired choice and click OK.
4. Select an existing user role to grant access to the selected cloud from the list of available roles in your scope or create a new user role (which will open the Create User Role Wizard).

Deleting a Cloud

When projects or customers no longer need their clouds, you can remove the clouds from the environment. Deleting a cloud releases all the associated resources so they can be reused.

Before you can delete a cloud, make sure no VMs, services, or other artifacts remain within the boundaries of the cloud. You may want to archive stored VMs from the library before you delete the cloud.

To delete a cloud, follow these steps:

1. In the console, open the VMs and Services workspace, and expand the Clouds node. Locate and select the private cloud you want to delete. On the Folders tab of the ribbon, click Delete.

2. VMM asks if you're sure. Click OK to delete the cloud. As with all jobs, you can monitor the deletion progress by opening the Jobs workspace to view the job status.

POWERSHELL SNIPPIT: REMOVING CLOUDS USING POWERSHELL

Removing a cloud using PowerShell is extremely simple; just use the following command sequence:

```
$myCloud = Get-SCCloud –Name "Production Cloud"
Remove-SCCloud –Cloud $myCloud
```

Summary

This chapter combines the materials we covered in earlier chapters to begin to form a cloud. It moves from discussing the capacity and capabilities of clouds through the creation of two sample clouds, one with the Create Cloud Wizard and the other with a sequence of PowerShell commands.

Roles, role-based access control, and profiles help simplify cloud security and management. They form the basis for the sample administrative and self-service roles you created for the sample clouds.

The chapter closes with a discussion of ongoing management tasks. Cloud administrators can quickly add capacity to a cloud or delete a cloud that is no longer needed. Self-service users can deploy and share resources without administrative intervention.

## Chapter 10

Working in the Cloud

So far we have focused on the ways administrators manipulate the fabric and create private clouds, using both the VMM console and the PowerShell interface. This chapter focuses on how Self-Service users create virtual machines (VMs) and use cloud services. It covers the following subjects:

◆ Using the Self-Service web portal

◆ The elements of VMs that Self-Service users need to know

◆ Creating, deploying, and managing VMs

VMM User Interfaces

VMM offers users three main ways to interact with it:

◆ The VMM console provides a rich and context-aware environment for working on the fabric and within clouds.

◆ The PowerShell command processor recognizes more than 450 commands, providing access to all of the functionality of the console and more.

◆ The Self-Service web portal provides limited functionality to Self-Service users who use the portal primarily to manage VMs.

Providing an Interface

You can offer users access to the console by sharing the installation files, using a software-based distribution system to deploy the console, or publishing the console utilizing a remote application technology.

By launching the VMM command shell (PowerShell with the VirtualMachineManager module preloaded), you can perform the same actions you can perform from the console.

The web portal is an installation option in VMM (see Chapter 4, "Setting Up and Deploying VMM 2012," for details). Once installed, the portal communicates directly with the VMM Management Service, just as the console and PowerShell do.

NOTE In a high-availability installation, although VMM Server will be installed on multiple systems, the VMM Service will be active on only a single instance at any point in time. Users will request the VMM Console or PowerShell to connect with the VMM management server; this request will be redirected transparently and automatically to the active VMM Service by Windows Failover Clustering.

Choosing an Interface

The console offers many useful features in a familiar interface, but there are situations in which the console is not the appropriate way to perform a given action on the fabric as an administrator, or on the cloud as a Self-Service user.

The console uses PowerShell for all its functionality, and it does so transparently. For example, at the end of every wizard, you can review the generated PowerShell script. Every property window has a View Script button that becomes enabled as soon as you modify a setting. This functionality enables you to review the commands the console is about to execute, so you can learn how to execute the same process directly from the PowerShell prompt.

One of the benefits of using PowerShell is its batch-processing capability. This process is much faster and more efficient than both the console and web portal, for example, consider the exercise required for deploying multiple VMs when executing the Create VM Wizard for each of the required VMs.

The Self-Service web portal provides a simple interface for users whose primary interest is managing VMs.

Both the web portal and PowerShell enforce the same private-cloud and user-role rules and restrictions that the console enforces. However, only users who are listed as Self-Service users can log onto the web portal.

Connecting to a User Interface

This section shows how to connect to VMM using each of the user interfaces described in the previous section.

CONNECTING WITH THE CONSOLE

When you launch the console to begin a new session, you'll see a dialog requesting the name of the VMM management server and asking for your authentication credentials.

VMM figures out which roles you belong to and lets you select one. The console then presents only the options that are valid for that role.

With the VMM console already open, perform the following steps to connect to a new session.

1. Click the down arrow at the top-left corner of the ribbon and then click Open New Connection. The Connection dialog reappears.

2. Establish the new session. If you have multiple consoles open, you can tell them apart because the title bar contains the name of the user role.

CONNECTING WITH POWERSHELL

After launching PowerShell, you can verify that the VMM module is present by issuing a simple query for commands:

```
Get-Command -Module VirtualMachineManager
```

NOTE The VMM PowerShell module can be loaded into a PowerShell instance if the module has previously been installed on the active computer. Installation of the VMM components is covered in Chapter 3, "Introducing the VMM 2012 Architecture." Once the module is installed it can be loaded into the session using the following command:

```
Import-Module VirtualMachineManager
```

PowerShell returns a list of more than 400 commands you can utilize if the module is loaded. Before you can use any of them, you must connect the PowerShell session to the VMM management server for your session. To do that, execute the following command (where `HAVMM1 .private.cloud` is the name of the VMM server):

```
Get-SCVMMServer -Computer HAVMM1.private.cloud
```

This establishes a link between your session and the VMM management server using the AD credentials of the user currently hosting the session. After the session is established, PowerShell autoconnects you with one of the user roles available to you. You can check which role you are using with the following command:

```
Get-SCUserRole
```

To open additional PowerShell sessions for different user roles, launch a new instance of PowerShell, connect to the VMM services, and specify the role that you would like to be active. To do that, issue thefollowing code:

```
Get-SCVMMServer -Computer HAVMM1.private.cloud -UserRoleName "Production
Helpdesk"
```

CONNECTING WITH THE VMM WEB PORTAL

After installing the web portal, the administrator establishes a URL to the new portal. Use a web browser to access that page. The logon dialog shown in Figure 10.1 appears.

FIGURE 10.1
The VMM web portal logon dialog box

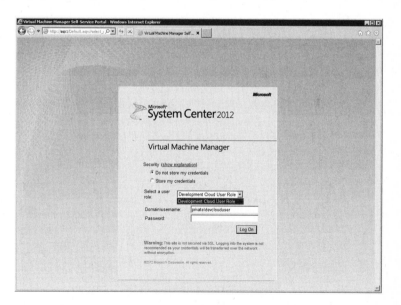

If the administrator has not enabled automatic authentication on the portal, the logon dialog box will not include the Select a User Role field. Log on with `Domain\UserName` credentials. The main screen, which is opened to the Computers tab, appears (Figure 10.2).

FIGURE 10.2

The main screen of the VMM Self-Service web portal

The name of the current user, with the active role in parentheses, appears at the top of the dialog. Also along the top are links to change the currently active role, contact the administrator, look up help, and log off the portal session.

In the View pane, you can select the Computer tab or the Library tab to choose a workspace. The Computers workspace lists the VMs currently deployed to the private cloud. The Library workspace lists the VMs in the Cloud Storage library.

The right pane lists the actions that are available. This list is context-sensitive. Actions are enabled or disabled based on the status of the VM selected in the window, and the action permissions granted by the administrator for your user role.

If you want to change your user role, click Change Role on the top line of the screen. A dialog similar to Figure 10.1 will appear. Select the new role and click Log On.

Working with Virtual Machines

Chapter 9, "Creating a Private Cloud," explained how administrators create private clouds and configure user roles to grant access to consumers. By defining Self-Service user roles, administrators also determine the actions those users can execute within the cloud (for example, creating and removing VMs, deploying applications, and sharing resources).

For the cloud to be of value, Self-Service users must be able to access the library resources. Those resources can range from base VM images and predefined VM templates and services to elements that can be combined to permit cloud users to define and create their own VMs. Figure 10.3 illustrates the workflow associated with preparing the cloud for use.

For example, the administrator can grant the user role the right to create VMs and deploy applications. Users can share these applications with other user roles. For example, they could share an approved service from the QA team with the production team.

VM templates define the information necessary to create a VM, including the following:

♦ The hardware profile, which specifies the amount of memory the VM will have

♦ The operating-system profile, which can, for example, specify the Active Directory domain the VM should join

♦ The OS product keys

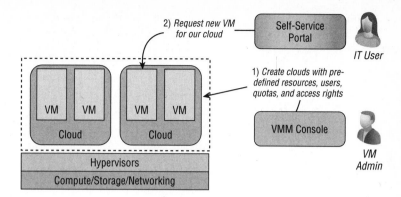

FIGURE 10.3
Creating clouds and
using them

As the development team focuses on creating new applications and revising existing ones, providing additional action permissions in VMM permits them to host their new code and its revisions as a service. With Author privileges, a service template can wrap together everything needed to deploy and run a multitier application. This includes the code for the application, descriptions of its database schemas, VM templates that describe the VMs it runs in, and more.

In order to define a service, the Self-Service user must know how the application is structured and how it should run. Normally, this person is a developer, a member of the QA team, or the person responsible for deploying the application. Chapter 8, "Understanding Service Modeling," explains services and describes how to use the VMM console's template designer to create service templates. These templates can be used to deploy new instances of the application and can be shared with other Self-Service users.

The rest of this chapter will explain how to use the VMM features and how to deploy and manage VMs. Chapter 11, "App Controller and the Public Cloud," will build on this chapter's foundation and explain how to use, deploy, and manage services.

Deploying a New VM

As a private-cloud user, the first thing you'll do is deploy a new VM. No matter which interface you use to deploy it, VMM will check to see if the requested VM is within the capabilities of the selected private cloud and that you and your role are within quota and capability limits. After verification, VMM will create the VM without additional approvals.

As a Self-Service user VMM will only ask which cloud (within your role's scope) to host the new VM; it will not tell you which host it was deployed to. As a Self-Service user, you are concerned only with the cloud and not with the fabric, which you cannot see. VMM makes placement decisions based on its knowledge of the resources available.

VMM creates a new job for every request. You can monitor the job-creation progress in real time from the Jobs workspace in the VMM console. Only jobs in the active user's scope appear in this view.

The process of deploying a VM to the private cloud is illustrated in Figure 10.4. For example, the developer interacts with VMM through one of the available interfaces and selects which resources to deploy. VMM checks the request and then deploys the new instance to the private cloud.

FIGURE 10.4
Deploying a new
VM

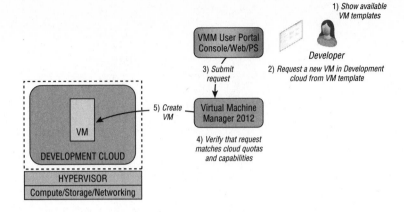

Using the Console to Deploy a VM

The VMM console offers the richest experience for deploying VMs to the cloud. To deploy a VM from a template that the administrator has provided, follow these steps:

1. In the console, open the VMs And Services workspace. On the Home tab of the ribbon, in the Create group, click the Create Virtual Machine drop-down and then click Create Virtual Machine.

   The Create Virtual Machine Wizard appears, displaying the Select Source screen (Figure 10.5).

FIGURE 10.5
Selecting a source
in the Create VM
Wizard

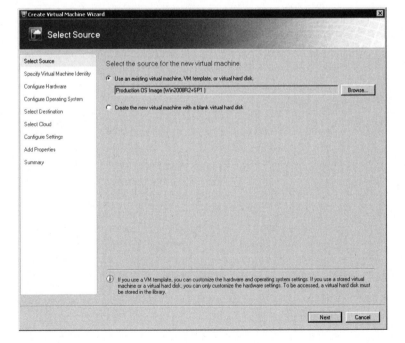

2. Select the source for the VM and click Next.

With Deploy permissions, Self-Service users and administrators can use previously created templates they can customize for their deployments. Self-Service users who have only the Deploy From Template permission cannot customize the templates when they use them.

3. Use the Browse button to select an existing VM, template, or VHD.

Administrators or Self-Service users with Author privileges can create a VM from scratch, using blank or prepared virtual hard disks (VHDs) from the libraries, ISO files for OS installation, and so forth to completely customize the new VM. They can also save these customization options as new templates for future deployments.

4. Click the radio button to create the new VM using an existing virtual machine, VM template, or virtual hard disk from the library. The Specify Virtual Machine Identity screen appears.

5. Enter a name and description for the VM and click Next.

All VMs in the private cloud must have an identity, which is simply a friendly name and an optional description. The name of the VM doesn't have to match the final computer name, but best practice is to keep them the same.

The Configure Hardware screen appears (Figure 10.6).

FIGURE 10.6
Configuring hardware in the Create VM Wizard

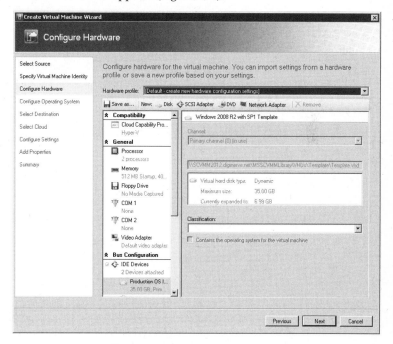

6. Configure hardware for the new VM and click Next.

If the selected source for the new VM is an existing template, the hardware profile is predefined as part of the template. The Configure Operating System screen appears (Figure 10.7).

FIGURE 10.7
Configuring the OS
in the Create VM
Wizard

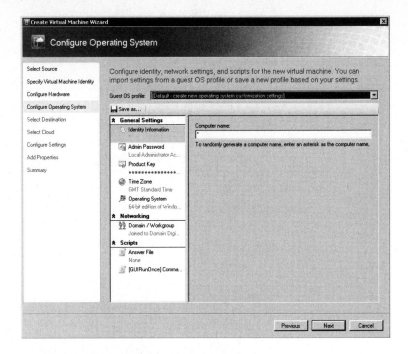

7. Configure the OS for the new VM and click Next.

   You can customize the operating system when you deploy VMs running certain versions of Microsoft Windows. You can set the system name, domain or workgroup, product keys, time zone, answer file, and GUI Run Once commands.

   Access rules for modifying OS profiles are the same as for hardware profiles (see Chapter 7, "Deploying Hosts and Clusters in VMM 2012," for more information about OS profiles).

   The Select Destination screen appears.

8. Click the radio button corresponding to the desired destination and click Next.

   You can deploy a VM to a private cloud or library within your scope. If you have administrative permissions, you can also deploy to a specific host.

   After a delay, during which VMM evaluates the available clouds and computes star ratings, the Select Cloud screen appears (Figure 10.8).

9. Select a destination cloud for the VM and click Next.

   If more than one cloud is available to your user role, VMM presents star ratings based on the hardware requirements of the VM template, the resources available on each destination, network services, and your quota. If you are an administrator, you can choose between seeing the hosts available on the fabric or the clouds that end users see.

You can help VMM fine-tune its ratings by clicking Expected Utilization and providing estimates of the CPU, disk, and network resources the VM should need. VMM recalculates its ratings based on your estimates.

FIGURE 10.8

Selecting a cloud in the Create VM Wizard

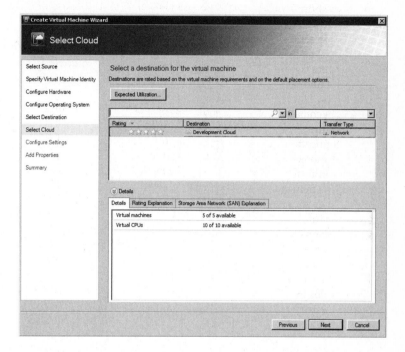

The Details pane shows how much of the quotas the selected cloud uses. The Settings screen appears.

10. Enter the computer name for the VM, adjust any other settings that VMM makes available, and click Next. The Add Properties screen appears if you have administrative permissions.

11. Select the actions to take when the virtualization server starts or stops and indicate whether to exclude the VM from optimization actions. Then click Next.

Chapter 6, "Integrating Networking and Storage into VMM 2012," provides additional information about optimization. The Summary screen appears.

12. Review your choices and click Create.

13. Monitor the progress of the Create Virtual Machine job in the Jobs workspace.

When the job is complete, you can find the newly created VM in the "VMs And Services" workspace. Expand Clouds, then locate and select the development clouds as used in our scenario.

Using PowerShell to Deploy a VM

As you can see from the previous section, the process of creating a VM includes a number of elements. You must define the hardware and optionally the OS, identify the target destination, and present an identity. In PowerShell we can repeat this process in individual steps, storing each as a variable; those variables are then combined as reference switches (parameters) to the command that instructs the VMM server to create the new VM. To do that, follow these steps:

1. In this PowerShell example, you'll create a variable and give it a reference to the template.

```
$VMTemplate = Get-SCVMTemplate | ? {$_.name -eq "Golden W2KR2 SP1 Image v2"}
```

NOTE The PowerShell command Get-SCVMTemplate will present a list of all templates currently available to the active user role. To select a single template we can filter this list to entries that match the unique name of the template we wish to use, as illustrated in step 1.

2. Combine the template with a name for the VM and store the result in a new variable.

```
$VMname = "Dev-Srv01"
$VMConfig = New-SCVMConfiguration -VMTemplate $VMTemplate -Name $VMname
```

3. Create a variable to hold a reference to the destination private cloud.

```
$cloud = Get-SCCloud -Name "Development Cloud"
```

4. Create variables to hold a description of the VM and start and stop actions.

```
$description = "Dev Test Server 01 - Test Deployment"
$startAction = "NeverAutoTurnOnVM"
$stopAction = "SaveVM"
```

5. Finally, ask PowerShell to create the VM and return control as soon as the job is started.

```
New-SCVirtualMachine -Name $VMname -VMConfiguration $VMConfig
-Cloud $cloud -Description $description -ReturnImmediately
-StartAction $startAction -StopAction $stopAction
```

Using the Self-Service Portal to Deploy a VM

In order to optimize the experience and reduce the amount of interaction required, the Self-Service web-portal process used to deploy VMs to the private cloud has a single-page wizard. To deploy a VM from the Self-Service web-portal main page (Figure 10.2), follow these steps:

1. In the Create area (located on the top right of the actions pane), click New Computer. The New Virtual Machine screen appears (Figure 10.9).

The Target Cloud drop-down contains a list of private clouds available to your user role.

2. Select the target cloud to which you want to deploy the new VM and wait for the Creation Source list to refresh.

3. Select a template from the Creation Source list.

4. In the System Configuration section, enter a name and description for the new VM and make any other necessary customizations.

FIGURE 10.9
One-page wizard
for Self-Service VM
deployment

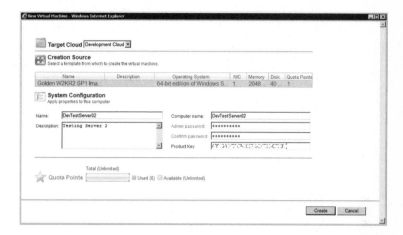

Any customizations that you can apply to the VM before deployment can be applied here.

If the template also supports guest-OS configuration, set any additional details, including the computer name and the administrative password.

5. Review the information in the Quota Points section

This area shows the quota points available for the deployment. However, this does not reflect all the new quota options available in VMM 2012. The information is usable only if the cloud uses custom quota points (see Table 9.2 in the preceding chapter).

If you deploy a VM without enough capacity, VMM stops the job after it completes its evaluation and it reports the details in the job status.

6. Click Create to deploy the new VM.

To check the job status from the Self-Service portal, follow these steps:

1. In the main screen, in the Computers view, select the VM.

2. From the Actions list, click Properties. The Properties screen appears.

3. Select the Latest Job tab, which is shown in Figure 10.10.

The view shows the progress of the current active job associated with this machine. If no job is active, it displays the status of the latest job executed. This feature enables you to monitor progress or understand job failure. To see more details or history, use the VMM console's Jobs view or contact the cloud administrator.

FIGURE 10.10
Self-Service VM job
properties

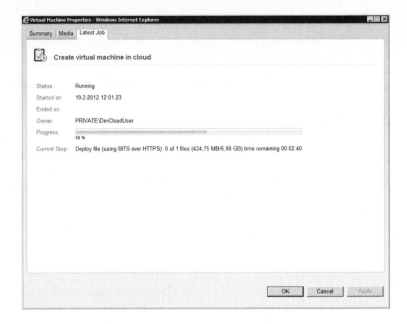

Managing Virtual Machines

The same three interfaces you use to deploy VMs give you options for handling VM-management tasks. The Self-Service portal is quick and simple to use, but it is limited. The console lets you access essentially all of the customization power of VMM, while PowerShell makes it easier to automate management tasks. In this section, you'll learn how to use each of these interfaces for typical management tasks.

One of the main benefits of clouds is Self-Service. Users feel a strong sense of ownership and control when they don't need administrator intervention to add and remove machines, power them on and off, and connect to the console or active desktop sessions.

Considering the additional advantages virtualization offers, you can empower your users to create snapshots and clones and to store and retrieve machines using inexpensive disks almost instantly. The following sections show how to perform the following VM-management tasks:

- ◆ Stop, start, or restart a VM

- ◆ Connect to a VM

- ◆ Attach an ISO to a VM

- ◆ Store a VM

- ◆ View a list of stored VMs

- ◆ Restore a VM

- ◆ Delete a VM

Stopping, Starting, or Restarting a VM

The console and Self-Service portal provide a simple DVD-style interface with DVD icons for start, stop, and pause that translate to their VM counterparts of on, off, and suspend activities. The interface additionally offers a Reset button to power on and power off the VM and a Shutdown button to tell the VM to start its OS power-down operations.

PowerShell also has commands for each of these functions; replace VMName with the actual identity of your desired VM:

```
Start-SCVirtualMachine VMName
Stop-SCVirtualMachine VMName
Reset-SCVirtualMachine VMName
Save-SCVirtualMachine VMName
Suspend-SCVirtualMachine VMName
Resume-SCVirtualMachine VMName
```

Each of these commands can take additional arguments, which are detailed in the PowerShell documentation.

NOTE   PowerShell has an inbuilt help system for all commands; to access help you can prefix any command with Get-Help and postfix with the options -Detailed, -Full, or -Examples. For example the following will present a detailed overview of the Start-SCVirtualMachine command Get-Help Get-SCVirtualMachine -Detailed

Connecting to a VM

Occasionally, you'll need to connect to the virtual machine's console (Figure 10.11). This interface is similar to viewing the monitor of a physical computer, where you can watch the normal power-on self-tests, interact with the BIOS settings, and install an OS.

FIGURE 10.11
Connecting to a
Linux VM

CONNECTING FROM THE CONSOLE

To connect from the VMM console, follow these steps:

1. Open the VMs And Services workspace, and select the VM with which to interact.

2. On the Virtual Machine tab of the ribbon, in the Window group, click Connect or View, and then click Connect Via Console. The virtual machine viewer appears.

    A window to the virtual machine's console appears in the viewer. Clicking on the view directs all input—except the key combination Ctrl+Alt+Delete (normally required to Unlock or Lock the OS console)—from the keyboard and mouse to the VM. You can use the drop-down menu or use the keyboard substitute sequence Crtl+Alt+End to send the Crtl+Alt+Delete input to the VM console.

    To release the focus from the window, you can use the key combination Ctrl+right arrow.

CONNECTING FROM THE PORTAL

To connect from the Self-Service web portal, follow these steps:

1. In the main screen, in the Computers view, select the VM.

2. In the Actions area, click Connect To VM.

    Microsoft Windows may ask you to install the Active-X component for the Self-Service web-console viewer.

    The Virtual Machine Viewer screen appears. Figure 10.11 shows the viewer for a VM running Linux.

NOTE The VM console viewer is suitable for use only in Microsoft Windows operating systems (XP SP3 and newer).

Attaching an ISO to a VM

If you are installing an OS on the VM or installing some special software distributions, you might need to attach an ISO to the VM.

USING THE CONSOLE TO ATTACH AN ISO

To attach an ISO to a VM using the VMM console, follow these steps:

1. In the console, open the VMs And Services workspace and select the VM. On the Virtual Machine tab of the ribbon, in the Properties group, click Properties. The VM Properties screen appears.

2. Select the Hardware Configuration tab in the Virtual Machine Properties dialog. In the Virtual Hardware list, in the Bus Configuration section, select the virtual DVD drive for the VM. If there are no virtual DVD drives attached to this VM you may add one using the Add Hardware button of the Hardware Profile, assuming you have permissions.

3. Select Existing ISO Image File, and click Browse.

The physical CD or DVD drive is not relevant because you do not have physical access and don't know from which host this VM is running.

4. Select the image and click OK. The path to the selected image appears in the text field.

5. Click OK to assign the new image to the VM.

USING POWERSHELL TO ATTACH AN ISO

The following example shows how to attach an ISO to a VM from PowerShell.

1. Create a variable to hold a reference to the virtual DVD drive (DEV_SVR01) on the VM.
```
$myVMDVDDrive = Get-SCVirtualDVDDrive -VM "DEV_SVR01"
```

2. Create a reference to the ISO file (CentOS6.0DVD1) in the library.
```
$myISO = Get-SCISO -Name "CentOS6.0DVD1"
```

3. Finally, attach the ISO to the VM via the virtual DVD drive.
```
Set-SCVirtualDVDDrive -VirtualDVDDrive $myVMDVDDrive -ISO $myISO
```

NOTE Get-SCVirtualDVDDrive may in some VMs return more than one virtual DVD; in these scenarios you may wish to filter the results to the bus or connection of the DVD drive to which you wish to attach the ISO. For example $myVMDVDDrive = Get-SCVirtualDVDDrive -VM "DEV_SVR01" | ? {$_.Bus -eq 1} will select only the DVD drives on bus 1 of the VM.

USING THE PORTAL TO ATTACH AN ISO

To attach an ISO to a VM using the Self-Service web portal, follow these steps:

1. In the main window, in the Computers view, select the VM.

2. In the Actions area, click Properties. The Virtual Machine Properties screen appears.

3. On the Media tab (Figure 10.12), in the Available Drives list, select the drive to use. In the Capture Mode list, click the Existing Image File radio button.

The media list becomes enabled.

4. Select the ISO image and click OK to assign the new image to the VM.

Storing a VM

In situations where the quota on your private cloud maybe almost exhausted, or you have a VM which is not currently required, but will be required at a later point, or possibly on a different cloud (assuming you have permissions). In cases like these, rather than request an increase, you can store the VM while it is not in active use. VMM can store VMs in a library and release their resources, making those resources and associated quota available for additional deployments.

Users who have Store and Recover Action permission (see Chapter 9) and who can access the library can easily store and recover VMs.

FIGURE 10.12
Self-Service VM media assignment

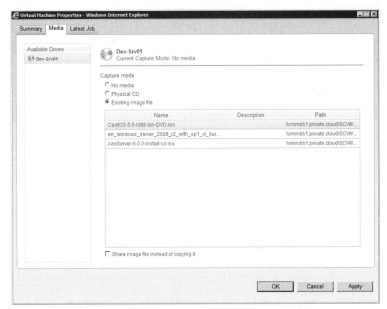

USING THE CONSOLE TO STORE A VM

To store a VM using the VMM console, follow these steps:

1. In the console, open the VMs And Services workspace and select the VM. On the Virtual Machine tab of the ribbon, in the Virtual Machine group, click Store In Library.

   For Self-Service users, VMM immediately begins storing the VM. For administrative users, the Store Virtual Machine Wizard appears.

2. Select the library server from the list and click Next.

   The list contains the library servers to which you have access. Ignore the star rating, which is not calculated.

   The Select Path screen appears.

3. Use the Browse button to select the path in the library where you would like to store the VM. Click Next. The Summary screen appears.

4. Review your choices and click Store. VMM stores the VM.

USING POWERSHELL TO STORE A VM

Using the `Save-SCVirtualMachine` command, you can store VMs to the cloud's VM-storage library (if one exists and you have permission for the action). Just follow these simple steps:

1. Create a variable to reference the VM you want to store.

```
$VM = Get-SCVirtualMachine -Name "Dev-Srv01"
```

2. Next, create a variable to reference the cloud's associated VM-storage library.

```
$LibraryServer = Get-SCLibraryServer | where {$_.Name -eq "vmmlib1.private.cloud"}
```

3. Finally, store the virtual machine in the library by providing the path to the storage location

```
Save-SCVirtualMachine -VM $VM -LibraryServer $LibraryServer -SharePath "\\
vmmlib1.private.cloud\SCVMMLibrary1\StoredVms"
```

USING THE PORTAL TO STORE A VM

To store a VM using the Self-Service web portal, follow these steps:

1. In the main window, in the Computers view, select the VM.

2. In the Actions area, click Store.

   The status of the VM changes to Under Migration. When the job is complete, the VM no longer appears in the Computers view. It appears in the Library view.

Displaying a List of Stored VMs

If a number of users share access to your cloud, or you can't recall which VMs are stored in the library, you can ask VMM to remind you.

USING THE CONSOLE TO DISPLAY STORED VMs

To display stored VMs using the VMM console, follow these steps:

1. In the console, open the library, expand Cloud Libraries, and expand the cloud containing the resources you want to display.

2. Select the Stored Virtual Machines node.

   The Cloud Library Objects list appears, containing any VMs in this library.

USING POWERSHELL TO DISPLAY STORED VMs

PowerShell adheres to the role-based access control configuration, so the level of detail it returns depends on your user-role settings. For example, Self-Service users do not see the Fabric view, so they do not see which library server stores a VM.

The following command lists all VMs that are available to you based on your user role, and resources which you have access to that are currently stored in a library.

```
Get-SCVirtualMachine | ? {$_.HostType -eq "LibraryServer"} | select name
```

Using the Portal to Display Stored VMs

To display stored VMs using the Self-Service web portal, in the main window, select the Library view. VMM refreshes the page, showing a list of VMs currently stored in a library.

Restoring a VM

To move VMs that are currently stored in a library back to the cloud, you only need to have enough quota capacity remaining for the process to complete successfully.

Using the Console to Restore a VM

To restore a VM using the VMM console, follow these steps:

1. In the VMM console, open the library, expand Cloud Libraries, and expand the cloud containing the VM to be restored.

2. Select the VM; and then on the Virtual Machine Tools tab of the ribbon, in the Actions group, click Deploy.

   If you are a Self-Service user, VMM asks whether to start the VM after deploying it and immediately starts restoring the VM to the cloud from which it was originally stored. Voilà! You are done.

   If you are an administrative user, the Deploy Virtual Machine Wizard appears (Figure 10.13) and you'll need to complete the following steps.

FIGURE 10.13
Selecting a host in the wizard

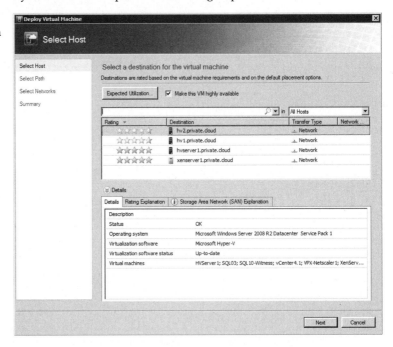

3. Select a host; optionally make the VM highly available, and click Next.

This screen functions like the Select Cloud screen in the Create Virtual Machine Wizard (Figure 10.8).

The Select Path screen appears.

4. Select a path and click Next. The Select Networks screen appears (Figure 10.14).

FIGURE 10.14
Selecting networks in the wizard

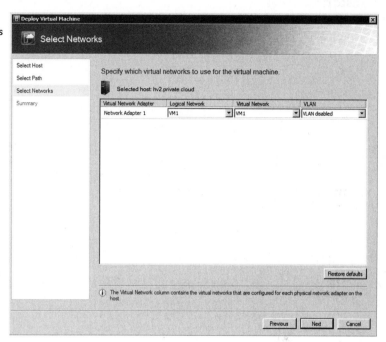

5. Specify the virtual networks to use for the VM and click Next.

Map the logical network, virtual network, and VLAN that the VM is configured to use to the networks in the scope of your role. You can change the network assignments before starting the deployment.

The Summary screen appears.

6. Review your choices and click Deploy. VMM starts the deployment.

USING POWERSHELL TO RESTORE A VM

Self-Service users can restore a VM only to the cloud from which it was originally stored. Administrative users have many more options. A Self-Service user can use the following commands to restore a VM from the library to the original cloud.

1. Create a variable to hold a reference to the stored VM.

```
$VM = Get-SCVirtualMachine -Name "Dev-Srv01"
```

Simply provide the name of the Virtual Machine as the parameter of the command Get-SCVirtualMachine, to identify the Virtual Machine that is to be restored.

2. Administrators can define the host to which the VM can be restored. Self-Service users cannot, because the VM is associated with a cloud and each cloud can have only one VM storage library. VMM moves the VM to or from this library.

```
$VMHost = Get-SCVMHost -VMMServer HAVMM1.private.cloud | where {$_.Name -eq "hv2.
private.cloud"}
```

3. Finally, issue a Move-SCVirtualMachine command to instruct VMM to restore the VM to the hosting private cloud.

```
Move-SCVirtualMachine -VM $VM
```

4. As an administrator, you can provide the name of the VM host to which you created a reference, and pass it also.

```
Move-SCVirtualMachine -VM $VM -VMHost $VMHost
```

USING THE PORTAL TO RESTORE A VM

To restore a VM using the Self-Service web portal, follow these steps:

1. In the main window, in the Library view, select the VM.

2. In the Actions area, click Restore.

   The status of the VM changes to Under Migration. When the job is complete, the VM no longer appears in the Library view. It appears in the Computers view.

Deleting a VM

The final stage in the life cycle of a VM is its removal from the cloud. Deletion is permanent, so be absolutely sure before you remove it. If there is any chance someone may need it again, consider storing it.

Before you delete a VM, place it into the powered-off state.

USING THE CONSOLE TO DELETE A VM

To delete a VM using the VMM console, do the following:

1. In the console, open the VMs And Services workspace and select the VM.

2. On the Virtual Machine tab of the ribbon, in the Delete group, click Delete.

   VMM will ask you to confirm the request. After you confirm it, the deletion will begin.

USING POWERSHELL TO DELETE A VM

Use the following command to remove the VM called DEV_SVR01.

```
Remove-SCVirtualMachine -Name "DEV_SVR01"
```

Note that PowerShell will prompt you to confirm the Request. After you confirm it, the deletion will begin. To suppress the prompt you can add the -Force parameter to the command.

USING THE PORTAL TO DELETE A VM

To delete a VM using the Self-Service web portal, follow these steps:

1. In the main window, in the Computers view, select the VM.

2. In the Actions area, click Remove.

   VMM will ask you to confirm the request. After you confirm it, the deletion will begin.

Summary

In this chapter, you finally reached the objective of deploying and managing VMs on private clouds.

VMM offers three interfaces for Self-Service users to interact with a cloud. Each interface offers a different degree of functionality to address the many scenarios that private clouds seek to address. These interfaces can be mixed and matched to harness the power of VMM and your ability to work in the private cloud.

VMs are the foundation for the service model that VMM offers for hosting software as a service within clouds. They function as a natural stepping stone to the public cloud as software engineers are introduced to software packaging for use within the cloud, and to the importance of developing stateless applications. The next chapter shifts focus to applications and the System Center App Controller.

Chapter 11

App Controller and the Public Cloud

Prior chapters showed you how to form a private cloud and manage VMs in it. This chapter focuses on hosting applications and introduces System Center Application Controller (App Controller), which is a feature-rich, self-service web portal created in Microsoft Silverlight and designed to replace the light-weight, self-service portal described in the previous chapter.

App Controller enables you to manage VMs and applications on your VMM private clouds, and it extends this reach to the Microsoft public cloud, Azure. App Controller is a fantastic new addition to the System Center suite of tools, and it needs a book of its own. This chapter focuses on a few of its key aspects and explains how to do the following:

◆ Obtain a free trial subscription to Azure

◆ Install App Controller

◆ Configure App Controller to connect with your existing VMM installation and your Azure subscriptions

◆ Use App Controller to perform common tasks

Introducing Windows Azure

Windows Azure is an application platform that Microsoft provides as a public cloud. As such, it is an example of the Platform as a Service (PaaS) model. It enables you to focus on business logic, not operational services, so you can quickly deploy production-ready solutions. Azure is a simple, comprehensive, and powerful platform for the creation of web applications and services. You can use it to deliver Software as a Service (SaaS) solutions.

The compute services hosted by Azure are generally categorized into two roles: Web and Worker.

Web roles provide an Internet Information Services (IIS) web server to host front-end web applications, enabling a quick and easy method to deploy sites on demand.

The Worker role, also called the Backend role, hosts longer-running tasks that are generally independent of user activities. Splitting applications to take advantage of these two roles permits better distribution of your application logic and greater control of how your business applications can scale.

Data is not persistent in either of these roles. The Azure fabric is designed to enable removing and replacing any running instance, transparently without notification or user knowledge. Applications deployed to Azure must be stateless, storing data to one of the provided Azure data-retention solutions, not simply hosting the data in a per-instance temporary folder, for example.

This stateless design means that Azure must provide a way for a role to continue processing data transparently when the active instance is swapped without warning. Azure enables application developers to persist their data in queues, tables, BLOBs (Binary Large Objects), and the SQL Azure role.

Microsoft has recently also included the Virtual Machine (VM) role, enabling the deployment of a custom Windows Server 2008 R2 (Enterprise or Standard) image (also referred to as a legacy application). The VM role runs a virtual hard drive (VHD) image of a Windows Server 2008 R2 VM. This VHD is created using an on-premises Windows Server machine and is then uploaded to Windows Azure. This new functionality extends the Azure service to offer "Infrastructure as a Service" functionality.

Windows Azure, like all public cloud services, shields users from the operational tasks of hosting a cloud, including the following:

◆ Fabric management

◆ Geolocation of hosting servers

◆ Real-time backup and failover for databases

◆ Deploying from staging to production environments

◆ Shared memory caches

As a consumer of Azure services, you are responsible for the following aspects:

◆ Application design

◆ Data persistence

The cost of using the Windows Azure public cloud is driven by a number of parameters, as described in Table 11.1.

TABLE 11.1:   Public-Cloud Billing Parameters

SUBSCRIPTION	DESCRIPTION
Compute Hours	A compute hour is basically the duration for which a service instance runs. If you were to keep an instance running for a single day, your compute cost would be calculated as *number of instances × hours in a day × cents per computer hour.*
Data Transfers	Data transfers (measured in GB) are charged based on the total amount of data going out of the Windows Azure platform data centers via the Internet in a given billing period.
Service Bus Connections	The service bus provides secure messaging and connectivity capabilities that allow you to build distributed and loosely coupled applications in the cloud, as well as build hybrid applications on-premises and in the cloud. Costs for connections are calculated by rate per 10,000 messages.

TABLE 11.1: Public-Cloud Billing Parameters *(CONTINUED)*

SUBSCRIPTION	DESCRIPTION
Access-Control Transactions	Access control provide identity and authentication to web applications and services, while integrating with standards-based identity providers, including enterprise directories such as Active Directory and web identities such as Windows Live ID, Google, Yahoo!, and Facebook. Some subscriptions include this service in their cost; others charge per 100,000 transactions.
Database Storage	SQL Azure is a highly available and scalable cloud database service built on SQL Server technologies. Costs are calculated based on the size of the database.

Microsoft offers a number of subscription models to suit different customer profiles and requirements. All of the offers, including free trails, require a credit card at the time of sign up. Microsoft charges your card if you use more than the plan's allocation. While evaluating Azure, you can monitor your account subscription summary to make sure you do not exceed your package limits and receive an unexpected bill.

Currently, Microsoft offers a free 90-day trial, in addition to three subscription offers available for the Windows Azure platform. Table 11.2 describes these offers.

TABLE 11.2: Windows Azure Subscriptions

SUBSCRIPTION	DESCRIPTION
Pay-As-You-Go	No commitment or up-front costs. Just pay for resources as they are used.
Subscriptions	Similar to the Pay-As-You-Go plan, with significant savings when agreeing to a six-month commitment.
Members	Special offers that are extended to Microsoft Software Developer Network, Microsoft Partner Network, and BizSpark members.

The monthly allowances vary for the different subscriptions. For example, the current free trial includes the following:

◆ 750 hours of a small-compute instance

◆ 20 GB of storage with one million storage transactions

◆ 20 GB of outbound data transfer

◆ Unlimited inbound data transfer

◆ 1 GB Web Edition SQL Azure relational database

◆ 100,000 access-control transactions

◆ Two service-bus connections

In order to select the most appropriate plan and budget for public cloud services, you must carefully consider infrastructure costs, which previously were taken for granted as a by-product of hosting an on-premise fabric. In many cases, the application must be re-architected before being hosted on the public cloud to make sure the solution is optimized in its new ecosystem.

NOTE   Each compute instance is a virtual server. There are currently 5 compute virtual server sizes offered on the Azure platform. These are defined as follows: Extra Small (Shared CPU Cores, 768MB RAM), Small (1 Core, 1.75GB RAM), Medium (2 Cores, 3.5 GB RAM), Large (4 Cores, 7 GB RAM), and Extra Large (8 Cores, 14 GB RAM)

Organizations using the Microsoft Enterprise Agreement license program can be licensed to use Windows Azure for periods of one, two, or three years. Some benefits of the licensing program include the options to consolidate existing subscriptions to simplify management and to use invoices rather than credit cards for billing. While standard subscriptions are limited to hosting six services each, Enterprise Agreement subscriptions are permitted additional services.

Subscribing to Windows Azure is relatively easy; all you need is a Windows Live account and a credit card so you can be charged for any service consumption beyond the trial or offer. Enterprise Agreement customers should work with their Microsoft Technical Account Managers. To subscribe to Windows Azure, follow these steps:

1. Start by pointing your browser to `www.windowsazure.com`.

2. Select among the try or buy options on the site. Then sign in with your Windows Live ID. A wizard guides you through the signup process.

3. After your payment method is verified, your subscription will be provisioned and you will have access to the Azure service. The Home screen appears (Figure 11.1).

FIGURE 11.1
Azure Home screen

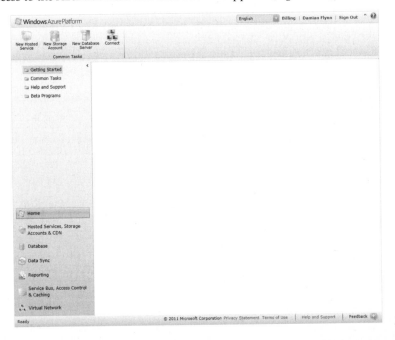

Introducing App Controller

Application Controller, the newest member of the System Center suite of tools, offers a unified web console to simplify the management of applications across private and public clouds.

Application Controller (App Controller) is designed as a self-service user experience and currently offers no functionality to design or administer components such as templates or services. They remain in the realm of VMM authors and administrators (see Chapter 8, "Understanding Service Modeling").

From this web console, you can easily publish new and updated templates to both private (VMM) and public (Azure) clouds using a simple graphical configuration experience, while also simplifying access and management of libraries and transferring resources to Azure storage.

Of course, App Controller provides the ability to manage the individual VMs, or VMs that are deployed within the services to which the user has access. All of the usual management capabilities are there: stopping, starting, mounting an ISO, opening a remote desktop connection, and so on.

Combining this functionality with the flexibility of managing more than one VMM server, App Controller allows you to seamlessly move resources between VMM servers (private clouds). Furthermore, role-based access to Windows Azure subscriptions (public clouds) and the ability to manage multiple subscriptions simultaneously solves many Azure-usage concerns. You can provide access through the App Controller interface based on Active Directory users/groups, without granting co-admin permissions directly to the Azure portal.

App Controller Performance and Scale

App Controller scale is not specifically affected by the number of hosts being managed in the fabric, because cloud information is the main exposure. The number of items that show up in a view (e.g., virtual machines or services) does impact App Controller's responsiveness. Assuming that most self-service users can see up to a few hundred items, response time will be reasonable to around 2,000 items in a view. Depending on the number of concurrent users and the number of items in the view, response times will slow down as the numbers increase. Server specifications will also contribute to the overall experience and scalability. Once App Controller begins to slow, you should consider adding additional instances following the App Controller "Highly Available Installation" section in this chapter.

Microsoft has published the current supported limits per App Controller instance at the following location:

`http://technet.microsoft.com/en-us/library/gg696060.aspx`

The maximum values are as follows:

◆ Objects in a Windows Azure storage directory: 900

◆ VMM management servers: 5

◆ Windows Azure subscriptions per user: 20

◆ Concurrent users: 75

◆ Jobs run in a 24-hour period: 10,000

Deploying App Controller

Before you begin to explore the functions of this new tool, you need to deploy it to your fabric. You can install it to either a physical node or a virtual node, depending on sizing requirements for the environment.

The deployment is a multiple-stage process (see the "Connecting App Controller" section later in this chapter):

1. Install App Controller.

2. Connect App Controller to your VMM service.

3. Connect App Controller to your Windows Azure subscriptions.

System Requirements

The system requirements for deploying System Center App Controller 2012 are similar to the guidelines in Chapter 4, "Setting Up and Deploying VMM 2012." The best scalable approach is to use a dedicated (virtual) machine and monitor the server's resources with System Center tools, such as Operations Manager, to determine whether additional resources are required.

The general requirements for the App Controller server include the following:

◆ The server needs to be a member of an Active Directory domain.

◆ The name of the server can have a maximum length of 15 characters.

◆ The minimum startup memory should be 1 GB if the App Controller Server is placed on a Hyper-V R2 SP1 host with dynamic memory enabled. Even then, it will warn you that at least 2 GB is recommended

The software requirements are outlined in Table 11.3.

TABLE 11.3: System Center App Controller Software Requirements

SOFTWARE REQUIREMENT	NOTES
A Supported Operating System	A full installation of Windows Server 2008 R2 (Standard, Enterprise, or Datacenter) with SP1 or higher
.NET Framework	.NET Framework 4 *(App Controller will install if required.)*
Web Services (IIS)	IIS Features: Common HTTP Features Static Content Default Document Directory Browsing HTTP Errors

TABLE 11.3:   System Center App Controller Software Requirements   *(CONTINUED)*

SOFTWARE REQUIREMENT	NOTES
	Application Development
	ASP.NET
	.NET Extensibility
	ISAPI Extensions
	ISAPI Filters
	Health and Diagnostics
	HTTP Logging
	Request Monitor
	Tracing
	Security
	Basic Authentication
	Windows Authentication
	Request Filtering
	Performance
	Static Content Compression
	Management Tools
	IIS Management Console
	(App Controller will install if required.)
VMM 2012	VMM 2012 Console Only
SQL Database	SQL Server 2008 or 2008 R2
	(For performance reasons, MS recommends that SQL not be hosted on the same server as App Controller.)

In addition, App Controller requires a service account to be provided during installation. This account must also be a member of the local Administrators group on the server on which the installation is being performed.

Client Requirements

In order for the App Controller web console to be used, certain client requirements must also be met. The client must have the following:

◆ Windows Vista, Windows 7, Server 2008, Server 2008 R2, or newer

◆ A 32-bit browser that supports Silverlight 4

◆ Internet Explorer 8, 9, or newer

Installing and Connecting to App Controller

Before you install App Controller on your selected server, you must be logged in as a domain user with membership in the local Administrators group. The account you use must also have at least DBO permission on the database that will be used.

As with the installation of the other tools in the Microsoft System Center Suite, you will be guided through the process by a wizard. During installation, the wizard asks you to provide an optional domain-user account to use as the service account for App Controller. You must also provide the IP address and TCP port to be used for hosting the site.

NOTE   Carefully choose the port you want to use for the web portal. The only way to change it is by uninstalling and then reinstalling the App Controller software.

Because the App Controller web interface should be secured using an SSL certificate, you will be offered the option to generate a self-signed certificate. (This is not really recommended because the certificate must then be distributed to every computer accessing the application.) Preferably, you can install an SSL certificate from your internal PKI solution or deploy a publicly signed certificate to the server prior to running the installation. The wizard presents these in a drop-down for you to select from while configuring the website.

NOTE   If self-signed certificates are used, the certificates must be added to the Trusted Root Certification Authorities store of each computer that will access the App Controller website.

To install App Controller, follow these steps:

1. Run setup.exe, and then click Run As Administrator. On the main Setup page, click Install. If it does not detect .NET Framework 4.0, the wizard offers to install it. The Product Registration Information screen appears.

2. Provide registration information and click Next. The License agreement appears.

3. Agree to the license and click Next.

   The wizard checks for the prerequisites. If any of them aren't met, the Installation Cannot Continue page appears with information about any issues and how to resolve them. After all the issues are resolved, the Select Installation Location screen appears.

4. Select an installation location and click Next. The Configure Services screen appears (Figure 11.2).

5. Specify an account for App Controller services and a port for internal App Controller communication, and then click Next.

   You can use a network service account or a domain account. Best practice is to use a domain account dedicated exclusively to App Controller. Use the default port if it is not in use. App Controller uses it only locally, so that port does not need to be open on the firewall.

   The Configure Website screen appears.

6. Specify the binding settings for the secure App Controller website, and click Next. Assign an IP address, port, and SSL certificate. The Configure Database screen appears.

7. Provide information about the database that App Controller will use and click Next.

   Provide the server name, instance name, database name, and port. If you have sufficient permissions, the wizard creates the database.

The Help Improve App Controller screen appears, followed by the Confirm Settings screen.

8. Review your choices and click Install.

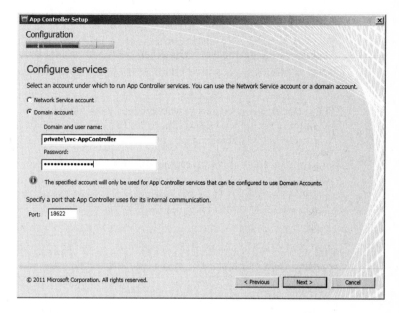

FIGURE 11.2
Configuring the
App Controller
services

The Installing Components screen appears and displays the progress until the installation is complete. Then the Setup Completed Successfully screen appears (Figure 11.3). The URL of the App Controller website appears at the bottom of the screen. You need this URL to access your App Controller installation.

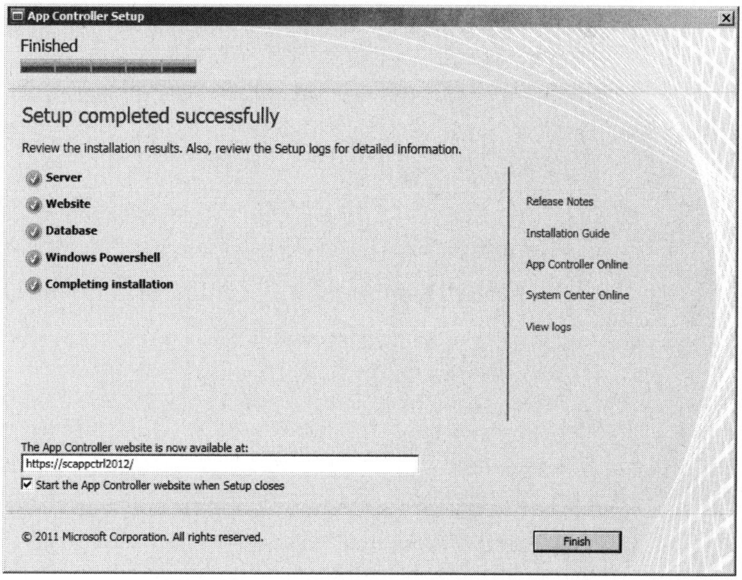

FIGURE 11.3
Finishing the
App Controller
installation

If the installation does not finish successfully, the wizard displays a list of items that were not installed and links to the related log files. The logs provide details about where or why the issues occurred.

In order to connect to App Controller, you'll need a browser and an OS that work properly with Silverlight 4.0 or newer.

To connect to App Controller, follow these steps:

1. Point the browser at the URL of the App Controller website.

   This is the URL displayed at the end of the preceding installation procedure. As the website loads, it checks your computer for a compatible version of Silverlight; if it does not find one, it provides a link to the Silverlight installer. You cannot use App Controller until you install Silverlight.

   If all is well, the Sign-In screen appears.

2. Enter your credentials and click Sign In.

   The username must be in the format *Domain\User*.

   App Controller supports more than one VMM and Azure subscription. If you are a member of more than one role, an additional screen appears showing subscriptions for any of those roles.

3. Select the desired role for each subscription. By refreshing the browser window, you can select a different role.

Enabling Single Sign-In

By default, App Controller prompts for your sign-in credentials every time you visit its web page. You can bypass this challenge by configuring Windows integrated authentication on the App Controller website. Then Windows presents your current credentials to App Controller whenever you visit its site.

To enable single sign-in, perform the following steps:

1. On the App Controller server, open the IIS Manager console.

2. In the IIS Connection tree, navigate to the AppController website and select the */api* node. The */api* Home screen appears (Figure 11.4).

3. In the IIS group, Features view, click Authentication. The IIS Authentication page appears, displaying a list of available authentication mechanisms.

4. Enable Windows Authentication and disable Basic Authentication.

   App Controller no longer presents the Sign-In screen when you connect to it with a browser. Instead, it goes directly to the Overview screen.

FIGURE 11.4
Select
Authentication in
the IIS group.

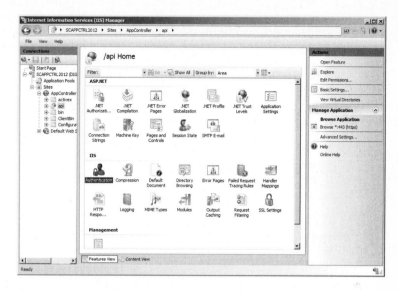

Installing the App Controller PowerShell Module

The App Controller PowerShell module is automatically installed when you install App Controller. To install the App Controller PowerShell module on a different computer, you must be a member of that computer's local Administrators group, and the computer must have PowerShell 2.0 or newer installed.

To install the App Controller PowerShell module, complete the following steps:

1. Run `setup.exe`, and then click Run As Administrator. On the main Setup page, click Install Windows PowerShell Module for App Controller. If it does not detect .NET Framework 4.0, the wizard offers to install it. The License agreement appears.

2. Agree to the license and click Next. The Installation screen appears.

3. Click Install.

   The installation proceeds; when it is finished, the module is ready to use.

NOTE   The App Controller PowerShell module currently offers primarily read commands. The most useful of them is used to retrieve the ACS key that is needed when you create a highly available installation.

Highly Available Installation

System Center App Controller supports the following options for highly available (HA) deployments:

◆ Employing clustered SQL Server databases

◆ Load-balancing multiple App Controller servers

◆ Using highly available VMs

If you install multiple App Controller nodes behind a load balancer, configure them to connect with the same SQL database, which can be clustered also.

After you install the first App Controller in a high-availability farm, you can retrieve its encryption key with the following App Controller PowerShell command:

```
Export-ACAesKey -FilePath C:\AppController.key
```

PowerShell asks for a password of at least eight characters, as follows:

```
Cmdlet Export-ACAesKey at command pipeline position 1
Supply values for the following parameters:
Password: *********
```

After you've supplied the password, you'll be ready to install additional App Controller servers. The installations will run as explained in the "Installing and Connecting to App Controller" section earlier in the chapter. After you've completed step 7 of that process, you'll be asked to supply the key file and the decryption password (Figure 11.5) created on the first App Controller server. By supplying this information, you are allowing the system to trust each additional server added to the farm.

FIGURE 11.5
Configuring encryption for an HA installation

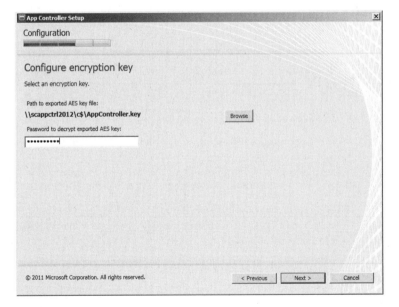

App Controller User Roles

App Controller supports just two distinct user roles:

◆ Administrator, for managing and configuring the App Controller environment, including subscriptions

◆ Self-Service, to permit App Controller to manage access by its users to public cloud services through Microsoft Azure subscriptions

All user access to private clouds managed by VMM is controlled within the user-role services of VMM, and exposed automatically in App Controller.

Managing the user roles in App Controller is also much simpler than the hierarchical wizard-driven experience in VMM. This section describes the process of managing the App Controller user roles.

App Controller Administrators

When you install App Controller, users and groups in the local Administrators group are automatically added to the App Controller Administrator role.

The following list defines some of the properties of the Administrator profile:

◆ Unrestricted access is available to all App Controller resources.

◆ No additional customizations are available or required.

◆ Administrators of Connected VMM Servers are not automatically added to the App Controller Administrator role.

◆ App Controller administrators can create one or more self-service user roles.

Only administrators can add or remove users of the Administrator role. To do so, follow these steps:

1. In the App Controller interface, expand the Settings node, click User Roles, and select Administrator from the list (Figure 11.6).

FIGURE 11.6
The App Controller
User Roles view

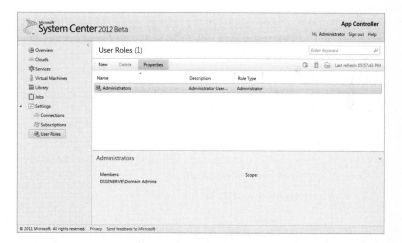

2. Click Properties. The Properties Of Administrators screen appears.

3. Click Members. Use the Add and Remove buttons to change the memberships. Click OK.

App Controller Self-Service Users

App Controller uses its self-service user roles only for managing access to Windows Azure subscriptions. Users can be scoped to specific Azure clouds, and they can be restricted with read-only access. Use VMM to manage self-service roles for private clouds.

The properties of the Self-Service role include the following:

◆ Used only to manage access to Azure subscriptions

◆ Scoped to a single Azure subscription

◆ Can be flagged as read-only — in which case, members will be unable to make any changes to the Windows Azure subscription

Creating a Self-Service user role in App Controller is simpler than doing so in VMM. To create a Self-Service role for access to an Azure subscription, perform the following steps:

1. In the App Controller interface, expand the Settings node and click User Roles.

2. Click New. The New User Role screen appears (Figure 11.7).

FIGURE 11.7
Adding a new self-service user

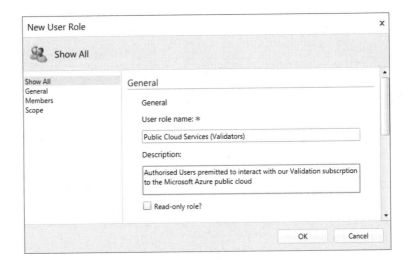

3. Provide a unique name and a description for the role. Check Read-Only if desired, and click Add. The Select Users Or Groups screen appears.

4. Pick a user or group and click Add. The system validates the selection and then presents a list of Azure subscriptions.

5. Select the subscription and click OK.

Connecting App Controller

Before anyone can use App Controller, an administrator must configure it to communicate with VMM for private clouds, or Windows Azure for public cloud services. Connecting App Controller to VMM is straightforward. Connecting (or subscribing) App Controller to an Azure subscription requires a little more work.

One of the coolest features of App Controller is its support for multiple connections and subscriptions. If for business reasons you implement different VMM deployments, you can connect App Controller to each deployment. Similarly, if you have multiple subscriptions to the Microsoft Azure service, you can add them to App Controller.

Connecting to the Private Cloud

To connect App Controller to VMM, the administrator must have the privileges of the following roles:

- App Controller Administrator
- Local Administrator on the App Controller server
- VMM Administrator
- Local Administrator on the VMM server

App Controller has the ability to copy files and templates to and from the VMM libraries if the SSL certificates are imported correctly while configuring the connection

To connect App Controller to VMM, complete these steps:

1. In the App Controller interface, expand the Settings node; click Connections. On the menu bar, click Connect. The Add A New VMM Connection screen appears (Figure 11.8).

FIGURE 11.8
Adding a new VMM connection

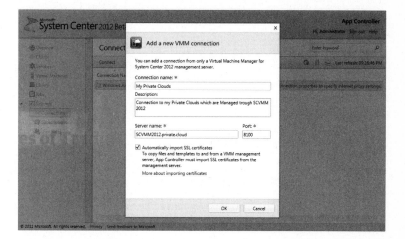

2. Enter a connection name, a description, the fully qualified domain name, and the TCP port of the VMM server. Check the Automatically Import SSL Certificates check box if you plan to copy files and templates to and from VMM cloud libraries (this option is recommended). Click OK.

   The connection name is the name that users see, so make it friendly. The server name is the FQDN of the VMM server with which you are connecting, along with its TCP port, which defaults to 8100.

   App Controller establishes the connection and begins a session with VMM. If your account is a member of more than one VMM role, VMM may ask you to choose a user role for this new connection session.

Connecting to the Public Cloud

The Azure management API, which is HTTPS based, is used to connect App Controller to Microsoft Azure. The certificates used to establish the trust for this SSL channel must be prepared and installed on both ends of the connection.

The service certificate (`.pfx` file) contains a private key, which App Controller stores in its database. Because the certificate contains the private key, you must provide the password so that App Controller can import and use the private key.

The management certificate (`.cer` file) contains only the public key, which is imported in Windows Azure for accessing the API. Windows Azure allows customers to create their own management certificates, either self-signed or from a certificate authority (CA).

Sharing these matching public and private keys permits the secure channel to be established, allowing App Controller and Azure to communicate.

CREATING A SELF-SIGNED CERTIFICATE

Before you create the connection between App Controller and Azure, you must first prepare, for this example, a self-signed certificate to secure the communications channel.

Open the Internet Information Services (IIS) Manager on the App Controller Server.

1. In the IIS manager on the App Controller server, with the IIS server highlighted, on the Features view, locate and double-click Server Certificates.

2. In the Server Certificates view, on the Actions menu, select Create Self-Signed Certificate. The Create Self-Signed Certificate screen appears.

3. Provide a friendly name for the certificate (for example, **App Controller to Azure Connection**) and click OK.

   IIS creates the certificate.

EXPORTING CERTIFICATES

You need to export the new certificate twice:

◆ As the PFX (service certificate), which contains the private key for use in App Controller

◆ As the CER file (management certificate) containing only the public key for importing into Azure

Open the Internet Information Services (IIS) Manager on your App Controller server.

1. In the IIS manager on the App Controller server, with the IIS server highlighted, on the Features view, locate and double-click Server Certificates.

2. In the Server Certificates view, double-click the friendly name of the certificate for this connection.

   IIS displays the certificate.

3. Export the certificate the first time:

   A. On the Details tab, click Copy To File. The Certificate Export Wizard opens.

   B. Click Next. The Export Private Key screen appears.

   C. Select Yes and click Next.

You need to export the key in order to create the services certificate to use with App Controller.

The Export File Format screen appears.

D. Check the Include All Certificates check box and click Next.

This step is relevant for CA certificates, but not for self-signed certificates, as in this example.

The Password screen appears.

E. Provide and confirm a password and click Next.

The password protects the new PFX file. You'll need the password whenever you import the certificate.

The File To Export screen appears.

F. Provide a path and name for the services certificate and click Next. The Completing The Certificate Export Wizard screen appears (Figure 11.9).

FIGURE 11.9
IIS – Exporting a certificate

G. Review your settings and click Finish. The certificate screen reappears.

4. Export the certificate a second time:

A. On the Details tab, click Copy To File. The Certificate Export Wizard opens.

B. Click Next. The Export Private Key screen appears.

C. Select No and click Next.

You need to do this in order to create the management certificate to use with Azure.

The Export File Format screen appears.

D. Select the default option, DER Encoded Binary X.509 (CER) and click Next. The File To Export screen appears.

E. Provide a path and name for the management certificate and click Next. The Completing The Certificate Export Wizard screen appears (refer back to Figure 11.9).

F. Review your settings and click Finish.

The Certificate screen reappears.

CONNECTING APP CONTROLLER TO THE AZURE SUBSCRIPTION

Using the certificates prepared in the previous section, you can establish a connection to the public cloud. The process takes two broad steps:

◆ Import the management certificate to the Azure subscription.

◆ Connect App Controller to the Azure subscription and import the services certificate.

To import the management certificate to the Azure subscription, follow these steps:

1. In the Azure management portal, in the lower portion of the Navigation pane, click Hosted Services, Storage Accounts & CDN. At the top of the Navigation page, click Management Certificates. The display changes to the Certificates group.

2. On the ribbon, click Add Certificate. The Add New Management Certificate screen appears (Figure 11.10).

FIGURE 11.10
Add New
Management
Certificate

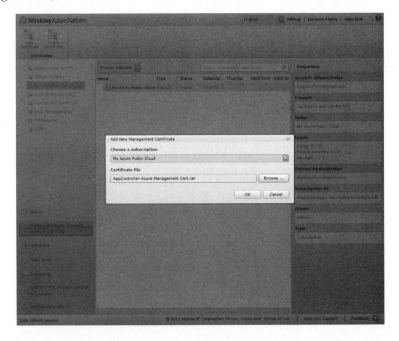

3. Browse to the management certificate (CER file) you exported for this connection in the previous section, and click OK.

   Azure imports the certificate. The display returns to the Certificates group view.

4. Click the subscription name, and then copy the subscription ID (Figure 11.11 illustrates the Subscription ID in the properties list on the right of the window) .

FIGURE 11.11
You can find the subscription ID in the Azure management portal.

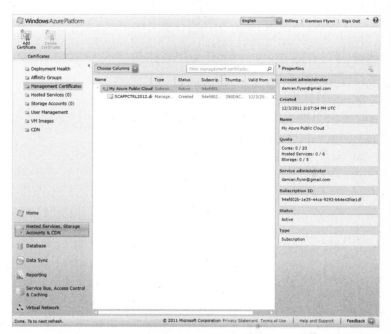

This completes the first of the two steps described at the beginning of this section. To connect App Controller to the Azure subscription and import the services certificate, you'll need to complete the second procedure, as follows:

1. In the App Controller interface, expand the Settings node, and click Subscriptions. On the menu bar, click Add. The Connect A Windows Azure Subscription screen appears, as shown in Figure 11.12.

2. Enter a name and description for the subscription. Enter the subscription ID you saved at the end of the last procedure.

   The name will be displayed in the Name column of the Clouds screen. The subscription ID is a globally unique identifier (GUID). If you misplace it, you can go back into the Azure management portal to retrieve it from the properties of the subscription.

3. Browse to the management certificate (PFX file) you exported for this connection, and enter the password. Click OK.

   In a few moments, App Controller completes the connection to the Azure subscription, and the new connection appears in the Subscriptions section of the App Controller Settings node. Congratulations!

FIGURE 11.12
Connecting to an
Azure subscription

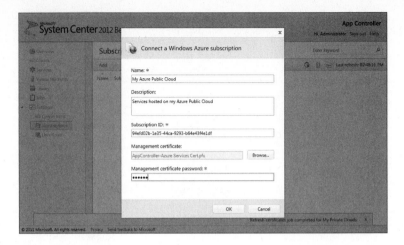

Exploring App Controller

As a light and fast web experience, App Controller offers a lot of really cool functionality to self-service users — certainly, far too much for us to do justice to in this chapter. With that in mind, let's look at the user experience and some key end-user operations.

So that you can become acquainted with the primary areas of the new portal, let's start with the Overview Home screen in App Controller (Figure 11.13).

FIGURE 11.13
The App Controller
overview

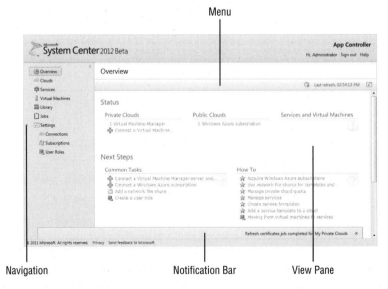

Table 11.4 describes the key areas of the screen. If you have already used VMM 2012, this is immediately familiar. Administrators will see additional options in the main pane.

All the Views and Panes are filtered so they present to the user only the actions, clouds, VMs, and services available for interaction from either the private or public cloud services, based on the active role.

TABLE 11.4:   App Controller User Interface

SCREEN ELEMENT	DESCRIPTION
Views/Navigation	Located on the left of the window, the View list is the access point to the different areas of control within App Controller. These include the primary views of clouds, services, VMs, libraries, and jobs, along with the secondary settings views of connections, subscriptions, and user roles.
Menu bar	The menu bar is located along the top of the view pane, and it offers context-aware options, along with a refresh button for the main pane, and a time stamp of the last completed refresh. A Settings icon lets you enable additional logging details if desired.
View pane	All of the relevant information for the active view is presented within the main pane, including status overviews, clouds, services, and VMs.

App Controller continues the VMM philosophy of keeping track of every job executed on the service, ensuring that an audit track of all activities is maintained, while offering a simple interface where users can check the status of their recent jobs and determine the reasons for any failures.

To view the status of a job in App Controller, use the Jobs view. The list of jobs presented is filtered based on the scope and role of the user viewing the history. Administrators can view jobs from all users.

To view the job status, in the App Controller interface, expand the Jobs node.

The main pane splits to show a list of jobs in the top half and details of the selected job in the bottom half (Figure 11.14).

FIGURE 11.14
The App Controller
Jobs view

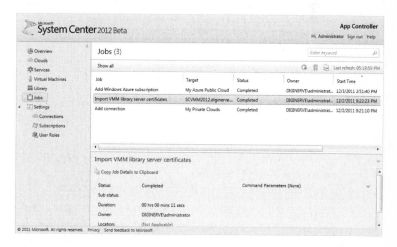

The List view includes the following columns for each job:

- ◆ **Job:** Friendly name for the job

- ◆ **Target:** Resources created or modified

- ◆ **Status:** Current completion status (In Progress, Failed, or Completed)

- ◆ **Owner:** User who initiated the job

- ◆ **Start Time**

- ◆ **End Time**

The Detail view provides more information about the selected job:

- ◆ **Cloud System Job ID:** Relates to the job on the underlying cloud environment, either VMM or Azure. This ID is very important for administrators who are tracing failed jobs to understand the reasons for failure.

- ◆ **Command Parameters:** The parameters provided to start the job

- ◆ **Errors:** Detailed error information if the job fails

When a new job is created, App Controller displays a job notification in the status bar. Clicking the notification brings up the Jobs view to allow the status of the job to be monitored as it progresses.

NOTE   To trace the Cloud System Job ID created in App Controller to the associated job in VMM., Select VMM Jobs View and ensure the ID column is enabled in the Recent Jobs list. Enter the Job ID in the filter box to locate the job quickly. Remember, VMM presents only the jobs that are available to the scope of the connected user role.

The App Controller Library

In VMM, libraries play a significant and important role in private-cloud functionality. App Controller extends this concept to a higher level of abstraction, which allows you to present a library share to end users who will deliver the content to either the private cloud (VMM) or the public cloud (Azure).

The library you define in App Controller allows end users to move, store, and share objects with VMM or Azure clouds.

NOTE   For App Controller to access and manage the content of shares added to its scope, the Computer account (not the Service account) of each App Controller server should be granted a minimum of read access to the share.

The App Controller interface contains a Library node (Figure 11.15), which presents a view similar to Windows Explorer.

App Controller supports the following library types:

Shares   Network file shares added by administrators. Depending on native file-server access control, users can store files and resources suitable for public and private clouds. These resources can then be copied to the Windows Azure or My Private Clouds shares.

Windows Azure Any subscription registered to Azure appears under this library. Initially each subscription may contain a single storage account called Image Repository, which is offered by Azure for the VM role. Additional containers can be added to each subscription to host additional resources.

My Private Clouds Cloud libraries offered from VMM for your private clouds appear under this library type, providing a unified experience for users to copy resources between private clouds, or from shares to both public and private clouds.

FIGURE 11.15

The App Controller interface's Library view

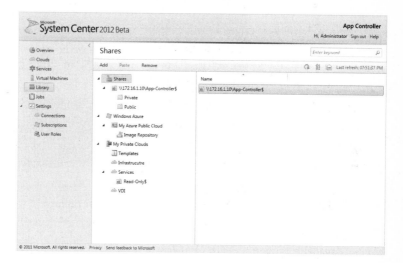

Adding File Shares to the App Controller Library

Any user with App Controller administrative privileges can add file shares to the library. The file server controls access to the shares, and prospective end users should have at least read access.

1. In the App Controller interface, click Library in the left pane. Click Shares in the left side of the Information pane (refer back to Figure 11.15).

2. On the menu, click Add. The Add A Network Shared Folder screen appears.

3. Enter the UNC of the share, and click OK.

   App Controller starts the job to add the share.

Adding an Azure Storage Account

After adding a subscription for Windows Azure, you should have an Azure storage account called Image Repository, which is used to store VHDs for use by the VM role in Azure. You can add a storage account so that you can upload resources to it for services publishing to the public cloud.

To add an additional storage account to the Azure subscription, follow these steps:

1. In the App Controller interface, click Library in the left pane. On the left side of the Information pane, expand the Windows Azure node and select the Azure subscription.

2. On the menu, click Create Storage Account. The Create A Windows Azure Storage Account screen appears (Figure 11.16).

FIGURE 11.16
You can add more storage to the Azure subscription.

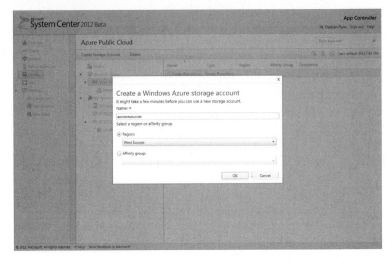

3. Provide a friendly name (between 3 and 24 characters), using only lowercase letters and numbers, with no spaces.

4. Select a geographical region or affinity group for the new storage account, and click OK.

   App Controller starts the job.

Copying Library Resources

After you add file shares to App Controller, you can copy resources from those shares to either your private cloud (VMM) or the public cloud (Azure). App Controller provides Copy and Paste buttons to make it easy to do.

Authorized users can copy VHD files from shares to their subscription's image repository for use by the Azure VM role. Only VHD files can be copied to the image repository.

Take the following steps to copy a resource from a library share to a cloud library:

1. In the App Controller interface, click Library in the left pane (refer back to Figure 11.15).

2. In the left side of the Information pane, navigate to the resource to be copied, select it, and click Copy.

3. Navigate to the desired destination in the cloud repository and click Paste.

   App Controller displays an appropriate screen, depending on the type of resource and the target.

   If the resource being copied is a VHD, and the target is the Windows Azure Image Repository, App Controller presents the Copy A Virtual Hard Disk screen.

   If the disk is a base disk, select a region or affinity group. If the disk is a differencing disk, click Select to select the parent disk. The differencing disk is placed at the same region or affinity group as the parent disk.

4. Click OK.

NOTE   Differencing disk is a virtual hard disk used to isolate changes from its parent virtual hard disk, by storing any changes (also referred to as differences or deltas) which might be applied in the dedicated differencing disk file.

NOTE   App Controller stages file copies by first copying the file to the App Controller server and storing the file in temporary storage. Next, the file is transferred from temporary storage to the destination target. It is important to ensure that the temporary storage location has enough available capacity to host any large files that might be copied. App Controller PowerShell offers the Set-ACTemporaryStorage command to modify the location.

Working with Services

So far, your journey to the private cloud has focused mainly on VMM and using it as an IaaS environment delivering VMs on demand to your consumers. Of course, having VMs on demand is very valuable for many business requirements. However, for the developers and application-hosting teams, it is just a means to an end, a step in their procedures to host applications.

VMM 2012 introduces the concept of services, a framework designed to enable users to deploy applications more efficiently by encapsulating VMs and applications as a service definition, which can then be deployed in a single step.

This approach offers a lot of benefits to the teams working with the applications — especially when you consider the work involved to deploy a moderately complex service, which then must be repeated multiple times for development, staging, quality assurance, and the production environments. The time required to complete this procedure can be quite long and prone to error — and once a deployment is complete, updates to these instances are inevitable.

One of the benefits of implementing a private cloud is to increase automation, and VMM's new Service model allows you to embrace these application deployments as part of the automated deployment process, vastly increasing the speed of deployment while reducing the potential for mistakes, on a standardized instance for each of the main environments.

Chapter 8 describes services and illustrates the key elements in creating a service and deploying it to a VMM private cloud.

With App Controller, these VMM service definitions, called *templates*, can be made accessible to cloud users for deployment — just as VM templates can (see Chapter 10, "Working in the Cloud"). Figure 11.17 shows the analogous process for deploying services.

FIGURE 11.17
The Service Deployment workflow

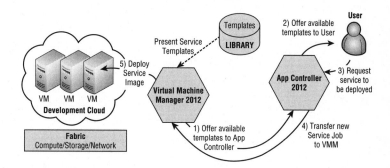

Chapter 10 explains how to deploy VMs using the VMM self-service portal (which Microsoft is deprecating in favor of App Controller). App Controller has a richer interface and built-in support for the new service templates, which Microsoft now recommends for all VM deployments, even single-VM installations that normally use VM templates. When a cloud user logs onto App Controller, a list of resources available for deployment, including any service templates created by the developers or the application team, appears in the Library view.

A self-service user can select the Deploy action and the service template to be deployed. App Controller requests additional information depending on the service template's requirements. After collecting the required data, App Controller coordinates with VMM and passes it the job for processing.

VMM accepts the job from App Controller, and verifies that the request matches the capabilities of the user role, the quota, and so forth. Then VMM deploys the VMs required for hosting the selected service, installs the application on these hosts, and applies any necessary customizations (for example, identifying the correct SQL server with which to connect).

Choosing an application in App Controller, in fact, chooses a service template. VMM examines the service template to determine what's required to create an instance of the application it describes; it then verifies that this request matches the cloud's quota and capabilities. If everything checks out, VMM creates one or more new VMs to run this application, installs the application in those VMs, and starts the app running.

Deploying applications through service templates has other advantages. A service template can specify that one or more of an application's tiers can be scaled out, with one or more VMs running in that tier. The template can specify a load balancer to spread requests across those VMs, and the application owner can control how many VMs run at any time.

Deployment with App Controller

Finally, you're ready to be introduced to App Controller's real value and rich interface for deploying VMs to private clouds and services to both private and public clouds. In this section, you'll work with examples of each of these deployments and be given an overview of the basic information App Controller needs to complete the deployments.

Deploying a VM to a Private Cloud

Chapter 10 explained how to deploy VMs to a private cloud using the VMM console, the self-service portal, and PowerShell. Deploying VMs in App Controller is a similar process.

To deploy a VM to a private cloud, just complete these steps:

1. In the App Controller interface, click Virtual Machines in the left pane. The Information pane shows VMs (Figure 11.18).

   Alternatively, you can start a service deployment by clicking Clouds or Services. If you start from Clouds with a cloud already selected, you can skip to step 4.

2. On the menu bar, click Deploy. The New Deployment screen appears. The New Deployment screen updates, showing the selected cloud.

3. Select a cloud and click OK. The Select A Cloud For This Deployment screen appears.

4. Select a VM template and click OK. The Choose A Template screen appears.

The New Deployment screen updates, showing the VM template with a Configure link (Figure 11.19).

FIGURE 11.18
In the App Controller interface, you can view the virtual machines.

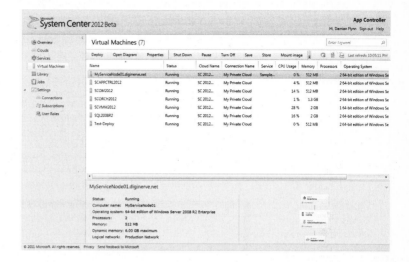

FIGURE 11.19
Configuring a new VM deployment

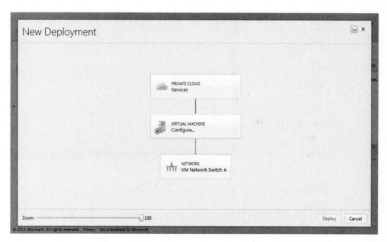

5. Click the Configure link in the VM box. The Properties Of New Virtual Machine screen appears.

6. Provide the VM name, computer name, description, name and password of the Administrator account, and a tag and cost center.

7. Provide the appropriate information about the virtual network adapter: logical network, static MAC address, and user static IP address. Click OK. The New Deployment screen updates again.

8. Click Deploy.

The New Deployment screen closes. After a few moments, App Controller displays a job notification in the status bar to signal that the job is active.

Deploying a Service to a Private Cloud

Deploying a service with App Controller is similar to the procedure in the previous section. To deploy a service to a private cloud, use the following steps:

1. In the App Controller interface, click Services in the left pane. On the menu bar, click Deploy. The New Deployment screen appears.

2. Select a cloud and click OK. The Choose A Template screen appears.

3. Choose a service template and click OK.

   The New Deployment screen updates again (Figure 11.20). Several boxes have Configure links.

FIGURE 11.20
Configuring a new
service deployment

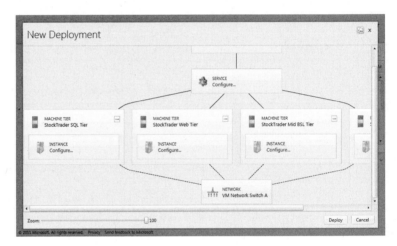

4. In the Service box, click Configure. The Properties screen for the service appears.

5. Enter the service name, description, priority, and cost center. Enter the service-specific settings. Click OK. The New Deployment screen updates again.

6. Click Deploy.

   The New Deployment screen closes. After a few moments, App Controller displays a job notification in the status bar to signal that the job is active.

Deploying a Service to an Azure Cloud

What differentiates App Controller is its ability to manage both private clouds (VMM) and public clouds (Azure) while masking the complex processes involved with deploying services. Deploying a service to an Azure public cloud follows a procedure similar to those in the previous sections.

You will never be asked to decide whether you should select a Web role or a Worker role; this decision is made by the developers when they create the package for deployment. The configuration file that you will select in step 6 contains the directives for Azure to process this decision.

To deploy a service to an Azure public cloud, perform the following procedures:

1. In the App Controller interface, click Services in the left pane. On the menu bar, click Deploy. The New Deployment screen appears, requesting the cloud.

2. Click Configure in the Cloud box, select an Azure public cloud subscription that you have configured, and click OK.

   The New Deployment screen updates, requesting the hosted service (Figure 11.21).

FIGURE 11.21
Deploying a new service in Azure

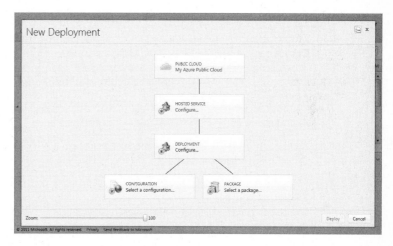

3. Click Configure in the Hosted Service box. Choose a service template and click OK.

   If the Select A Hosted Service dialog box presents no templates, or presents an unsuitable template, follow instructions in the "Create an Azure Hosted Service" section.

   The New Deployment screen updates again and requests the deployment.

4. Click Configure in the Deployment box. The Properties Of New Deployment screen appears.

5. Enter the name of the server instance, the version of the Azure guest OS to use, and whether to deploy to the Staging or the Production environment. Click OK.

   The New Deployment screen updates again, requesting the Configuration file.

6. Click Select A Configuration in the Configuration box. The Select A Windows Azure Service Configuration File screen appears.

7. From the Image Repository, select a configuration file and click OK. The New Deployment screen updates, requesting a package.

8. Click Select A Package in the Package box. The Select A Windows Azure Service Package File screen appears.

9. From the Image Repository, select a service package for the service to deploy and click OK. The New Deployment screen updates again.

10. Click Deploy.

The New Deployment screen closes, and after a few moments App Controller displays a job notification in the status bar to signal that the job is active.

Creating an Azure Hosted Service

The definition of a hosted service is constructed from a service name and a location to host the service on the public cloud. The hosting location you choose may affect the cost of your subscription.

As a Software as a Service public cloud, Azure requires you to define a URL to access the service (as a subdomain of `cloudapp.net`, which you can alias with your own domain name anytime). You can also select the region on the Azure public cloud to host the application. You must define at least one hosted service to deploy an application to Azure.

To create a hosted Azure service, perform the following procedures:

1. In the App Controller interface, click Services in the left pane. On the menu bar, click Deploy. The New Deployment screen appears, requesting the cloud.

2. Click Configure in the Cloud box, and select an Azure public-cloud subscription you have configured and click OK. The New Deployment screen updates, requesting the hosted service (refer back to Figure 11.21).

3. Click Configure in the Hosted Service box. Click on the Create button. The Create A Hosted Service screen appears (Figure 11.22).

FIGURE 11.22
Creating a hosted service

4. Provide a service name, description, public URL, and location. Click OK.

The public URL is the subdomain of `cloudapp.net`. For example, if you specify **MyAzureService**, the public URL of the service becomes `MyAzureService.cloudapp.net`.

The location offers a drop-down list to select the Azure data-center region to which the service will be deployed. Different regions may have different charges and rates.

Removing a Virtual Machine

Of course, some day you may have to remove a VM from a private cloud. The simple process involves just two steps:

1. In the App Controller interface, click Virtual Machines in the left pane. The Information pane shows the VMs.

2. Right-click the VM to be deleted and select Delete from the context menu.

   App Controller requests confirmation and then launches the deletion job.

Upgrading Services with App Controller

App Controller has many more features than could possibly be covered in a single chapter. The rest of this chapter will focus on using the App Controller interface to upgrade services to new versions on both public and private clouds.

Upgrading Services

Deploying an application more quickly is all but certain to please that application's users. Yet an application (and the platform it runs on) is probably updated more often than it's deployed, and so making the update process simpler also has significant value. Reflecting this, the Microsoft private cloud contains several technologies aimed at making it easier to update applications deployed from service templates.

For example, suppose your developers update their business application, which you have already deployed as a service to the VMs hosting your applications. The VMM service model allows you to deploy a new version of the business application with all the new updates included, and then reapply the application, as illustrated in the flowchart in Figure 11.23.

FIGURE 11.23
The Service Update workflow

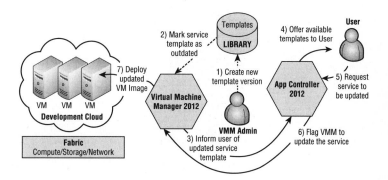

Let's assume that the updated application packages (for example, a Web Deploy) are deposited into the VMM library by the development team and then tagged as a new revision of a current package family. VMM scans each service template to flag ones that use the package just upgraded.

App Controller users can select the Services view. If VMM has flagged any of the services within their scope as out of date, they will be notified. They can update the instances now, later, or not at all. If a user chooses now, App Controller initiates a job to update all affected VMs in the service, bound by the defined upgrade domain setting for the service's tier.

This scenario is slightly simplified. The service template itself also has an owner who must accept the change before the application owners are notified. Still, it illustrates the key concept: an update made to a single package can be automatically deployed to all services that use the image. This automation makes updates faster and less error-prone. This model also permits VM images to be updated separately from applications and lets organizations create and manage fewer base images. Rather than using a distinct VM image for each application, administrators can reuse a smaller set of images across multiple applications. To use VMM effectively to update VM images and applications, the hosted applications should be stateless. When this is not possible, VMM offers Server App-V to package the application and its associated state (refer to Chapter 8 for additional details).

One last point to understand is that this kind of automated update is available only with service templates; it's not possible with VM templates.

Upgrading in a Private Cloud

Private cloud services are upgraded by selecting a new version of the service template. If your service has a status of Pending Servicing, this selection has already been done for you by an administrator or via template authoring outside of App Controller. Cancelling an upgrade for a service with the Pending Servicing status deselects the upgraded template.

To upgrade a service, follow these steps:

1. In the App Controller interface, click Services in the left pane. Right-click the service and select Upgrade from the context menu. The service diagram appears.

2. Select the desired version of the template.

   To change global settings, select the current version of the template. To downgrade, select an older version.

3. To change global settings, click the hyperlink in the Service node, provide the required information, and click Upgrade.

Upgrading in a Public Cloud

Public cloud services can be upgraded in one of two ways:

◆ **Environment swap:** Place the staging environment into the production environment and the existing production environment into the staging environment.

◆ **In-place upgrade:** Replace the existing binaries and settings with new binaries and settings.

SWAPPING ENVIRONMENTS

A swap works only if there is a deployment in the staging environment. If the staging environment is empty, you cannot perform a swap upgrade.

To perform an environment swap, follow these steps:

1. In the App Controller interface, click Services in the left pane. Select the service and choose Upgrade from the menu.

   The service diagram appears. The Deployment node expands to show the staging and production environments.

2. Select the production environment and click Upgrade.

NOTE   Upgrade in place is applicable to service's deployed either to private or public clouds.

UPGRADING IN PLACE

An upgrade in place is performed one upgrade domain at a time. A deployment is made up of one or more roles, which you can view in the diagram. A role's instances are automatically divided into the upgrade domains. So, if your role has six instances and your deployment has two upgrade domains, the upgrade occurs on three of the role's instances at a time. Once all three are upgraded, the next set of role instances is upgraded. By default, the whole process of moving from upgrade domain to upgrade domain is automated. You can optionally specify that you want to manually signal when the upgrade should proceed to the next upgrade domain.

To perform an in-place upgrade, do the following:

1. In the App Controller interface, click Services in the left pane. Select the service and choose Upgrade from the menu. The service diagram appears.

2. Select the package or configuration file for this upgrade. A red asterisk marks the required information.

3. Click the Role node, provide information on the Properties screen, and click OK.

   Information on this page can include the instance count, certificate selection, remote-desktop configuration, and custom settings.

4. Click Upgrade. The confirmation dialog appears.

   Unless you specify otherwise, the upgrade proceeds automatically from upgrade domain to upgrade domain until the upgrade is complete.

   If you select manual upgrade, you must click Resume Upgrade each time the process stops.

Summary

App Controller is a feature-rich self-service web portal created in Microsoft Silverlight and designed to replace and extend the original light-weight VMM self-service portal. App Controller simplifies the process of deploying software as a service both in VMM-managed private clouds and in the Windows Azure public cloud.

Additionally, App Controller is currently the only application that offers a simple friendly interface to Windows Azure. It permits organizations to finally consolidate all their subscriptions centrally and efficiently manage them through user roles. At the same time it simplifies currently complex exercises, including copying resources such as Azure VMs.

This chapter is much too short to offer a complete overview of all the features of App Controller, its ability to work with the Services Model, and its flexibility to work with VMM and Azure. The objective is to set the seed in your mind so that you can begin to appreciate the beauty of this application and begin to dig deeper into its hidden depths.

Over the last three chapters you have been introduced to the process of delivering and consuming clouds, both private and public. Old concepts mixed with new, but you should clearly see that this is truly a Version 1.0 solution that can only get better and better.

Windows 8 Server will become Microsoft's standard hypervisor for the coming years. When compared to previous offerings, it is jam-packed with exciting new technologies such as network virtualization, VM replication, extensible switches, and so on — all of which will influence future private-cloud foundations into far more scalable and feature-rich offerings.

You don't have to be a genius to see that this is only the beginning of a journey that can lead to a very exciting future. The management framework will evolve to embrace all the features exposed in Windows 8 Server and other hypervisors, offering even more sophisticated options for building rich and powerful clouds simply!

Just imagine hybrid solutions, offering the ability to host services on private clouds hosted in-house, with hosting providers, or on the public cloud, all working smoothly together within the VMM/App Controller environment. IT pros will be able to obfuscate the underlying fabrics so they can make smart and easy business decisions to extend the fabric on demand, and instantly!

The next chapter completes the Microsoft private cloud vision by introducing Microsoft's approach to providing infrastructure as a service. This solution is still in its infancy. Read on to see how it's hatching.

## Chapter 12

Cloud Services Process Pack

Self-service is a key feature of private clouds. Self-service users can access IT resources automatically, with no human intervention required. If you, as an administrator, are comfortable creating a cloud for a subset of your organization, defining services and quotas for that cloud, and letting people use the cloud as they like, this approach can work well.

However, if you sometimes want your IT users to go through a more formal approval process to get resources, you'll need to go outside VMM or even App Controller. For such situations, Microsoft provides the System Center Cloud Services Process Pack (CSPP). CSPP enables you to attach Information Technology Infrastructure Library (ITIL)–style workflows to self-service requests generated by VMM or App Controller.

With CSPP, your enterprise can realize the benefits of Infrastructure as a Service (IaaS) while simultaneously leveraging your existing investments in System Center components. This chapter introduces these aspects of the final component of the Microsoft private-cloud solution:

◆ The Infrastructure as a Service vision

◆ The components of Cloud Services Process Pack and how they integrate with System Center components

◆ Setting up and using runbooks

◆ The role of the configuration-management database

Introducing the Vision

The goal of Service Manager is to support IT service management in a broad sense. The goal of the ITIL is to establish standard practices for managing IT services, such as change management and incident management. Service Manager's role includes implementing ITIL processes, such as change management and incident management, and it can also include processes for other things, such as allocating resources from a private cloud. For example, suppose an organization wants to let developers allocate VMs from a private cloud but decides that these requests should sometimes require approval from the developer's manager. Figure 12.1 shows an example of how this can be implemented in the Microsoft private cloud.

Within this scenario, Service Manager maintains a configuration-management database (CMDB). The Private Cloud Request flow is outlined in the following steps, which correspond to the numbers in the figure:

FIGURE 12.1
A Private Cloud
Request flow

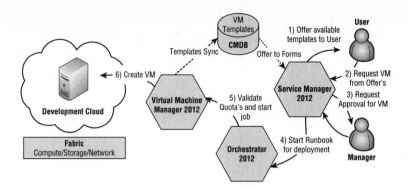

1. Service Manager provides its own self-service portal and, using the information contained in the CMDB, presents each user a catalog of services and resources available to that user.

2. The user in the figure chooses an available resource template to create a VM in the Development cloud.

3. Unlike App Controller, Service Manager does not pass this request to VMM for action. Instead, it initiates a workflow to process the request. This workflow can do pretty much anything from its custom logic. In this example, the workflow executes two processes.

   The first process of the workflow obtains approval from the developer's manager. This enables the development manager to monitor and limit chargebacks for resources used by developers.

4. After the manager approves the request, the second process in the workflow begins. It starts an Orchestrator runbook. The runbook, implemented as part of CSPP, communicates with VMM to create a new VM in the Development Cloud.

5. VMM handles the request in its usual way, checking whether the approved request is within the requester's quota and cloud capabilities.

6. VMM creates the requested VM. The developer can work with it using the VMM and App Controller self-service interfaces.

The *configuration-management database* (CMDB) is the repository for nearly all configuration- and management-related information in the System Center environment. With the CSPP, this information includes VMM resources (such as VM templates, VM service templates, and so on), which are copied regularly from the VMM library into the CMDB.

A *workflow* within Service Manager is designed to implement an ITIL-style process, applying actions dependent on the results of the previous stages of the workflow.

A *runbook* is a workflow defined within Orchestrator. In the private cloud, the runbook is designed to interact directly with the other modules of the System Center suite using a range of prepackaged components in a Visio-style visual layout.

The Components

One of the clear differences between the CSPP and all the solutions you have encountered in this book so far is that the architecture of the solution is not created from a built-in function within System Center, but rather a customizable integration of functions and features offered through the components of the System Center suite.

CSPP is a solution accelerator, designed to help implement a highly customizable private cloud service offering while permitting easy modifications to address specific business requirements. These can span from simple changes within the approval process to extending the runbook to provision library shares, or far more-complex scenarios if necessary.

Differing from the functions offered with App Controller, this approach permits adding functionality to the solution, including the ability to implement human approval processes, and creating new service offerings that can be embellished with highly creative automation extensions.

Let's take a few moments to introduce the additional members of the System Center suite, which enrich the experience of private clouds through their integration.

Cloud Service Process Pack

Organizations considering IaaS must examine and adapt their existing tools, processes, workflows, and automation to meet the requirements of an effective cloud-services implementation. While it is critical that the underlying components (such as self-service portal, ticketing infrastructure, notifications, workflows, and automation) integrate well with each other and follow industry-wide best practices, the work involved to ensure an effective cloud-services implementation can be daunting and time-consuming.

CSPP addresses these concerns by enabling IaaS while incorporating domain expertise and best practices from enterprises that have successfully deployed IaaS. These best practices are made available out of the box and are evident in all aspects of the solution.

Created on the System Center platform, the process pack exposes the flexibility it inherits from this suite of applications, permitting solutions to be customized to address the requirements of the business. For example, Service Manager allows organizations to customize individual questions and inputs of CSPP on the self-service portal, and Orchestrator allows creation of custom runbooks that can be run as part of infrastructure service requests.

The benefits offered by CSPP for the enterprise include the following:

◆ A well-tested and fully supported cloud-services solution that follows industry-wide best practices

◆ Deep customization and extension of the cloud-services experience natively supported by the System Center suite of products

◆ Reduced cost, effort, and time to deploy cloud services to organizations that already leverage the System Center platform

The benefits offered by CSPP for consumers of IT within the enterprise include these:

◆ Standardized and well-defined processes for requesting and managing cloud services, including the ability to define projects, capacity pools, and VMs

◆ Natively supported request, approval, and notification to enable businesses to effectively manage their own allocated infrastructure capacity pools—for example, project administrators can approve or reject capacity pool and VM requests

Operations Manager

Operations Manager (OM) is a cross-platform data-center-management system for OSs, network devices, and hypervisors. It uses a familiar System Center interface to display state, health, and performance information of monitored infrastructure, while providing alert generation according to rules covering availability, performance, configuration, and security information.

It installs a small software component (agent) on each computer to be monitored. The agent watches relevant information sources on the computer for specific events or alerts generated by the applications executing on the monitored computer. These alerts are then forwarded by the agent to the OM server, which maintains a database on the history of these alerts.

As alerts arrive, OM uses filtering rules and can trigger notifications such as an email or a pager message, generate a network support ticket, or trigger some other workflow intended to correct the cause of the alert in an appropriate manner.

The rules are stored in management packs that Microsoft and other software vendors provide for their products. OM also provides for authoring custom management packs.

OM delivers integration, availability, performance, and security of IT services in the following ways:

◆ Enhances application performance and availability across heterogeneous platforms in the data center, with the ability to monitor Windows, Linux, and UNIX servers and their workloads—all through a single console

◆ Improves management of applications in the data center through enhanced reporting that shows how actual application performance and health map to target levels of service, as well as monitoring capabilities that scale to required workloads

◆ Increases speed of access to information and functionality to drive management with efficient problem identification and actions to quickly resolve issues before they become incidents

OM and VMM have a special connector functionality, which permits bidirectional communications between these products, as overviewed in Table 12.1.

TABLE 12.1:   Operations Manager and VMM Integrations

COMPONENT	INTEGRATION
Operations Manager	Powerful interoperability and automation using PRO-enabled management packs provide an automated or advised response to incidents within virtualized environments (for example, live migration of workloads between servers in response to a hardware issue on the virtualization host).
VMM	VMM service definitions are synchronized to Operations Manager as distributed applications.

Orchestrator

Orchestrator is an automation platform for orchestrating and integrating IT tools to decrease the cost of data-center operations while improving the reliability of IT processes. It enables

IT organizations to automate best practices, such as those found in Microsoft Operations Framework (MOF) and ITIL. It operates through workflow processes that coordinate System Center and other management tools to automate incident response, change and compliance, and service–life cycle management processes.

Through its workflow designer, Orchestrator automatically shares data and initiates tasks in OM, Configuration Manager, Service Manager, VMM, Active Directory, and third-party tools.

Orchestrator workflow automates IT infrastructure tasks, while Service Manager workflow provides automation of human workflow. The combined offering ensures repeatable, consistent results by removing the latency associated with manual-coordination service delivery.

Orchestrator enables integration, efficiency, and business alignment of IT services by doing the following:

◆ Automating cross-silo processes and enforcing best practices for incident, change, and service–life cycle management

◆ Reducing unanticipated errors and service delivery time by automating tasks across vendor and organization silos

◆ Integrating System Center with non-Microsoft tools to enable interoperability across the data center

◆ Orchestrating tasks across systems for consistent, documented, compliant activity

Orchestrator and Service Manager have a special connector functionality enabled through the Orchestrator ODATA web service, which permits bidirectional communications between these products, in addition to the integration packs that are published to Orchestrator servers as explained in Table 12.2.

TABLE 12.2: Orchestrator Integrations

COMPONENT	INTEGRATION
Service Manager	Using Orchestrator ODATA web services, Service Manager extends its workflow functionality by consuming and executing runbooks hosted in Orchestrator in a fully integrated experience.
Orchestrator Integration Packs	Add-on packs that extend the functionality of Orchestrator to manage additional products are available from Microsoft and third parties (including open-source offerings hosted normally on the CODEPLEX site).

Service Manager

Service Manager is an integrated platform for automating and adapting IT-service-management best practices, such as those found in MOF and ITIL, to provide built-in processes for incident resolution, problem resolution, and change control. By providing an integrated service-management platform, Service Manager can reduce costly downtime and improve the quality of the services in the data center.

Service Manager delivers integration, efficiency, and business alignment of IT services by doing the folllowing:

◆ Optimizing processes and ensuring their use through templates that effectively guide IT analysts through best practices for change and incident management

◆ Reducing resolution times by cutting across organizational silos, ensuring that the right information from incident, problem, change, or asset records is accessible through a single pane

◆ Extending the value of the System Center platform through automated generation of incidents from alerts and the coordination of activities among System Center products

◆ Enabling informed and cost-effective decision-making through the integration of knowledge from disparate IT-management systems and delivering out-of-the-box reporting and flexibility of data analysis through Microsoft SQL Server 2008 reporting services and Microsoft SQL Server 2008 Analysis Services–hosted cubes

Through its CMDB and process integration, Service Manager automatically connects knowledge and information from the products that integrate with Service Manager. The features provided by this integration are illustrated in Table 12.3.

TABLE 12.3:   Service Manager Integrations

COMPONENT	INTEGRATION
OM	Automatically creates configuration items in the Service Manager CMDB based on computers discovered in OM.
	Automatically creates incident tickets based on alerts generated in OM. Incident tickets in Service Manager create work items for analysts.
	Extends and augments the knowledge-base information in Service Manager with the knowledge-base information in OM.
Configuration Manager	Automatically creates configuration items in the Service Manager CMDB based on computers discovered in Configuration Manager.
	Automatically creates incident tickets based on changes in managed-computer configuration using the desired configuration-management (DCM) feature in Configuration Manager.
Orchestrator	Automatically extends Service Manger functionality to execute and monitor runbooks published in Orchestrator as part of the Service Manager workflow.
Active Directory	Automatically creates configuration items in the Service Manager CMDB based on computer, user, group, and printer objects in Active Directory.

Using Service Manager, a private cloud can also handle requests that require human approvals or carry out other processes.

WARNING   The steps covered in the section are relevant to the currently available version of the process pack, which at the time of writing is still Release Canidate. Many of the steps covered, along with the personas, are quite likely to change in the final version of the pack.

Implementing the Cloud Service

Prior to implementing CSPP, the following components of System Center should be deployed and functioning within your fabric:

◆ Service Manager

◆ Orchestrator

◆ OM

◆ VMM

Once the prerequisite components are in place, some additional configuration work needs to be completed by first creating the VMM, OM, and Orchestrator connectors.

A connector imports data from the System Center component to the Service Manager CMDB. Connectors can import logical networks, VM templates, storage classifications, and so on from VMM; import policies from Orchestrator; and import operational data from OM.

After the imports are complete, we will configure the VMM resources in the Service Manager console, and complete the final configuration settings for the process pack. These are the tasks we will be performing:

◆ Create the VMM connector.

◆ Create the OM connector.

◆ Create the Orchestrator connector.

◆ Configure the VMM resources.

◆ Create the user roles.

◆ Create the notification channels and subscriptions.

◆ Configure the general properties (global settings).

◆ Create the cost centers.

◆ Configure offerings.

Integrating VMM and OM

The VMM to OM connector enables PRO integration services between the two products. One of the key benefits of enabling this integration is the services feature in VMM. With the integration enabled, VMM can keep the service model of the distributed application up-to-date in OM, including dynamically updating the service diagram because of scale-out (for example, add a web server to a load-balanced web tier) or scale-in (for example, remove a business-logic server from a load-balanced middle tier), as well as display the health of the virtual machines, tiers, and the overall service in OM.

For this feature to function, you must first import the VMM management packs to your OM server and deploy an OM agent to the VMM server. The management packs to be imported reside on the VMM server, normally in the products' installation directory, typically at the following folder location:

`C:\Program Files\Microsoft System Center 2012\Virtual Machine Manager\ManagementPacks.`

The packs, once imported into OM, appear as follows:

- System Center 2012 Virtual Machine Manager Discovery

- System Center 2012 Virtual Machine Manager Monitoring

- System Center 2012 Virtual Machine Manager PRO Diagnostics

- System Center 2012 Virtual Machine Manager Reports

- System Center Virtual Machine Manager 2008 R2 PRO Library

- Virtual Machine Manager Library

- Virtual Machine Manager Overrides

- Virtual Machine Manager PRO Library

- Virtual Machine Manager PRO V2 Hyper-V Host Performance

- Virtual Machine Manager PRO V2 Library

After the management packs are imported, you can also add an account to the OM Administrators role to use for VMM integration.

On the VMM server, install the OM management console before starting the Integration Wizard. The Integration Wizard is located on the Settings workspace, under the System Center Settings view. The first time you launch the OM Server option, a simple wizard requests the name of the OM server, and the account that has administrative access for the integration. Additionally the wizard offers the opportunity to enable the PRO features, along with enabling maintenance mode in Operations Manager automatically. When the wizard finishes, double-click the Operations Manager Settings view again; this time you will be presented with the Settings dialog, as illustrated in Figure 12.2.

FIGURE 12.2
The VMM Operations Manager settings

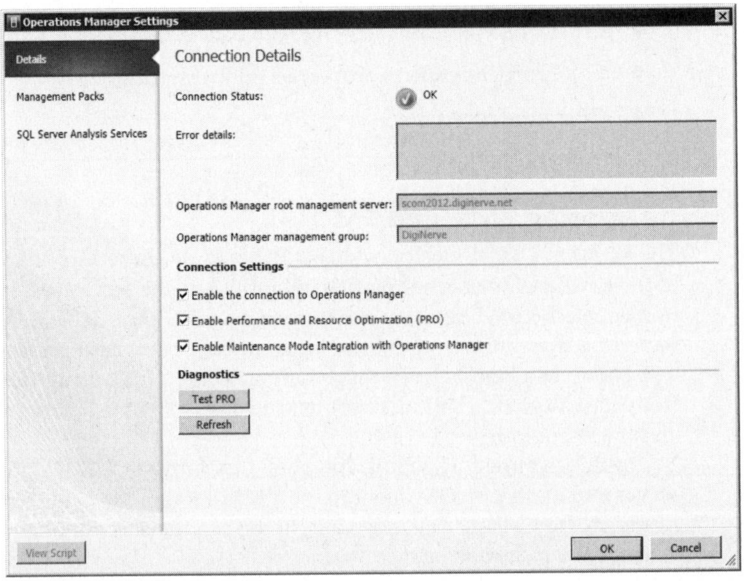

Test the integration by clicking Test PRO. This raises a test PRO alert, which pops up a new dialog with the relevant information for your attention and should self-resolve a few moments later.

Adding the Management Packs to Service Manager

In Service Manager, you need to import some of the same management packs to meet the requirements of the CSPP installer and to ensure that the OM connector provides the required packs for synchronization.

Unlike Operations Manager, however, Service Manager does not automatically resolve the management-pack dependencies and download the missing ones. Only some of the management packs need to be imported so that Service Manager can understand the objects with which you are working. The main required pack is called System Center 2012 Virtual Machine Manager Discovery.

Table 12.4 lists the dependent management packs you must import into Service Manager, and the sequence in which they should be imported, so that the main pack can be successfully imported. The management packs are supplied with the Cloud Services Process Pack in a folder called "ManagementPacks".

TABLE 12.4:   Service Manager Management Pack Import Order

IMPORT ORDER	MANAGEMENT PACK	FILENAME	SOURCE
1	Data warehouse library	`Microsoft.SystemCenter.DataWarehouse.Library.mp`	MP
2	IIS library	`Microsoft.Windows.InternetInformationServices.CommonLibrary.mp`	MP
3	Generic report library	`Microsoft.SystemCenter.DataWarehouse.Report.Library.mp`	MP
4	Windows Server IIS 2003	`Microsoft.Windows.InternetInformationServices.2003`	MP
5	Windows Server OS library	`Microsoft.Windows.Server.Library.mp`	MP
6	Windows Server 2008 OS (Discovery)	`Microsoft.Windows.Server.2008.Discovery.mp`	MP
7	Windows Server 2008 IIS 7	`Microsoft.Windows.InternetInformationServices.2008.mp`	MP
8	SQL Server core library	`Microsoft.SQLServer.Library.mp`	MP

TABLE 12.4: Service Manager Integrations *(CONTINUED)*

IMPORT ORDER	MANAGEMENT PACK	FILENAME	SOURCE
9	System virtualization library	`System.Virtualization.Library.mp`	MP
10	VMM library	`Microsoft.SystemCenter.` `VirtualMachineManager.Library.mp`	VMM
11	VMM 2008 R2 PRO Library	`Microsoft.SystemCenter.` `VirtualMachineManager.PRO.2008.Library.mp`	VMM
12	VMM PRO library	`Microsoft.SystemCenter.` `VirtualMachineManager.PRO.Library.mp`	VMM
13	VMM PRO V2 library	`Microsoft.SystemCenter.` `VirtualMachineManager.PRO.V2.Library.mp`	VMM
14	VMM Discovery	`Microsoft.SystemCenter.` `VirtualMachineManager.2012.Discovery.mp`	VMM

TABLE 12.5: Management Pack Source Locations

SOURCE	PATH
MP	.\Setup\ManagementPacks
VMM	.\Setup\ManagementPacks\VMMMP

Creating a VMM Connector

The VMM connector is important because it imports VM templates, service templates, logical networks, VIP profiles, clouds, and VMM user roles to Service Manager to provide automation in the infrastructure when provisioning VMs.

To complete this process, you need Administrator privileges on the Service Manager system. In the Administration view in the left pane of the Service Manager console, select Connectors. A Create Connector action appears in the Tasks pane (Figure 12.3). In subsequent sections, you'll create each of the listed connectors.

FIGURE 12.3
Creating connectors
in Service Manager

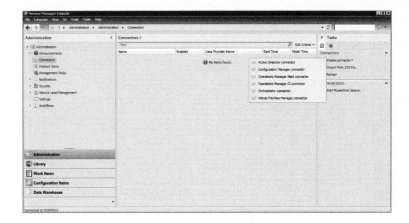

Select Virtual Machine Manager Connector. The VMM Connector Wizard opens.

Enter a name for the connection, a short description, the fully qualified name of the VMM server, and a Run As account to complete the connection. On the Summary screen, review your choices and read the Additional Information field. For example, if the wizard detects that the VMM server is configured to push data to OM, it reminds you to create an OM connector too.

Click Create to begin creating the connector.

Creating Operations Manager Connectors

Figure 12.3 shows Service Manager's two OM connectors: the Alert connector and the Configuration Items (CI) connector. Together they enable Service Manager to populate the CMDB with information from the managed environment.

Create these connectors using the same procedure as for the VMM connector. First select Operations Manager CI Connector. The OM CI Connector Wizard appears.

Provide a name for the connection, a short description, the fully qualified name of the OM server, and a Run As account.

On the Management Packs tab (Figure 12.4), the wizard lists all the management packs present on both OM and Service Manager and suitable for synchronization with the CMDB. Select all of them and ensure that the list includes the Discovery management pack:

`Microsoft.SystemCenter.VirtualMachineManger.2012.Discovery`

This management pack is required for CSPP to be updated with changes detected by OM. Click OK, and the Summary screen appears. Click Create.

Following the same procedures you just used, select Operations Manager Alert Connector (see Figure 12.3) to create the Alert connector. This connector is not required for the CSPP to function. Its purpose is to transfer alerts detected by OM to Service Manager to process as incidents. The connector can be filtered to the type of alerts transferred, and associated with specific templates in Service Manager.

FIGURE 12.4

Selecting management packs for the connector

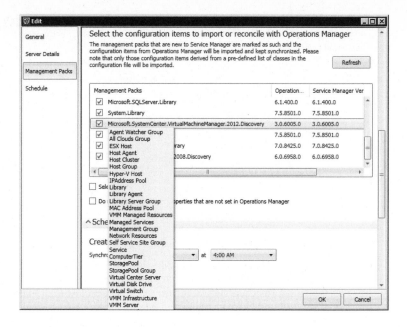

Creating an Orchestrator Connector

The Orchestrator connector enables the integration and use of runbooks hosted on the Orchestrator server as part of the Service Manager workflows.

Following the same procedures as in previous sections, select Orchestrator Connector. In the wizard, provide the following:

◆ Name and description of the new connector

◆ A web service URL for Orchestrator web services (for example, `http://scorch2012` `.private.cloud:81/orchestrator2012/Orchestrator.svc`)

◆ A Run As account with permissions to access to the runbooks

◆ The runbook folder to synchronize

Select the root folder; you can reduce scope later.

◆ The URL of the Orchestrator web console to enable hyperlinks for users to monitor active jobs

Review the summary and click Create.

Installing the Cloud Service Runbooks

In the CSPP installer, select Cloud Service Runbooks to install the runbooks on the Orchestrator server. The installer requests administrative access to the Orchestrator server and the name of the Service Manager connector. Figure 12.5 shows a sample runbook installed for creating new VMs in VMM.

FIGURE 12.5
A sample Cloud
Services runbook

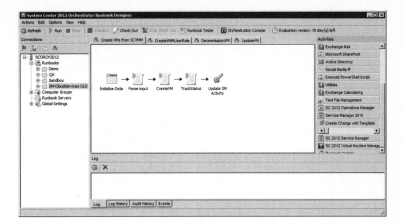

These new runbooks deployed to the Orchestrator server are used by CSPP to interact with VMM (for example, deploying a new VM to a cloud after it is approved).

Installing the Cloud Service Process Pack

On the Service Manager server, start the CSPP installer. The prerequisite check verifies that everything is ready for the deployment. In particular, the OM management pack must be synchronized with the VMM Discovery management pack. The installation should proceed without issue and begin importing new management packs into the Service Manager server for the new cloud processes.

After installing CSPP, close any open Service Manager consoles and reopen them to see the new Cloud Services view in the Administrator workspace (Figure 12.6).

FIGURE 12.6
Viewing cloud ser-
vices in the Service
Manager console

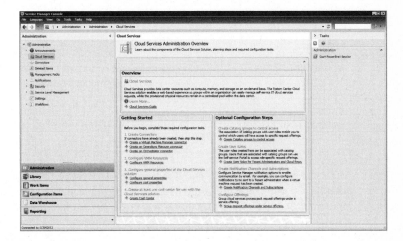

Configuring VMM Resources

In the Service Manager console, Cloud Services view, select Configure VMM Resources from the solution checklist. The wizard (Figure 12.7) steps you through the tabs.

The Placement Tags tab enables you to offer end users input choices that you can use to determine where infrastructure requests should be placed (for example, in which data center, on which server). Figure 12.7 shows a sample tag. Other tags might include location, business impact, and compliance requirements. You can customize this list at any time.

FIGURE 12.7
Configuring place-ment tabs in the Service Manager console

Creating User Roles

CSPP bases user roles on the two personas described in Table 12.6.

TABLE 12.6: CSPP Personas

PERSONA	RESPONSIBILITY
Tenant Administrator	The tenant administrator manages the cloud subscriptions. This person decides that using the cloud for a project is a good idea and requests a new project thought the portal
Cloud Subscription User	The Subscription users, are the end users. They request and use VM's for project clouds

These personas are represented in Service Manager as user roles. Defining them is simple, because you don't need to assign users or configure the roles. Initially, they are empty groups for users who later join these roles. The process of joining users to the role is addressed by the actual cloud process workflows once users begin to use the environment.

To set up the user roles, select Create User Roles for Tenant Administrators and Cloud Resources Subscription Users (refer back to Figure 12.6). This redirects us to the User Role node of the Security branch on the same pane. Select Create New User Role from the Tasks pane, and select End User as the role type.

Working through the wizard, enter the name of the first persona (Tenant Administrator). On the Management Packs screen, select All. This page filters the options that appear on the follow-ing screens. For now, simply click through the wizard to finish setting up the role for the persona.

Repeat the previous procedure for the second persona (Cloud Resources Subscription User). For clarity, as illustrated in Figure 12.8, you can name this persona CSPP Cloud Resources Subscribers.

Creating Notification Channels and Subscriptions

If your Service Manager installation is new, create an entry for your SMTP server. Otherwise, it probably already exists.

To check, find the Email Notification Channel configuration on the Administrators view, expand Notifications to show the Channels node, and select it to view and edit its properties.

Once the notification channel is configured, check to see if any subscriptions are enabled; they tell Service Manager which notifications to send and when to send them (for example, notify an agent when a new ticket is logged or update the requestor when a ticket is complete).

While still on the Notifications branch of the Administrators view, select the Subscriptions node to see or edit current notifications or create new ones.

Configuring General Properties (Global Settings)

Hidden in the middle of the configuration is the Cloud Services Settings screen (Figure 12.8), which is accessed by selecting step 3 of the getting started list. These important settings determine how the process-pack routes received requests for review and implementation. First, you should define the prefixes to be used within Service Manager for both Tenant and Cloud Resources Subscription requests.

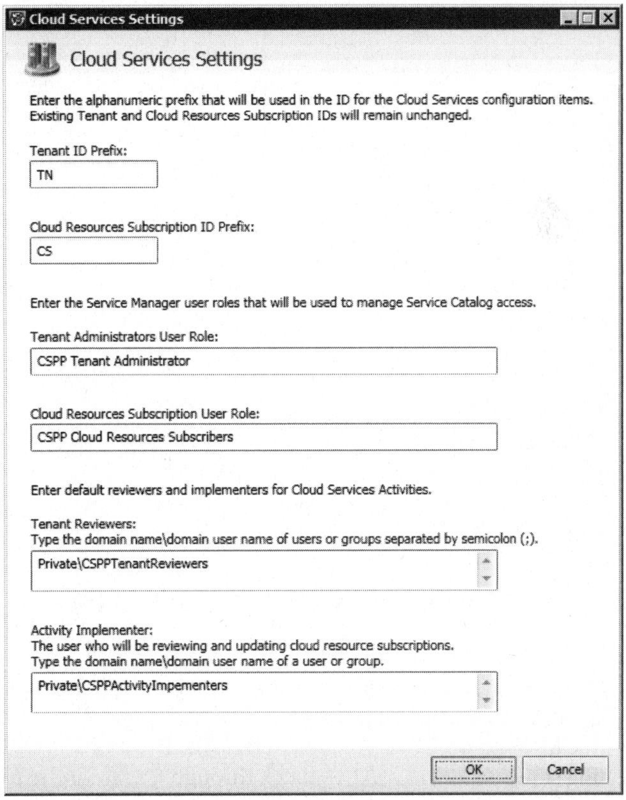

FIGURE 12.8
The Cloud Services settings

The *personas* (user roles) you created earlier—that is, Tenant Administrator and Cloud Resources Subscribers—are now connected to the Cloud Services process pack in the dialog section titled "Enter the Service Manager user roles that will be used to manage Service Catalog access." Defining both of these user roles enables CSPP to automatically update the user-role membership with the relevant user accounts after requests have been reviewed and approved.

The lower area of the dialog is where you specify the default reviewers and implementers of cloud-service activities—that is, the person or group that approves requests before you can process them. The Active Directory User or Groups identified for these roles must already be contained in the Service Manager CMDB; If the objects were only recently created in AD, then ensure that the AD connector has successfully completed a synchronisation to import these objects, otherwise you will be unable to store these settings when closing the dialog. Figure 12.8 shows the two additional personas in action here:

◆ *Project Administrators* whom request capacity in the cloud, initially as a Tenancy, and then as a cloud subscription for there respective projects within the Tenancy.

◆ *Activity implementers* prepare the user roles and clouds in VMM and associate the newly created VMM cloud and resources with the subscription request.

Figure 12.9 presents an overview of the CSPP personas.

FIGURE 12.9
The CSPP personas

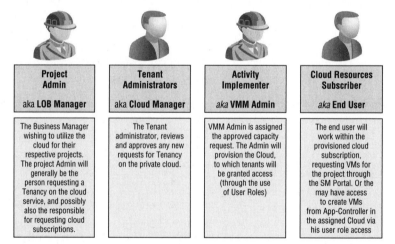

Project Admin	Tenant Administrators	Activity Implementer	Cloud Resources Subscriber
aka **LOB Manager**	aka **Cloud Manager**	*aka* **VMM Admin**	*aka* **End User**
The Business Manager wishing to utilize the cloud for their respective projects. The project Admin will generally be the person requesting a Tenancy on the cloud service, and possibly also the responsible for requesting cloud subscriptions.	The Tenant administrator, reviews and approves any new requests for Tenancy on the private cloud.	VMM Admin is assigned the approved capacity request. The Admin will provision the Cloud, to which tenants will be granted access (through the use of User Roles)	The end user will work within the provisioned cloud subscription, requesting VMs for the project through the SM Portal. Or the may have access to create VMs from App-Controller in the assigned Cloud via his user role access

Creating the Cost Centers

CSPP offers very basic chargeback support. On the Virtual Machine Cost Settings screen, specify the following costs for VM resources:

◆ Memory cost (GB/day)

◆ Storage cost (GB/day)

◆ CPU cost per unit per day

◆ Miscellaneous cost per day

All of these costs must be supplied, even if you do not plan to use the chargeback feature; in such cases, just supply a zero value.

The memory, storage, and CPU costs are pretty much self-explanatory. The miscellaneous cost is for any additional, daily fixed cost for your offered services—a tax of sorts.

Don't get too excited, though; the costing here is very simplistic and does not take different classes of storage or fabric infrastructure into account, nor does it consider whether the VM is running, stopped, or in the library! Therefore, you will want to begin with an average value.

As Chargeback/Showback is a key feature of Private Cloud and Infrastructure as a Service, Microsoft will be offering an updated Process Pack which will focus on this area in greater detail very soon.

Configuring Offerings

Now you are ready to offer the new services to end users. Installing CSPP creates additional request offerings, as described in Table 12.7.

TABLE 12.7:   CSPP Requests

OFFERING	PURPOSE
Register a Tenant	Request to host a new tenant. You specify the urgency, tenant name, tenant administrators, and a cost center.
Update Tenant Registration	Identify a tenant to be updated, and provide details on the changes required—for example, adding new administrators.
Cancel Tenant Registration	Provide information about the tenant to be decommissioned.
Subscribe to Cloud Resource	Request a Cloud subscription for your project. This includes VM templates and quota requirements, such as storage and memory.
Update Cloud Resource Subscription	Identify the Cloud subscription to be updated, and provide details on the changes required—for example, additional RAM quota.
Cancel Cloud Resource Subscription	Provide information about the Cloud subscription to be decommissioned.
Request Service	Specify the information needed to request a service.
Request Virtual Machine	Specify the information needed to request a VM.
Update Virtual Machine	Identify the VM to the updated and provide details on the changes required—for example, adding a virtual processor.

The CSPP Request offerings are initially installed in Published status. As a best practice these should be changed to Draft status, and then copied to a new management pack, permitting you to version and customise the offering prior to being published.

To copy and publish the service requests

◆ In the Service Manager Console, switch to the Library workspace, expanding and selecting the Service Catalog ➢ Request Offerings ➢ All Request Offerings node.

- The main view will refresh and present a list of all request offerings currently defined, In this list locate the 9 request offerings as listed in Table 12.7

- In the Tasks pane select the option Unpublish, to change these to Draft status.

- Select one of the Cloud Services request offerings, and in the Tasks pane, select the option Create a Copy.

- A new dialog lets you define which management packs to place the copy in.

- You can Create a new management pack to store your CSPP requests and customizations by clicking the New button on the dialog.

- From the drop-down list, select the management pack you want to use and then click OK.

- With a new copy of the request created, edit it to provide a friendly title, for example, and then publish the request offering to the portal.

- To publish, select the request and click Publish from the Tasks pane.

- You may want to repeat this exercise for each of the service requests you changed back to draft format, so the original offerings remain unaltered or customised.

After these are published, you'll see the offerings in the portal when you switch to List view. The next logical level is to group these request offerings under a service offering, which will be presented on the home page of the portal and allow you to group and scope these request offerings.

- To publish a service offering, switch to the Library workspace, expand and select the Service Catalog ➤ Service Offerings ➤ All Service Offerings node.

- The main view changes to a list of all currently defined request offerings. Click the Create Service Offering option from the task list; this will launch the Create Service Offering Wizard.

- Provide a name for the Service offering, and select the target management pack to which you will be storing the customizations.

- On the Request Offerings tab, add the new Cloud Services Request offerings you want to present.

- You may set the Offering status to Publish and complete the wizard.

Using the Cloud Service

With the connectors live and the services presented, let's take a quick tour of the service offerings that users will be presented through the Self-service portal.

While implementing CSPP you created personas. These personas take a major role in the daily use of private cloud services. The illustration in Figure 12.9 shows the responsibilities of each of these characters so that you can decide whether you can combine some of these personas in your organization.

After becoming acquainted with the different personas, you should consider the process flow that occurs while using this solution and how this flow interacts with the VMM environment.

Figure 12.10 shows the stages that CSPP guides the users through, from the initial request of hosting a project, to finally automatically provisioning the VM to cloud users. You will return to this figure at the end of the chapter to explore opportunities for further automation.

FIGURE 12.10
The CSPP personas
in workflows

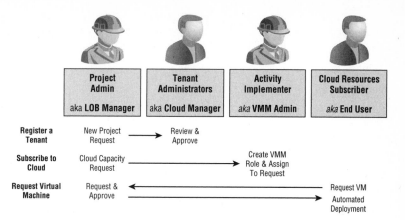

NOTE In the remainder of this section, information will be provided specifically for different personas, as you experience the CSPP in action and monitor what is happening behind the scenes in Service Manager.

Register a Tenant

For the following instructions, assume the Project Administrator persona.

Start the cycle by selecting to Register a Tenant in the Service Manager self-service portal. The Register a Tenant screen, shown in Figure 12.11, appears. Provide details about the tenant, including its name, urgency, and the associated cost center. Supply an email address for the tenant contact and domain usernames of the project administrators.

FIGURE 12.11
Making a project
request

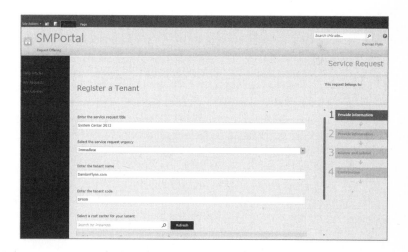

For the following instructions, assume the Service Manager Administrator persona.

In the Service Manager console, Work Items view, expand the Service Request Fulfillment node to view and select All Open Service Requests to see the service request that the project administrator just submitted. Open the properties of this service request and select the Activities pane (Figure 12.12) to see the progress of the associated activities.

FIGURE 12.12
Viewing the request

CSPP requests must be reviewed by the project reviewer for approval prior to completing the rest of the configuration. Activity RA19 in Figure 12.12 is in that state.

For the following instructions, assume the Tenant Reviewer persona.

In the Service Manger self-service portal, select the My Activities view to see the new request awaiting approval. Approve or reject the request. For the purpose of this scenario, approve the request and supply a short comment with the decision.

Subscribe to Cloud Resources

For the following instructions, assume the Project Administrator persona.

After a successful request for a new project, you can request to Subscribe to Cloud Resources in the Service Manager self-service portal. On the Subscribe to Cloud Resources screen, provide details about the pool to configure, including name, urgency, and the associated project for this pool. Provide storage capacity, CPU quota, and RAM allocations. Provide the *domain names/group* of users to be granted access to this pool resource.

For the following instructions, assume the Service Manager Administrator persona.

In the Service Manager console, on the All Open Service Requests node, refresh the view to see the new request, and open it to check progress persona.

For the following instructions, assume the Activity Implementer persona.

In the Service Manager console, click Work Items in the left pane. Expand the Activity Management node and its Manual Activities subnode to view and select the Activities Assigned To Me node. Figure 12.13 shows the manual activity you must now complete to fulfill the request.

FIGURE 12.13
Completing your
manual activities

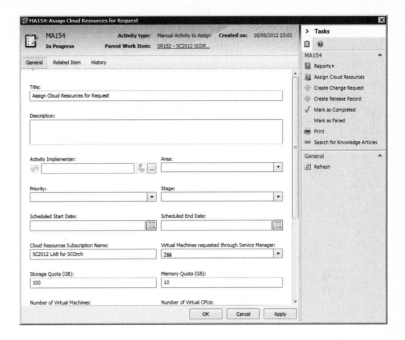

A manual activity requires you to complete some work before updating the activity to indicate that the associated task is complete. The Assign Cloud Resources for Request activity first requires that you have previously created Clouds in Virtual Machine manager to select from.

The VMM Clouds are Synchronised into the SCSM CMDB across the System Center Operations Manager connector. If you have created clouds recently, you will require the Service Manager administrator to manually synchronize the Connector in order for them to be available.

The Assign Cloud Resources wizard will prepare to create a new VMM user role which will be granted access to the selected Cloud, with the assigned resources, quota's and members (Figure 12.14) based on the information which was submitted in the request.

After the Manual activity is marked as completed, the following activity will invoke an Orchestrator runbook to create the defined User Role Launching the VMM Console, on the Administration view, under Security ➤ User Roles, we will then see this role, and its configuration as illustrated in Figure 12.15

FIGURE 12.14
Configuring the
new user role in the
wizard

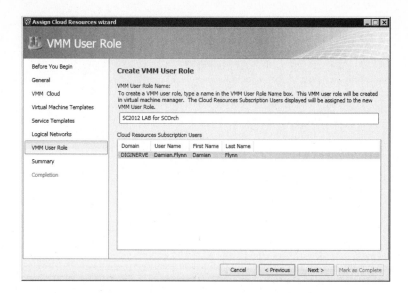

FIGURE 12.15
Newly created
VMM User Role

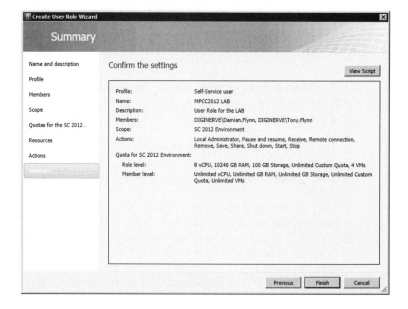

After the Runbook activity has completed provisioning the new VMM User Role with access
to the selected cloud, the remaining automated activities will provide access to the subscription users. These will also configure the subscription depending on whether the VM resource
request for this cloud should only be available only trough the Self-Service portal, or as an
Action permission on the VMM User Role.

Request Virtual Machine

For the following instructions, assume the Cloud Resources Subscriber persona.

You can use the Service Manager self-service portal to request a VM. As in previous requests, use a form to provide details on the VMs requested, including name and description, the subscription, the VM template, the network to connect the VMs to, and a potential decommissioning date.

For the following instructions, assume the Service Manager Administrator persona.

In the Service Manager console, Work Items view, All Open Service Requests node, you can refresh to see the new request. Open the request to check the progress. Because the request might generate charges to the project, the project administrator must approve.

For the following instructions, assume the Project Administrator persona.

In the Service Manager self-service portal, select the My Activities view to see the new request. Approve or reject the request. For the purpose of this example, approve the request and supply a short comment with the decision.

For the following instructions, assume the Service Manager Administrator persona.

Because the request is approved, the activities on the service request proceed. This example invokes an Orchestrator runbook. The CSPP installer created runbooks to automate transferring the approved VM request to VMM to provision this exact VM based on the criteria in the request. Refer back to Figure 12.5 to see.

For the following instructions, assume the Cloud Resources Subscriber persona.

Once the runbook automation has completed, the request will be marked as resolved. The resolved request will have being updated, and contain information confirmed that your new Virtual Machine is ready for use.

Automation: The Sky Is the Limit!

Throughout this book, you have learned that private clouds are an effective way to give IT users the computing resources they need. Yet while providing resources automatically is useful, it still might not be enough. In this chapter, you learned that with the help of additional System Center family members, you can do more. Service Manager enables you to add ITIL processes to the cloud environment, and with its integrated CMDB, it can reach out to the rest of the ecosystem and learn a lot about what is happening.

Integrating VMM and OM is a useful extension, even when you do not need all the functionality of a private cloud. The ability to dynamically monitor the virtualization environment and intelligently distribute the load based on changed fabric conditions is not new, but extending this with the services functionality of VMM to enable OM to create distributed application monitoring for each of the services is new—and it is very cool, and quite easy to implement!

Orchestrator is the dark horse of the family. This is the unexploited jewel in the crown, which will return dividends for the time you invest in learning and using its capabilities; automating every conceivable IT process as a runbook will change your working days forever. Consider Orchestrator as your junior assistant—spend a little time teaching it how to deal with an issue, and you'll never need to teach it about this problem again, as it sits obediently on the network waiting for the job to be needed and running a repeatable process every time.

Service Manager integration with these products opens the door to really changing your imagination from *what if* to *can do*.

Let your imagination run free for a moment, and consider the Pet Shop application introduced in Chapter 8, "Understanding Service Modeling," as a VMM service template. This service is designed to scale in and out, depending on load. It uses a load balancer to connect users to the changing nodes as the service is adapted to the current demand.

Today, OM is used to monitor the server's load—which it now does quite nicely with the VMM integration, detecting and monitoring new nodes as they are deployed, and letting you know the pressure they are under so you can react accordingly.

Now, let's assume that this application is managed completely with the System Center environment; OM can direct its alerts to Service Manager, and Service Manager creates and directs incidents based on these alerts, which can now have workflows attached to engage Orchestrator to automatically address the situation. This reaction could be simply instructing VMM to deploy a scale-out instruction to part of the service that is under pressure—and before you know it, VMM will inform OM of the new node and begin monitoring it, too. Closing the loop and letting Service Manager know that the incident can be closed completely automates the process.

This is not a dream anymore, but actually quite achievable with the functions offered by System Center. Look again at Figure 12.1, and let's take a deeper look at how this process might really flow.

1. Deploy an OM agent to each web-tier VM to generate an alert whenever the load on the member servers has risen too high.

2. After OM receives the alert, it sends an incident to Service Manager.

3. Service Manager records the incident in the CMDB and (optionally) notifies someone via email.

4. Depending on the scenario, Service Manager might decide to have a human approval before proceeding.

5. Service Manager starts a workflow to remedy the problem.

6. The workflow starts an Orchestrator runbook to interact with VMM.

7. VMM starts its own job, updating Orchestrator about its progress and notifying OM about the changes to the deployed service so that OM can monitor the service correctly.

Conclusion

Over the last four chapters, you were introduced to the foundations for a new world built on today's technologies. As you begin to embrace the private cloud, and the management suite that Microsoft is offering to simplify and enrich this new experience, you should understand that we are only touching the surface of what is achievable.

Starting from role-based access controls and the flexibility they offer, you can implement a private cloud to enable users to interact with this once-inconceivable resource. They can use a range of interfaces designed to address all potential scenarios—from the thin web-based graphical UI to the automation-ready PowerShell service.

Moving from VMs to application services is a big step, and the benefits this will deliver over the next few years are yet unknown. But it is already clear that embracing these new ways of working will not only enhance our private-cloud objectives and enable highly serviceable and automatable solutions, but also begin to dissolve the gap between private and public clouds.

We are on the cusp of a new computing generation, and there is no better time to join us as we embrace the evolution of computing.

Index

Note to Reader: **Bolded** page numbers refer to main discussions of a topic. *Italicized* page numbers refer to illustrations.

H